D0741977

The Indiana University School *of* Music

A History

The Indiana University School *of* Music

A History

George M. Logan

INDIANA UNIVERSITY PRESS
Bloomington & Indianapolis

This book is a publication of

Indiana University Press
601 North Morton Street
Bloomington, IN 47404-3797 USA

http://www.indiana.edu/~iupress

Telephone orders 800-842-6796
Fax orders 812-855-7931
Orders by e-mail iuporder@indiana.edu

The paper used in this publication meets the minimum requirements of American National Standard for Information Sciences—Permanence of Paper for Printed Library Materials, ANSI Z39.48-1984.

Manufactured in the United States of America

Library of Congress Cataloging-in-Publication Data

Logan, George M., date
The Indiana University School of Music : a history / George M. Logan.
p. cm.
Includes bibliographical references (p.) and index.
ISBN 0-253-33820-4 (cl. : alk. paper)
1. Indiana University, Bloomington. School of Music—History.
2. Music in universities and colleges—Indiana—Bloomington—History.
3. Music—Instruction and study—Indiana—Bloomington—History. I. Title.

MT4.B6 I5345 2000
780'.71'1772255—dc21

00-039630

1 2 3 4 5 05 04 03 02 01 00

For my children, Adam and Sarah

The life of a university is long, and, as a result, its achievements are the work of many, over many decades. And so it is with the School of Music. It had a humble beginning. . . .

—Herman B Wells, President (1937–1962) and Chancellor (1962–2000) of Indiana University

What gives the School its importance is the importance of the repertoire it's done. That's my way of evaluating how good a school is: what do you play, what do you sing? . . . I have said, and it's been repeated, "We have the horses."

—Wilfred C. Bain, Dean of the School of Music, 1947–1973

Contents

Illustrations

Preface

This book has its origins in a sabbatical year I spent in 1994–95 as a Visiting Scholar at the Institute for Advanced Study of Indiana University. I had chosen this venue partly because of the reputation of the University's School of Music. Having just concluded a long stint as Head of the English Department at my home university, I felt entitled to spend the evenings and weekends of my year hearing, for once, as much music as I wanted to; and I knew just enough about the size and quality of the School to surmise that Bloomington would be a good place to satisfy that ambition.

In the event, the School far exceeded my expectations. I had not really grasped what it would mean to live in a town where one had, a matter of minutes from home, what is certainly the largest, and is widely regarded as the best, classically centered music school in North America. What it *did* mean was that, apart from some vacation periods, I could attend at least one musical event every weekday evening and several more on Saturdays and Sundays. During the course of the year, these events included seven fully staged operas and a musical comedy, several studio operas, twenty-nine concerts by the School's six regular orchestras (plus several by pickup orchestras formed to accompany students performing concertos), seventeen choral concerts, numerous band concerts and jazz concerts, several ballet programs, and literally hundreds of solo and chamber recitals.

Moreover, the average quality of these events proved to be astonishingly high. A relatively small number of the recitals were by faculty or guests, and I was not surprised that these were generally splendid. I was, though, amazed at the quality of the student performances: with rare exceptions, they provided satisfying, professional-level musical experiences; and scores of times they were simply superb.

In 1994–95 (the situation has changed since then) the vast majority of the musical events were presented in the venerable Recital Hall of the School's main building, B. Winfred Merrill Hall. Sitting there night after night, I sometimes found myself wondering how this marvelous school had come to be. How had it happened that there was so much classical music to be heard, in performances of such quality, in a small Indiana town—a place that, though exceedingly pleasant, seemed an improbable setting for one of the world's major musical institutions? A trip to the

Music Library failed to provide an answer to this question: there was no history of the School (though one of its former Deans—Wilfred Bain—had surveyed his own long regime in two massive and not especially disinterested tomes). I thus left Indiana in the late summer of 1995 with my question unanswered; and it was this fact that led me to ask it of the man who was then Dean of the School—Charles Webb—when I first spoke with him, by telephone, just after Labor Day. (Our conversation resulted from a letter I had written him, shortly before leaving Bloomington, to express my feelings about the School.)

Webb was able to give me a partial answer to the question, but he shared my regret that there was no comprehensive history of the School; and at some point in the conversation the idea—outlandish as it at first seemed—occurred to me that *I* might write that history. Webb enthusiastically encouraged me to do so; and since I was at a stage in my career where I felt free to reallocate some of my research time from English studies, I decided, after a few days of rumination, to undertake the project.

The book that has resulted naturally reflects my particular interests and experiences. Since it stemmed from my fascination with the question of how the School came to be what it is (a question that especially intrigued me, no doubt, because I had spent a decade in academic administration), the book includes a good deal of material about administrative matters—about the Deans of the School and their relationships with their colleagues and with the central administration of the University. In general, my criterion for the inclusion or exclusion of particular topics has been that of whether they had bearing on my overriding question. Compared with other histories of music schools, then, this one is more analytic and less annalistic. It is also written from a position of much less familiarity with the general culture of music schools: unlike the authors of these other books, I have neither attended nor taught at any of these institutions. Much of what I do know about their culture derives, in fact, from two fascinating books, Henry Kingsbury's *Music, Talent, and Performance: A Conservatory Cultural System* (Philadelphia: Temple University Press, 1988) and Bruno Nettl's *Heartland Excursions: Ethnomusicological Reflections on Schools of Music* (Urbana and Chicago: University of Illinois Press, 1995). I am happy to refer lay readers to these books, as a sort of complement to mine.

Of the many debts I have incurred in writing my book, the greatest is to Dean Webb, without whom it simply could not have existed in anything like its present form. As head of the School during the years in which I was collecting materials, he accorded me unrestricted access to all the relevant documents in his files and devoted many hours of his scarce time to interviews and informal conversations with me about the institution, giving remarkably full and candid answers to my questions. Moreover, he opened all the necessary doors for me, especially by arranging interviews with key members of the School and the University. In the years since his 1997 retirement, he has been unfailingly diligent and patient in answering—or tracking down the answers to—the innumerable queries I have addressed to him; and he has read the book in draft form, saving me from many errors. Nor did his largess come with strings attached. From the inception of the project, he believed—correctly, I hope—that the School would be better served by a book that attempted an honest portrait, including any warts, than by an uncritical panegyric, and he never made the slightest attempt to exert, in return for his candor and for supplying me so richly with materials, any control over the contents of the book. From first to last, his attitude toward the project has seemed to me utterly—and admirably—impeccable.

I am also deeply indebted to John Gallman, Director of Indiana University Press during all but the final months of the project, not only for his shrewd counsel—and the gratifying enthusiasm that succeeded his prudent reserve, once he had read some chapters in draft form—but also for choosing an absolutely perfect reader to assess the manuscript for the Press. This was (as, after a favorable assessment, I was permitted to know) the illustrious ethnomusicologist Bruno Nettl of the University of Illinois, who is both the son of a faculty member of the School and a graduate of it. He has given me invaluable advice on all aspects of the book.

I owe a tremendous debt to Mary Wennerstrom and Leonard Phillips. Mary, who was a student at the School and stayed on to become a key member of its faculty, has been, after Charles Webb, the person with whom I have talked most about the School; and she and her husband, Leonard—who has his own longtime insider's knowledge of the place—read the penultimate draft of the book and gave me pages of extremely helpful comments on it.

Further, I am greatly indebted to other faculty members of the School who consented to be interviewed for the project: former Dean Wilfred Bain (now deceased), former Dean David Woods, Professor Emeritus Ross Allen, Distinguished Professor David Baker, Professor Emeritus Malcolm Brown, the late Newell Long (together with his wife Eleanor), Distinguished Professor Thomas Mathiesen, Distinguished Professor Menahem Pressler, and Professor Emeritus Oswald Ragatz (together with his late wife Mary). I also interviewed the great former President (and only Chancellor) of the University, the late Herman B Wells, as well as the wise and delightful Dorothy Collins, who worked for many years in a number of key staff positions in the University and, after retirement, co-authored a splendid pictorial history of it. Catherine Smith, a graduate of the School and an authority on many aspects of its history, generously shared her knowledge with me in conversation; and she and David Cartledge (a longtime pupil of Gyorgy Sebok who now directs the School's program in secondary piano) allowed me to use, as the basis of one of the book's appendixes, a comprehensive list they had compiled of the many individuals who have taught at the School over the years. I have also profited greatly from a number of conversations about the School with James Scott, formerly Associate Dean at Indiana and now Director of the distinguished School of Music of the University of Illinois, and with Henry Upper, who retired in May 2000 after a career at Indiana that included many years as Assistant and Associate Dean in the Webb and Woods administrations. Upper also assisted me with various practical matters related to the project.

Mildred Blake, who studied at the School in the 1930s, sent me detailed reminiscences of it in that era. Through my friend Valery Lloyd-Watts, I met, and over time acquired as a Bloomington friend, Sara Pressler. My conversations with her have often included the Music School—a subject over which her deep intelligence moves with the same acuity as over all others. My first friends in Bloomington, though, were my fellow literary scholars Al and Linda David, whose presence there constituted one of the reasons I chose it as the venue for the sabbatical that led to my writing the book; and they helped me by reading drafts of some of the early chapters.

Many members of the School's non-academic staff have given me unstintingly generous assistance. These include Carrie Root, who was Director of Publicity during the first years of the project, and her successor (under the title of Director of Communications), Arizeder Urreiztieta; Sue Trotman, who before her retirement worked for many years in the administrative offices of the School and who was extremely helpful in guiding me to a range of internal documents; Richard Lathom, the longtime manager of the School's Musical Arts Center, who gave me the benefit of his great knowledge of what has gone on in that splendid edifice; and Susie Allen, Susie Buzan, Jan Cobb, Tami Davis, Pam Duncan, Tammy Nichols, Hae Sook Park, Dorothy Riggle, Betty Robertson, Rhonda Spencer, Brenda Strombeck, Jan Wellman, and Ted Yungclas.

Staff members of other units of the University have also greatly assisted me. First among these are four members of the staff of the University Archives, William Baus, Bradley Cook, Dina Kellams, and Thomas Malefatto. Throughout the many long days I spent in their domain (as, more recently, in endless e-mails and faxes), I found them to be unfailingly knowledgeable, helpful, patient, and friendly. Julie Stein and Mia Williams of the University Architect's office dug out information about various buildings for me. Sharon Leigh of Indiana University Photographic Services guided me through the vast holdings of that office. Barbara Truesdell of the Oral History Research Center went out of her way on more than one occasion to help me. The staff of the Lilly Library were unfailingly courteous and helpful to me in my several visits to that great repository of rare published and unpublished materials.

I also owe a large debt to James Clemens of Ottawa, Ontario. As a graduate student at the School in the early 1990s, he wrote a Master's thesis on the administrative philosophies of the first four chief executives of the institution, a project for which he did much archival research and conducted extremely valuable interviews (printed as appendixes to his thesis) with Herman Wells and Newell Long. For the period through 1973, his work has been a tremendous help to mine.

I have enjoyed my association with Jeffrey Ankrom, who, as Music Editor, was involved with the book from the first day I approached the Press about it, and who has been extremely helpful to me since it went into production. I feel lucky to have had Michael Baker as copy editor, and to have had Jane Lyle, the Press's very able Managing Editor, looking after the book as it moved through the production process. In the final stages of that process, Marvin Keenan, the Press's Editorial Assistant, provided indispensable aid.

At home, I want to thank the two individuals who have, over the years, helped me more with my work than anyone else, and to whom is owed much of whatever merit it may have had. One of these is Karen Donnelly, who has (as on many occasions in the past) gone far beyond her duties as Head's Secretary in the Queen's University Department of English to assist me with the transcriptions of my taped interviews and with the keyboarding of successive drafts of the manuscript; and this though I am no longer Head. The other is my wife, Catherine Harland, who, a scholar herself, saved me, by acute readings of drafts and needfully frank comments on them, from many obscurities, errors, and gaucheries. Any remaining ones are entirely my fault.

A Note on Documentation

This is a book without footnotes. It is, however, a work of scholarship, and I have been conscious of my obligation to enable those readers who may be interested in the sources of quotations, or my authority for various claims, to satisfy their curiosity. I have attempted to fulfill this obligation with a minimum of fuss and pedantry. In many cases, the source or authority will be clear from the way in which the materials are introduced in my text. For all other quotations, and for those claims of fact that seem likeliest to evoke curiosity or skepticism, I have recorded the source in the commentary that constitutes the bulk of the appendix on sources. This appendix also includes an annotated list of the major published sources for the history of the School, together with a list of the collections of unpublished materials on which I have drawn.

I have been deliberately unfaithful to my sources in one respect. When quoting from transcripts of interviews conducted by others, I have felt free to alter what bibliographers call the "accidentals" of the text, namely, punctuation and (occasionally) spelling. My justification for taking these liberties is that the accidentals are not attributable to the interviewee but to the transcriber—and in some cases transcribers are not masters of the minutiae of standard punctuation and orthography.

The Indiana University School *of* Music

A History

Prelude

Since the 1960s, the Indiana University School of Music has been, by general consent in the profession, the all-round best music school in North America. During that era it has also been one of the four or five largest music schools in the world. Without spending some time at the School, it is hard to grasp what these facts mean in conjunction.

An ideal opportunity to find out was provided in November 1995, when, over the course of an extended weekend, the newest of the School's major facilities, the Bess Meshulam Simon Music Library and Recital Center, was dedicated. Dedications of its buildings have long been, at the School, occasions not only for celebration but for displaying the quality and scope of its musical operations, and its stature in the musical world; they have also become object lessons in the amounts of private money now needed to sustain high-level musical education, even at a publicly supported university.

The first of the special musical events of the dedication weekend was a Friday evening concert by the hundred-member Indiana University Philharmonic Orchestra, the ranking orchestra among the four full symphony orchestras maintained—without overlapping personnel—by the School. (There are, in addition, a Chamber Orchestra and a Baroque Orchestra, as well as two concert bands, a marching band, four jazz bands, and other ensembles, including a dozen choral groups.) On this occasion, the Philharmonic was conducted by the Music Director of the New York Philharmonic, Kurt Masur, who had lent his prestige to the event in token of his esteem for the School.

Since the concert required a large stage, it took place not in the Simon Center but next door in the School's opera house, the Musical Arts Center—a magnificent building completed in 1972 at a cost of $11,200,000. Although the MAC (as it is called) seats a modest 1,460, it has stage facilities rivaled, in size and sophistication, on the North American continent only by a handful of the finest professional theaters.

On Saturday the festivities moved to the Simon Center. Constructed at a cost of $18,500,000—all of it private money—the Center received its "naming gift" of $2,100,000 from the late Mrs. Simon's children. It occupies 100,000 square feet in a renovated limestone building adjacent to the MAC and the School's other two main buildings, Merrill Hall (40,000 square feet), which was dedicated in 1937, and its extension, the Music Annex (100,000 square feet), dedicated in 1962. (The School also has, across the street from Merrill Hall, a Music Practice Building, with eighty practice rooms, opened in 1979; and at the time of the Simon dedication it had some offices—most of them now being moved to the new facility—in Sycamore Hall, adjacent to the Annex.)

One end of the Simon Center is taken up by the three-story William and Gayle Cook Music Library (named in response to a gift of $1,000,000), which now houses what is the fourth-largest American music library, comprising some 500,000 print items (including 312,000 full scores and performance parts) and 126,000 audio recordings. At a cost of $2,000,000 and in partnership with IBM, the "Variations Project" is digitizing the library's core holdings in scores and analogue audio recordings. Doing so allows the electronic distribution of these materials to computer workstations both within the library and outside it, enabling many users to have simultaneous but independent access to the same score and recordings of it; and this without the gradual degradation of the source material that inevitably occurs when printed material is handled or an analogue recording played. (In 1995, the library was providing about 125,000 analogue playing services per year.) In addition to the library and the Elsie I. Sweeney Lecture Hall—a 200-seat auditorium fitted out with audio-visual equipment and made possible by a $300,000 memorial gift from the family of one of the School's great patrons—the Simon Center's major facilities are two concert halls. The first of these is the Ford-Crawford Recital Hall, sponsored by a $350,000 gift from Richard E. Ford and the Ford Meter Box Company. This is an intimate 100-seat auditorium, in which the first row of seats is only four feet from the stage, which is itself raised just sixteen inches above floor level. The hall was unofficially inaugurated on Saturday afternoon by two student chamber recitals, the first offering nineteenth-century music as well as the premiere of a brass quintet by Bernhard Heiden (an emeritus faculty member), and the second consisting of sixteenth- and seventeenth-century works performed by members of the School's celebrated Early Music Institute.

The Center's third major facility is the Ione B. Auer Concert Hall, made possible by a million-dollar gift from Mrs. Auer. Her hall is a beautiful 400-seat auditorium with a high beamed and coffered ceiling, and with main-floor seating supplemented by three levels of side terraces. Here as in Ford-Crawford Hall, the accouterments include two new Steinway concert grands. (All told, the School owns nearly 500 pianos.) As the Saturday evening inaugural offering in the hall, the School mounted a performance of Monteverdi's Vespers of the Blessed Virgin. For this massive work, the forces included the University Singers, the University Children's Choir, a chamber orchestra of students from the Early Music Institute, and two faculty tenors—Alan Bennett and Paul Elliott—supplementing the student soloists who emerged at intervals from the choir. Sometimes the soloists, like the Children's Choir, sang from the front of one of the high terraces, to thrilling effect.

On Sunday afternoon, another recital was given at Ford-Crawford Hall, by twenty-one members of the School's New Music Ensemble, directed by faculty composer David Dzubay; this was followed by a concert at Auer Hall featuring student soloists playing concertos with the Chamber Orchestra. In the evening, the festivities reverted to the MAC, where PBS filmed a special for broadcast during its March 1996 fund drive. Hosted by television's Tyne Daly, the program offered a broad spectrum of love songs, from opera through Broadway and American popular standards, sung, in solos and different combinations, by Sylvia McNair (an alumna), Frederica von Stade, Jon Garrison, and Kurt Ollmann—and sometimes by Ms. Daly. The singers were accompanied for part of the program by the New York pianist Steven Blier but mostly by the eighty-four members of yet another School ensemble, the Concert Orchestra, which was, together with the forty-member Opera Chorus, conducted by another guest, the Bernstein protégé Michael Barrett.

The dedicatory festivities concluded with two additional chamber recitals. On Monday evening, an alumni concert in Auer Hall displayed the talents of three of the most celebrated recent graduates of the School's string program: violinist Joshua Bell, cellist Gary Hoffman, and bassist Edgar Meyer. On Tuesday evening, in the final event of the five-day celebration, Ford-Crawford Hall had its official inauguration. Corey Cerovsek, the prodigious Canadian violinist who in 1987 had become, at fifteen, the youngest graduate in the history of the University, joined with Hoffman, student violinist Michael Lim, and two faculty members (violist Atar Arad and pianist Evelyne Brancart) to perform the Dvořák piano quintet; afterward, Schubert's "Trout" quintet was performed by Bell, Arad, Hoffman, Meyer, and another faculty pianist, Shigeo Neriki.

Although the number of visiting and faculty artists on display during this extended weekend was unusual for the School, the number of scheduled musical events was not. With over sixteen hundred students, almost all of whom have recital and ensemble requirements to fulfill, and a good many of whom give extra recitals in preparation for competitions, the School mounts over a thousand musical events each year—on average, that is, a little over three per day. Except for vacation periods, there are few nights without at least one recital; on weekends, especially toward the end of the academic term, they come in batches. I've known thirty-six recitals—plus an opera and a studio opera—to be mounted on a single weekend. Nor is it unusual to have two major performances at the MAC during a weekend: there are frequent orchestral concerts there, and it was long a tradition of the School that opera was presented every Saturday night of the regular academic year, and some Friday nights as well.

The School mounts six fully staged operas, in addition to various semi-staged Opera Workshop productions, from September through April; there are two additional fully staged operatic productions in the summer (one of them usually a Broadway musical).

Apart from the scale of the School's operations, the biggest surprise it offers a visitor is likely to be the seeming dissonance between its high-culture sheen and its small-town setting in Bloomington, Indiana. Located fifty miles south of Indianapolis, Bloomington is a town of some 60,000 (swelled, for most of the year, by 30,000 out-of-town students). It is about twenty miles deep into the hill country of southern Indiana, of which, despite its modest size, it is the second-largest city, after the Ohio River town of Evansville a hundred miles to the southwest. This is limestone country—karst topography, a land of hills, ravines, sinkholes, and caves. Throughout the region, rolling farmland, punctuated by wooded areas, encompasses the towns.

By European or eastern American lights, the area is unsophisticated. With the partial exception of Bloomington, its culture is country and Midwestern. The next-door town is Nashville, which on a small scale emulates its Tennessee namesake in being a center of country music. The dominant religion of the area is Protestant and fundamentalist, the politics Republican and conservative. In these respects, it is like Indiana in general.

Like most other towns, Bloomington itself is either attractive or unattractive, depending on where one looks. The older part of the University, which occupies the center of town, is extremely handsome, appearing not so much like a publicly supported institution as like one of the well-endowed private universities. Most of the buildings are of the local limestone. A small stream runs through the old campus, and the eight-acre Dunn's Woods constitutes a particularly pleasant feature of it. One is not surprised to learn that Thomas Gaines's *The Campus as a Work of Art* lists the Bloomington campus among the five most beautiful in America. Spreading east and north, the newer part of the University is less attractive, with huge student-housing structures, numerous fraternity and sorority houses, and a miscellany of other buildings, though also much green space.

Fanning out from the campus are residential neighborhoods, which vary, in the customary American fashion, from astonishingly affluent to distressingly impoverished. Skirting the town on the north and west is the bypass of the highway to Indianapolis, flanked by the usual commercial sprawl. The town's one substantial shopping mall—thus universally known as "The Mall"—lies to the southeast of the University. I've seen deer crossing the road two hundred yards past its southern edge, where a wooded strip buffers the suburbs. There is an excellent park system; and in the spring the many blooming trees and flowering bushes justify the town's lovely name.

Hardly any place in Bloomington is more than a ten-minute drive from the performance venues of the School of Music, and in the evening and on weekends the parking is easy. This must be the most cost-effective place in the world to listen to classical music. There is a large number and variety of performances to choose from, the average quality is high, and the cost is exceedingly low: almost everything is free except the opera, where the best seat in the house goes for $28.

The question, though, is why the music is there to listen to in the first place. Charles Webb, who was Dean of the School at the time of the Simon Center dedication, is fond of pointing out that with the addition of the new building the School has better facilities than any of its world rivals: "Better than the Berlin Hochschule, better than the Paris Conservatory, better than the Toho School of Music in Tokyo." But all those schools, and other nationally preeminent ones such as the Moscow Conservatory and London's Royal Academy, as well as most of the best American conservatories, are in major world cities—that is, in the metropolitan settings where elite musical training and performance have always been concentrated. How did the foremost American music school, a major world cultural institution, come to be at a state university in a provincial town, amid the cornfields of southern Indiana?

1

Beginnings (1824–1919)

There was always music in Bloomington, but in the nineteenth century very little of it was in the Western classical tradition. William Lowe Bryan, who had joined the faculty eighteen years before becoming President of the University in 1902, put the matter succinctly: "The Empire of Beethoven was as far from our people generally as the Empire of Genghis Khan."

The Indiana Territory became a state in 1816. Two years later, the "New Purchase" treaty opened the central portion of the state to white settlement; and in 1824 Indiana University opened, as the Indiana Seminary, in a town that was itself only six years old. In a retrospective account of his "seven and a half years in the far west," the Seminary's original, sole professor, Baynard R. Hall, recalls the sensation created by the piano that he brought for the fledgling institution from Philadelphia. Supposedly the first piano in the Purchase, its arrival was awaited with "expectation . . . on tip-toe, and conjecture never weary. 'A pianne! what could it be?'"

This passage is quoted in the survey of music at the University in the nineteenth century that the first Dean of the School of Music, Barzille Winfred Merrill, contributed to Burton Myers's history of the University in the Bryan era. The bulk of the survey consists of anecdotes that, like this one, confirm the accuracy of Bryan's assessment. At the 1829 inaugural reception for the University's first President, Andrew Wylie, according to a report Merrill quotes from Dean D. D. Banta, the speeches were interspersed by a flutist and a fiddler playing "their most enlivening airs, such as 'White River,' 'Fire in the Mountain,' 'Jay Bird,' and 'Bonaparte Crossing the Alps.'" For the trustees' inspection of 1832, Professor Ebenezer Elliott recorded, the University had "a fine brass band"; but Elliott also noted that the orchestra for the 1833 Commencement "was composed of two flutes, one of them cracked." The program for an 1849 meeting of the Philomathean Society has the university band playing various marches and waltzes. Since the society was a literary club, this program may, as Merrill says, "be considered as representing music at its best at Indiana University in the middle of the nineteenth century." During the brief history of the University's first teacher-training program—1852–58—vocal music was listed as a required part of that course of studies (though there is no indication as to who might have taught it). In the 1880s, classical and light classical numbers began to appear on Commencement programs. A major aspect of the University's history—its association with opera—began modestly in 1889, when the program included a Donizetti aria.

Music reappeared as a subject of instruction, though only on an extracurricular footing, in the University Catalogue for 1893–94, which records that "Mr. M. B. Griffith is the director of the college choir and the University Glee Club, and, also, by the authority of the University, teaches private classes in vocal music in the University buildings." The 1895–96 catalogue announces that Griffith had organized a non-credit course in elementary sight reading; the following year's catalogue announces classes in choral singing. In 1896, Griffith was succeeded as Director of Music by Charles N. Hassler, who was in turn succeeded by Lucius M. Hiatt in 1899. Hiatt continued with the classes in choral singing and with the Glee Club (supplementing that all-male organization with a Women's Glee Club), and he organized an orchestra and a band, as well as "first and second mandolin clubs" and other ensembles. Burton Myers, who had just come from Johns Hopkins to head the new medical school (and was an accomplished singer), heard Hiatt's orchestra at the 1903 Commencement, and reports, with an aptly musical metaphor, that it was "the one sour, discordant note of the occasion."

Of the several musical organizations, the male Glee Club was undoubtedly the most important in the development of music at Indiana, for it first set the school's administrators to thinking about the potential benefits of music for it. The earliest report of the club's activities dates from the spring of 1893, when it journeyed to Indianapolis in support of the University's representative at the state oratorical contest; it also serenaded the new President, Joseph Swain, and his wife, upon their arrival in Bloomington in June. In the following years, as the club undertook a growing number of out-of-town engagements, Swain became aware of the considerable benefits, in terms of advertising and public relations, that might accrue to the University from musical performance. This was a lesson that his successors also apprehended.

In June of 1898, Swain reported with pride to the Board of Trustees that the Glee Club had enjoyed unprecedented success in the past year. It had made tours, during school vacations, to both ends of the state, and had several engagements for the summer. Presumably it was Swain's sense of the importance of the club as an advertisement for the University that caused him to be so distressed when, a year later, he had to inform the trustees about Glee Club publicity of the opposite kind. At a stopover on the club's spring tour in the southern part of the state, three of its members "were drinking and became somewhat intoxicated"—that is, made a public spectacle of themselves; a perennial hazard in having a university represented by its undergraduates.

In 1902, Swain left Indiana for the presidency of Swarthmore College. He was succeeded in Bloomington by Bryan, a distinguished Professor of Psychology who had also taught English and philosophy, and had served as Swain's Vice President since 1893. Bryan was to be President for thirty-five years, and it was in his long reign that the University assumed its modern form.

Reshaping the school was Bryan's major concern from the beginning. As Thomas D. Clark says in his four-volume history of the University (1970–77), Bryan was "obsessed with the subject of enrollment," perhaps because "he had lived through a period when professors watched anxiously to see if there would be enough returning students each fall to open classes." In order to maintain and increase its enrollment, Bryan thought, the University needed to diversify its curriculum. Shortly after assuming office, he reported to the trustees that, of the University's 748 students, eighty-five were registered in its only professional school, Law, and the rest were liberal arts majors. Having made a study of enrollment patterns in other universities, Bryan knew that this proportion of liberal arts students was unusually high, and he saw in it a serious institutional weakness. To correct the problem, he proposed, in the first years of his administration, the establishment of several other professional schools. The implementation of this proposal was the major accomplishment of his long presidency.

As well as schools of medicine, architecture, engineering, and graduate studies, Bryan urged the establishment of a school of music. The idea of incorporating music into the curriculum of the University had, in fact, a double impetus. In the first place, Bryan believed that music formed an important part of a liberal arts education; from this point of view, it was incumbent on the University to mount courses in music appreciation. At the same time, music could be viewed as a profession, for which the University might offer training. The kind of professional musician Bryan had in mind was not the elite performer but the music teacher, especially in the public schools of the state. Most graduates of the University became teachers; the University could extend teacher-training into this additional field. One special incentive to do so lay in the possibility of thereby attracting more female students, music-teaching being a profession open to women. As the *Bloomington Telephone* put it, "It has been recognized . . . that if Indiana were to hold her own as a co-educational institution she must have a first-class music department." With such considerations in mind, Bryan in June 1904 persuaded the trustees to approve the creation of a music school.

If the school had been founded at that time, Indiana would not have lagged much behind most other universities in the teaching of music. As Merrill noted in his account of music at the University in the nineteenth century, the field was slow to gain acceptance as a part of the curriculum in American universities, partly in consequence of the Puritan heritage. If music was first mentioned in an Indiana catalogue in 1854, it was first mentioned in a Harvard catalogue only in 1856, 220 years after the founding of the college! And though by the end of the century Harvard and many other universities—including a number of Midwestern ones, with Michigan, Illinois, Iowa State, and Northwestern among them—did have departments or schools of music, the continuing resistance to music as a subject of formal academic instruction is apparent in the observation of Harvard's President Charles W. Eliot, in his 1916 pamphlet *Changes Needed in American Secondary Education,* that "by many teachers and educational administrators music and drawing are still regarded as fads or trivial accomplishments not worthy to rank as substantial educational material." Even where music was accepted into the curriculum, formal academic credit was often extended only to courses in the theory, history, or appreciation of music, not to practical training in musical performance.

We touch here on a fact of fundamental importance. The development of postsecondary musical education in North America has been heavily influenced by the bipartite model of musical education found in Europe and especially Germany (whose educational system has had such a strong impact on the form of the modern American university). In the customary European practice, universities grant credit only for musicological studies; performance training is restricted to conservatories. The European model was generally adhered to in late nineteenth- and earlier twentieth-century North America, where the serious study of what was (and is) revealingly called "academic" music—music theory and musicology—was effectively confined to the universities, while instruction in musical performance—quaintly called "applied" music in the universities, where "applied" has generally not been a term of approbation—was, especially at the highest level, the province of independent conservatories such as the Juilliard School or the Curtis Institute.

Over time, though, the curricula of the two kinds of institutions have grown less distinct, especially because many universities have come to grant credit for, and even to have degree programs in, applied music as well as academic; in a number of important cases, such as those of Oberlin, Michigan, and Rochester, universities have actually absorbed nearby conservatories. In cases of this latter kind, but also in many others where the development of musical studies has been purely internal to the university, music has been constituted as a separate school or institute within the university; elsewhere, it has been constituted as a department within the college of arts and science. These alternative administrative arrangements have resulted in the partial preservation, within the family of universities, of the bipartite model of musical education: for where Music is constituted as a department within a college of arts and science, the curriculum is normally dominated by academic music, and credit for performance studies is limited or even (as at Harvard) non-existent; by contrast, where Music is constituted as a separate faculty or school within the university, performance study has tended, over time, to become more important than academic music.

In the light of Eliot's remarks on the widespread suspiciousness, among academics, toward music as a university subject, these contrasting patterns of development are not hard to understand. In a college of arts and science, music is likely to be fully respectable as a subject of study only when it is restricted to the historical and analytical modes that are standard in the other arts fields. But when music is made a separate school or faculty within the university, academic status for performance study is much easier to achieve, for two reasons. First, most faculty members in such schools are apt, even if they are specialists in academic music, to regard performance training more favorably than do most arts and science faculty. Second, the director of a school of music, being (in effect, and often in title) a dean, deals directly with the central university administration rather than with the Dean of Arts and Science; and central administrators are keenly aware of the importance of public relations and readily able to appreciate the fact that musical performance is of almost infinitely greater importance in this sphere than is academic music. Bryan's decision to create a *school* of music, then, was the most fateful one in the history of the subject at Indiana.

It was not, though, possible to establish the school nearly as soon as he wished. The trustees had authorized him to search for the single appointee he thought would be necessary to launch the school, a "Professor or Dean" of Music. But a few months after having received this charge, Bryan reported that securing such an individual had so far proved to be impossible: "It is extremely difficult to find a man whose musical training is quite first rate and who has also the good sense and executive ability required."

As some of Bryan's letters acknowledge, his difficulty in recruiting a suitable musician derived partly from his relative ignorance of the field. Another source of difficulty, surely, lay in how little he had to offer, in terms both of remuneration and of the local amenities. Throughout its history, Indiana University has been cursed with low faculty salaries, as a result of a chronic shortfall of state funding. A major problem for Bryan was the difficulty of offering able faculty sufficient financial inducement either to come to Bloomington or, when they began to achieve some distinction, to remain there. Then too, what person of first-rate musical training, as well as "good sense and executive ability," would want to move to such a town as Bloomington then was? At the time of Bryan's accession, streets in both the town and the campus were dirt and gravel, and the town lacked a reliable water supply and a sewage system. The creek running through the campus—christened the River Jordan after one of Bryan's predecessors, the illustrious David Starr Jordan—served as the University's sewer. In consequence of the poor sanitary conditions in the town and the fact that, as Clark reports, "many students came from counties where vaccination rules were unenforced," the University was subject to recurrent epidemics of typhoid, scarlet fever, and smallpox. Furthermore, vandals and vagrants infested its wooded environs. In 1903 (the year after Bryan's accession) the Governor was so incensed by reports of "violent lawlessness" in the town that he threatened to ask the legislature to relocate the University.

Bloomington was also geographically isolated. Roads were poor, and, had it not been for the Monon Railway's north-south line—supplemented in 1906 by the east-west line of the Illinois Central—travel to and from the town would have been next to impossible. Even the railroads did not provide wholly satisfactory transportation, due to the condition of the equipment and the rowdiness of some of the passengers. According to a student account of 1912, trains consisted of a "neurasthenic engine" and "three prehistoric passenger coaches which will stop at the least provocation." The roughness of the ride suggested the absence of a roadbed. To while away the hours, one could "shoot craps, chew tobacco, smoke, take a swig of whiskey, or play poker in any of the coaches."

Although the search for a music professor dragged on, the musical life of Bloomington improved rapidly in the early years of Bryan's tenure. There were not merely local efforts, such as concerts by the university band and the glee clubs, but a number of visits by individual artists or ensembles from the larger world. Professor Guido Stempel, a philologist and musical amateur who for the first half of the century wrote music criticism for the Bloomington and University newspapers, noted that these visits included two appearances (the first as early as 1899) by the Chicago Symphony under its founding conductor, Theodore Thomas. The Pittsburgh Orchestra, under the direction of Victor Herbert, also played in Bloomington, as did the Spiering String Quartet and, among individual performers, Ede Reményi and Rudolph Ganz.

For the development of music instruction at Indiana, though, the most important visitor was the pianist Edward Ebert-Buchheim. Born and educated in Germany, Ebert-Buchheim was by all accounts a highly accomplished performer; and he had taught music in Europe for seventeen years before emigrating in 1897 to the United States, where he held, at the time he began giving occasional recitals in Bloomington in 1903, the position of head of the Piano Department at Central Normal College, a teacher-training institution in nearby Danville.

In 1906, Bryan engaged Ebert-Buchheim to give a series of recitals for the University, and to offer piano lessons to its students. The next year Ebert-Buchheim, having been appointed Instructor in Piano, moved to Bloomington, where he was supplied with a studio, guaranteed twenty-five lessons per week for thirty-six weeks of the academic year (at a dollar per lesson), and engaged to give fifteen recitals (at $15 each) during the same period. Certificates of achievement were awarded to students who completed the courses of study Ebert-Buchheim set up at the elementary, advanced, and "artist" levels, but no University credit was given. Ebert-Buchheim also offered instruction in harmony and counterpoint to advanced piano students; and for this work in academic music, students *could* earn credit.

Ebert-Buchheim's recitals, presented free of charge at the Student Building and centered in works of major composers, were well attended and received, and in general his presence in Bloomington must have contributed greatly to the enhancement of both music appreciation and piano performance in the University. He was the first in a long line of émigré European musicians who have played a vital role in the development of music at Indiana. The arrangement with Ebert-Buchheim was continued in the following year; and perhaps Bryan began to entertain the possibility of eventually bestowing the professorship of music on the pianist. Unfortunately, in the summer of 1908 Ebert-Buchheim suffered a stroke, which left him paralyzed on his right side. By the following spring, he was able to give a series of recitals exploring the rich piano literature for the left hand; and the next year he gave, with his wife, a series of duet recitals. Eventually he was able to offer a few more solo recitals. But he was, as Myers (who knew him) says, "a stricken man unable to exert leadership in the expansion of the work for which the time was ripe." He died in January 1912.

In 1910, Bryan, despairing of hiring a suitable "Professor or Dean" anytime soon and painfully aware of the fact that, as he told the trustees, "we have had a very unsatisfactory and inadequate provision for Music," felt it necessary to establish a better interim arrangement. Lucius Hiatt was still Director of Music, but, as Bryan informed the trustees, "it became evident years ago that Mr. Hiatt was not equal to the demands of this place." He added that Hiatt "has understood this and has been ready to retire whenever we think best." As an alternative to continuing with Hiatt, Bryan proposed the seemingly desperate expedient of promoting a thirty-two-year-old Assistant Professor of German, Charles Diven Campbell, to the position of Associate Professor of Music. Campbell was to become Head of a new Department of Music, serving on a year-to-year basis until such time as a satisfactory outside appointment could be made.

Campbell had in fact good qualifications for this role. A native of Anderson, Indiana, he had completed his undergraduate degree at the University and, after two years as a teacher at the depressingly named Manual Training High School in Indianapolis, had proceeded to graduate studies at the University of Strassburg, where in 1905 he attained a doctorate in philology. He then returned to the United States for a year at Harvard, engaged in what Guido Stempel described, in his obituary of Campbell, as an "effort to adjust his German training to American conditions." In 1906 he was appointed Instructor of German at Indiana, rising to Assistant Professor two years later. Stempel says that Campbell pursued his philological studies "because they promised him an assured livelihood" (an interesting statement in itself), but that "his passionate interest was music." While at Strassburg, he had "found time for extensive and intensive studies in the history and theory of music." In addition, he had "become a pianist of no mean ability, and he had devoted much time to dramatics." He soon began to indulge these passions in Bloomington, where he produced and conducted *The Mikado* at the Harris Grand Theater in 1909, and, in 1910, Reginald de Koven's operetta *Robin Hood*. These were the earliest full productions of opera or operetta in Bloomington; the second one was such a success that it was repeated in Indianapolis.

From his earliest years on the Indiana faculty, Campbell shared Bryan's desire for a School of Music. In 1907 he arranged for a recital of the Schellschmidt Quartet of Indianapolis, with the proceeds used, as the student newspaper explained, to establish "a music fund, to lead ultimately to the equipment of a school of music in the University." In 1909, he offered a series of lectures (not for credit) on the history of music, and wrote to Bryan outlining several courses in music history and musical form that he thought should be mounted.

It was in this context, then, that Bryan wrote to Campbell on May 30, 1910, proposing that he "should become Associate Professor of Music, giving certain courses in Music and having next year general charge of the musical interests of the University." Campbell agreed to this arrangement, which was subsequently endorsed by the Board of Trustees; and thus a Department of Music was created, and the glorious history of music as a regular subject of study at Indiana University began.

Given Campbell's German (and Harvard) training, one might expect that applied music would play no role in his plans for the curricular development of music at the University. But President Bryan had always been interested in music not only as a liberal art but as a field in which the University might offer professional training, and his charge to Campbell had been, as he explained to the trustees, "to submit plans for some courses in Music as part of the Department of Liberal Arts, and also to submit plans for some enlargement of the work in applied Music." Moreover, Campbell himself had—as his operatic productions indicate—a strong interest in applied music.

He also sensibly believed that academic music and applied music were not wholly separable. The fullest exposition of Campbell's philosophy of musical education is found in a twenty-four-page appendix to a 1913 report to Bryan and the trustees. In this document, he argued that the study of music had two components, which he was trying, in his Department, to balance: "that leading to a knowledge *about* music, and that leading to a knowledge *of* music." Knowledge about music could be gained from courses in music history and music theory. Knowledge of music could be gained from listening to it, but *making* music was also an invaluable source of this knowledge. It was not so much public performance that was useful in this regard as the practice that *precedes* performance—"the thorough familiarity gained in the rehearsals, through the constant repetitions and the continued hearings." But just as a complete education in academic music required experience in applied music, so also the education of performers required knowledge of music history and theory. Thus, as Campbell put it in a 1915 report (a disquisition announced as a sequel to the 1913 appendix), academic and applied music "merge into each other so gradually that the drawing of a definite line between them is difficult, and must, for the most part, be purely arbitrary."

Campbell's organization of the Department of Music was consistent with these views. He was completely clear on the point that the business of the Department was academic music, music treated as a liberal art. As he explained in the University Catalogue, the Department's aim was to cultivate "a better understanding and appreciation of music, rather than of technical proficiency in any one of the various branches of applied music." Thus "the courses offered are . . . mainly historical and theoretical in character: lectures and recitations, supplemented by illustrations on the piano, and by collateral reading and reports." But two of his five original courses were Orchestra and Chorus, and he allowed academic credit for these applied-music courses, provided that the student also took one of the courses in music theory—provided, that is, that the applied-music courses could be construed as adjunctive to those in academic music.

In addition to the courses in Orchestra and Chorus, Campbell mounted one on the History and Development of Music and two on music theory (Elements of Music; Musical Forms). He taught all three of the academic courses himself, and shared responsibility for the applied courses with three musicians appointed as Assistants; another Assistant replaced Hiatt as band director. (Band was listed as a sixth course, but no credit was given for it.) As had been the case before the creation of the Department, private, non-credit lessons in vocal and instrumental music were also offered to students who wanted to pay for them: one of the Assistants—John L. Geiger, who came down from Indianapolis on a part-time basis—taught voice, and Ebert-Buchheim gave piano lessons.

Enrollment in the Department grew rapidly. In its first year of operation, there were 214 enrollments in the credit courses. The band and orchestra each had about thirty members, the chorus about sixty. By the second year, course enrollments had increased to 281, and they continued to grow. The number of courses offered also grew. By 1918, there were thirteen on the books, including courses in Wagner, Nineteenth-Century Opera, Oratorio, the Symphony, Modern Composers, and Public School Music.

The number of Assistants did not keep pace. They came and went, some of them appearing in the catalogue for only one year; and their overall number never exceeded half a dozen. Of the Assistants of the first several years, Geiger alone became a permanent member of the Department. (Archibald Warner, who became band director in 1916, remained until 1926.) Starting with the 1915 catalogue, Geiger's title is Tutor rather than Assistant, a promotion connected with the fact that from this time forward he was the only person other than Campbell who had sole charge of credit courses. (Under Merrill, Geiger was promoted to Instructor and later to Assistant Professor, a rank he held until 1938, when he retired.)

Facilities and equipment for the new Department were very basic, as for the liberal arts in general in this era of the University. In 1883, a fire had destroyed most of the original campus, at Seminary Square, about a mile from the present campus. When the University was rebuilt, at the Dunn's Woods site, the available money totaled $110,000. Since the initial plan was to keep the liberal arts at Seminary Square, in the one surviving building, these funds were committed to raising two handsome science buildings, each of brick and costing a little more than $50,000; they still grace the campus. When the impracticability of having two separate campuses became clear, the princely sum of $3,800, formerly earmarked for scientific equipment, was diverted to the construction of a two-story wooden building, sixty feet by forty, for the arts. This building was to play a major role in the history of music at Indiana for three decades.

Even when it was new, in 1885, the building (first christened Maxwell Hall and renamed Mitchell Hall when Maxwell was honored with a better one) was, especially in juxtaposition with the science buildings, unimpressive. The *Indiana Student* characterized it as "a poor little frame." Its main floor was used as a chapel; "and stored away in its attic are four or five little rooms, about 12 × 16, where the student must get his philosophy, political economy, literature, languages, etc." In 1896 the building became a gymnasium for female students, pending the completion of the Student Building; and this was its use when, in 1905, the *Student* announced that Mitchell was to be made available to the promised music school. By the next year the band and the glee clubs were installed there. There, too, Ebert-Buchheim gave his piano lessons and his first Bloomington recitals. And this was the building in which the new Department of Music conducted all its operations. (Recitals could be mounted in the Student Building, which opened in 1906, and large-scale productions such as opera were presented at Assembly Hall—the former men's gymnasium, a ramshackle building of 1896.)

Already by the time the Department of Music opened, Mitchell Hall was in wretched condition. In an appendix to his first report to Bryan, Campbell pleaded for repairs. A new roof was needed, and repainting. Carpentry was required outside and in, most urgently to brace and strengthen the stairway. One of the rooms was unusable, because of the condition of the plaster and the floors, and a second was scarcely better. The wiring was deplorable; and there were no fire hoses. Evidently these requests evoked little or no response, for the next year Campbell again called attention "to the condition of Mitchell Hall, particularly to the unsafe condition of the stairway, and to the lack of fire protection, there being no water connections in the building." Again little or nothing was done, and in a 1917 report Campbell once more pointed out to Bryan, and through him to the Board of Trustees, that Mitchell Hall was in "an extremely bad condition": "Not only are the walls bulging outward at places, and plastering falling from the ceilings, but every rain causes water to leak through two stories."

Finally, in 1918, the trustees appropriated $1,800 to remodel the building. That summer, the second story was removed and the first expanded by constructing a sixteen-foot addition to one side, resulting in a building seventy-six feet by forty. A large principal classroom and rehearsal room occupied most of the interior space, while there were, around three sides, a room for the Head and half a dozen instrumental studios and practice rooms. Throughout Campbell's headship (and afterward), equipment was also a problem—one which, like that of accommodations, grew worse as enrollment increased. Laments about shortages of instruments, and about repairs needed by the few the Department *did* have, are another leitmotif of Campbell's reports. There was a constant shortage of pianos, and most of those the Department owned were in poor condition (not that this is not also the case with the School's practice pianos in the current era). In 1995–96, the equipment inventory of the School was a book of 125 pages, including 477 pianos and, among many other instruments, 17 tubas; but in 1911 the demise of a single tuba created a crisis serious enough to be referred to Bryan and the trustees: for this was the only tuba. In the nature of things, the band depended heavily on it; and there was no money to replace it.

Among Campbell's highest equipment priorities, for which he did get funding, were a Victrola and records for it, and a player piano together with a number of rolls. The second purchase may seem outlandish for a music department, but at the time the player piano was the only high-fidelity recording device in existence; and like the phonograph it was standard equipment for music-appreciation courses. Campbell nourished the dream of putting the Victrola and piano, together with the books and scores he was accumulating, into what he liked to call a "musical reading room." He never got the soundproofed quarters he wanted for this purpose, but his acquisitions were the nucleus from which the audio and print collections of the School's library grew.

Campbell also did the best he could to supply live music, both by local performers and by visiting artists. In this endeavor he was aided by the management of the Harris Grand, who not only opened the theater to his operatic productions but occasionally brought in musical troupes from elsewhere, and by the Friday Musicale, a women's club founded in 1905, which for many years sponsored a variety of performances. Campbell, too, brought in visiting artists for concerts whenever he could, and he saw to it that the Department itself mounted a constant series of public performances. Performance, after all, played a role not only in the education of music students but in helping the students of the University in general to acquire what Campbell described in a 1911 report as "such acquaintance with the names and works of the great composers, as is generally expected in the world at large of an educated and cultivated man." (Just as exposure to classical music would have a beneficial effect on students, Campbell thought, so would the performance of what he regarded as bad music have a corrupting effect on them; and his 1913 report warned against letting the management of the Student Union concert series fall into the hands of students "with low ideals of music," who would mount minstrel shows and vaudeville. If the eminent danger of such "degeneration" should be realized, "the Union should lose its right to University support, and should be forbidden to continue its series of musical entertainments.")

As is suggested by his early productions of *The Mikado* and *Robin Hood,* which were supplemented in 1911 by another de Koven operetta, *Rob Roy,* and in 1912 by Victor Herbert's *Babette,* Campbell initially thought that opera was perhaps the most efficacious means of cultivating the appreciation of music. According to Guido Stempel, though, in time Campbell came to regard opera as not entirely suitable as the "focal center of activity" for the Department: operatic performances "awakened an interest in music, but also in things extraneous, and they dissipated more energy than they conserved." Whatever exactly these objections may mean, Campbell did turn away from opera and, in its place, developed the orchestra as the focal point. As I noted above, early in his tenure the orchestra was small. A 1912 photograph of it shows twenty-three players—nineteen men and four women. (See Figure 4.) The program for a 1916 concert, though, lists forty-two members, including some non-students, with Campbell conducting.

In these same years, Campbell emerged as a composer. His great triumph in this field came in May 1916, when, as part of the centennial celebrations of the state, forces numbering more than a thousand—men, women, and children, students and faculty of the University, and citizens of the town—mounted a historical and partly allegorical "Pageant of Bloomington and Indiana University." For the nine parts of the pageant (and for two other pageants, at the current and former capitals, Indianapolis and Corydon), the text was written by William Chauncy Langdon, and Campbell composed and directed the music.

The allegory of the Pageant is not to modern taste. In the summary found in the extensive, highly laudatory account of the event published in *Musical America* for June 24, 1916, we read that

> The introduction began with the full orchestra pronouncement of the Indiana theme, and passed immediately into graceful dance music as the Spirits of Hope and Determination poured back and forth over the pageant grounds like endless beds of irises waving in the wind. The approach of a band of pioneers interrupts this free nature dance. Indians attack the pioneers, and the Spirits first of Determination and then of Hope fly to the rescue and lead the pioneers onward into the vision of the future in which the ideal of the State of Indiana attended by the Angel of Inspiration appears to them as they march to the strains of the new State hymn.

Campbell's music was highly praised. According to *Musical America,* he had shown himself "an able musician, a thorough scholar," whose music had "nobly justified" his selection as the pageant's composer. The musical centerpiece was the stirring "Hymn to Indiana," which concluded the first scene and was reprised to end the Pageant as a whole.

The Pageant was the high point of Campbell's tenure, a watershed event deploying as many as possible of the performance resources of the Department and, in addition, displaying his own skills as a composer. For the first time, the event brought Music at Indiana to attention in the national press. In the sequel, Campbell was elected to membership in two honorary music fraternities. For a musical amateur, Head of Music only *faute de mieux,* these marks of professional acceptance must have been sweet.

Throughout his years as Head, though, Campbell never lost sight of the fact that he was fulfilling only half of the charge that Bryan had given him. Like Bryan, he wanted the University to provide not just music for liberal arts students but a thorough training for professional musicians. Like Bryan too, he saw this training as properly the business of a separate administrative unit, a School of Music outside the College of Liberal Arts. The outline of courses and material requirements for a Department of Music that he submitted to the President in June 1910 had appended to it a sketch of the requirements for a "school of applied music." Such a school could be established by the appointment of as few as three teachers, one each for voice, piano, and strings. It could confer "a special musical degree," although, since the school would be functioning as part of a university, students would be required to supplement their music courses by certain courses in the College of Liberal Arts. In his covering letter to Bryan, however, Campbell acknowledged that instituting this second music program was "possibly more than the University can do at present."

By the time of his 1913 report, though, he was ready to make a formal proposal of this kind, urging Bryan and the trustees to establish, as a complement to the Department of Music, a School of Music offering the professional degree of Bachelor of Music. He confidently shared Bryan's old dream that such a school would be a money-making proposition: "Music schools are for the most part not only self-supporting but very profitable institutions as well"; the examples of the University of Michigan and nearby DePauw University showed that this was so. There was every reason to think that the same would be true at Indiana.

Recognizing that the trustees would be unlikely to create such a school at a stroke, Campbell recommended (as he had in the plan submitted to Bryan in 1910), as "an experimental step," the appointment of a small number of Instructors in applied music. Their salaries would be offset by lesson fees collected from their students. News of these appointments would bring young musicians flocking to the University; before long, additional appointments would be justified, and the School of Music created. Further, Campbell urged that a program to train public school music teachers be developed.

The trustees did not act on either of Campbell's recommendations. In 1915, though, he went on and mounted the course in Public School Music referred to previously (Jack Geiger taught it), and in his report that same year he reiterated the proposal for the incremental development of a School of Music, this time urging the appointment of three particular individuals as Instructors in violin, cello, and piano. Again the minutes of the trustees' meeting include no mention of Campbell's proposal.

But finally, in the fall of 1918, the trustees approved his experimental step. Campbell was allowed to appoint, as Assistants, three instrumentalists: Gaylord Yost, an Indianapolis violinist who had since 1914 been advertised in the Catalogue as being available for private lessons; Adolph Schellschmidt, a cellist, also of Indianapolis, who had played and taught in Bloomington for years; and Pasquale Tallerico, a Spanish pianist. Tallerico did not actually come, but in the next year's Catalogue, Yost and Schellschmidt were announced in a new paragraph explaining that in addition to its regular courses the Department also offered non-credit ones in voice, piano, and various orchestral instruments. The new appointees were paid a token salary, but their main income derived, in accordance with the suggestion Campbell had originally made in 1910, from lesson fees, of which 90 percent went to the appointee, the rest to the Department. (Arrangements of this kind were standard practice in conservatories.)

From the point of view of the development of Music at the University, it was probably the best possible outcome that Campbell's plans for applied music got this far and no farther. The principle of appointing to faculty positions (if only as Assistants) people who simply gave music lessons was established, as was the mechanism of paying them through lesson fees collected by the University. Winfred Merrill was to make great use of these advances. But it was doubtless a good thing that Campbell did not get past this first stage of his plan to develop a discrete School of Music as a complement to the Department of Music.

To be sure, dividing music studies between two separate academic units—a liberal arts department and a professional school—offered a way around the prejudice against applied music as a credited subject in a liberal arts college. There is, moreover, a certain enduring appeal in this kind of segregation, which, in contrast to the European model, allows professional musical training to take place within the rich cultural matrix of the university (a matrix it further enriches) while recognizing that the musical needs of liberal arts students and professional music students are partly different and even competing. On balance, though, the interests of music as a whole in the university are surely not well served by this kind of administrative segregation. In terms of university politics, the musical enterprise is weakened by dividing its forces into different and partly rival camps. More important, such a division does not really make sense in academic terms. As Campbell himself had recognized, the division between academic music and applied music is ultimately arbitrary, and students need, in order to become fully competent in either field, a good deal of work in the other.

One may wonder why it took the trustees five years to approve even Campbell's modest experimental step. The only recorded explanation is found in a 1915 letter from Bryan to Campbell, which claims that the obstacle was, at least that year, monetary: "the present financial condition of the University has prevented the Trustees from making the additions to the musical faculty which you have recommended." But this explanation does not seem to bear scrutiny, since Campbell had said from the first (though not explicitly in his 1915 submission) that the salaries of the applied-music teachers would be generated from lesson fees. Moreover, since the trustees seem always to have followed Bryan's lead on the development of music at the University—acceding, as far as one can tell, to every suggestion he made on the subject—it seems likely that the real obstacle to Campbell's plans was Bryan himself.

If so, the President's objection was not to applied music, whose development in the University he had always supported. He may not have wanted to make any expansionary move, however modest, in those wartime years. (When the trustees finally did act on Campbell's proposal, the World War was coming to a close.) Or perhaps Bryan hesitated to take a serious step in the development of an applied-music program before he had in place his real Professor of Music. This latter possibility—that the President was reluctant to act on Campbell's proposal at least in part because he lacked entire confidence in his interim Head—is strengthened by the fact that in these same years he steadfastly declined to accede to another of Campbell's requests, namely, that he be promoted to Professor, with a commensurate increase in salary.

By 1916 Campbell appears to have lost the optimism with which he had formerly approached his work. After 1915, his reports include no more expositions of his theory of musical education. His 1916 report is a melancholy document, sadly contrasting with the grand musings of the earlier ones. Though he noted that "considerable progress has been made" in the establishment of music at the University, he was also aware, "probably better than any one else, . . . of the defects in the work": "I have fallen short of my ideals." He went on to request that he be promoted to the rank of Professor, with an increase in salary from $2,200 to $3,000. While ruminations about his shortcomings did not provide an especially good context for this request, Campbell had in fact previously made the same one in a letter to Bryan dated May 18—which, as the final day of the great Pageant, would seem to have been an ideally propitious moment. Pageant or no, Bryan and the trustees turned him down. (His salary was increased by $100.) Campbell raised the matter again the next year, pointing out his length of service and the unusually heavy teaching load that, as the sole professorial appointee in his Department, he was forced to carry. He reiterated the request a third time in 1918, arguing that "in consideration of the amount and kind of the work, of the difficulties, the lack of facilities and of assistants I have had to contend with and of the rapidly growing importance of the work, I believe that I am justified in making this request, particularly in comparison with the heads of other departments." Again the request was fruitless.

By this stage, Campbell had passed from melancholy through disgruntlement to embitteredness, not just on his own behalf but on that of music at the University. He was especially outraged by the fact that, while financial difficulties were cited as the reason why matters could not be improved in Music, money continued to be found for other purposes that were no more—in some cases, surely much less—worthy. Departments established later than Music had already had additional professorial appointments. In a 1917 report, he requested "most earnestly" that some way be found of paying the band leader (Archie Warner) more generously. To supplement his income, Warner had been doubling as janitor of Mitchell Hall—a position in which he earned $624 per annum, as compared to the $150 he received as band director. The latter amount was, Campbell said, "absurdly small . . . when the time and the training and experience necessary to do the work are taken into consideration." He added parenthetically (perhaps not helping his cause) that "I might suggest here a comparison with the work and the pay of the various athletic coaches." This same report concludes with one of his pleas for repairs to Mitchell Hall. In this matter, too, he could not resist comparison: "I hope that the time is not far distant when Music will have its turn, and will receive some much needed support." Though Music *did* soon have a turn, in the form of the 1918 renovations, it is difficult to see how, unless he had been promoted, Campbell could have gone on working for Bryan much longer.

In 1919, death abruptly terminated the impasse. On a spring evening, Campbell was taking his infant daughter (and only child) for a walk in her carriage. Something went wrong with one of the wheels, and, trying to fix it, he skinned his finger. As could easily happen in those days before antibiotics, the infection that followed led to septic pneumonia, and he died within a week, on March 29, at the age of forty-one.

His death was greatly lamented in the University and the community at large. The *Student* and the *Bloomington Evening World* printed eulogistic accounts of his contributions to the University, as well as several articles about the elaborate memorial service given him. The service was, naturally, musical, and was performed by faculty members, the two glee clubs, the University Chorus (composed of members of these clubs), and Campbell's orchestra. The program consisted of standard works, including the first movement of the Unfinished Symphony, as well as three of Campbell's own compositions. At the end, the "Hymn to Indiana" was performed by orchestra, chorus, and soloists.

The memorial resolution passed by the University faculty stresses Campbell's "lofty ideals of scholarship," his service to "the larger interests of the University" as well as to the Department of Music, and the "lasting monument of art" he created in the Centennial Pageant and especially in the hymn. To a later observer, though, the most significant tribute is found in the statement that "under his care music in the University was made to take its rightful place among the humanities." This claim accurately summarizes Campbell's achievement. Yet, as he had known, the humanities were not the only rightful place for music, which also had legitimate aspirations to a place among the array of professional schools. Bryan had pledged that it would be so; but it was not for Campbell to lead Music into this promised land along the Jordan.

The Merrill Years (1919–1938)

Symbolism and Uncivil Strife

Following Campbell's death, President Bryan named an English professor, William D. Howe, to oversee the Department of Music while he pursued with new urgency the appointment of the "Professor or Dean" of Music he had been seeking intermittently since 1904. Howe served only four months, for on August 1, 1919, Barzille Winfred Merrill became Professor of Music and Head of the Department.

In several respects, Merrill was the opposite of the first Head. Campbell had been a musical amateur, albeit an unusually knowledgeable one. His education had been primarily in philology and had followed the traditional academic path, culminating in a doctorate and a university appointment. His advanced musical studies were taken at the same German university where he earned his doctorate, and these studies were, therefore (given the European practice of excluding performance study from the universities), restricted to academic music.

By contrast, Merrill was a thoroughly professional musician, a violinist, conductor, and composer. Born in Elgin, Illinois, on May 20, 1864 (and thus thirteen years older than his predecessor), he had graduated from the Gottschalk Lyric School in Chicago, with majors in violin and composition. It is a mark of the seriousness of his aspirations as a performer that he returned to school at the age of thirty-six, spending the years 1900–1903 in advanced studies in Germany. Unlike Campbell, though, Merrill enrolled not at a German university but at one of the state-supported conservatories, the Berlin Hochschule für Musik, where he studied with the preeminent violinist of the time, Joseph Joachim, as well as with Andreas Moser. Later still, in the period 1909–12, he studied composition with the noted theorist Bernhard Ziehn in Chicago.

Again in contrast to Campbell, who had, when Bryan tapped him in 1910, no professional experience as a music teacher, let alone as a music administrator, Merrill had had an extraordinary range of teaching and administrative experience before he came to Indiana. Following his graduation from the Gottschalk School he had directed the Tacoma Academy of Music from 1888 to 1893. He subsequently moved to Atlanta, where he established the Merrill School of Music and, from 1895 to 1900, was Conductor of both the Atlanta Symphony Orchestra and the Atlanta Orchestral Society. Upon his return from Germany in 1903, he was appointed Professor and Head of the Department of Orchestral Music at Iowa State Teachers College in Cedar Falls, where he remained until he came to Indiana in 1919. With this appointment, then, Bryan seemed finally to have succeeded, and beyond all reasonable expectation, in achieving the goal he had set himself in 1904, of appointing, as head of music, "a man whose musical training is quite first rate and who has also the good sense and executive ability required."

Indeed, we may wonder why, at the age of fifty-five, Merrill was willing to come. According to his daughter, Winifred, he was happy in Iowa. Nor was he, when Bryan brought him for an interview, impressed with Bloomington, which in comparison with Cedar Falls seemed to him but a poor provincial town. Nevertheless, on July 18 Merrill accepted Bryan's offer, effective two weeks later, of an appointment guaranteed only for one year, at a salary of $3,300. (This was not a lavish offer, since at the time department heads averaged about $4,200 and full professors about $3,000. But the salary would be supplemented by lesson fees.) Perhaps this adventurous man, who was a success in practical matters but an idealist bold enough to return to school in his thirties, and who had been at Cedar Falls sixteen years, simply wanted a new challenge.

And indeed the situation in Bloomington *was* challenging. Though the town now had (in contrast to its state when Bryan became President of the University in 1902) paved streets and a sewage system, it was still, with a population of 13,000, small and distinctly unsophisticated. This was a city where the local newspaper recorded, in the year of Merrill's arrival, such momentous events as (on the front page) that "Mrs. Grant Hazel, South Madison street, is visiting Mrs. Charles Burch at Bedford" (a community several miles to the south).

The Department of Music was also a small-scale provincial operation. At first, Merrill was, as Campbell had been, the only faculty member at professorial rank. The teaching staff he inherited consisted of Jack Geiger, the voice teacher who had been one of Campbell's original Assistants (and now held the rank of Tutor), and two of Campbell's more recent appointees: the band director Archie Warner and the cellist Adolph Schellschmidt; the latter had just been appointed as part of Campbell's "experimental step" toward developing an applied-music program. (The violin teacher whose appointment had been approved at the same time, Gaylord Yost, was rendered superfluous by Merrill's arrival.) In his first year, Merrill was able to add a faculty wife, Mrs. Ruby Mosemiller, as Instructor in Piano—a position she retained until her retirement in 1950.

At the same time, he managed to have Geiger and Schellschmidt promoted to Instructor.

As for accommodation, the Department had the recently remodeled but still grossly inadequate Mitchell Hall. In a reminiscence published in 1987, Winifred Merrill vividly evoked the place in which her father spent all but the final year and a half of his career at Indiana: Mitchell was a "hot little building where there were no 'facilities' and not even a drinking fountain but instead an old sink in the corner of the rehearsal room with a tin cup attached by a chain. In those hot summers the temperature in the hall sometimes rose to 110 degrees." Here Merrill "'fried' his brains." And though major performances could be held in Assembly Hall, that aging structure was also a poor venue. A 1921 article in the *Indiana Daily Student* characterized it as "the wretched object of mingled mirth and scorn of all who come into contact with the University. . . . it can seat only about half of the students in the University and . . . only about a fourth of that half . . . can get a satisfactory view of the stage."

But the main problem with the Department, in Merrill's view, was that it was not fulfilling the mission that Bryan had set for it. From the first, Bryan had been interested in music not just as a liberal art but also as a field in which the University could provide professional training, thus boosting its enrollment. Campbell had shared this conception of the mission of the Department but had not been allowed to go very far toward fulfilling it, and at the time of his death the Department's activities were still centered in the cultivation of music appreciation. The consequence of this orientation was, as Merrill reported to Bryan and the trustees in his first October in Bloomington, that Indiana University was "not in evidence in the state as a place where boys and girls can come for a musical education, in piano, violin or public school music."

In Music at Indiana, the prior administrative experience, or lack of it, of the chief administrative officer has usually made a huge difference. As a professional, conservatory-educated musician, Merrill wholeheartedly agreed with Bryan (who would presumably not otherwise have offered him the headship) that Music should be organized as a professional school. And as a vastly experienced music administrator, he knew exactly how to achieve that goal.

The key lay in stressing music as a *business,* both for the students and for the University. Merrill's fullest exposition of his view of the matter came several years after his arrival, in a 1926 article he wrote for the *Student.* There he explained that music was not merely a solace for the soul and the inevitable accompaniment of activities in "the church, the school, the theater, the parade, and the home" but also "a business proposition in the state and in every city of Indiana." The most obvious form of this business was music-teaching, but, as Merrill showed in a comprehensive and galvanizing survey, it encompassed much more: "The radio business (music is its raison d'être), the manufacture of its sets, of phonographs, organs, pianos, small instruments; opera and concert companies, the thousands of musicians in the moving picture theaters [in those days when live music served as the soundtrack], dance orchestras and church organists and choirs—the millions of Indiana's music business is astounding." But, since all these musicians had to be trained somewhere, music was also a tremendous business proposition for higher education. How foolish Indiana was to let this business go elsewhere; and in this perspective spending money to expand and enhance the School of Music was simply a sound investment.

One thing businesses did was advertise, and in his first report to Bryan and the trustees, in October 1919, Merrill requested funding for "a course of state-wide advertising." This campaign evidently paid off, for the next October Merrill reported (in the context of requesting additional facilities and equipment) that "I have so many letters of inquiry from music students and prospective music students and we are so crowded for necessary room that it is worse than useless to advertise at present." Crowding was so bad that the Department's seven pianos were "in constant use from seven o'clock in the morning till seven at night and I have had to find pianos in private houses in order that our students may be able to practise."

To teach this crowd of students, Merrill clearly needed, in addition to more room and more instruments, more faculty. He did not, however, simply want more Assistants or Instructors. He recognized (as Campbell also had) that the Department could not advance far without additional regular faculty positions. Good musicians would not come to teach at Indiana unless they were offered, as Merrill himself had been, professorial rank and, as emolument, not merely lesson fees (which in any case did not exist for academic musicians) but a substantial fixed salary.

Despite the poor financial condition of the University, Bryan was willing to make what he doubtless regarded as sound investments in "Indiana's music business." In 1920, the trustees approved two additional appointments at the full professorial rank. One of these, the Professorship of Piano, was filled by a graduate of the Oberlin Conservatory, Charles Wing (who, however, remained for only two years). The other professorship was to be in the field of Public School Music—that is, in the field where, because of its size and because of the tradition of teacher-training at Indiana, the University could most plausibly hope to turn a profit in the music business. For this position, Merrill recommended Paul J. Weaver of the University of North Carolina. For whatever reason, nothing came of this suggestion, and the person appointed, in 1921, was in fact Bryan's candidate, Edward Bailey Birge, a graduate of Brown University and the Yale School of Music who had held a series of positions in the administration of school music and was, at the time Bryan approached him, Director of Music in the Indianapolis Public Schools. Merrill acquiesced in the appointment without visible reluctance.

By February of 1921, Merrill was ready to give the President and trustees the chance to make good on Bryan's twenty-year-old commitment to creating a School of Music. "In view of the fact," he wrote to Bryan, "that the Department of Music is not only filling its place as a department of the College of Liberal Arts and a cultural part of university life, but is taking its place as a professional school for the making of the musicians and music teachers of Indiana and the country in general, I hereby recommend that, with organization similar to the other Schools of the University, it be known hereafter as the School of Music of Indiana University." It seems almost laughable that the head of such a small department should think it merited the grand status of a School. But Schools at Indiana in that era were not necessarily large—in 1921 the School of Law had four professors—and Bryan, who had so long cherished the idea of a School of Music, endorsed Merrill's recommendation, putting it before the trustees on March 12. They approved the proposal, establishing the School, with Merrill as Dean, effective August 1; and thus the single most significant event in the history of music at Indiana had occurred. The Department was now reconstituted on a basis that would not only guarantee the new School's chief administrative officer direct access—unmediated, that is, by the Dean of Arts and Sciences—to the central University administration but would also redirect its focus from musical acculturation to the training of professional musicians.

Three months after achieving the goal of reconstituting his Department as a School, Merrill was campaigning for an improvement to its overcrowded facilities. Reporting to Bryan and the trustees in June 1921, he included a request for funds to reconfigure the space in Mitchell Hall and to erect a small separate annex to it. The request was approved, and in the summer of 1921 the annex, containing a classroom, two studios, and four practice rooms, was constructed to the north of the parent building, at a cost of $3,500. Together with the reconfiguration of Mitchell, this development tripled the practice space available to students.

To be sure, the space was less than ideal. Mildred Blake (who was a student at the School in the early 1930s) recalls that, due to the thinness of the walls, "everyone knew what his neighbor was working on. One had to really concentrate on his own lesson material." Each of the hot little rooms had a window that opened onto the woods behind the School, and "sometimes it was tempting to crawl out the window and take off."

The following October, Merrill concluded his first campaign for improved facilities by requesting that Mitchell be repainted the same color as the Annex, so that

> it might be more attractive and less disfigure the beautiful spot in which it is located. The feeling would be that the School of Music is an entity and the impression abroad among the students would be improved. With this done, the changes made and the floor of the entrance covered with linoleum—solid color—our room equipment would be ideal for some time to come.

This request, too, was approved. "Ideal," though, was clearly hyperbolic, and the preceding "less disfigure," especially when taken together with the enrollment trend, must have suggested to Bryan that he had not heard the last from Merrill on the subject of facilities for his School.

Merrill's next item of business was to establish a series of new programs for the School. Prior to 1922, the only degree available in Music was a Bachelor of Arts with a major in that field. In the first year of the new School's existence, though, the Dean secured approval for a broad range of programs within the School itself. There were, first, non-degree programs in applied music, with studies in piano, organ, violin, cello, or voice (harp was added the following year), leading to a Certificate of Musical Proficiency. Those who combined applied-music studies with practice teaching could earn a Teacher's Certificate; and an Artist's Diploma was to be "granted only to those who show a marked ability to play or sing intelligently and artistically in public and whom the Faculty of the School of Music feel can justly be called artists." Second, there was a four-year applied-music program leading to the degree of Bachelor of Music with a major in either piano, violin, or voice. Merrill had thus secured the fundamentally important point that applied music was to be not merely a credited subject of study at Indiana but a degree program. (Like all the School's undergraduate degree programs up to the present—and just as Campbell had proposed as early as 1910—the Bachelor of Music program included a substantial liberal arts component: students were required to take Arts courses in such subjects as educational psychology, aesthetics, and English.) Third, there was a four-year academic-music program leading to the degree of Bachelor of Music in Theory and Composition; additionally, a Master of Music degree, requiring a fifth year, was offered in the same field. (This was the first of several graduate programs that came and went in the early years of the School, in a sporadic and puzzling fashion. By 1932 the list had stabilized, with a Master of Music offered through the School of Music and the academic degrees of Master of Arts and Doctor of Philosophy offered through the Graduate School.) Fourth, there were several programs in Public School Music, including a two-year course "fulfilling the requirements of the State Teachers' Training Board," a three-year course leading to a Certificate in Music Supervision, and a four-year course leading to the degree of Bachelor of Public School Music. The four-year undergraduate Arts degree with a major in Music remained; and it was supplemented by a combined six-year program leading to Bachelor's degrees in both Arts and Music.

In the early years of the School, in fact, the number of degree programs exceeded the number of degree candidates. There were no graduate students at all, and the first graduating class in the Bachelor's programs, in June 1923, consisted of one Bachelor of Public School Music and one Bachelor of Arts in Music. (As the graduate in Public School Music, Gertrude V. Schaupp had the distinction of being the first graduate of the School of Music itself.) To be sure, several hundred students were taking music courses as electives or taking music lessons from members of the School's faculty.

In addition to applied-music lessons, the School of Music in the first year of its existence offered twenty-two courses, ranging from theory, composition, orchestration, and music history and appreciation through ear training, dictation, and sight singing, various ensemble courses (orchestra, band, chamber music, chorus, *a cappella* choir, and the boys' and girls' glee clubs), and courses in public school music offered in conjunction with the School of Education. Over the next few years the number of courses grew at a modest pace, reaching thirty-one by 1930.

The expansion of the faculty was yet more modest. In 1922, the Danish-born Axel Skjerne, a product of the Royal Conservatory of Copenhagen who had been the accompanist of the violinist Maud Powell and had also had something of a solo career, replaced Charles Wing as Professor of Piano; for the following year only, his wife served as Instructor in Piano. In 1924, Montana Grinstead, an Assistant who was a graduate of the School, was elevated to the position of Instructor in Piano and Secretary to the Dean. During Edward Birge's leave of absence in 1925–26, he was replaced by Douglas Nye, who had studied at New York's Institute of Musical Art (which later became Juilliard) and was, at the time of his appointment to Indiana, teaching at Stuyvesant High School in that city; when Birge returned, Nye stayed on in a regular appointment as Assistant Professor, teaching voice and theory. In June 1926, the band director, Archie Warner, resigned, in consequence of his inability to keep track of instruments loaned to students; he was replaced by a new Assistant, Mark Hindsley, who became an Instructor in 1929. (Later, at the University of Illinois, whence he removed in 1934, Hindsley achieved great professional distinction, serving as President of both the Band Directors National Association and the American Bandmasters Association; in 1982 he was inducted into the National Hall of Fame of Distinguished Band Conductors.)

In its first few years, the School of Music was a small and seemingly pleasant place nestled in a university which could be characterized in the same terms. The University, with its score of buildings strung along an arc skirting Dunn's Woods and linked by paths of brick or board, still numbered fewer than 3,000 students. Thanks to the School of Music Bulletin, which began to be published separately from the University Catalogue in 1923, and which included a large amount of information for prospective students, we know much about how students lived in that time, and what it cost them. (The Bulletin notes that "with the present student body economy is the rule, not the exception.") Most students lodged in clubs or private houses. In 1923, "modern rooms" for men cost $3 to $6 a week; for whatever reason, the range for women was $3 to $5. Some "not modern" rooms could be had, by students of either sex, for $2. For women, there were also the University Residence Hall and two Cooperative Houses. Board in the cooperatives (where meals were planned and prepared by the students) averaged $3.50 a week; elsewhere it ranged from $5 to $7. Overall, "probably most of the students spend (exclusive of railroad fare and clothing) from $350 to $500 a year." Tuition was free, though students paid a "Contingent fee" of $25 per semester, and a $5 activities fee. Applied-music students, of course, also paid lesson fees, and were charged a rental fee for practice rooms.

For information about what students—some of them, at least—did in their spare time, we may consult a very different, unofficial source. In Bloomington as elsewhere, the dominant culture of the day was that of the Roaring Twenties. Its musical component was personified at Indiana not by Dean Merrill but by a highly gifted law student (whose primary gifts and later fortune lay, however, not in law), Hoagy Carmichael. Much later, Carmichael wrote about the Twenties in an autobiography, *Sometimes I Wonder* (1965), which must surely be one of the shrewdest and most vivid accounts of the mores of the era, at Indiana and in general.

Carmichael is especially eloquent on the relation between popular music—jazz—and the sexual emancipation of students—especially female students—in the period. "We saw jazz, already in the dives and moving into the speakeasies," he writes, and it "set the tone and color of the country. . . . Jazz didn't change the morals of the early twenties. But it furnished the music, I noticed, to a change in manners and sexual ideas. Women wore less and wore it in a slipping, careless way on the dance floors. Every girl wore silk stockings—and many rolled them beneath the knees so that every sitting-down showed the American female thigh, nude and lush, anywhere from kneecap to buttocks. ('You just know she wears them,' said the ads.)" "Our girls," Carmichael writes a few pages later, "were trying to make he-men of us but we were still hicky kids. Every girl I knew wanted to own long strands of pearls in a hangman's knot and borrow the college boys' pull-over sweaters of fuzzy wool, to which were pinned Greek letter frat pins; the more the merrier. . . . Ball bearing hips, jello haunches free of girdles or even underwear. Soft felt styles and the first of the shoddy, shiny rayons. Seated on their spines, legs in the air, in the Stutz Bearcats or the high-nosed Packards, wrapped in school colors at games, kicking the lock step in hotel rooms and country clubs, while the band played *I'll Get By If I Have You* and *As Time Goes By*."

How could classical music—the sole concern of the School of Music, whose embrace stooped no lower than operetta—compete? The School's only formal connection with popular musical culture was through the university band—"The Marching Hundred," as it came to be called—which, though it had, since the World War years, been linked with and financed by the U.S. Army's Reserve Officers Training Corps, was based in Mitchell Hall and directed by an appointee of the School. Naturally, the band drew many of its members from the School. One notable example was the trombonist Newell Long, who later became a member of the faculty. (As an undergraduate, Long also directed his own band, to accompany the silent movies at the Indiana Theater; during the same years, Hoagy Carmichael directed a band at the Princess Theater.) But the band also drew students from other academic units, such as School of Business student Herman B Wells, who was to become Bryan's successor, and who, as a baritone horn player, marched just behind Long.

While jazz and band music were in abundant supply, the classical music community continued to suffer from a shortage of good performances. In his section of Burton Myers's *History*, Merrill says that when, in 1920, "contemplating bringing an orchestra to the University, I asked a Convocation audience of faculty and students for a show of hands of those who had ever heard a symphony orchestra, there were only seven students who responded out of an audience of more than a thousand." (Presumably the Music Department's own modest orchestra didn't count.) But at least by the twenties radio was available, and in 1922 Merrill arranged with a physics professor to equip the Mitchell Hall stage to receive the broadcasts of the Chicago Opera.

Merrill's great coup in the provision of live music, though, through which he enabled classical music to compete with popular by securing a tilted playing field, was to persuade Bryan to allocate to the creation of a Music Series a substantial portion of the $5 activities fee collected annually from every student of the University. The students having paid for the series, Merrill graciously allowed them to help choose the artists for it. The Music faculty drew up a list of potential visitors (taking suggestions from whoever cared to offer them), which was then submitted to the students and faculty of the University as a ballot. And each year Merrill tried to engage for the series the artists who had received the largest number of votes.

The results were simply astonishing. In an era when major musicians performed for far less money than now, and thus much more often and in some smaller places, the concert series attracted over the years not merely many first-rate musicians but a number of the truly legendary names of the early twentieth century. Starting in the 1923–24 academic year, the series offered, among pianists, Hofmann, Rachmaninoff, Paderewski, Bauer, Gieseking, Iturbi, Grainger, Petri; among string players and chamber groups, Kreisler, Heifetz, Zimbalist, Szigeti, Elman, Huberman, Feuermann, the Budapest String Quartet; among singers and choral groups, Ponselle, Swarthout, Garden, McCormack, Martinelli, the Vienna Choir Boys. Charles Humphreys and Doris Weidman with their dance company appeared, as did other dance and theatrical troupes, including the Abby Irish Players. The Cleveland, Minneapolis, and Cincinnati Orchestras were presented. In 1924 there was a production of *The Impresario* and the next year one of *The Marriage of Figaro*. The only unfortunate feature of the series was that its venue was Assembly Hall, where music competed for dates with athletic events; and the patrons contended with the obstructing posts and scraping chairs.

Within the School of Music itself, Merrill was the dominating presence (though Birge was, as we will see, to some extent an independent power), not just because he was the Dean in an era when heads of academic units were something close to absolute (and lifelong) monarchs within their fiefdoms, but also because of his musicianship and the force of his personality.

Merrill had had opportunities early on to display his musicianship. In January 1920 the University marked with gala festivities the hundredth anniversary of its legislative charter. For the culminating "Ceremonial," designed by William Chauncy Langdon (he of the Indiana Centennial pageants) and presented in Assembly Hall before the Governor and other dignitaries, the music was drawn from Campbell's Centennial music; Merrill conducted the orchestra. If this event cast him somewhat in the shadow of his predecessor, he had his turn for undimmed glory when warm weather arrived and the festivities resumed out of doors, with a full-scale "Centennial Pageant of Indiana University," spread over the first three days of June and including in its cast some 2,000 students. Like the state pageant, this one boasted a lofty, partly allegorical libretto by Langdon; but this time the music was by Merrill, who also provided, for the printed program, a three-page analysis of it.

In the quotidian musical life of the School, the orchestra was Merrill's primary concern, as it had been Campbell's. (Orchestration was Merrill's main scholarly interest, and he published a book on the subject in 1937.) In this era—and for a generation to come—the orchestra consisted of a mixed bag of players, it being necessary to recruit players from outside the student body to round out the instrumentation. A chemistry professor played bassoon. The eminent folklorist Stith Thompson was the principal cellist, while a piano tuner played the oboe and a Bloomington jeweler the flute.

In training such an orchestra, the Dean's all-round musicianship was invaluable. He could play any instrument and was, moreover, a fine singer. (He created an *a cappella* choir for the School shortly after his arrival.) Merrill's omnicompetence—and his energy, which was evidently not diminished as he moved toward, and then passed, sixty—also figured in the diverse teaching that he undertook. Newell Long—who, as the only person to have given detailed reminiscences of the School in this era, was, until his death in 1999, a uniquely valuable witness—recalled that Merrill taught "most anything that came along," ranging as far afield as clarinet and harp. He also taught the ensemble class, in addition to courses in harmony, counterpoint, and composition.

In general, Merrill must have been an impressive figure, charismatic and often eloquent. Long reported that he was "a delightful person," who "had a sense of humor and had a European air about him even though he was an American." Another shrewd observer of Merrill's early years at Indiana, Herman Wells, remembered him as having "a personality that stood out in the University community. . . . There was much talk of developments in the School of Music during that era, and no one was unaware that we had a Dean in the School of Music, a School of Music that was on the march."

Though Merrill had complete authority in the administration of the School, in the early years of his tenure he appears often to have been happy to rely on the advice of his colleagues. In various matters, large and small, the minutes of faculty meetings show him governing democratically, as *primus inter pares*. As time passed, though, the importance of faculty meetings as a mechanism for the governance of the School strikingly diminished. After the ten recorded meetings of 1921–22, they rapidly became much less frequent, averaging three a year for the next fourteen years. For some years only one meeting is recorded.

The decreasing importance of faculty meetings in the governance of the School was, in fact, only one manifestation of a rapid and startling deterioration of collegiality that became the greatest problem of Merrill's deanship. In its earliest years, the faculty of the School appears to have been a happy little band. The first recorded meeting (December 6, 1921) was held in the evening, at Birge's home. In 1924 it became the custom to meet "at 12 o'clock in the University Cafeteria," a convivial practice that persisted into 1926. Yet in December 1925—that is, in only the fifth year of Birge's appointment and the fourth of Skjerne's—Merrill wrote an extraordinary letter to Bryan strongly criticizing both his fellow Professors.

Skjerne's offense was moonlighting. Without informing Merrill, he had accepted the "so-called deanship" of the Piano Department of the Associated Artists School in Indianapolis. Merrill resented Skjerne's deception, and he saw him as an ingrate. "From a musician with his reputation to make, the university has elevated him into a professorship"; his acceptance of the Indianapolis position connotes "disloyalty to the school that supports him and through whose standing *his* standing was made." More important, his behavior did actual harm to the School: "the Music School cannot afford to employ teachers connected with other schools. It removes from us any prestige the possession of a good man may give and gives the other school the benefit of what we pay for."

But the accusation against Skjerne (which seems fair enough) pales beside those leveled at Birge. First of all, he is responsible for the perfidy of Skjerne, whom Merrill is surprisingly willing to let off the hook in order to sink it more deeply into Birge. Despite Skjerne's "sneaking" behavior, Merrill was somehow convinced that the pianist was basically too honest to have chosen this bad course "of his personal initiative." The culprit, he was sure, was Birge. Merrill cited no evidence for this view, but he felt no need to do so, for he was convinced that the Birges—both Edward and his wife Mary—were responsible for *all* the problems in what would otherwise be an idyllic place. "The School of Music is an art school," he wrote. "Nothing worth while in art can grow in commotion. The sensibilities of the artist are cultivated to such a degree that his surroundings must be quiet and peaceful so that he can hear the voice from within." This being the case, "one person of the aggressive, forcing, scheming, stirring-up type can put the whole instrument out of tune and set it jangling." And unfortunately the School was beset by *two* such individuals: "Shortly after the Birges came, ructions began to exist."

The instances Merrill cited were takeover bids directed at Bloomington musical organizations, especially the Friday Musicale (Mary Birge's special target) and the Bloomington Choral Society. With respect to established community institutions, the stated policy of the School of Music had been "*development* and *not revolution*." But despite plans to help Professor Birge (who was choral director for the School) "make so good a chorus in the School of Music that the Choral Society folks would in time and of themselves want to come under his leadership, they rode roughshod over the policy stated with the result that the Society no longer exists and a feeling of antagonism—something I try so hard to avoid with the city people—was engendered."

At the base of the problem, according to Merrill, was the fact that "Mr. Birge is not an artist nor has he the instincts of one":

> He is a public school man, and is not happy in the intenser, deeper work of the serious music students. It is plain that his long service in the public schools has peculiarly unfitted him for University work. You are not unaware of the tendency of the public school man toward mass-production and mediocrity and his antagonism toward individual high endeavor.

Not surprisingly, then, the academic program that Birge directed for the School was contemptible: "While it is necessary to have public school music taught as a subject in the Music School, it is so rudimentary in content that it must not be considered an advanced or even a relatively important course at present." (This despite the fact that almost all of the School's students were enrolled in Public School Music.)

Naturally Merrill had tried to rid the School of the pair of vipers. He had given Birge "information of an opportunity that means an income of from eight to ten thousand a year" (that is, at least twice Birge's Indiana salary), but Birge had evidently not pursued the matter.

At this distance of time, it is impossible to assess the validity of Merrill's charges against the Birges. Who knows whether Skjerne's perfidy was instigated or abetted by them? From correspondence, Mary Birge is seen to have been a power in the Friday Musicale by 1923, but whether for good or for evil is not clear. (She eventually became President of the Indiana Federation of Music Clubs.) As for the Bloomington Choral Society, we know, from Guido Stempel, that "from the winter of 1918–19 through the spring of 1925" it "ran its vigorous course" under the direction of Rudolph Heyne. Stempel says the Society's high point "was the performance in 1922, for the first time in Bloomington, of Handel's *Messiah.*" But the next year Edward Birge directed a University ensemble—though with an admixture of townspeople—in the *Messiah.* (He continued the practice, establishing what became a cherished annual event, for which he received much credit, and which was carried on by others after his retirement in 1938.)

What is absolutely certain from Merrill's letter, though, is that by late 1925 he had conceived a rabid dislike for the Birges and a suspiciousness of them that can only be described as paranoid. These attitudes would be conveniently explained if the Birges were in fact the monsters that Merrill thought them, but this does not appear to have been the case. Bryan, for example, seems to have regarded Birge highly. Thus in 1932 he wrote Birge to tell him how much he appreciated the annual *Messiah,* and three years later, congratulating Birge on a laudatory piece on him in a recent issue of *The Musician,* he took the occasion "to express my appreciation of your fine service to the University." Nor was Birge the philistine that Merrill thought him. He had had extensive keyboard studies and, according to Eleanor Long (Newell's wife), loved to play both the piano and the organ. (See Figure 7.) He was also a violinist, and often invited others to his home to play quartets with him.

But it is not necessary to attribute monstrosity to the Birges in order to understand the enmity: there were a number of more ordinary causes for it. First, as Eleanor Long (a shrewd observer) says, the dislike between the two men reflected their very different temperaments and backgrounds. Merrill was a product of conservatories; Birge was a university man, and an Ivy Leaguer at that. Their enmity was further exacerbated—to a very significant extent, according to Eleanor Long—by social rivalry between their wives. The two couples developed, in effect, rival salons. It was hard to be a member of both; one did not mention the Birges to the Merrills, or the Merrills to the Birges.

Merrill's hostility toward Birge surely also derived in part from the fact that Birge alone among the faculty had an authority that in some ways rivaled his own. A well-published scholar, who wrote a standard history of public school music, Birge like Merrill was a formidable figure, and only four years younger than the Dean. Moreover, unlike the rest of the faculty, he was not Merrill's creature, having been, as I noted earlier, Bryan's choice—a fact that in itself might understandably account for some hostility on Merrill's part. It is striking, too, how much Birge is treated, in the minutes of faculty meetings, as the clear second-in-command, almost an equal. After a while, he had his own letterhead, as Director of Public School Music. Then too, as this last item suggests, Birge rapidly came to rule a large satrapy within Merrill's empire, one that was indeed larger than the rest of the empire put together. He designed and nurtured the program in Public School Music. Newell Long's impression, implicitly validated by Merrill's 1925 letter to Bryan, was that the sensitive-artist Dean never "bothered his mind . . . much at all" with this program; for him, the real work of the School was that "intenser, deeper work of the serious music students." Yet—and this must have been a galling fact for Merrill—almost all the graduates of the School throughout his deanship were in Birge's program. In 1938, Merrill's last year as Dean, of the 113 undergraduates enrolled in Music degree programs, 24 were in the Bachelor of Music program, 9 in a combined program leading to a Bachelor of Music degree together with a Supervisor's license for public school music, and 80 in the Bachelor of Public School Music program. That June, the School graduated eighteen candidates in Public School Music, four candidates for the Master of Arts, and one for the Master of Music.

The tension between Merrill and his two key faculty members did not diminish, and by August 1927 Skjerne was writing to Bryan to confirm his resignation from the School. Bryan had either not sided with Merrill in his dispute with Skjerne or had at least not thought the problems with Skjerne outweighed the benefits of retaining his services, for he offered to "do everything in my power to make your situation more agreeable." Skjerne's reply expresses his appreciation of Bryan's "power to improve the conditions for me"; but merely mortal intervention could not solve the problem: "having given the matter most careful consideration from all points of view I feel it is beyond human power to improve the situation in a way that would enable me to give my best. Even if surface conditions are improved I cannot build up where there is no good understanding and cooperation." To be sure, there does seem to have been, as Merrill had claimed in 1925, a certain weakness and propensity for "sneaking" in Skjerne's character. The account he gave Bryan of his situation in the

School does not jibe with his letter of resignation to Merrill, which is quite friendly, and attributes his defection only to the irresistible offer of a professorship at Oberlin; and Bryan himself was irritated and, at the end, quite cold toward Skjerne for leaving the School with very short notice, just before the fall semester was to begin.

As if Merrill did not already have, by the mid-1920s, sufficient problems with his faculty, in 1926 he took a step that would inevitably—and obviously—exacerbate these problems, appointing his daughter Winifred to a unique, non-professorial position as "Violinist"—in effect, artist-in-residence. (In 1930, Merrill unsuccessfully recommended that she be named Associate Professor, and, in 1937, Professor. The following year, she was made Assistant Professor—not clearly a promotion, since she had previously been listed above the Assistant Professors in the masthead.) Although Winifred had completed advanced studies at New York's Institute of Musical Art, had subsequently had Nadia Boulanger as a coach, and had soloed with the Minneapolis Symphony, she was not, at least on the evidence of those who heard her during the latter part of her career at Indiana, a good violinist. Nor was she, on the evidence of the results she is reported to have gotten with her students, a good teacher. (Apart from her father, she was the only violin instructor on the faculty until 1948.) Moreover, the nepotism of her appointment, together with the widespread feeling that she had undue influence in the administration of the School, was a constant irritant in Merrill's relations with the rest of his faculty. (One of the Merrills' grievances with the Birges was that they did not sufficiently appreciate Winifred.) With gracious understatement, Newell Long said that Winifred "had less acclaim perhaps than she would have had otherwise, or respect, because he had brought her in. I suspect that she might have shown better in another school."

In 1928, Merrill was able to replace Skjerne as Professor of Piano with Ernest Hoffzimmer, a German who had studied at the Liszt School in Cologne and with Busoni; he had previously taught at the Stern Conservatory in Berlin and at the Düsseldorf Conservatory. The Dean must have thought him an ideal appointee: a thoroughly professional, conservatory-educated performer and teacher who was, all the better, a European. Still, within four years Hoffzimmer was writing to Bryan to complain about Merrill's treatment of him.

The trouble began when Merrill failed to involve Hoffzimmer in consultations over the University's purchase of new Steinway pianos. Hoffzimmer wrote a brief and, under the circumstances, notably temperate letter of protest to Merrill about the matter. Merrill's reply, which infuriated the pianist, patronizingly explained to him that he had been misled by his inexperience of the mores of American universities: "The subtle independence of old American Universities like this is not so quickly learned, and it is for this reason that the one wholly responsible has to meet these problems." Moreover, he reminded Hoffzimmer that, while it was up to him to select his own pianos, "the one sharp critizism" of him had come when he played on a Baldwin piano in Indianapolis. Seemingly the point here was to suggest that Hoffzimmer's judgment of pianos was not altogether trustworthy. Finally, having written a letter whose expression is in several places so oblique as to be almost impenetrably obscure, Merrill closed with the hope "that this clears the situation with not the slightest reflection on you." And then he added that "I stand ready at all times to be of service in whatever is not clear for I realize that there are those existing who are officiously anxious to mislead for your undoing."

Hoffzimmer sent copies of his letter and Merrill's reply to Bryan, together with a lengthy comment on the reply. He called attention to his long association with Steinways, to the fact that a pianist's reputation was damaged if pianos were purchased in his own domain without consulting him, and to the fact that, since pianos even of the same model vary considerably, the skills of an expert assessor were always important in buying them. As for the Baldwin in Indianapolis, it had come with the engagement. The "sharp critizism" referred to in Merrill's letter was the opinion of one reviewer that the piano, in this chamber recital, had been too loud. But Merrill had been present, had been asked to assess the balance, and had declared it good. Hoffzimmer protested the meanness of spirit that allowed Merrill to bring up the hurtful and irrelevant matter of the review; and he was caustic about the Dean's offer to guard him against unnamed enemies:

> I have not found out yet, who is here officiously anxious to mislead for my undoing. . . . But I have heard this threatening warning not the first time. The first time it came, when I had accepted a dinner in the house of Prof. Birge.
>
> The second time I heard it, when I gladly followed the . . . request of Mrs. Bryan, to play at her Senior reception together with Miss Haralan, who is, an excellent violinist.

In 1929, Merrill had been able to appoint the School's first Professor of Cello (the last of his appointees at the full-professorial rank), Lennart von Zweygberg, a Finnish-born and Finnish- and German-trained musician. Within three years Merrill was also at odds with him, as we learn from a remarkable letter that Bryan wrote to the Dean in the aftermath of the Hoffzimmer affair. The letter, which alludes to Merrill's problems with von Zweygberg only in passing, as one instance of a general problem, focuses on a painful fact: since Merrill had had full power in selecting appointees to the School, his problems with faculty must be regarded as, in a very real sense, of his own making. "I have," Bryan wrote, "been for a long time seriously concerned by the continued lack of harmony between the Dean of the School of Music and various members of the faculty of that school":

> You were made Head of the Department of Music in 1919, and have been Dean of the School of Music since 1921. You have had throughout these years entire freedom to discover and recommend your associates. Your nominations have been promptly concurred in. In effect you have chosen your own faculty. [Birge was, of course, the exception.] You have in each case when proposing men praised them with enthusiasm. In no case have you later reported any lack of musical ability or training in the men recommended by you. But there has developed between you and various ones among them strained relations which affect most seriously the success of the School of Music. Professor Skjerne left the university on account of these strained relations. It has long been apparent that such strained relations exist between yourself and Professor Birge. It is within my knowledge that a similar situation exists as between you and Professor Hoffsimmer [*sic*] and between you and Professor Von Zweygberg.
>
> You may adduce evidence to show that the fault in these cases lies with those men. The question then is: when you have had eleven years as Dean with entire freedom to build a harmonious faculty and have failed to do so, what ground have we to hope that you can do so in the future?

Merrill was, as one would expect, devastated by Bryan's despairing reprimand: "I am stricken with your letter," he wrote in reply; "I do not know what to say." He instantly recovered the power of speech, however, and proceeded to defend his conduct with respect to every single one of his colleagues (and to one colleague's wife). He led off with the Birges, who "in 1926 . . . succeeded in alienating a friendship of years and causing an artist [clearly Skjerne] to be sacrificed." Buoyed by this success, the Birges had subsequently "pursued a campaign of state-wide belittlement of the music school"; and so on. As for Merrill's differences with other faculty, he simply denies that there are any: "discord and strained relations do not exist, and never have existed, between me and the teachers." The discontents of Hoffzimmer and von Zweygberg result simply from their ignorance of American ways, their nostalgia for the old country, and, naturally, from the machinations of the Birges. When Europeans arrive,

> I tell them not to mix up with anything that will lead to the school's unpopularity. This is all that I can do. I feel guilty in getting distinguished people knowing that their standing will be assailed, as was the case with Hoffzimmer through comparison with his predecessor for the ruin of his work, and efforts be made to lose them to the School as in the former case.

Von Zweygberg is as easily victimized as Hoffzimmer: he is "a sensitive soul, . . . dependent upon the things he has formerly been used to, a home and an old housekeeper to look after him." As for the lesser faculty members, a few have small discontents, but in general they are a happy and productive lot. All in all, "the school is solid as a rock, in spite of ten years of racketeering against it. . . . This unbalanced, if not insane, effort to drag in the dust honesty, industry and the love of God and humanity is not so simple or this school would have been effaced and we only a memory."

This response doubtless did nothing to alleviate Bryan's concerns, and in the event he was right to despair of any improvement in the situation. In 1936, Merrill precipitated a major brouhaha in the School by relieving Montana Grinstead of her position as his secretary. At the same time, he tried to persuade Bryan to dismiss her from the faculty. It would be impossible, he wrote to the President, "to retain Miss Grinstead in any capacity." She was "erratic and partisan," habituated to meddling with both faculty and students, "settling matters out of her province without my knowledge until too late to prevent the consequences." Recognizing the need to explain why he had retained such a person as his secretary for a dozen years, he added that "in the beginning her lack of training and her eccentricity were partly compensated for by her willingness and apparent self-effacement." Now, though, she had become "a liability to both the dignity and usefulness of the school." In an interview with Bryan a few weeks later, Merrill added (according to Bryan's careful memorandum of the conversation) that Grinstead's conduct was "damnable," and he insisted that she not be allowed to continue as an instructor even for the upcoming summer term.

In response, Bryan told Merrill that he could fire Grinstead as his secretary if he wanted to, but that "the tenure of a member of the faculty is on a different basis." The University did not dismiss a faculty member "except where a case is made which is just in the judgment of members of the faculty." He commanded Merrill to give Grinstead the students she had been promised for the summer. In a subsequent conversation with Grinstead, he urged her to ignore "any and every factional situation in the School" and to "devote herself wholly to her own work." Informing Merrill of this interview, Bryan took the occasion to remind him of their 1932 exchange of letters on dissensions within the School. These dissensions obviously continued, "to the grave injury of the school." And again the melancholy refrain: "Since you chose almost if not quite all the members of your staff and warmly commended them in the beginning, what hope is there that conditions will ever be better?"

He received no reply to this letter, but two weeks later (on July 14) had a letter from von Zweygberg complaining that Merrill had disparaged him to a prospective private pupil and assigned him to teach a class of students in Public School Music. To Bryan, Merrill defended himself, in a letter that is scarcely comprehensible (whether because of deliberate ellipticality or for some other reason), by claiming that his actions in steering the pupil away and giving von Zweygberg the class assignment had been taken in the latter's own interest, "to give him time." And he directed at von Zweygberg charges he had formerly made against the Birges: the cellist had not acted "loyally or even sanely" in the matter. As with Skjerne's case, too, the problem was ultimately attributable to a nest of vipers: "The domination of Montana Grinstead and her family has contributed to pull down the school to their level, and he [i.e., von Zweygberg] goes to you for the explanation." As always, Merrill portrays himself as a sensitive artist dismayed by these barbarous proceedings: how can he deal with people who do not observe "the finer courtesies"? To a person of his delicate organization, such behavior is simply incomprehensible (though he is again ready to find its explanation in madness): "I do not see how human beings who have had every chance known to me to take what they most desire, without the thorn—the ranting is almost like the demented." He closes with a sentence that I include only to show how incomprehensible his prose sometimes is: "To be someone else for the benefit of anyone makes a gap between the other self."

In response to this letter, Bryan declined to assess the rights and wrongs of the case, but simply pleaded with Merrill:

> I wish to ask you to join with me with all your heart in abating the dissension within the School. . . . I make this appeal because it is evident to me, as I hope it is evident to you, that the success or failure of the School of Music, and therewith the success or failure of yourself as Dean, depends upon whether there can be now established at least a *modus vivendi* of peace and cooperation within the School. This means the setting aside of all less important considerations in order to secure the one essential end. It means on your part the complete setting aside of all resentments and hostilities toward all members of your faculty, whatever you may judge their faults to be.

He added that those who were friendly with Merrill (this is the only evidence that there were such people, other than Winifred) should be made to understand that "whoever with the intention of aiding you does anything against this peace is unwittingly preparing for your downfall." I take it that this last phrase was meant to be understood as a warning that Bryan might, if matters did not improve, remove Merrill from the deanship. How could the President do less, if he thought that the dissension that swirled around Merrill would be the ruination of the School?

Merrill's six-line reply (still long enough to be festooned as usual with the flowers of rhetoric) was submissive—"There is no fire too hot to go through with you. . . . Let me see in this what you see"—but evidently did not put Bryan's mind at ease, and two days later he met once more with Merrill, traversing again, according to Bryan's memorandum, "the ground which I have covered with him in recent letters." He expressed the regret he still felt at the loss of Skjerne, "a result due to dissension." He also recalled Hoffzimmer's complaint, four years previously, about not having been consulted in the purchase of pianos. This time, in contrast to the elaborate, self-exonerating explanation he had given to Hoffzimmer himself, Merrill said simply, "I never thought of it." Bryan suggested that it might be helpful for Merrill to have more contact with his faculty, in "individual friendly conferences" and in faculty meetings. Throughout the interview, Merrill avowed his willingness to do anything that might bring peace to the School, though he professed not to know either "why members of the faculty were against him" or how "to secure their friendship and cooperation." He did allow, though, that he had been at fault in not having more individual conferences and faculty meetings. (Two months later, in what was only the second regular faculty meeting of 1936, Birge moved that meetings should be held every two weeks. The motion was carried, and, afterward, meetings were indeed held more or less regularly on alternate Tuesdays. They were also memorialized by minutes that, with the advent that fall of Grinstead's replacement as Secretary to the Dean, Vera Norton, suddenly became far more detailed and authoritative than in the past.)

Following this second interview with Merrill, Bryan had a second conversation with Grinstead. Unlike the Dean, she was very clear about the causes of dissension in the School. The "underlying trouble-maker," Bryan recorded her as saying, was Winifred Merrill. She supported this view with examples, and added that "she had spoken to Miss Merrill, and in her father's presence, a year ago telling her plainly of her faults as Miss Grinstead understood them." Though the point is not made in Bryan's memorandum, one assumes that Grinstead attributed her own downfall to this frankness. (Von Zweygberg had expressed similar views in an interview with Bryan on June 26. Grinstead's dismissal as secretary had, Bryan recorded him as saying, been a shock to the other members of the faculty, who were left feeling insecure in their own positions. He added "many complaints against the Dean and Miss Merrill who together, he said, controlled everything in the School. He complained that his salary is less than hers [as indeed it was, though not by much]; that she is given every advantage over other members of the faculty.")

Surveying this astonishing series of documents, one can scarcely avoid laying most of the blame for the School's dissensions at Merrill's feet. This was the view of Bryan, who knew all the principals and made diligent efforts to understand what was going on in the School; and surely anyone who reads the documents is forced to the same conclusion. There is no reason to doubt that Merrill could be, as Newell Long said, "delightful," and pleasant and easy-going as conductor and teacher. But his personality also evidently included other, less attractive features. (Long himself acknowledged that Merrill must have had an "ornery streak" in him.) After his first few years at Indiana, he allowed himself to become isolated and estranged from his faculty. Lacking much real human contact with his colleagues, he was always ready to attribute any disagreements with him to baseness, weakness, or ignorance—or, indeed, insanity. His habitual presentation of himself as a sensitive artist bewildered by the depravity of others, a pose that would be unappealing at best, is rendered all the more so by the alacrity with which he descends to any level, however low, to discredit or discomfit his adversaries. Though exhibiting, on public occasions, real eloquence, in correspondence with his faculty he routinely resorted to an obfuscatory style that he seems to have imagined somehow cushioned, or dissociated himself from, the nastiness of his innuendos. Repeatedly, too, the paranoia and obsessiveness of his attributions of dire machinations to others bespeaks in himself something not so far removed from the derangement he so readily attributes to his opponents. Finally, his appointment of his daughter, together with the preferential treatment he clearly gave her, was about as bad a mistake as an administrator could make.

To be sure, Merrill's was not the only difficult personality or large ego in or around Mitchell Hall. The Birges had their airs, and Skjerne was at least a bit of a sneak. Grinstead, too, was not an easy character. In her interview with Bryan, she freely confessed that she had, even after her dismissal from the secretary's position, taken it upon herself to advise students, sometimes countering what they had been told by Merrill. When Bryan urged her to desist from this practice, she agreed, he recorded, only "with great reluctance." In general, the faculty appear to have been a cantankerous lot. Long recalled that there were, at least when he joined the faculty in 1935, "some feuds between other members too besides the Merrills, outside the Merrills"; "there was one period there when I was probably the only one on the music faculty who was on speaking terms with every other member." He never knew the reason for some of the feuds: "Just a clash of personality or maybe some decision or something, I don't know."

Bryan feared, plausibly enough, that these manifold dissensions might destroy the School. But they did not, for three reasons. First, Merrill had the power to do whatever he wanted (other than dismiss regular faculty), whether his colleagues liked it or not. As Long said, Merrill "pretty much handled everything; he was in charge." Second, members of the faculty did not, in the Depression years when the worst infighting occurred, have much opportunity to go elsewhere. Skjerne had left, in the booming twenties, but the rest of them were stuck. Third, however much Merrill's colleagues disliked him, they generally endorsed his view of how the School should develop, which was that it should become, in effect, a conservatory. How could they fail to endorse this view, given that all of them above the rank of Instructor were, with one notable exception (the one whom Merrill had not recruited), conservatory products themselves? Of the senior faculty, only Birge held a university degree.

The faculty's project, then, was to build—insomuch as one could be built within a state university—a conservatory. Despite personal enmities, they proceeded without strife through the successive steps of this project. Indeed the minutes of faculty meetings do not record a single dissenting vote on any motion before June 1, 1935—when Grinstead recorded her own dissent on a motion to confer a degree with distinction. (We'll leave aside, for the moment, the fact that a public university, where almost all the music students were training to be school teachers, had no discernible need for a conservatory.)

To be sure, the Dean and his faculty were happy to have the School of Music play a role in the acculturation of liberal arts students to the European musical tradition. Throughout Merrill's tenure, Jack Geiger taught music-appreciation courses that were, according to Long, "very popular with non-music students": "they were some of our larger classes. He had quite a sense of humor, he was a jolly sort of person. And it was probably the easy way to get credit. But at least he played the records for them and sang some of the parts." Then too, the Music Series that Merrill started in 1923 offered a great benefit to all students of the University—as well it should have, since their activities fee paid for it. (In the Depression year of 1933, though, the fee was canceled, after which the Music Series was replaced by a subscription series, fully comparable to its predecessor, except that large orchestras were no longer brought in.)

But music appreciation was a merely adjunctive function of the School. So too, really, was academic music. Merrill had to battle the traditional prejudice against music as a university subject, and in this connection he was doubtless happy to have bridges to the liberal arts core of the University, in the form of the Bachelor of Arts degree with a major in music and the graduate degrees of Master of Arts and Doctor of Philosophy. (Not that anyone ever enrolled in the latter program.) Nor is there any reason to doubt that he respected the work of academic musicians and was happy to have the School foster it. He was himself, in a small way, a composer, and he taught composition, harmony, and counterpoint. The overriding concern of the School, though—indeed the reason why Merrill (and Bryan) had wanted it to be a School in the first place—was to train not music scholars but working musicians. For the time being, the great majority of these had to be public school music teachers, or private music teachers.

But, as Merrill had pointed out in his 1926 interview in the *Daily Student,* the musicians he hoped the School would train included performers in "opera and concert companies, . . . in the moving picture theaters, dance orchestras," and so on.

Apart from the recruitment of core faculty, the first step in the creation of the conservatory was the implementation of the Bachelor of Music programs in piano, violin, and voice (along with theory and composition), accomplished in the earliest days of the School. If these were really to be degree programs in applied music, then instrument and voice study in them, and even required practice, must be credit courses: it was Birge who moved, in a meeting of March 1923, that such credit should be allowed "on a laboratory basis."

Over the course of Merrill's deanship, the School also developed a varied program of recitals. From the beginning, final-year Bachelor of Music students in instrument or voice were required to present a recital before the assembled faculty, for which, if successful, they received course credit. Perhaps more significant (in the context of traditional academic hostility to crediting applied music), final-year candidates for the College of Arts and Sciences degree of Bachelor of Arts in Music could also elect to present a recital for credit. From 1924, there were two general recitals at the end of each school year, the first displaying the best student performers and the second for composition students. By 1925, the recital requirement for Bachelor of Music candidates had doubled to include a Junior Recital, played before the faculty, and a public Senior Recital; but the recitals were no longer given formal academic credit. The next year the faculty agreed that the first week of May—"Music Week"—should be devoted entirely to recitals. By 1934, the general recitals had become biweekly. (As the number of recitals rose, attendance at them predictably fell. In 1936, by which time there were some fifty recitals annually, the faculty passed a motion—surely too weak, since it included no sanction—that students will be "expected in their own interest" to attend all general recitals in which the program contained selections for their own instrument. Moreover, students were required to attend all Music Series events.)

In addition to their function in the education of music students, recitals also served to raise the public profile of the School and, presumably, to increase its acceptance in the general academic community. While these effects were only local, other events began to spread the reputation of the School beyond its immediate surroundings. In 1929, Hoffzimmer and von Zweygberg, apparently not yet on bad terms with Winifred Merrill, formed with her the first resident chamber group of the School, the International Trio. In the same year, Merrill instituted a European summer program, with six weeks of touring followed by six weeks of study in Munich. This venture, which he proudly described to Bryan as "the first Invasion of Europe by the Music School of an American University," continued for a second summer, but then fell victim to the stringencies of the Depression.

Also in 1929, the School launched the first of what later came to be known as its "outreach" programs for high school students: programs that had the double function, first, of enlarging the School's contribution, as a unit of a public university, to the general level of educational opportunity in the state and, second, of helping the School to recruit students of high musical attainment. With these ends in view, and in collaboration with the Extension Division of the University, the School sponsored regional music contests, which were judged by members of the faculty. The best regional performers became finalists in a second-level competition held in Bloomington; and the winners in this round were offered scholarships to the School. By 1936, this program had grown to such an extent that the three-day Music Festival at the University, which combined the School's solo contests with the state contests for high school vocal and instrumental ensembles, attracted groups from 102 schools, comprising 1,990 students competing in contests of bands, orchestras, and choruses, as well as 332 finalists in vocal and instrumental contests. In addition, "Hoosier Music Festival" competitions in strings, winds, and brass were held annually at the State Fair, with, again, scholarships offered to the winners. The School also established an alumni association, in conjunction with a quarterly newsletter for alumni. In financial terms this venture was not a success, for in one of Merrill's last meetings he lamented the fact that the cost of the newsletter exceeded the dues collected.

The shortfall mattered, for throughout Merrill's tenure the School was constantly strapped for money. In consequence, the development of the applied-music program was handicapped by an inability to provide all the needed equipment, including especially instruments. Organ was a particular problem. In 1927, Mrs. Fred Chew found herself unable to complete her organ major because there was no instrument available either for practice or for her Senior Recital. (She had played her Junior Recital at the Methodist Church, but that arrangement was evidently not replicable the following year.) The solution to this problem, not altogether satisfactory, was that Mrs. Chew studied piano instead of organ during her senior year, was excused from her Senior Recital, but was still granted a degree with a major in organ. The situation did not dramatically improve during the rest of Merrill's tenure. Shortly after his arrival, his successor, Robert Sanders, lamented "the glaring bar to our completeness as a School of Music, the singular absence of any kind of pipe organ on the campus."

But what the School in Merrill's time most needed—ever more desperately as the years passed—was not equipment but accommodation. Although in the fall of 1921 Merrill had assured Bryan and the trustees that once the past summer's remodeling of Mitchell Hall was completed the School's accommodations would be "ideal for some time to come," the very next year he launched a campaign for a new building. This campaign lasted for fifteen years, but Merrill could not but persevere in it, for the growing inadequacies of Mitchell pressed in on him every day.

These inadequacies were of several kinds. First, the building, even when supplemented by the Music Annex of 1921, rapidly became too small to house the growing faculty and student body of the School. This problem was exacerbated by the special nature of some of the activities that took place in it, for Mitchell housed not only classrooms but studios and practice rooms, and the noise from the second set of rooms posed a considerable hindrance to the activities of the first. The faculty minutes of February 7, 1927, report a request "by several members of the Faculty that the students practicing trumpet, Saxaphone [*sic*] etc. be removed as far as possible from recitation rooms." Second, the remodeled building was no cooler in summer, and no less fundamentally shabby, than it had been in its previous form; and conditions in it grew steadily worse. In addition to everything else, as Newell Long remembered, "animals got underneath the building. One time there was so much barking they had to call off rehearsal."

Then too, though the large room in Mitchell doubled as a recital hall, this venue was inadequate for many of the performances mounted by the School. A few student recitals were given in the Commerce Auditorium; and from 1934 the general student recitals were held in the Alumni Hall of the recently completed Memorial Union. Performances involving large forces (such as orchestral concerts) or anticipating large audiences (such as the Music Series) still had to be held in Assembly Hall.

There were, then, quite sufficient practical reasons for wanting a new music building. Merrill, though, who had a keen sense of the importance of advertising and public relations, had still another reason for wanting one: he recognized the great *symbolic* value of a good building. Even in the case of poor Mitchell, as I noted earlier, he had requested that it be repainted to match the Annex, since then "the feeling would be that the School of Music is an entity and the impression abroad among the students would be improved." But his full argument along these lines could be made only in the campaign for a *new* building. "My great desire," he wrote to Bryan in February 1924 (in a letter that reminds one of how genuinely eloquent he could be, when not writing about his colleagues), "is to see here a Music School of solid dignity and worth; to see the frivolous and false notions of music, held by a great majority of our students, supplanted by a serious-minded and true conception." For this desire to be realized, it was not enough simply to have a school filled with able people. When outsiders deplored the School's lack of a decent building, he could only answer that it was men that counted. But in his heart he knew "that Polonius was right in the matter of his son's apparel, and that the pupil who joyfully announces to me that he is going to a 'Conservatory' next semester, only voices the general feeling that we haven't a 'School of Music' here because we lack the visible sign." This remark (which, incidentally, makes clear that for Merrill "school of music" equaled, or ought to have equaled, "conservatory") embodies what appears in retrospect to have been a strikingly accurate and important perception. For the superb physical facilities that the Indiana School of Music has had, from the building that Merrill's campaign finally brought about to the Simon Center, have not only physically accommodated its burgeoning activities but have played a large part in creating and sustaining its powerful mystique: in conveying its size and stature with immediate force, and in operating as a recruiting tool for both students and faculty.

In the chronically underfunded condition of the University, though, a new music building was not easy to come by, however clear the need for one. On more than one occasion, hopes were raised only to be dashed. In a faculty meeting just before Christmas of 1925, expectation ran so high that "it was unanimously decided . . . to apply the present amount in the Steinway Piano fund on the purchase price of a choice Steele painting to be hung in the future Music School." (T. C. Steele was the preeminent member of the artists' colony in adjacent Brown County.) There could scarcely be a clearer indication of the importance Merrill (and his faculty) attached to symbolism, which was here ranked above what was surely a pressing material need of the School. The painting should, Merrill suggested, be one "suitable for use on the cover of Music School bulletins and publications of all kinds connected with the School so that it might come to be recognized as a sort of trade mark of the School of Music." One is not sorry to read that the decision was reconsidered the following February, when it was decided that only *after* the purchase of the Steinway would a fund be established for acquiring one or more Steele paintings.

According to Burton Myers, in this same year of 1926 Bryan raised hopes by suggesting that Merrill discuss a new building with the Bursar; a building also seemed eminent in 1927, when an application for funding was made to the Presser Foundation. There was recurrent talk about housing the School in the proposed University auditorium. Merrill favored this idea, but year after year the auditorium project failed to get beyond the talking stage. In 1932, the School was offered, as an interim solution, larger quarters in Residence Hall (not far from the current location of the School), but Merrill declined the offer, fearing that once it was seen that the School had "sufficient room, no matter how inappropriate," the authorities might decide that a new music building was no longer necessary. This misgiving was surely justified. The decision to turn down the larger quarters was hard to make while sitting in Mitchell Hall, but it had enormous long-term benefit for the School.

Ironically, it was the financial catastrophe of the Depression that at last made it possible to finance a new building. In 1933, one of the New Deal recovery agencies, the Public Works Administration, instituted a matching-funds program for construction projects. This and other recovery programs enabled the University to make a prodigious improvement and expansion of its physical plant. In June 1935, in the new climate created by the PWA, Merrill appeared before the Board of Trustees to urge the case for a music building. Following his presentation, the President of the Board proposed that its members inspect Mitchell Hall after their meeting. No doubt this inspection helped to convince the trustees that a new building was a great desideratum. In any case, at their meeting on October 9 they approved an arrangement, which had been worked out in the interim, whereby the PWA would provide a grant of $155,000 toward the construction of a music building; the University would be responsible for the remaining $141,000 of the cost. (The University would finance its share through a bond issue, to be amortized, over thirty years, from the School's practice-room and lesson fees.) At the same meeting, Bryan announced the selection of Robert Daggett of Indianapolis as architect for the building. A few days later, the President received a petition from many members of the School, protesting the proposed siting of the building at a location which was at that time on the eastern edge of the campus, "a very great distance," as the petition said with some hyperbole, "from the remainder of the buildings where all of the School of Music students have classes." Bryan told Merrill it was too late to reconsider the site—which was, in the long run, just as well.

Merrill, who was sufficiently confident of his architectural talents that he designed his own house, played a major role in the design of the Music Building. Indeed, Daggett supposedly became so displeased with the Merrill-influenced building that he at first declined to have his own name on the cornerstone, which was laid on May 16, 1936; a decision that, upon maturer consideration, he reversed.

And well he should have (if the story is true), for the Music Building was a splendid structure. It had an exterior of the local limestone, with steel casement windows, above which were incised the names of great composers; inside, there was marble and oak wainscoting, and, on the functional level, elaborate soundproofing. Almost best of all, the building had central air-conditioning—a rarity at the time. There were three above-ground floors and a full basement. The top floor was partitioned into forty-eight practice rooms. The other floors comprised studios, classrooms, a large rehearsal room, the Music Library, a "radio and recording room," and a music museum (which included Baynard Hall's "pianne").

The centerpiece—literally and figuratively—of the building was Recital Hall, which, with its balcony, seats 435. Chaste in design, the hall was decorated with six bas-reliefs of composers above its white oak wainscoting. Most important, it was (and is), as the Bulletin quite fairly said, "a marvel of acoustical perfection" (though frankly one could sometimes wish for less noise from the air-conditioning).

On August 5, 1936, Merrill conducted the summer school orchestra in "The Last Serenade in the Court of Old Mitchell," and over the next several months the School moved from what was surely one of the poorest accommodations of an American music school to what was unquestionably one of the very best.

The first program in Recital Hall was given on January 15, 1937. The move to the new building did not, though, signal the end of the School's financial problems. It was still the Depression, and no federal largess was available to equip the new structure, which was therefore very sparsely equipped. In 1937, Merrill's budget submission for the School included a grand request for $20,000 for "a pipe organ, orchestral instruments, desks, piano truck, radio with loud speaker, lockers, furniture for the reception room." But the actual budget appropriation for equipment—which, to be sure, represented a 10 percent increase over the previous year's—was $533.50 (in a total budget of $1,138.50). For want of a curtain for Recital Hall, the Gilbert and Sullivan production by the Pro-Music Club (a student organization founded in 1936) scheduled for the fall of 1937 had to be postponed.

This was a temporary setback; but the preceding year a more ominous financial note had been sounded. At a faculty meeting in December 1936, Merrill reported the contention of the University administration "that the music school should pay for its operation." The School was not turning out to be the money-making proposition that Bryan had hoped (and Merrill confidently predicted) it would be; on the contrary, it was a drain on the general University economy.

In response to the Dean's announcement, the faculty approved a motion, proposed by Birge, that Merrill ask Herman B Wells, who was by this time Dean of the Business School, to recommend someone who would study the School's financial situation and, among other things, advise the faculty whether it would be worthwhile to try to increase enrollment by an advertising campaign. Evidently Wells undertook the assessment himself, for on the following March 3, Merrill reported "the proposal of Dean Wells to survey the openings in music houses and Indiana cities for music teachers, with the hope of placing some of the graduates of the School of Music." Placement had not been one of the matters on which the faculty resolution had asked for guidance, but one may surmise either that Merrill decided to broaden the request or that Wells had thought that a demonstrated ability of the School's graduates to find employment would (especially in the Depression) be necessary in order for an advertising campaign to be successful or even conscionable. In any case, the minutes also record Wells's suggestion that the School advertise through the University Publicity Department. Hoffzimmer moved that an advertising campaign be started using national music journals. Though the minutes fail to indicate whether or not either this proposal or Wells's was approved, those of the next meeting record Merrill's announcement that his budget request for the following year included $1,000 for advertising. The request was not granted. Advertising is heard of only once more in Merrill's deanship: at a meeting in March 1938, he proposed an unlikely-seeming venture whereby the School would sell postcards featuring autographed "pictures of the faculty in action in their studios." The sale of these cards would not only raise money (a rather small amount, one would think) but would "advertise the School of Music in a way that other schools are doing in their view books."

In addition to the School's cost to the University, the central administration was also concerned about its cost to students. As far back as November 1936, Merrill had advised his faculty that the Director of the Summer School "had commented on the fact that Music School credits cost a good deal more than credits of other schools." These extra costs were the fees charged for applied-music lessons and for the rental of practice rooms. In May 1938, Merrill had to explain to the members of the visiting University Self-Survey Committee (of which more later), one of whose members had raised the matter of "the tremendous cost of the training in the School of Music," that the levying of fees was standard in good music schools. Those schools "which did not charge extra were never heard of for their pupils." Fees were necessary to support the faculty in an educational situation where individual instruction must partially replace classroom instruction.

Apart from increasing the number of Music majors through an advertising campaign, there were two obvious ways to improve the School's financial situation. The first was to attract more non-Music students to its cost-effective music-appreciation courses and large ensembles (for which students received course credit), as well as to applied-music lessons, for which the fees they paid would, *pace* the Self-Survey Committee, enrich the treasury. In the last Bulletin he prepared, Merrill greatly expanded the School's statement of purpose so as to woo these students who might study music as an elective: "While the purpose of the School of Music is to give its students a complete education in the science and art of music and to prepare them for professional careers, it does not overlook the fact that thousands of doctors, lawyers, and business men are unusual performers on the piano, violin, cello, or other instrument, or singers. For these amateurs the best of instruction is offered and extraordinary opportunity to participate with others in all kinds of ensembles and larger groups. Interesting courses are also offered to the University student who simply wants an understanding of music sufficient to enjoy its beauty and realize that to him it is not a closed book."

The second way to make Music less costly, to its own students if not to the University, was to reduce the emphasis on applied music within its degree programs, whether by reducing the number of credit hours required in applied music—which was high, by the standards of the discipline's accrediting body, the National Association of Schools of Music (to which the School did not yet belong)—or by reducing the amount of individual instruction students were expected to pay for; in either case, by backing down some distance from the conception of the School as a conservatory. Almost all its students were in Public School Music anyway, preparing for careers as educators rather than as performers. The acceptability of group lessons was, however, a matter on which academic and applied musicians took predictably different positions. To Merrill in particular, any retreat from the conservatory model of training was unacceptable. It was evident, he told the Self-Survey Committee, that "music students prefer to pay for a half hour's private lesson rather than share the time in a class of 4 for an hour at half the price. Each student is different and has to be diagnosed accordingly." In response, Birge "raised the question of what standard of proficiency was required of the public school music teacher, the private lesson standard or the class standard"?

The issues raised in these meetings have echoed through the subsequent history of the School. The University still wishes the School were not so expensive to run. Partly (though only partly) because Music Education programs are more cost-effective than performance programs, discussion continues within the School as to the appropriate relative numbers of students in the two areas; some faculty members feel that the School should do more to attract non-Music majors to its courses; and there is still disagreement about the appropriate standard of performance to require of academic-music students.

Merrill, however, remained to fight just the opening round of these conflicts. Before 1937, the University had only a bare-bones pension plan sponsored by the Carnegie Foundation, and, since low salaries made it difficult to save for retirement, many faculty members kept working indefinitely. Bryan himself had entered the employ of the University in 1884; by the spring of 1937 he was seventy-six years old and was completing his thirty-fifth year as President. He hadn't, according to Herman Wells, really wanted to serve that long, but had continued for the same reason that applied to other faculty. In that year, though, Bryan persuaded the state legislature to approve the University's participation in a much better national academic pension plan, the Teachers Insurance Annuity. Under the new system, retirement became mandatory at age seventy; and so in the summer of 1937 the President himself retired along with a host of others. Merrill—who was seventy-three—was allowed to stay on until a successor to the deanship could be secured. He retired in the summer of 1938, together with his nemesis Birge, and Jack Geiger.

According to Newell Long, Merrill didn't want to retire. Given the scars his long battles surely left on him, it is hard to see why not; but the School had, one supposes, come to seem his life. Despite his appalling relations with his faculty, and his failure to deliver on his promise that music would be a paying proposition for the University, his accomplishments had been great. Beginning with a small department centered in music appreciation, poorly staffed and miserably housed and equipped, he had made the case for a School of Music, had recruited an international faculty for it, and had shaped, with his colleagues' support on this key matter, what was (as much as might be) a conservatory within a university. In Merrill's final year as Dean, the School had 116 students enrolled in its degree programs, with another 383 taking courses or music lessons or participating in ensembles. All told, fully a tenth of the University's students were doing work in the School. There was a Music Library of 1,500 volumes, supplemented by collections of scores and recordings. Within five years of his arrival, too, Merrill had created a permanent and astonishingly good concert series; and his culminating work had been the erection of a superb new building for the School.

The only thing missing was the high-quality performance students for whom Merrill had built his conservatory. In his final year as in his first, almost all the School's students were enrolled in its program in Public School Music, in whose mundane business the Dean had no real interest. Only a handful of graduates had positions as orchestral musicians. But Merrill took long views, and, in his remarks at the dedication of the Music Building, on June 13, 1937, he tried, speaking from the stage of Recital Hall, to impress these views upon his students and colleagues:

> This music building was not built in a year. It is the product of thought, composite thought, the thought of multitudes of students, your great-grandfathers, grandfathers, and fathers longing for musical expression; of the subtle influence of performers, writers, and speakers. . . .
>
> We believe that America is in the midst of a spiritual and esthetic renaissance, a rebirth of creative art; that Americans, having revolted from formal respect for dead tradition, have awakened to the stimulus and inspiration to be gained from the humanities, the husbanded resources of human wisdom and human vision. . . .

> We believe that from this very spot will issue composers, executive musicians, teachers, and amateurs . . . [of importance] out of all proportion to their numbers.

He lived until 1954, remaining in the Bloomington area, and saw his dream beginning to come true. In 1989, his building became Merrill Hall.

Figure 1. William Lowe Bryan. As President of Indiana University 1902–37, he conceived and brought to fruition the idea that it should have a School of Music. *University Archives*

Figure 2. Charles Diven Campbell (1877–1919), the Associate Professor of German whom Bryan chose, in 1910, to found a Department of Music. *University Archives*

Figure 3. Mitchell Hall (before 1918).
The "poor little frame" served as the first home
of Music at the University.
University Archives

Figure 4. The University Orchestra, 1912. *University Archives*

Figure 5. Mitchell Hall after its 1918 renovation.
In this form, it continued (together with an annex)
as the home of Music until 1937.
University Archives

Figure 6. Barzille Winfred Merrill (1864–1954). Brought to the University as Campbell's successor in 1919, he became, in 1921, its first Dean of Music. *University Archives*

Figure 7. Edward Bailey Birge (pictured in 1936). Appointed Professor of Public School Music in 1921, he quickly rose to the top of Merrill's enemies list, where he remained at least until they both retired in 1938. *University Archives*

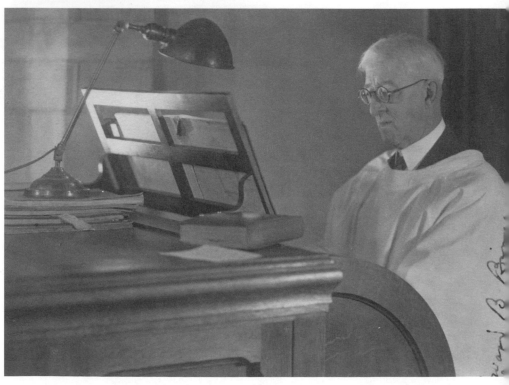

Figure 8. Winifred Merrill (1947), whose appointment to the faculty—by her father, in 1926—caused untold strife in the School. *Indiana University Photographic Services*

Figure 9. Ernest Hoffzimmer (1948), appointed as the Professor of Piano in 1928. The cigar was a fixture.
Indiana University Photographic Services

Figure 10. Lennart von Zweygberg (1944), who was appointed in 1929 as the School's first Professor of Cello.
Indiana University Photographic Services

Figure 11. The Music Building (now Merrill Hall). Opened in 1937, it was the realization of Dean Merrill's great dream, the "visible sign" of "a Music School of solid dignity and worth."
University Archives

Figure 12. Herman B Wells (with the white hat), President of the University 1937–62, pictured in his Packard Phaeton, 1932. Ward Biddle, later the University's Comptroller, holds a cigar. *University Archives*

Figure 13. Robert L. Sanders (1906–74). Brought in by Wells as Merrill's successor, the composer served as Dean until 1947. *University Archives*

Figure 14. *Top right,* The Universit Auditorium. Opened in 1941, the Auditorium gave the University a superb venue for the full range of musical and theatrical performances. *University Archives*

Figure 15. The 3,700-seat hall of the Auditorium; the building also includes the 400-seat University Theater.
University Archives

Figure 16. The Metropolitan Opera Company, in its first appearance at a university, performs *Aida* (April 13, 1942) in the Auditorium. *University Archives*

Figure 17. Paul Nettl and Dorothee Manski conduct the Mozart Seminar (1947). *Indiana University Photographic Services*

Figure 18. Wilfred C. Bain (left), Dean of the School 1947–73, pictured in 1948 with the "twin geniuses" of his Opera Theater, the conductor Ernst Hoffman and the stage director Hans Busch. *Indiana University Photographic Services*

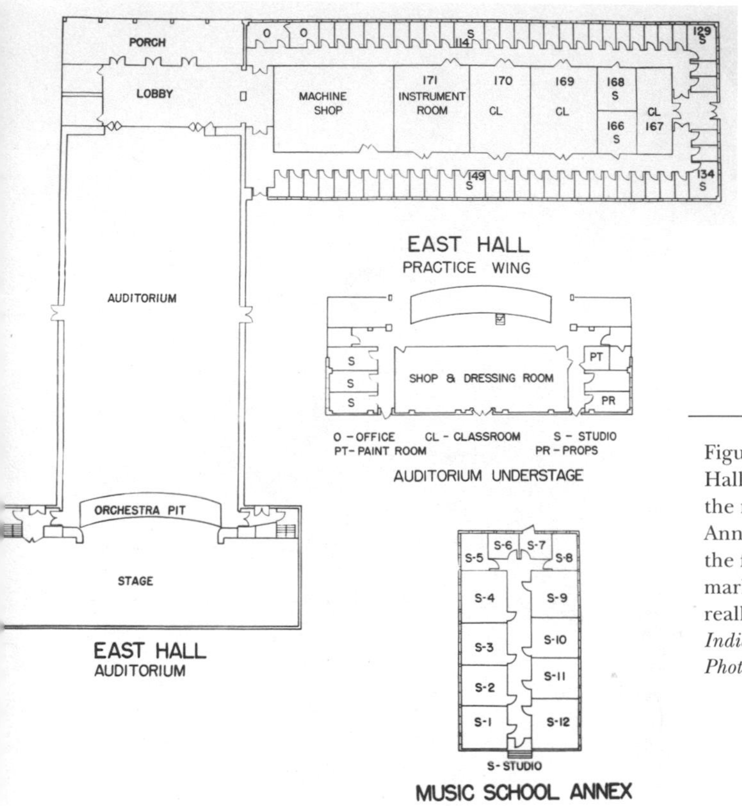

Figure 19. Plans for East Hall (opened 1948) and the modest Music School Annex (opened 1947). In the former, the tiny rooms marked "S" (for studio) are really practice rooms. *Indiana University Photographic Services*

Figure 20. East Hall in its glory (1950). *Indiana University Photographic Services*

Figure 21. The auditorium of East Hall, the former movie theater for soldiers that served as the School's opera house until 1967 (when the productions were transferred to the auditorium of the University School). *Indiana University Photographic Services*

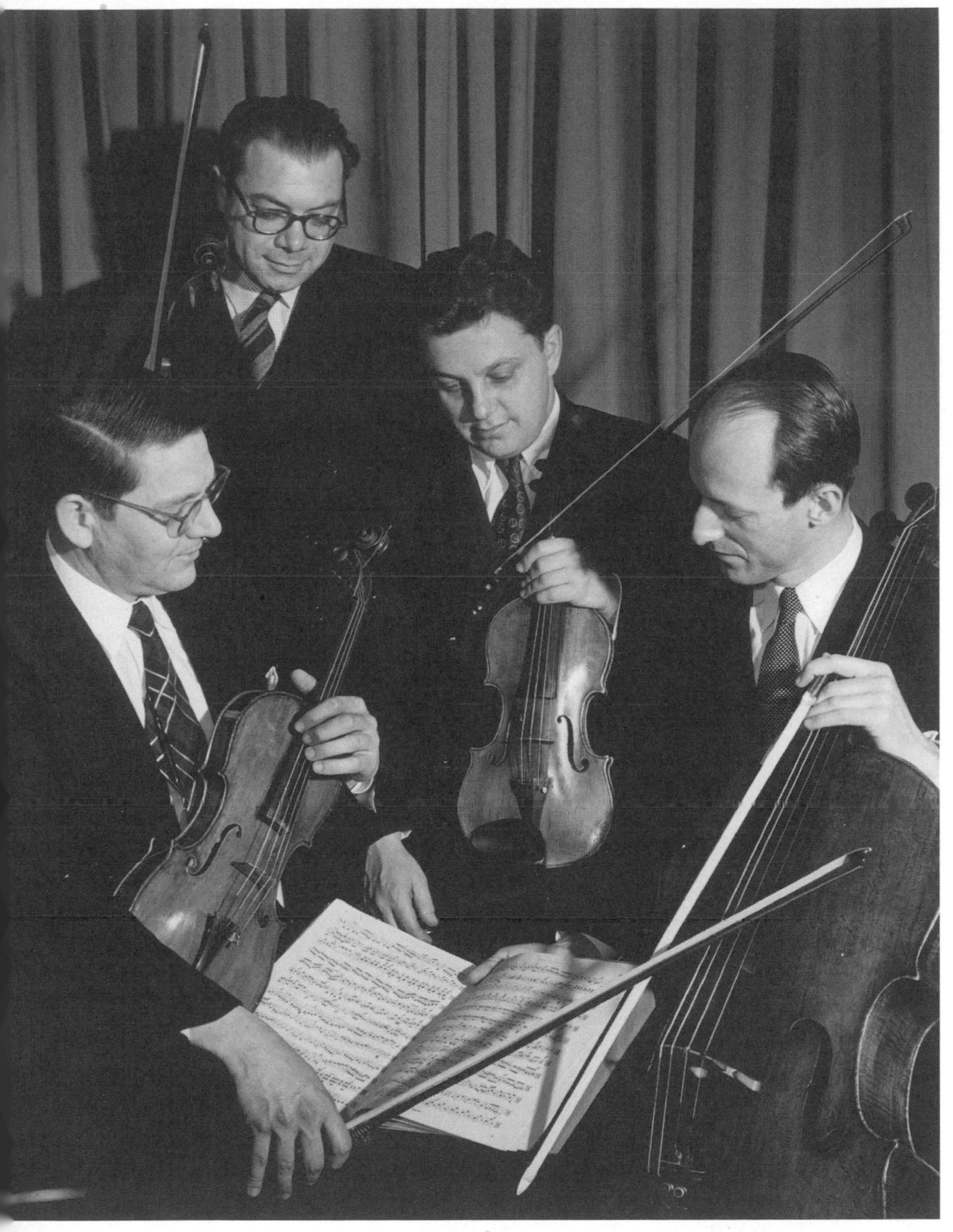

Figure 22. The Berkshire Quartet (appointed to the faculty in 1948), pictured in 1950: David Dawson, Albert Lazan, Urico Rossi, Fritz Magg.
Indiana University Photographic Services

Figure 23. *Top left,* The Belles of Indiana (1952), posed in the foyer of the University Auditorium, with one of the Thomas Hart Benton murals behind them. *Indiana University Photographic Services*

Figure 24. *Bottom left,* The pianists Walter Robert and Sidney Foster (1954). Robert followed Bain from North Texas; Foster, appointed in 1952, had been the first Leventritt Award winner and became the first faculty member of the School to combine academic duties with a major concert career. *Indiana University Photographic Services*

Figure 25. Frank St. Leger, who came to the School in 1953 after a long stint as artistic administrator of the Met and a brief one at Twentieth Century–Fox. *University Archives*

Figure 26. The third Music Annex (opened 1960). *University Archives*

Figure 27. The labyrinthine interior of the Music Annex.
Indiana University Photographic Services

Figure 28. The Beaux Arts Trio, with its 1968–87 personnel: Isidore Cohen, Menahem Pressler, Bernard Greenhouse.
Office of Publicity, School of Music

Figure 29. Josef Gingold, who in 1960 left his position as concertmaster of the Cleveland Orchestra to become the School's superlative violin pedagogue and its most beloved member. *University Archives*

Figure 30. Tibor Kozma. Hired in 1957 to replace Hoffman as the School's principal orchestral conductor, he became Bain's nemesis. *University Archives*

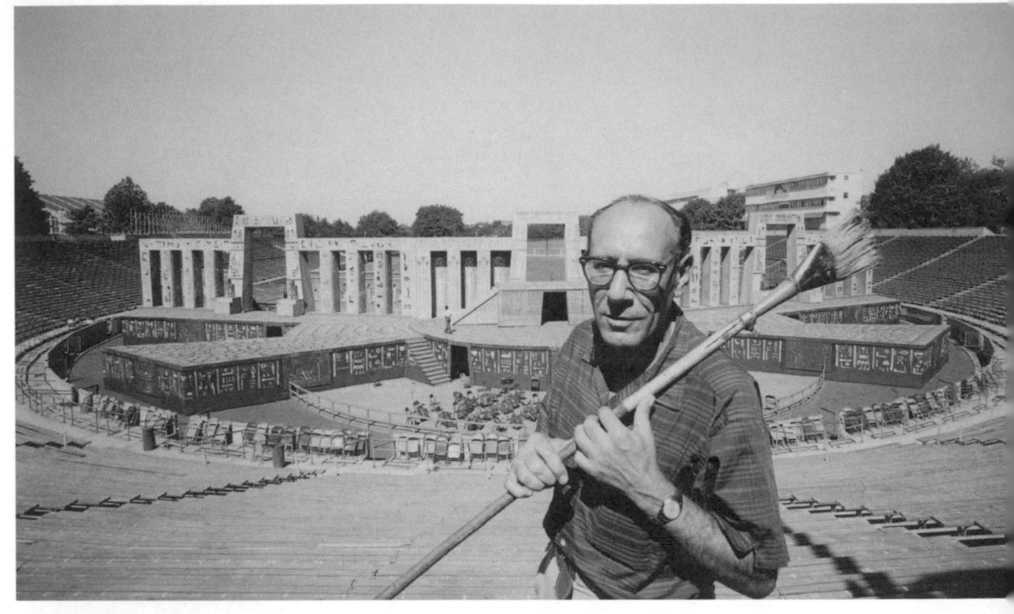

Figure 31. Mario Cristini, the School's great scenic designer, in the University football stadium as fitted out for *Aida* (1963). *University Archives*

Figure 32. Margaret Harshaw as Kundry in the 1967 production of *Parsifal*. *Office of Publicity, School of Music*

Figure 33. The American Woodwind Quintet (ca. 1965): Harry Houdeshel, Jerry Sirucek, Philip Farkas, Leonard Sharrow, Earl Bates. *University Archives*

Figure 34. Rehearsing *Lucia di Lammermoor* (1970), Wolfgang Vacano pauses to study the score. *University Archives*

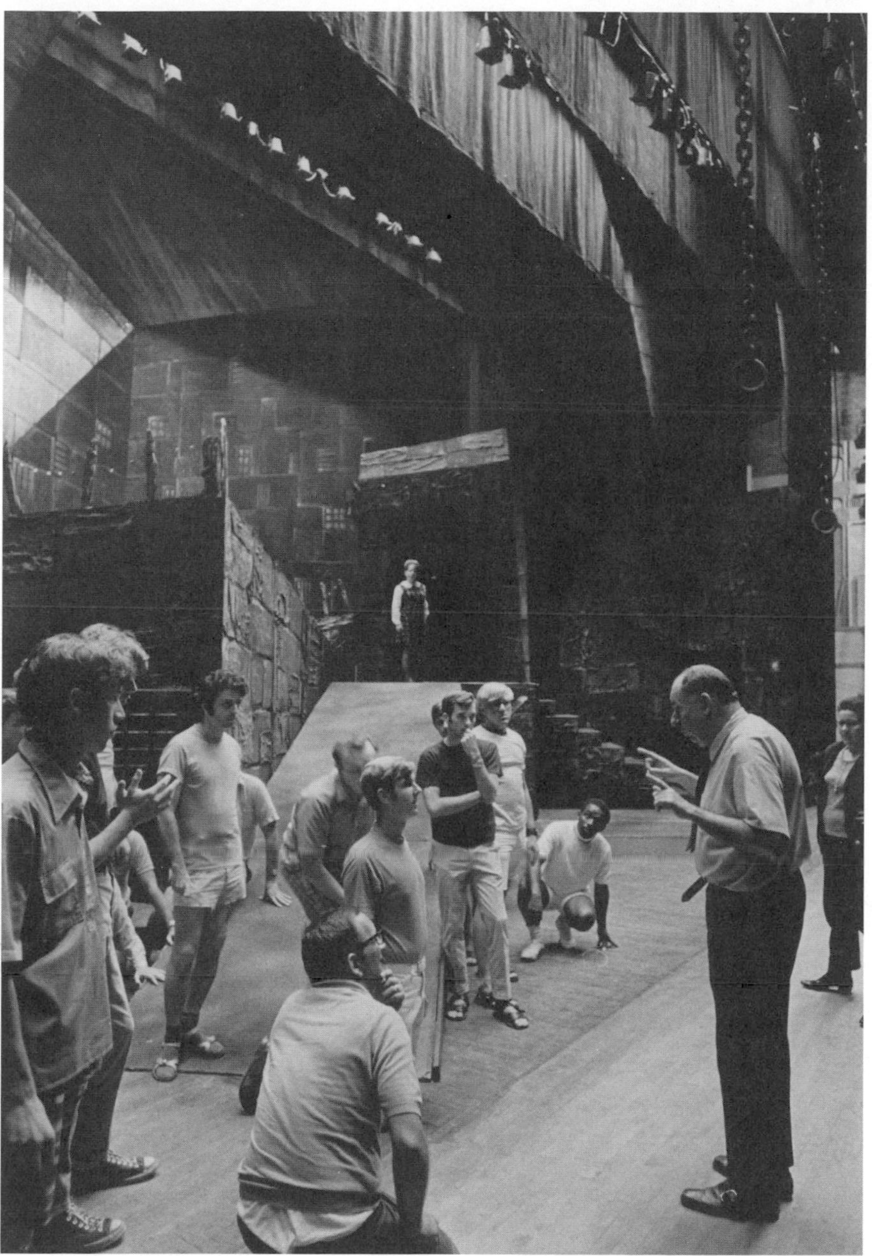

Figure 35. *Top left,* Linden Hall of the Trees Center. Its thin walls did not ideally suit it for its longtime use as a practice building; at one point students were asked to collect egg cartons as soundproofing materials. *Indiana University Photographic Services*

Figure 36. *Bottom left,* The Wagnerian conflagration of East Hall (January 24, 1968). *Indiana University Photographic Services*

Figure 37. *Above,* Ross Allen, as stage director for *Fidelio* (1970, at the University Auditorium), instructs the chorus. *University Archives*

DO NOT
ENTER

Figure 38. The Musical Arts Center, opened in 1972; its Calder stabile ("Peau Rouge Indiana") is on the right.
University Archives

Figure 39. *Above,* The MAC's Hoagy Carmichael Foyer. *University Archives*

Figure 40. *Top right,* Bain addresses the audience at the dedication of the MAC (April 15, 1972). *University Archives*

Figure 41. *Right,* On-stage reception after the dedicatory performance of John Eaton's *Heracles:* "the stage filled up with prop girls and crew, . . . the center wagon complete with turntable and temple of Zeus moved back (about halfway to Indianapolis, it seemed), . . . and then, as the climax of this animated, delightful, and tautly-paced show, the wagon stage from the right rolled on front and center, bearing buffet tables, student waitresses, and beef stroganoff and quiche lorraine for 2000" (Michael Steinberg). *Office of Publicity, School of Music*

Figure 42. Charles and Kenda Webb, the School's Dean and its First Lady, 1973–97. *Courtesy of the Webbs*

Figure 43. *Below,* Janos Starker in a master class (1976). *University Archives*

Figure 44. *Above,* Robert Stoll rehearses the Singing Hoosiers. *Office of Publicity, School of Music*

Figure 45. Prof. Eileen Farrell (ca. 1975). The MAC is in the background. *University Archives*

Figure 46. *Above,* The Music Practice Building (opened 1979). *University Archives*

Figure 47. Harvey Phillips as TubaSanta (1979). *University Archives*

Figure 48. *Rigoletto* (1980), the second cast: Sylvia McNair and Gran Wilson. *University Archives*

Figure 49. *Below,* Max Röthlisberger, the School's second great scenic designer, prepares a model for *The Abduction from the Seraglio* (1982). *University Archives*

Figure 50. *New Yorker* music critic Andrew Porter, as visiting stage director, rehearses *The Abduction. University Archives*

Figure 51. In the lobby of the MAC, Gianna d'Angelo and Nicola Rossi-Lemeni discuss *The Barber of Seville* (1982). *University Archives*

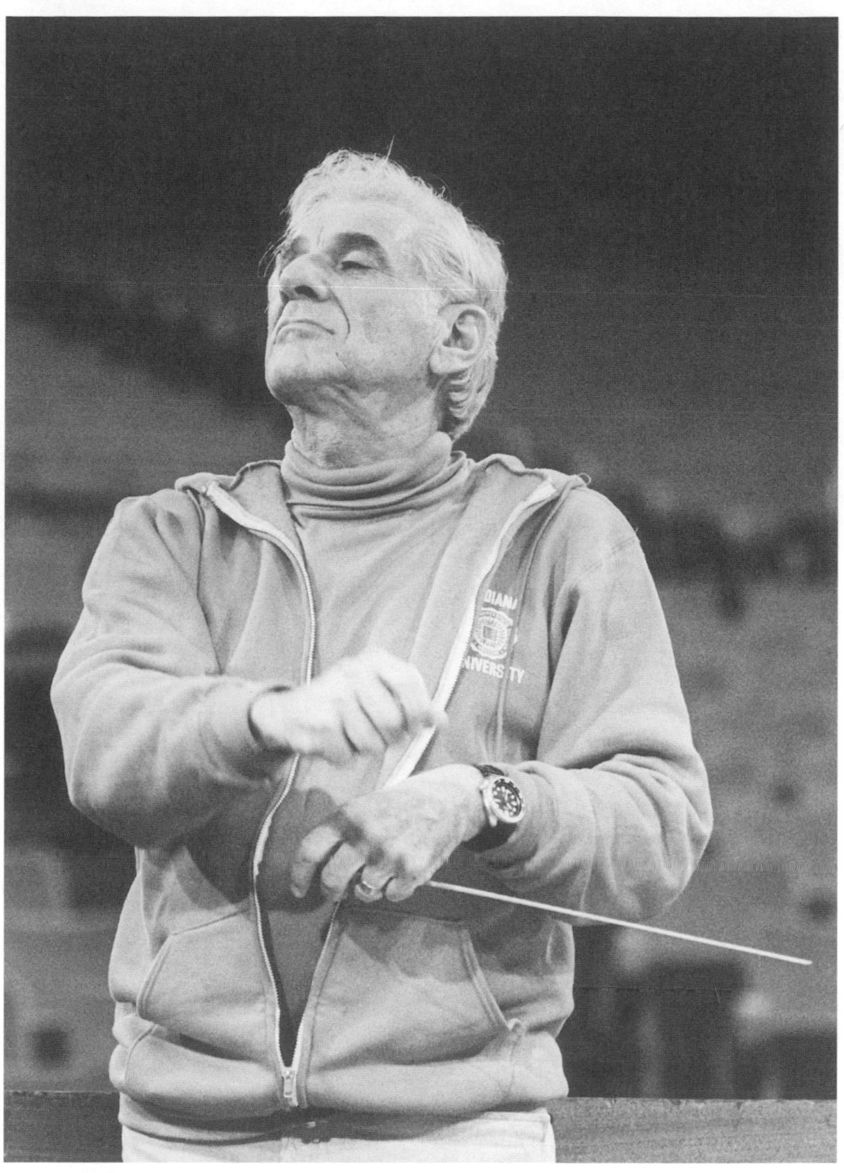

Figure 52. Two months after his sojourn in Bloomington (January–February 1982)—when he had "fallen in love" with the School—Leonard Bernstein rehearses the London Symphony Orchestra. *Photo © Suzie Maeder*

Figure 53. Stanley Ritchie, the superb baroque violinist who joined the faculty in 1982. *Office of Publicity, School of Music*

Figure 54. David Baker, the gifted composer and cellist who first came to the School as an undergraduate in 1949 and returned to it for good in 1966, becoming the founding head of the Jazz Department. *University Archives*

Figure 55. Virginia Zeani. She and her husband Nicola Rossi-Lemeni became the only married couple in the history of the University who both achieved the rank of Distinguished Professor. *Office of Publicity, School of Music*

Figure 56. Gyorgy Sebok in his celebrated monthly chamber music master class. *Office of Publicity, School of Music*

Figure 57. Thomas Binkley, the founding director of the Early Music Institute. *University Archives*

Figure 58. Patricia McBride and Jean-Pierre Bonnefoux (ca. 1989), teaching in the Ballet Department they transformed. *University Archives*

Figure 59. The Simon Center (opened 1995), seen through the McKinney Fountain. *Photograph by Nancy Webber, Indiana University*

3

The Sanders Years (1938–1947)

Experiment in Democracy

Whenever a visitor to Indiana University asks a denizen how the institution acquired one or another of its many impressive academic units or physical facilities, the answer is invariably "Herman B Wells." Wells served as President from 1937 through 1962 and then, until his death in the spring of 2000 at the age of ninety-seven, as the University's first Chancellor. He was one of the greatest of American educational administrators; and no individual played a more important part in the rise of the School of Music to preeminence.

The key fact about Wells was his unabashed patriotic love for Indiana and Indiana University. A small-town Hoosier, he was born in 1902 in the village of Jamestown, northwest of Indianapolis and less than 100 miles from Bloomington. In his attractive and modestly titled autobiography, *Being Lucky,* Wells reported that his parents "shared a great love for learning" and therefore began saving for their son's college education at the time of his birth. (Why, at the same time, they gave him the middle name "B"—not an abbreviation—is unknown.) When Herman was about ten, his schoolteacher father began moonlighting as a teller at the local bank, of which he eventually became President. As the only child of a banker (who was also twice elected county treasurer, with his wife serving as deputy), Wells after high school not surprisingly matriculated as a student of business—not at Indiana but at the University of Illinois, whose business school was better established than the one at Bloomington. After a year, though, he secured parental permission to transfer to Indiana: its business school, as he says in *Being Lucky,* "was beginning to move forward and, since I expected to spend my life in Indiana, I thought that my Indiana University associations would be useful in the future." From the very beginning, he reports, "I fell in love with Indiana University (and the romance has continued to this day)."

After completing his business degree in 1924, Wells, who had thought to make small-town banking his career, took a position as assistant cashier in the bank in Lebanon, near Jamestown. But he was bored by the job, and returned to the University in 1926 for a Master's degree in economics and, in 1927, proceeded to the University of Wisconsin for an additional year of graduate studies. Meanwhile, the essence of his Master's thesis, on Indiana country banks, had been published in *Hoosier Banker,* where it attracted favorable notice from the profession; a fact, Wells says, that led the Indiana Bankers Association to offer him the position of field secretary when he came back from Wisconsin in 1928. In 1930 he returned to Indiana University as Instructor of Economics; and in the first half of the Depression decade, when banks were a central matter of state and national concern, he also occupied successive positions as Secretary and Research Director of the Study Commission for Indiana Financial Institutions, Supervisor of the Division of Banks and Trust Companies and the Department of Financial Institutions of Indiana, and Secretary of the Indiana Commission for Financial Institutions. In these roles, Wells became a key figure in banking reform not only in Indiana but nationally. He also rose apace in the University, and in 1935 President Bryan elevated him to the rank of Professor and appointed him Dean of the School of Business Administration.

On March 15, 1937, Bryan conveyed to the University trustees his desire to be retired from the presidency at the Board's earliest convenience. Presumably because they thought he would be willing to serve at least until the end of the year, the trustees made little progress in finding a successor during the first months after Bryan's announcement. At a meeting on June 10, however, they were galvanized into action by his request that he be allowed to retire twenty days hence, on June 30. At this juncture, the trustees decided that they must appoint an Acting President while they searched for a permanent successor; and late that same night Judge Ora Wildermuth, the Board's Vice President, called Dean Wells, at his summer cottage in neighboring Brown County, to offer him the position. Wells was a person who loved to repeat favorite stories, and he often told the one about this telephone call. He had protested to Wildermuth that he was a young dean and still a new one; there were much more plausible candidates for the presidency among the more senior deans, one of whom could be tried out in the acting role. Wildermuth's reply, as Wells remembered it in *Being Lucky,* effectively disarmed this argument: "to be perfectly frank with you, the reason we don't want to take one of the other men is that we might want him for the president. We know we won't be considering you. We can make you acting president without prejudicing the choice of any of the others." Under these circumstances, Wells replied, he would accept the job, "if you will promise me that during this period you won't consider me for the Presidency . . . [and] will get me back to my dean's job as soon as possible."

Wildermuth made these promises, but he had to break them the following spring, when the trustees decided to offer Wells the full presidency, on the ground that he had surpassed all their expectations during his stint as Acting President. Wells acceded to the offer, and on March 22, 1938, he became, at thirty-five, the youngest president of a major state university.

He had indeed been extremely active in the interim role, partly because of his own character, experience, and energy, and partly because the times demanded action. As Wells said, he came to office near the beginning of "a fluid and dynamic period" in the life of the University. The end of the Depression was in sight, but the federal recovery programs that had created an unprecedented opportunity for improving the institution's physical plant remained in place. The mandatory retirement policy, which came into effect on the same day that Wells became Acting President, presented him with an equally unprecedented opportunity—and necessity—to rejuvenate the faculty with a host of appointments.

Faced with this situation, and supported by a faculty and Board of Trustees who recognized the need for action without delay, Wells set to work especially on three fronts. In the area of the fiscal affairs of the University—which his education and experience made him far better equipped to manage than his predecessor had been—he moved rapidly to secure funding for additional buildings from the recovery programs that had made possible the erection of the Music Building, and he also launched a multi-faceted exploration of ways of improving the long-term financial situation of the University. (The main conclusion of this study was that state funding would never be adequate, and that the University should therefore develop more effective means of obtaining money from private donors and federal government sources.) Second, Wells began an extremely vigorous recruitment campaign for new faculty. Finally, he established a Self-Survey Committee, charged with assessing the current state of the University and formulating a strategic plan for its development. (Self-surveys were common in American universities in the 1930s. The report compiled at Northwestern was especially influential in the design of Indiana's survey.) Few university committees can have had a greater impact than this one: its report did in fact become the blueprint by which Wells operated during the twenty-five years of his presidency. Still, it would be impossible to say that this self-study initiative had a greater beneficial effect on the development of the University than did Wells's initiatives in restructuring its finances and in recruiting a largely new faculty.

Wells threw himself into the task of recruitment with a will, not only because the rash of retirements demanded immediate attention to the matter but also because he recognized that, as he expressed it in *Being Lucky*, "the quality of the faculty is the most important ingredient in the success of the university." Consequently, "the recruitment and retention of superior faculty members must be the first objective of any administration and must have top priority in the use of the administrator's energy, mind, and body."

He proved to be an astonishingly industrious and persuasive recruiter. In the sciences, Dean Fernandus Payne of the Graduate School, a biologist, carried part of the load, as did Dean Henry L. Smith of Education in his own field and others. But Wells himself devoted a huge amount of time to the process. Especially time-consuming, in those days before easy air travel, were his trips to interview prospective appointees. (He thought it important to interview candidates "first in their home situations," so as "to learn how they measured up in the institution where they had been.") In *Being Lucky,* Wells says it seems to him that he must have spent about 40 percent of his nights the first year in sleeping cars, and, even if this is an exaggeration, the sample itineraries he gives—one involving thirteen stops from Louisville to Florida and up the coast to Washington, and the other encompassing twelve stops in five Midwestern states; and these only two of many such trips—indicate what a grueling schedule he maintained. Altogether, as Wells reported to the trustees, representatives of the University traveled, in the 1937–38 academic year, a total of 33,414 miles, and had interviews with 190 prospects, "besides numerous conferences with approximately 50 advisers."

Immediately after taking office, Wells interviewed all faculty members aged seventy or over, and decided (sometimes with the welcome backing of an advisory committee appointed by the trustees) which were to remain "for a semester or year in an acting capacity and which were to have retirement at once." In the case of Music, it was agreed that Merrill and Geiger should stay on until their successors were in place; Birge, who would turn seventy in 1938, could retire on schedule.

To advise him on a replacement for Merrill, Wells consulted principally Howard Hanson, who was Director of the preeminent music school, Eastman, and Casey Lutton, who handled music for a Chicago academic recruiting firm, the Clark-Brewer Teachers Agency. Acting on the advice of these individuals and others, he eventually narrowed the choice to two composers: Roy Harris, who was then teaching at the Westminster Choir College, and the less well-known Robert L. Sanders, who was on the music faculty of both the Bush Conservatory (which later became the Chicago Conservatory) and, since 1935, the University of Chicago.

Wells's method for deciding between these two candidates was to bring both to Bloomington for luncheon meetings with the faculty of the School, and then to determine the preference of each member through a private interview. As often happens in these matters, the faculty members appear to have based their choice about as much on a desire to have an administration as different as possible from the outgoing one as on an objective comparison of the merits of the candidates. Sanders visited first.

Newell Long was highly impressed by him: he spoke well, and he seemed "a very intelligent person." Then Harris came "and brought his wife [the pianist Johana Harris], and we'd have some question, and he'd turn to his wife and ask her what the answer to it was." For a faculty sick to death of a situation in which the Dean's daughter appeared to rule jointly with him, this deference was more than sufficient to ruin Harris's chances. By contrast, Sanders had, as Wells later recalled, "a very attractive wife and a very attractive family; and Bob himself was a very attractive guy." The faculty was unanimous in preferring Sanders. It is not clear whether Wells regarded himself as bound by the result of his poll, but in any case he offered Sanders the job. (Years later, in 1957–60, Harris came to Indiana as Visiting Professor and Resident Composer.)

To be sure, Sanders had, in addition to faculty support, impressive musical credentials. He had earned Bachelor's and Master's of Music degrees from the Bush Conservatory. He was a Fellow of the American Academy in Rome, where he had studied under Ottorino Respighi and others from 1925 through 1929. After returning to Chicago, he had taught at Bush and the University, been a church organist and choirmaster, and served as Assistant Conductor of the Chicago Symphony Civic Orchestra and guest conductor of the Chicago Symphony itself. He came highly recommended by, among others, Frederick Stock. In 1938, he received the New York Philharmonic Award for his Little Symphony in G, and he conducted the Philharmonic in a performance of the work early in 1939; his compositions had also been performed by the Chicago Symphony and the Minneapolis Symphony.

For all that, Sanders was, as Wells later acknowledged, "a rather unconventional appointment" to the deanship. Though evidently charismatic and talented, he was only thirty-two years old, and he had had no administrative experience when he became Dean on July 30, 1938.

Among the other candidates Wells had considered for the deanship had been Samuel T. Burns, the Director of Music for the State of Louisiana. Having settled on Sanders, Wells decided to pursue Burns for the Professorship of Public School Music that would be vacated by Birge's retirement. Sanders was enthusiastic about this idea, and Burns, who might understandably have been miffed by being passed over for the deanship in favor of a man ten years his junior, succumbed to Wells's characteristically intense recruiting effort and accepted the position on August 12.

The other position to be filled was that being vacated by Geiger, for which Wells commissioned Sanders to look for a suitable person. Geiger had taught both voice and music appreciation, and Sanders successfully urged Wells to let him appoint *two* people, one for each half of Geiger's work. By September 7, Sanders was ready to recommend William E. Ross (a Chicago acquaintance) for the position of Assistant Professor of Voice. His choice was based partly on the fact that Ross had a "trait in his personality which I might describe as a bit of the perennial undergraduate. . . . That is, when occasion warrants, he is able to enter into the mind of the midwestern university male undergraduate to an amazing extent." Sanders had consulted Burns on the matter, and he quoted from Burns's letter the opinion that Ross "would be extremely valuable in bringing music forcibly to the attention of the general student body and in making it felt throughout the state. [Ross would be expected to take choral groups on tour.] He would make a Kiwanis, Rotary, or school group sit up and take notice. This consideration at the present perhaps ought to outweigh others." This was *not* a consideration that Merrill would likely have entertained in choosing an appointee, though arguably it should have been, given his avowed intention of promoting music as a "business proposition." But it is completely consistent with the orientation of Wells—whose administration was fundamentally defined by the seriousness of his commitment to making the University serve the people of Indiana—and it signals an important shift of priorities in the administration of the School of Music.

To cover the history and appreciation courses, as well as to teach theory, Sanders recruited Robert S. Tangeman, who would probably not have so much power over undergraduates and Rotarians but who had impeccable credentials in academic music, with Bachelor's and Master's degrees (of Arts, of course) from Harvard. Thus Sanders began his first year as Dean, 1938–39, with twelve faculty members (as compared to Merrill's eleven), four of whom—Burns, Ross, Tangeman, and himself—were new.

In addition to expanding the faculty, the other main item on Sanders's initial agenda was a thorough review of all the School's operations, prompted by a realistic appraisal of its current condition and its position as a unit of a state university. To be sure, this was necessarily the main item on the agenda of every unit of the University at this juncture, for Wells's self-survey initiative demanded it. It seems likely, though, that Sanders would have conducted such a review in any case, since the situation of the School at the time of his arrival so clearly called for one. In his first annual report, submitted to Wells in June 1939, Sanders began by summarizing the condition of the School as it appeared to him in his early months as Dean; it is hard to fault this summary in any particular:

> I found the School but recently provided with an adequate physical plant and already beginning to experience the growth which must inevitably follow such provision. The School was not uniformly prepared for such growth. Its library was very little more than a good beginning and was without effective supervision. Its studentbody [*sic*], though containing a certain number of professional talents, seemed also to include much mediocre material giving little promise of future professional distinction. Its faculty, in most cases able and well equipped, seemed in some respects disunited, especially in the

> field of applied music. There was much concentrating of the attention on the single narrow field and not enough consideration of the problems of the School as a whole. It also appeared to me that the School (perhaps unavoidably for lack of adequate equipment) had failed to keep pace with noteworthy developments of music in the public schools and was not offering some of the essential training available as a matter of course in the music schools and departments of Northwestern, Michigan, Illinois, Iowa, Ohio State, to name only a few of our nearest neighbors.

To this intelligent observer from outside, that is, it appeared that there was a large discrepancy between the School's pretensions and its actualities, and that in some ways it was a hollow shell: a training school for music teachers that masqueraded as a conservatory, and that was not even doing a good job of training the music teachers.

Still another consideration made a review of the School's operations desirable. Sanders (and his colleagues) decided early on that it would be greatly advantageous to the School to gain membership in the National Association of Schools of Music (NASM): in order to do so, the School would have to make substantial revisions to its programs and procedures, and raise its standards.

The question of whether the School should apply for membership in NASM had been discussed at two meetings in the fall of Merrill's last year as Dean. Merrill pointed out that the purpose of the organization was "to keep up the standards" of degree-granting music schools, and he noted that as of 1936 only Music, Education, and Nursing among the University's professional schools lacked accreditation by national organizations in their fields. The faculty passed a motion approving application for membership in NASM, but nothing more is heard of such an application until the second meeting under Sanders, when the question was raised as if it were a new one. In this meeting, the principal incentive for application was said to be the leverage it would give the School in prying money from the University administration for the purpose of raising standards. By mid-November, the faculty had agreed to invite a NASM examiner to inspect the School on three days just before Christmas.

Sanders had, then, several incentives for launching a fundamental and comprehensive review of the School's operations, and he immediately got busy with one. His procedure for the review—as indeed for everything else—was thoroughly democratic. Long characterized Sanders as a "liberal," and surely this orientation was apparent nowhere more vividly than in the new Dean's conception of his role in the School. His colleagues, who had long chafed under Merrill's imperium, must have been electrified to hear Sanders, in his first faculty meeting, on September 15, 1938, explain his "concept of the duties of the Dean": "namely, transmitting the collective will of the faculty to other parts of the University." He added that "any changes in the work of the School will be effected by the group."

In the same meeting, Sanders announced that the faculty would conduct a thorough review of the School and its programs, which would begin with fundamental questions—"What is music? What are we supposed to be doing here? What are our aims?"—and thence proceed to practical matters: "What is the curriculum that will best achieve those aims? What is the best credit structure?" Since in addition to formulating its collective views on these great matters the faculty must also make determinations on all the quotidian ones (in Sanders's early years, almost nothing was left to the Dean or given over to committees), it would need to meet constantly: every Monday evening for two hours, Sanders explained. In the event, meetings during his first year often stretched to two and a half or even three hours. As Long noted, Sanders would "give everybody a chance to have their say." Governing the School, then, began to occupy vastly more man-hours than had been the case under Merrill.

Though one member—Montana Grinstead—ventured, after eight grueling months of the new regime, to suggest that meetings be scheduled for the afternoon and limited to an hour, the faculty as a whole appears, during Sanders's early years, to have retained a remarkable tolerance for the endless stream of meetings. This was partly because the meetings did, much of the time, deal with—and decide—important matters, and also because their social tone was pleasant. Long recalled that "we had a big table, and we'd all sit around the table and talk. Across the street there was . . . a restaurant and bar. And so we'd send someone over with a list of drinks, and they'd come back with a beer or two and a lemonade and so forth. It had that kind of social atmosphere." (By contrast, in the Bryan regime, one wouldn't even "dare serve wine with your meals at home.") While the mostly male faculty met, "the wives had their own meeting." As a consequence, presumably, of these democratic and pleasant if sometimes inordinately time-consuming procedures, collegiality improved rapidly under Sanders. It is striking to find, in the minutes (carefully recorded in the Sanders era by Vera Norton), evidence of genuine mutual support between performers and academic musicians. And, happily, the pace slackened a bit with passing time. By Sanders's second year, he sometimes failed to maintain the once-weekly schedule, and meetings often fell short of two hours. Moreover, as the years passed he grew increasingly willing to shift the preliminary discussion of issues to committees.

To structure the review of operations, Sanders hit on the sensible expedient of leading the faculty in a detailed review of the text of the School's Bulletin; and for several months, beginning on the evening of September 26, the weekly meetings were largely taken up by a sentence-by-sentence examination of the 1938–39 edition. Setting aside the historical sketch of the development of the School, the listing of faculty, and the University calendar for the year—all of which could be left to the Dean to update—the Bulletin began with the statement of the School's purpose; thus a sequential examination launched the faculty immediately into the fundamental questions that for Sanders constituted the first order of business for the review.

Historically, the statement of purpose had been the clearest indicator of a Dean's vision of the School. For Campbell, the overriding aim was "the cultivation of a better understanding and appreciation of music, rather than of technical proficiency in any one of the various branches of applied music"; Merrill's statement had reversed this emphasis, locating the School's primary purpose in preparing students "for professional careers"; music appreciation for the generality of students became a distinctly secondary concern. Sharply contrasting with Merrill's formulation, the draft statement that Sanders presented for the consideration of the faculty in the fall of 1938 listed, as the first of three aims for the School, the provision of a program "for the orientation of all University students who seek to understand the place and scope of music in their world." The second aim was to train public school music teachers; and only third and last do we find the aim of offering instruction "designed to aid in preparation for a professional career in the field of music." After discussion, a partly reworded but essentially unchanged revision of Sanders's statement was approved.

In retrospect—given that the School's primary function and glory now lies in its performance programs—this reversal of Merrill's priorities is likely to seem misguided. Viewed in the context of the time, though, with Wells's Self-Survey Committee insisting that every unit develop a sound strategic plan in harmony with the overall purposes of the University, it seems the only rational course. From the point of view of the state university in which the School existed, the musical acculturation of the student body and the training of teachers for the state's public schools were clearly its primary functions; and a glance at the lists of graduates in these years not only confirms that Public School Music continued to be by far the most important of the School's degree programs but strongly suggests that its faculty members, in order to justify their positions, needed to teach many students from other divisions of the University. In the spring of 1939, the supposed conservatory that Sanders had inherited graduated twelve students—as it were, one for each faculty member. Eleven of these graduates earned the degree of Bachelor of Public School Music; one of them earned the Bachelor of Music in Piano. Meanwhile, there were 290 students from other parts of the University taking lessons or registered in at least one course in the School. It is not surprising to find that Wells wrote to Sanders that he was "in hearty accord" with the revised statement of aims.

If the aims of the School as stated by Merrill did not match its current realities, this was also true of its array of programs. The faculty agreed to drop the applied-music course of study leading to the Certificate of Musical Proficiency "since these had never been granted." For the same reason, Sanders secured permission from Dean Payne to drop the degree of Doctor of Philosophy in Music. The faculty did, though, agree that the Master's programs should be retained and strengthened—because they served the School's Public School Music constituency: teachers got larger salaries if they had a Master's degree. Subsequently, the distinction between the Master of Music and the Master of Arts in Music was discussed: should the former be exclusively an applied-music degree? One would have thought that this matter (which was referred, seemingly with no result, to the "Graduate Council," consisting of Sanders, Burns, and Tangeman) would have been determined long since. But there had never been enough graduate students to make it a more than notional issue. (The matter was raised again, also inconclusively, several years later, when the faculty was formulating plans for the postwar era.)

Sanders introduced the discussion of the curricula of the undergraduate programs by noting that the applied-music requirements for the Bachelor of Music degree were more extensive than those of many other schools or than recommended by NASM: the heavy requirements in this area were, of course, a reflection of Merrill's ambition to create a conservatory. The main objections to this weighting were that it was at the expense of giving students an adequate grounding in ear training and music theory, and that it left them insufficient room in their programs for liberal arts electives. The upshot of the discussion was a revised curriculum for the Bachelor of Music with a major in applied music, in which the number of credit hours in applied music was reduced by one-fifth and the academic music sequence—theory, history, and appreciation—increased by a fifth. Ear training, now made a requirement for all four years, was incorporated into the theory courses for the first two. The number of credit hours stipulated for liberal arts electives, however, despite the good intentions, actually decreased, from fifteen to fourteen.

An attractive feature of curriculum revision in the Bachelor of Public School Music program was that it was undertaken in the light of hard information, supplied by the University placement office, about the pattern of demand for graduates of the program. The data showed that there were four times as many requests for teachers qualified in music plus one or two other subjects as for those qualified in music alone. In consequence, Burns proposed, and the faculty agreed, to decrease modestly the applied-music requirements in the program so as to make room for electives in other teaching areas. The faculty also approved a new five-year degree program issuing in a Bachelor of Music degree and a Supervisor's license—in effect, a combination of the Bachelor of Music and the Bachelor of Public School Music—which was to be recommended to students as "the wise thing for the person who wants to be a good musician and good school teacher."

Having dealt with programs and curricula, the faculty undertook a streamlining of the Bulletin section on Rules and Regulations, which, over the years, had grown in the usual incremental fashion until it comprised twenty items. The list was reduced to eight, partly by rearrangement and combination but also by deleting some rules, including several on practice—how much, when, where, forfeit of credit as the penalty for unexcused absences—which were replaced by a hortatory paragraph speaking of expectations rather than requirements. Earlier, the requirement that students keep practice records had been dropped. One should not imagine, however, that these changes signaled a genuine liberalization in the treatment of students. Although Sanders did establish a Student Council, which met with the faculty once a month, in general the new liberalism and democracy did not extend beyond the faculty. The minutes of Sanders's era, like those of his predecessor's, include numerous discussions of how best to coerce students to do things the faculty thought good for them. As in Merrill's time, a particularly sore point was incomplete attendance at Music Series concerts and School recitals. In 1939, the faculty instituted compulsory attendance at recitals; nonetheless, for the first recital of 1940, sixty-three of 150 students were absent; and finally, in 1942, loss of academic credit was enacted as the penalty for unexcused absences.

The 1938 review of operations also included an extremely significant revision of the policy on applied-music fees. In the earliest years of Music at Indiana, lessons were on a purely extra-curricular basis, so fees were naturally charged. This practice persisted after it became possible to take these lessons as credit courses. Indeed this was the norm in university music schools. (In 1941, Sanders reported the finding that in most universities 20 to 30 percent of the operating expenses of the School or Department of Music derived from fees; the figure for Indiana was 26 percent.) At first, applied-music teachers at Indiana had received no pay other than their fees; and even after they were granted regular University appointments, fees constituted a substantial part of their emolument. (In accordance with the arrangement established by Campbell, the University, which collected the fees, deducted 10 percent for overhead.) Moreover, fees varied—as in the traditional practice of conservatories—with the stature of the teacher. At Indiana, the level of the fee was a function of academic rank: in 1937–38, two lessons per week cost $90 per semester with faculty at the rank of Professor (and Winifred Merrill), $75 with Assistant Professors, and $45 with Instructors.

By the last years of Merrill's regime, the levying of fees for credit courses in the School, which made Music more expensive to students than other programs, had begun to draw unfavorable attention from the University administration. In the first meeting of the School with the Self-Survey Committee, it will be recalled, Merrill had had to defend the charging of fees against a complaint by one member of the committee about "the tremendous cost of the training in the School of Music."

Early in Sanders's first year, the matter of fees was raised at a faculty meeting, in a discussion of agenda items for an upcoming meeting with the Self-Survey Committee; and indeed the following spring the committee proposed that there should be no applied-music fees whatever. Sanders's counter-proposal, which was approved by the faculty of the School, was that a blanket fee of $40 per semester for music majors be substituted for the differential fees; but this change should be accompanied by a move to higher, fixed salaries for applied-music teachers to compensate for the loss of income from fees, as well as by the institution of standard teaching loads.

This proposal, which was accepted by the University administration (though a system of differential fees was retained for the Summer School), had great benefits not only for the students but for the School as a whole. First, the new system put the School in a stronger recruiting position, especially for graduate students, where, as Mr. Moore of the placement office had explained to the faculty, Indiana was at a great competitive disadvantage because its fees were unusually high, particularly in comparison with those at state teachers colleges. Second, the new flat fee—which was lower even than the fee formerly charged for lessons with Instructors, and much lower than those charged for faculty at higher ranks—worked to improve the level of applied-music achievement among students in the Public School Music program. As Sanders explained to Wells, under the old system, some of these students, "forced by financial stringency to do so, . . . dropped all music applications at their first opportunity." Third, the system benefited the faculty in its provision of stable income; and along with the enactment of fixed salaries went a cap on the hours of teaching required of a member. The new system also tended to increase faculty harmony. As Newell Long observed, "stratified fees tend to stratify your applied-music faculty." The new system "was more democratic."

The various revisions to the School's programs and procedures had been undertaken in part to meet the requirements of NASM membership, but for this purpose they proved to be insufficient—if only because some of them had not yet come into effect by the time of the NASM examination in December 1938. After the Christmas break, Sanders reported to Wells and the faculty of the School that, although NASM had, at its annual meeting, admitted the School to associate membership, full membership would be withheld pending a second examination in two years. The deficiencies cited by the NASM examiner were, as Sanders summarized them, in the School's theory program and in the inability of students in Public School Music "to give decent performance on any instrument." No one disputed this assessment. To be sure, the School did have some good undergraduates, as well as an occasional superb one. In the mid-1940s, for example, several Indiana students were accepted into graduate programs at Eastman. In general, though, the students were (as Sanders had observed in his first annual report) not highly accomplished. At one point, the cellist von Zweygberg asked why the piano students weren't required to play more chamber music: "they can't read anything; they can't count." The cello students too were mostly unremarkable; and in 1941 the School took the unprecedented step—but one that prefigured the future—of awarding its scholarship in cello to a student from outside Indiana.

The faculty had already agreed on a restructuring of the theory program, so presumably the deficiency in that area would be corrected when the revised program went into effect in the fall of 1939; and the new, lower applied-music fee would presumably improve performance by encouraging students to take lessons for more semesters. The basic problem, though, was the generally poor quality of the students, in terms of both ability and level of accomplishment, at the time of entry to the University. This problem was intractable, because it was bound up with the admissions policy of the University as a whole, which remained, as it always had been, to accept any graduate of an Indiana high school. (By contrast, in these years Eastman is reported to have accepted fewer than a tenth of its applicants.) As a result, the University had many poorly prepared undergraduates. Nor could the problem be solved simply by instituting a selective admissions policy: to do so would have had a calamitous effect on enrollment.

Moreover, Music had special problems of its own in this area. First, aspiring music teachers had an alternative route open to them: they could take a Bachelor's degree in the Faculty of Education, with a program that included only a few courses in Music. Thus any attempt to raise standards in the Public School Music program would simply result in the defection of many students to Education. In 1940, Hoffzimmer proposed that students should be required to have had at least one year of piano lessons before being admitted to Public School Music. This would seem to be a very modest proposal, especially in view of the fact that NASM's guideline was that students entering music school should have had three or four years of piano. But Burns responded to the suggestion by pronouncing that "it would work a hardship" on the students, "who might go elsewhere"; and Sanders added that one of those other places was the Bachelor of Science in Education program. So the proposal was dropped. In the same year, of the forty freshmen in Public School Music, thirty-four were reported to be at the beginning level in piano.

Nor did the School's recruiting tool for top-level instrumental and voice students—the State Music Contest it had run for several years—bear much fruit. An ongoing problem was that winners declined the proffered scholarships in order to enroll elsewhere—or, worse, accepted them but subsequently backed out, when it was too late to bestow them on runners-up. Other contests were sponsored by the state's music teachers. In 1942, Winifred Merrill reported the discouraging fact that of the fourteen violinists rated in the highest category in these contests, not one had enrolled at Indiana.

As if the general level of student accomplishment were not low enough, proposals by the Self-Survey Committee threatened to make it lower still. By the Music School (as surely also by many other units), the committee had quickly come to be regarded with alarm. We have already seen it questioning Merrill's faculty, in the spring of 1938, about the high cost of instruction in the School. Far worse, there was by that time already a rumor that the committee might recommend the amalgamation of Music with Drama and Art in a School of Fine Arts. Merrill raised this matter in the faculty's meeting with the committee, protesting the proposal on the grounds that there was no real relation among these diverse fields and that the prestige of the School of Music, and thus its power to attract students, depended on its remaining a separate academic unit. (Hoffzimmer supported the Dean, making the point, which he doubtless thought should settle the matter, that "there were no combined schools in the old country.") The response of the committee was non-committal: Wendell Wright, chairing the meeting, "explained the administrative weakness of the present system with 54 separate administrative units dealing directly with the President."

Indeed the committee's final report, which was submitted to the trustees in March 1939 and made available to faculty the following July, recommended that the University be reorganized into eleven academic divisions. What must have been especially galling to Sanders and his colleagues was that all the professional schools save Music were, in this plan, left as before, except for their names being changed from "School" to "Division." But the School of Music was to disappear into a "Division of Music and Fine Arts."

Music was thus threatened with the reversal of Merrill's most important victory, its organization as an independent administrative unit. This threat continued to exercise the Music faculty greatly through the fall of 1939 (by which time the committee's proposal had acquired the odd additional feature that Home Economics would be included along with Music, Drama, and Art in the proposed Division). In the event, though, the proposal was not adopted, and the School avoided a change of status that would surely have precluded its rise to eminence.

A second proposal of the Self-Survey Committee threatened to exacerbate the problem of the low level of accomplishment in applied music exhibited by the School's students. In an attempt to improve the breadth and quality of the general education the University provided to its students, and influenced by similar initiatives in other American universities, the committee proposed that the four-year undergraduate program be divided into Junior and Senior Divisions. The former, comprising the initial two years, would be largely given over to general education, in the form of interdisciplinary survey courses in the major liberal arts areas. Thus concentrated education in a particular discipline would not begin until the third year, when students entered the Senior Division.

From the point of view of Music, this proposal was almost as disturbing as that to incorporate the School into a Division of Music and Fine Arts. The School of Music was unique in requiring professional training at the undergraduate level; because of the poor preparation of most of its students, it could (as the NASM report had underscored) scarcely bring them up to a professional level in four years. What hope could it have of doing so if professional education were to be restricted to a two-year Senior Division?

As finally enacted, though, the proposal for Junior and Senior Divisions was purely beneficial to the School. When the committee's recommendations were voted on by the University faculty in 1940, this one was narrowly rejected. The Board of Trustees exercised its prerogative to overturn the vote, and decreed the reorganization; however, the Junior Division, as actually enacted, comprised only the first year of studies, not the first two, and in fact the reorganization did not materially affect the education of music students. The proposal for interdisciplinary survey courses for Junior Division students having come to naught, the curricula of undergraduate programs in Music remained unchanged. Then too, under pressure from the administrators of the Junior Division, the College of Arts and Sciences and the School of Business joined Education in granting credit, in degree programs, for applied-music courses—a development that brought the School increased enrollment.

Meanwhile, in April 1940 the reexamination of the School by NASM had taken place. The examiner, Burnet Tuthill, found the situation in music theory—where the redesigned course sequence had gone into effect—now quite satisfactory. In performance, too, he found the situation improved, as a result of the new, lower applied-music fee, which meant that "now practically all students are regularly enjoying lessons in some field of applied music." The improvement on this front was, however, insufficient. There were actually two related problems. First, most of the students in the graduating class could not play at an acceptable level: at almost any school where they might teach, the examiner's report said, "students in their bands and orchestras will be able to outplay them." Second, the grades these seniors had been awarded were far higher than Tuthill, having heard them play, thought appropriate.

In consequence of these remaining problems, as Tuthill reported to Sanders two weeks before NASM's annual meeting (held just after

Christmas), the association's Commission on Curricula decided that the School's application for full membership would be tabled for one or two years, "until such time as you deem that satisfactory progress in the field of applied music has been made to warrant a further examination." Hearing this report, the School's faculty voted that Sanders should inform Wells that the Commission's decision was justified. Sanders had, though, been invited by Tuthill to discuss the decision with the Commission at the annual meeting, and, while reporting the faculty's vote to Wells, he added that he would attend the meeting of the Commission and "use every reasonable effort to put before them more concretely the realities of our situation in an endeavor to amend their decision." On December 28, an elated Sanders reported to Wells by telegram that the School had been granted full membership. In his reply, Wells said that the Dean "must have performed a miracle . . . in light of Tuthill's report."

The report had occasioned a good deal of earnest discussion, which continued even after acceptance to full membership, about how to improve the situation in the Public School Music program. Tuthill's own suggestion had been that the School either extend the course to five years (or even more) or that it establish entrance requirements such that students could plausibly expect to attain the required level of proficiency within four years. But neither of these solutions could be implemented, for the same reason: they would drive down enrollment. What could be hoped was that the School's accreditation by NASM would make it a more attractive choice for good students. Another possibility would have been to increase the number of credit hours in applied music required for graduation; but here the main obstacle was simply a shortage of instructors (in part because students from the rival Bachelor of Education program in music were taking lessons in the Music School). At one point the possibility of stretching faculty resources by instituting more group lessons was mooted. But the only positive steps actually taken by the faculty were to enact a requirement for performance before a jury (juries were mandated by NASM) and a recital requirement for Public School Music students.

While the School labored over the modest improvements that were within its power, the University administration at last brought to completion a building project that was to have enormous benefits for the School, supplying, indeed, one of the major contributing factors in its ascent to eminence. As a venue for large-audience events, the University still had, at the time of Wells's accession, only the ancient Assembly Hall, with its 1,200 wooden chairs and jerry-rigged stage. As early as 1914, Bryan's administration had listed an auditorium as among the University's greatest needs. When the Memorial Union was being planned in the 1920s, the assumption was that it would include an auditorium with a seating capacity between three and four thousand. But when it opened in 1932, the Union had, by way of an auditorium, only Alumni Hall, a room that, fitted out with folding chairs, could be made to seat five or six hundred.

Finally, in March 1937, a few months before he left office, Bryan was able to present to the Board of Trustees a preliminary floor plan for a large auditorium. It was left to Acting President Wells to secure financing for the building—which was fortunate, since he was far better than Bryan at this kind of work. Whereas the courtly Bryan had been uncomfortable and not very effective with the state legislature, Wells was, as a result of his previous involvement in banking reform, thoroughly at ease with politicians. The story of how he secured funding for the auditorium was one of his favorites.

As it happened, Purdue University was, at the time, seeking money for the same purpose. In July 1938, Wells was (as he explained to James Clemens in a 1992 interview) "out at Kansas or someplace in Iowa, recruiting some faculty member," when President Edward Elliott of Purdue telephoned to inform him that the legislature was in special session to appropriate money, which would be matched by federal Public Works Administration grants, for building projects:

> "I think that we could get these two auditoriums that we want if we went in together on it." So I got on the train and came back, and we went in together. . . . Well, finally it got down to the last minute, and it looked like we had lost it. Everybody had left but me, and the chairman of the budget committee came up to me at the last minute and said, "I think you can get that in the morning, if you put a little pressure on." I tried to get Ed, but he had gone off to crown a Tomato Queen someplace [or, as Wells told me, "to shuck some corn someplace"], and nobody knew where he was; and I got word that Ward Biddle [the Comptroller of the University and a former state senator] . . . [, who] had been helping out on this, . . . was on his way out to California, and I got him back the next morning. The Lieutenant Governor was a friend of ours, and he . . . stood up there waiting to gavel the start of session until he saw we had enough votes. We stirred up and down the aisles working on votes, and when we gave him the high sign, he started: Bang!

The legislature appropriated $300,000 for the project and authorized a bond issue of $305,000; these monies, added to a $495,000 federal grant, made up the $1,100,000 cost of the auditorium.

The building that resulted was a marvel. First called the Hall of Music (because a bureaucratic oddity precluded federal funds being used for a building called an auditorium or theater), the Indiana University Auditorium, which was dedicated March 22–26, 1941, included a hall seating 3,700, as well as the 400-seat University Theater. There was a huge stage, with up-to-date equipment. Apart from the great hall itself, the most impressive feature of the building was (and is) a splendid series of murals by

Thomas Hart Benton, mounted in the foyer. Depicting the social history of Indiana, the murals had been painted for the Indiana exhibit at the Chicago World's Fair of 1933. Afterward, they had been stored in a barn at the state fairgrounds in Indianapolis, until Wells had offered to take them off the state's hands, for free.

The Auditorium provides an unsurpassed example of the benefits, both material and symbolic, that superior physical facilities can provide for the development of an educational institution. The perennially embarrassing Assembly Hall had epitomized the provinciality and relative poverty of the University and had strongly suggested that it was a place where the performing arts did not enjoy a high priority. By contrast, with the opening of the Auditorium the University suddenly had a cultural facility that rivaled or surpassed that of any other American university, and most commercial halls. This fact gave an enormous boost to the self-esteem and reputation of the University, and it enormously enriched the cultural life of students, faculty, and the surrounding community (indeed, of the state as a whole), by making Bloomington an attractive venue for the full range of musical and theatrical performers.

The elaborate five-day dedicatory celebrations included a joint recital by Lotte Lehmann and Lauritz Melchior, and a Lunt and Fontanne production of Robert Sherwood's *There Shall Be No Night.* The Lunts declared the Auditorium the finest theater they had ever played in. After a start of this kind, it was easy to keep the hall lit with the brightest of luminaries. Merrill's Music Series concerts had, over the years, attracted to the University an astonishing number of first-rank artists, mostly soloists but also a few major orchestras and an occasional opera company. The Auditorium Series that succeeded it was able to do even better, especially (as one might guess) with respect to larger ensembles. The 1940–41 series included fifteen events, among them, in addition to recitals by Alexander Kipnis, Marian Anderson, and José Iturbi, appearances by the Ballet Russe de Monte Carlo and the San Carlo Opera Company. Over the half-dozen remaining years of Sanders's deanship, the series presented, among many others (and some non-musical events), Rubinstein, Horowitz, and Brailowsky, Kreisler, Heifetz, Menuhin, Stern, Szigeti, and Francescatti, Pons, Tibbett, Traubel, and Pinza, the Philadelphia and Minneapolis Orchestras, the Budapest String Quartet, opera productions (including several by Charles F. Wagner touring companies replete with Metropolitan Opera stars), dance troupes, and the Trapp Family Singers. The Indianapolis Symphony was a staple, appearing each year, sometimes twice.

To a large extent, the success of the Auditorium Series was due to the Comptroller, Ward Biddle, who was, like Wells, an intensely serious music lover, and who had not only helped Wells secure financing for the Auditorium but had been involved in the design of the building and the fine-tuning of its acoustics. Biddle also directed the performance series.

Biddle's ambition for Auditorium presentations knew literally no bounds. Though he had settled for Metropolitan Opera stars Lehmann and Melchior for the dedication, he had wanted to have the Met as a whole. At first thought, this aspiration may appear simply laughable. But in fact the Met did, in those days, make annual spring tours (though these included only major cities, not provincial hamlets); and now suddenly Bloomington had a facility fully adequate to accommodate the company. As it happened, the Met had a prior engagement for the dedication week, in Boston, but in 1941 Biddle, assisted by Lee Norvelle, who was in charge of speech and drama for the English Department (and who later became the first head of the Department of Speech), launched a serious campaign to bring the Met to Bloomington, involving both correspondence and visits with Edward Johnson, the General Manager of the company. Johnson declared that no college facility in America could accommodate the Met; this claim was refuted by a perusal of the Auditorium blueprints. (Biddle's widow recalled that it had been Wells who first suggested that the stage of the auditorium be built large enough to accommodate grand opera; Biddle had made sure that this was the case.) But even though the facilities were adequate, the cost would, Johnson said, be prohibitive: $13,500. Biddle and Norvelle, however, estimated ticket sales of $9,000, and the University could underwrite the remaining $4,500. And so one of the most unlikely and charming events in the history of American music was contracted: the Metropolitan Opera Company, making its first appearance on a university campus, would perform in Bloomington, Indiana.

Not satisfied merely to *have* the Met, Biddle and Norvelle asked that it offer an especially splashy opera, *Aida*. The resulting performance, on April 13, 1942, drew spectators from as far away as Chicago, St. Louis, Cincinnati, and Louisville (a prudent clause in the contract had enjoined the Met from including on the tour cities within 200 miles of Bloomington), and in the end the University netted $380 on the venture. Far better yet, Johnson was highly satisfied with the occasion. He told Biddle that "the Metropolitan likes Indiana University, and Bloomington. So we are not saying 'goodbye' but only '*au revoir*.'" The war would affect the Opera's touring plans, "but when we again leave New York, Indiana University need only beckon."

In fact the Met returned just after the war, in April 1946, and then fifteen more years in a row, presenting two operas on each visit (with an additional single production at rival Purdue, which had, after all, its own large new auditorium). The company enjoyed performing in Bloomington; and it was on the railroad, strategically located on the tour route between various major cities (a fact that increased its attractiveness for other performers as well). The series of appearances concluded in May 1961, by which time the Met had decided that the increasing economic and transportation problems of the tour made it impractical for the company to go anyplace where it couldn't stay for an entire week.

It is impossible to overstate the importance of the Met visits for the School of Music. First, they exposed members of the School to operatic performance at a high level. Especially under Rudolf Bing (who succeeded Johnson in 1950), the touring productions were simply the best the Met had to offer. Second, the fact that the Met was willing to come to Bloomington must have acted to dissipate, in other troupes, any lingering resistance to scheduling this small town: if the Met would come to Bloomington, obviously *anyone* might safely do so. Third, the visits of the Met and other musical headliners greatly raised the cultural profile of the University as a whole and of the School of Music. Finally, the personal contacts between Met performers and the faculty of the School made possible the establishment of an appointments pipeline that has been of incalculable benefit to the School both in itself and in the precedent it established for other professional musicians whom the School would seek to recruit to its faculty.

Again at first thought, the idea that Met stars would accept appointment to the faculty of the School seems as implausible as the idea that the Met itself would perform in Bloomington. Its visits offer a study in cultural dissonance. The Met company that arrived in April 1942 comprised 300 individuals—two trainloads on the Monon Railroad. Since Bloomington lacked commercial establishments that could have come near housing them, most members of the company were accommodated, for this and subsequent visits, in a dormitory (Rogers Hall), alongside students. Management and stars occupied the twenty-eight lodging rooms of the Memorial Union. Ross Allen, who came to the School as a graduate student in 1949 and stayed on to become a distinguished stage director in its Opera Theater, recalls, from his early years at the School, the odd after-hours jostling of townspeople and the visiting metropolitan sophisticates:

> There was a restaurant on the Square in those days. When the Met would come, there weren't too many places open to eat afterward, and so at the place called Gib & Denzil's they would go down and eat after the Met performance, and there would be Rudy Bing with some of the ballet people, and there would be some of the singers that didn't work that night in one group and some of the singers that did would all be around, and then there would be a lot of people who were getting to know the people because they were visitors, trying to be nice to them, also dazzled by some of the personalities, and here at this little place there would be, "Well, hey, girlie, bring me some of that!" along with the whole Met in that very same place.

But the members of the Met took as much of a shine to Bloomington as Bloomington did to them. In the 1948 visit, students in the dormitory adjacent to that housing the company undertook to serenade the visitors with the Indiana loyalty song. The opera singers serenaded them in return. The following night, students packed the Rogers dining hall, where the Met cast presented an impromptu comic program. This event became a standard part of the annual visit, the "After-Opera Antics." In 1949 the venue was changed to the new Men's Quadrangle dormitory complex, where President Wells joined some 1,500 others in attendance. The Antics, which included songs and musical skits both by members of the Met company and by students and faculty of the University, began after the evening's opera, at about midnight, and continued until about 2 A.M. On at least one occasion, the festivities lasted until shortly before the Met company caught an early-morning train to the next stop on its tour.

If Bloomington was a congenial place to visit, it might also be a good one in which to live and work. All accounts from the period agree that the town was very pleasant. (To be sure, these are accounts from people who *stayed.*) It is often described as "a good place to raise children." Moreover, thanks to the Met visits and the Auditorium Series, it offered a substantial slice of big-city cultural life, without big-city overheads. Allen recalls a friend who would sunbathe "until 5:05 in the afternoon, stir up a bit of dinner, and then walk over to hear the Met at 7 o'clock."

And then what was an opera singer supposed to do, when her voice began to fade? Or what, for that matter, was a singer or a director or a designer supposed to do when he simply grew weary of the round of performances or of the road, those long train trips with stopovers of a few days' duration dotted across the continent? There were no pensions (in contrast to the situation of Indiana faculty); few had saved enough by midlife to be able to retire; and in any case they would normally want to continue living and working with other musicians, and might reap both pleasure and the satisfaction of duty fulfilled from transmitting their craft to students. Then, too, performers could be permitted absences from the School—brief ones during the regular school year, longer ones in the summer—to take engagements. For such reasons, neither Sanders nor his successors (until the recent radical improvement of the financial picture for first-desk players and successful soloists) had any difficulty in attracting eminent performers to the faculty of the School.

Natural as it now seems to pursue such appointments, though, one should be aware that in the early 1940s the fact that Indiana University would offer an appointment to a performer required explanation just as much as the fact that a performer would accept the offer. Applied music as a whole had, not long before, been suspect as a field for university study; and while the University had of course by this time appointed many faculty in applied music, an important distinction operated in these appointments: the applied-music teachers whom the School had employed were teachers first—with university degrees or previous appointments in teaching positions—rather than people who supported themselves as performers. As a rule, full-time performers lacked what had been regarded as the minimum academic credentials for university faculty. And while the possibility of appointing performance stars to teach performance was, in the early 1940s, beginning to be exploited, such appointments did, not infrequently, turn out to be fraught with problems, both because of the "artistic temperament" and because performers, with their typically limited experience of the academic world, did not always conform well to its mores.

In the case of Indiana University, these problems are nowhere more evident than with the first two opera singers appointed, the American soprano Ora Hyde and—as the first of the true star appointees—the German-born soprano Dorothee Manski.

With Hyde, who had had a considerable operatic career in Germany and Italy before she was appointed to the faculty in 1940, the problem was not lack of familiarity with university mores, for she held a Bachelor's degree from the University of Minnesota. Nonetheless, she did not get along well either with students—who called her Formaldehyde—or with colleagues. Having been appointed as Assistant Professor of Voice at a salary of $2,600, six months later she was writing to Sanders to ask for promotion to Head of the Voice Department, at the rank of Professor, with a salary of $5,000. Sanders passed the letter on to Wells without comment, and set out to look for a replacement.

The way in which he did this provides the first illustration of the benefit that the existence of the Auditorium constituted for the School's faculty recruitment. As I noted earlier, Lauritz Melchior had sung at the dedication of the Auditorium. During his visit to Bloomington, Sanders asked his advice about a replacement for Hyde. Shortly after returning to New York, Melchior wrote to recommend his Met colleague Manski, who, as he explained, wanted very much "to get out of New York and into the country, particularly, because of the health of her husband. That is why there is a possibility of getting her."

Sanders was understandably thrilled with the prospect. Born in Berlin in 1897, Manski was an important figure, a dramatic soprano who had sung at the Met a number of Wagnerian leads and other major roles, including the Marschallin. Before coming to America, she had sung Isolde with Bruno Walter at Salzburg in 1934, and been reengaged for it the following year at Salzburg and Vienna. Melchior also assured Sanders that she was an excellent teacher, "of classic and modern songs as well as opera repertoire." Sanders opened negotiations, Manski responded with enthusiasm, and in the summer she became Assistant Professor of Voice. Sadly, removal to the "country" did not help her husband, who died in December; but Manski herself remained at the School until her retirement in 1965.

Madame Manski (as she was always called) was a figure whom it is very difficult to imagine living in Bloomington even with its improved cultural life; and the discordance between her personal style and the local mores was the source of an unparalleled number of indefinitely repeatable anecdotes. No one ever speaks of Manski without smiling, or without recounting one or more of these stories.

Leaving the Music School, Manski would flag down cars to transport her to her next destination. Possibly she thought them taxis (or perhaps this and other characteristic gestures were parts of a persona she chose quite deliberately to create). For Auditorium events, she had a favorite seat, which she treated as her personal property, and from which she would eject anyone else who happened to be occupying it. One seat might as well be hers as another, since she disdained the purchase of tickets, sweeping imperiously by those stationed to collect them.

She was an excitable person. Ross Allen recounts a charming anecdote of her as the Witch in an Indiana production of Humperdinck's *Hansel and Gretel.* (The Witch was Manski's most familiar role; she had, for example, sung it in her 1927 Met debut.) The Witch's effigy, flying about the stage on its broomstick, somehow failed to exit by the time Manski's cue arrived. Undeterrable by those who pointed out that the effigy was still on stage, "she says, 'I must go! I must sing!' She runs out, and there were *two* witches for a while. I really don't know what the children thought in that performance. It was a very bizarre introduction to opera." This excitability made her easily teased. Once when her beloved dog Gogo (whom she was accustomed to bring to the School) wandered off and could not be found in the Music Building, a colleague mischievously suggested to her that it might have fallen into the hands of the murderous medical students. "So first of all," according to Allen, "she bothers to get dressed up like a Christmas tree, very fancy. And she runs down to the Medical School, . . . starts pounding on the first door she comes to, and says, 'Give me Gogo! Where is Gogo?' And everyone thought, 'who is this madwoman with all her jewelry?'"

Yet Manski rose rapidly through the academic ranks, being promoted to Associate Professor in 1943 and Professor in 1946. Sanders's successor Wilfred Bain, though recalling that Manski "had no concept of fulfilling requirements for degrees," acknowledged that she was a good voice teacher: "everybody wanted to study with her, both men and women." Such an appointee represented, after all, the full realization of Merrill's principle that music should be taught by professional musicians. And Manski's appointment proved to be an important precedent for the series of appointments of eminent performers that has done more than anything else to give the School its current celebrity and its drawing power for first-rate performance students.

While Manski was flamboyantly laying a path for other performers, Sanders made a substantial number of conventional appointments, which over the course of his tenure more than doubled the size of the faculty. The explosive phase of growth occurred in his final two years, in consequence of the postwar boom in enrollment as returning soldiers flooded campuses. But the faculty also grew steadily both before and during the war.

Having begun in 1938 by adding Burns, Ross, and Tangeman as regular appointees, in the following year Sanders persuaded Wells to fund several part-time appointments, especially of first-desk players of the Indianapolis Symphony. Arrangements of this kind continued throughout Sanders's tenure, though by his last year he had managed to replace all but one of the part-timers with full-time appointees. Newell Long recalled that a problem with part-timers from the Symphony was that when it went on tour, members of the regular faculty had to "take up the slack." Long himself "even taught clarinet," which he "had no business teaching." (The School went through four Part-Time Instructors in Clarinet before Sanders was finally able to make a regular appointment in that field, in 1945.)

Two Instructors in Piano were added in 1939, and several others were appointed during the war years of 1941–45. There were also appointments in voice and theory, and, in 1942, the School's first appointment in organ, Oswald Ragatz. (The School's only organ at the time was a Holtkamp baroque organ, purchased the year before; but shortly afterward a small Möller pipe organ was acquired.)

By the end of World War II, the regular faculty complement had increased to twenty—though two of these were on leave for government service from 1942 through 1945. The faculty was also supplemented in each of these years by about half a dozen Assistants, almost all of whom were graduate students doing lower-level undergraduate teaching. (The practice of using graduate assistants began in Sanders's second year, 1939.) In 1939, too, Sanders was able to appoint a music librarian, Ethel Lyman, who had formerly done the same job at Smith College. Lyman continued at Indiana until 1959, and oversaw a major expansion of the library.

The enlargement of the faculty appears paradoxical, in view of the fact that enrollment in degree programs in Music declined substantially during the war. In September 1943, for example, Sanders announced that the total number of degree students was eighty-nine—larger than expected, though about sixty fewer than in the past. There was a "fully normal quota of girls," but, of course, many fewer boys. Despite this decline in the number of music majors, though, there was a chronic shortage of faculty, especially in applied music, because of the influx of students taking music as an elective or as part of the Bachelor of Education program with a specialization in music. The former group increased dramatically as a result of the establishment of the Junior Division, which, it will be recalled, led to the College of Arts and Sciences and other units agreeing to grant credit for applied-music courses. These developments resulted in what Sanders called a "horde of students from all over the campus."

To supplement the faculty, Sanders managed to bring in a few Visiting Professors, whose presence surely tended to broaden the horizons of the permanent faculty and the students. Ruggero Vené, a Respighi protégé whom Sanders had met in Rome in 1926, was Visiting Assistant Professor for three semesters in 1941 and 1942, teaching advanced composition and conducting the Concert Choir. The outstanding Russian violinist Tossy Spivakovsky, who had emigrated to the United States in 1941 and become concertmaster of the Cleveland Orchestra the following year, was Visiting Professor in the summer of 1944. When Winifred Merrill was on sabbatical leave that fall, another Russian violinist, Leo Lehrman, served as Visiting Professor.

There was also, of course, the opportunity of bringing in European émigrés as regular faculty. In January 1940, the faculty discussed the official position of NASM concerning Jewish émigré musicians, said to be that while truly superior individuals such as Hindemith (who was, in point of fact, not Jewish) should be cordially welcomed, Americans should be given preference over Europeans of equal ability. Indeed Sanders would have been very happy to appoint Hindemith. In March, having heard that the composer was settling in the United States, he offered him a position at Indiana; but Hindemith declined.

Were no other suitably superior émigrés available? In 1940, Imre Englander, a Hungarian Jew, spent one semester as an Assistant in Violin. But no émigré was given a regular appointment until 1946, when two were added. One of these was the composer Bernhard Heiden, a German Jew who had studied with Hindemith before emigrating in 1935, and who joined the School after wartime service in the U.S. Army. The other was the Czechoslovakian-born musicologist Paul Nettl, who had been put in mortal danger in Nazi-occupied Europe by his Jewish background.

Nettl, who was by far Sanders's most illustrious appointee, had taught in the German University of Prague until 1937; in 1939 he and his family were brought to America by means of a fund raised by the faculty and students of Westminster Choir College. After his arrival, Nettl was given a special (non-permanent) appointment at the College, on a small salary. The College took these steps, as its President, John Finley Williamson, explained in a letter of recommendation to Sanders, "because we considered him one of the five greatest musicologists in the world, and knew he would be killed" if he stayed in Europe. The references listed in the *curriculum vitae* that formed part of Nettl's application to Indiana included Albert Einstein, Alfred Einstein, and Thomas Mann. Indiana offered him a two-year probationary appointment as Professor of Music History and Literature (replacing Tangeman, who had resigned to accept a position as head of musicology at Juilliard); his wife, Gertrud, was appointed Instructor in Piano. Nettl's presence enriched the School in various ways, including his organization, in the fall of 1946, of a Collegium Musicum, which gave frequent concerts. His English, though, caused some problems in the classroom, and perhaps it was for this reason that on June 16, 1947, he was notified that he would not be reappointed after the second year of his probationary term. When, two weeks later, Wilfred Bain became Dean, he reversed this decision, and Nettl remained to bring distinction to Indiana for the rest of his career.

In response to the "horde of students from all over the campus" who were already crowding the School by the fall of 1944, and to the anticipated, and then real, flood of returning veterans, the rate of appointments changed radically in Sanders's final two years. In 1945–46, eight regular appointees were added. (One of these—Thurber Madison—replaced Burns, who had resigned in 1944 to become chairman of the Department of Music Education at New York University, while a second—Richard Clayton—replaced von Zweygberg, who retired in 1945.) The following year, an astonishing thirteen regular appointees were added. Thus by the end of Sanders's deanship the faculty numbered thirty regular members—and was supplemented by one Part-Time Instructor, eleven Graduate Assistants (including William Christ, who was eventually to become Associate Dean), and four Accompanists.

Even with this great increase in faculty, the School remained, in Sanders's last year, badly overcrowded. There was an acute shortage of studios and practice rooms. The number of music majors had increased to 247, up from the 154 of Sanders's first year; thirty prospective majors had to be turned away, as did 180 non-majors who had wanted to take applied music as an elective.

To be sure, this crowding had one highly beneficial effect. In his 1945–46 report, Sanders noted that the superabundance of applicants had compelled a policy of declining to accept into the School's degree programs students with little previous training. But this was precisely the class of students whose inability "to give decent performance on any instrument" had constituted, in the view both of the NASM examiner and of the faculty, the School's single biggest problem. As a solution, the examiner had proposed that admissions standards be raised; but this solution could not be implemented because it would drive down enrollment. By the final years of Sanders's tenure, though, the situation was reversed: enrollment pressure left the School no choice *but* to apply higher standards.

The result was twofold. First, there was an improvement in the quality of the Public School Music program. Under Burns's successor Madison, the curriculum of the program was changed, as Sanders's report explained, to place "much greater emphasis on instrumental and choral technics, in line with the advance in leading schools for teacher training." (At the same time, and also in accordance with the practice elsewhere, the name of the program was changed to Music Education.) Second, in a highly significant development, the balance of enrollment between this program and the Bachelor of Music program began to shift. In this same report, Sanders elatedly announced that current trends indicated that students in the Bachelor of Music program would before long outnumber those in Music Education. He added that this development did not mean a decrease in the number of students in the latter program but that "the School of Music is acquiring a sound reputation for preparing students for artistic performance and teaching at the University level, as well as preparing students for teaching in secondary schools." (In actual fact, B.M.E. students continued to outnumber those in the B.M. program for a good many years—though by 1949 B.M. and M.M. students *together* outnumbered those in undergraduate and graduate programs in Music Education.)

Wells, who was always scanning the horizon, had of course recognized that a period of rapid expansion in the University would follow the conclusion of the war. In June of 1944—on D-Day, as it happened—Sanders informed his faculty that the President had "been carrying on a series of conferences with heads of divisions to check up on what was being done about post-war planning." In the case of Music, the answer was "that we hadn't done very much about it." To remedy this situation, Sanders's characteristic proposal was another exercise in direct democracy: "We have got to have a series of meetings before the summer is over to formulate, shape up and swap ideas, reactions." And the floor was immediately opened to random suggestions. Over the years, though, Sanders's initial disinclination to relegate business to committees had considerably eroded, and, in the aftermath of this meeting, he sensibly decided to appoint a committee to develop a coherent set of proposals to be discussed by the faculty. This committee—chaired by Douglas Nye and including Burns, Grinstead, and Gerald Doty (who had been appointed in 1941, as Instructor in Music and Director of the University Band)—collected some views from other members of the faculty and was able to complete its report by early July. The plan for a series of summer meetings evidently having been dropped, the faculty began detailed discussion of the report in the fall.

As at the beginning of Sanders's tenure, then, the School was launched on a strategic review. This one did not, however, descend to the same fundamental level as its predecessor—there was no talk, this time, about revising the School's mission statement, or of basic revisions to its core undergraduate degree programs—and in fact the changes of direction that resulted from the review were not great. The committee made recommendations under ten headings, but most of these recommendations were either voted down, not acted on, or not implemented.

In the area of curriculum, the only significant change was the institution of a combined Bachelor of Science program in music and a second field: business, journalism, or speech (which included drama and radio). The curricula for these pioneering programs were essentially the Public School Music curriculum with the education courses replaced by courses in the second field. The aim, obviously, was to render musicians more employable; the program was launched after broad consultation with businesspeople. Evidently it was successful, since it has continued up to the present, in the generalized form of the Bachelor of Science in Music and an Outside Field.

The committee's report also resulted in the institution of a number of additional outreach programs, undertaken with a view both to improving music education at the pre-university level and to enhancing the School's recruitment efforts. With Wells's encouragement, a "field man" (C. Lawrence Kingsbury, an Assistant Professor of Public School Music) was appointed by the Division of Extension to visit high schools on behalf of Music, Fine Arts, and Speech. The number of scholarships was increased. A two-week summer performance clinic for high school students was established, as well as an annual conference for music teachers from around the state. There was discussion, too, of the public-relations importance of radio broadcasts of performances by faculty and students. Members of the School had frequently been featured in programs produced in the University's radio studio for broadcast on commercial stations in Indianapolis and Muncie. Beginning in October 1940, a series of programs by the University Studio Ensemble had even been broadcast nationally, on the Mutual network. But since commercial stations could not be relied on to program a sufficient amount of classical music, the faculty passed a motion urging the establishment of a University-owned FM station. This goal was achieved in 1950, with the creation of WFIU.

From the point of view of the subsequent development of the School, though, the most interesting topic of discussion stemming from the Post-War Committee's report was the possibility of establishing an opera department. A recommendation to this effect had been made to the committee by the voice teacher William Ross, who had noted that implementing it would require the appointment, for half the year, of an experienced stage director. The committee felt that such an appointment would be, at least for the next several years, "rather too specialized for a school of this size," but it endorsed the proposal for a department, provided that its emphasis "would be on the preparation and production of light operas and operettas, and if it linked itself closely with similar work in the high schools." Burns added to the report a note saying that the pioneering Opera Department at Louisiana State University "has done a fine job in the presentation of opera, but that its work has proved distinctly detrimental to the work of the School of Music as a whole." (He did not elaborate.) In the ensuing discussion, Sanders observed that Indiana had, in the Auditorium, a wonderful *facility* for opera. In the end, the faculty did not approve the recommendation to create a department, but settled instead on giving, once a year, "a group of one-act operas or one full opera."

In fact the School had already taken serious steps toward the development of an opera program. In addition to the ongoing extra-curricular series of Gilbert and Sullivan operettas presented since 1937 by the Pro-Music Club (rechristened Alpha Mu Omega in 1943), the School had staged *Cavalleria Rusticana* in April 1942 and, the following December, *Hansel and Gretel.* The further development of opera was interrupted for the war years 1943 and 1944, but in the spring of 1945 the School again staged *Cavalleria Rusticana,* together with *Trial by Jury.* Sanders reported to Wells that the performances on this double bill "were reasonably satisfactory though they involved considerable compromise with perfection." In August 1946, the School presented the Garden Scene from *Faust* and scenes from *Pagliacci,* and, on the same long program, repeated *Trial by Jury.* Thus it was not actually the case, as Wilfred Bain later liked to suggest, that opera at the School was created *ex nihilo* by him.

The foregoing summary of the faculty's decisions on the most significant matters raised in the Post-War Report obscures the fact that these decisions were arrived at only after an astonishingly meandering and protracted course of discussion, one that provides a vivid illustration of the problems entailed in Sanders's conception of democratic procedures. When Nye, as chairman of the committee, formally presented the report, on September 11, 1944, discussion immediately broke out on the first of its sets of recommendations. A motion was made, and an amendment to it passed, before Montana Grinstead brought the precipitous proceedings to a halt by the commonsense suggestion that "we go through the whole report and discuss it all before we accept any one part of it."

Sanders acceded to this suggestion; but he should not have needed it, if only because Grinstead had made similar ones before. She had long been disgruntled by the length of the meetings under Sanders (as well as by the fact that they were held at night), which she saw as resulting from the Dean's failure to give them a definite agenda or to enact clear rules of procedure. On September 18, at the end of the first meeting devoted to the kind of section-by-section examination of the Post-War Report that she had recommended, Grinstead moved that "faculty meetings be limited to 2 hours, begin on time and end at 9:30." The motion was carried. In October, at the conclusion of a meeting in which discussion of two sections of the report was tacked onto the end of an already long meeting, Grinstead raised again the matter of the length of meetings, moving this time that they be limited to 1½ hours. She was seconded by Hoffzimmer, who made it clear that the problem was not simply the length of the meetings but their formlessness: "Maybe we could save a lot of time if we knew before hand exactly what would come up so that everybody would prepare for it. Sometime[s] we sit here for an hour [discussing something that] we know nothing about and have no interest in."

Although this motion failed, discussion of the report was suspended until February 20, when its first set of recommendations was discussed again, amended, and passed. For whatever reason, though, there were only two regular meetings for the remainder of the 1944–45 academic year, at neither of which the report was discussed. Discussion finally resumed in October 1945 and, tacked on at the end of agendas, proceeded through the other sections of the document, finally terminating on January 14, 1946, sixteen months after the report had been presented—and five months after the end of the war for whose aftermath it was supposed to plan. In the meantime, in November 1945, Wells had made a written request to Sanders that his annual report include a statement on trends in music education and how the School meant to respond to them. (Sanders's reading to the faculty of this request evoked a series of fifteen off-the-cuff, random suggestions.)

Sanders's democracy had, then, lost its forward momentum—had become almost incapable of dealing with strategic issues. The most obvious reason for the encroaching paralysis was the steadily increasing size of the faculty: a *modus operandi* that had already been cumbersome with a faculty of twelve became simply unworkable with one over twice that size. A more vigorous and skillful Dean, though, could have coped with this situation, in part simply by instituting different administrative procedures. Many faculties, after all, are larger than Sanders's, and not all of them are incapable of sustained action. Moreover, there is evidence, in the eruptions of discontent with the desultory nature of the faculty meetings, that he would have had some support in effecting such changes.

But Sanders himself had apparently lost momentum: in the second half of his deanship, he seems merely to be responding to events rather than shaping them. Perhaps he, too, like at least some of his faculty, was worn down by the endless series of meetings; and meetings are only the most visible part of an administrator's work. Sanders was, for one thing, constantly engaged in the recruitment of faculty: a time-consuming and sometimes frustrating and disheartening business. In Newell Long's view, "things just got too big for him, with the size growing and the new faculty and all. It was too much of a problem, and he just wasn't interested in that side of it."

As this remark suggests, part of the trouble lay in the fact that in serving as an administrator Sanders was going against the grain. His primary professional interests were in teaching and composition, for which the deanship left him little time. A democratic idealist, he also did not relish power and did not understand what to do with it. And he had only a limited number of ideas for the development of the School, namely, those he expended in his first year, in the fundamental review of aims and operations: after that task was accomplished, he had, as James Clemens has observed, no real agenda beyond refinement of the model put in place in the review.

He could have made the job less wearing if he had delegated more of its responsibilities. But here, too, he suffered from his lack of the skills or instincts of an administrator. Long told Clemens that Sanders "didn't know how to simplify his job," adding that "he had just the one secretary in that one office"; and though she was very good, "she couldn't keep up with him."

In the spring of 1945, Sanders informed his superiors that if the pressure of his administrative duties were "to continue with anything like its present weight," he would "shortly cease to be a musician of any kind." He referred particularly to the burdens of faculty recruitment: "The cumulative effect of resignations from faculty, war time shortage in competent available people, and increasing difficulties of travel and communication have produced a situation in which during the entire academic year I, for the first time, have written no music nor thought of any to write."

In the aftermath of this lament, an arrangement was worked out whereby Douglas Nye assumed charge of recruiting and of various routine administrative tasks; at some point he officially became Assistant Dean. This transfer of responsibilities salvaged the situation for a while, but in March 1946 Sanders submitted his resignation from the deanship, effective as of September. Though he was persuaded to stay on for an additional year, his delegation of duties became something close to an abdication: from October 1946 Nye chaired all faculty meetings. On December 11, Sanders informed the faculty of his resignation, which had been accepted for June 30, 1947.

He would, he explained, remain on faculty as Professor of Composition. But the following May he submitted his resignation from the School (effective at the end of August), having accepted a position at Brooklyn College. Given his lament that the deanship was destroying him as a musician, it is amazing to learn that he went to Brooklyn as Chairman of the Music Department. Perhaps Brooklyn's offer was simply too good to refuse. But the fact that he went to another such position raises the question of whether he may have been not so much tired of administration as tired of Indiana. In characterizing Sanders as a "liberal," Long referred specifically to his politics (though perhaps he was also thinking of the Dean's freewheeling social life, which is, for example, reliably reported to have involved many coeds). Long added that liberalism was anomalous at Indiana in the 1940s, and that Sanders's liberalism may have resulted in some unpleasantness between him and his superiors: "I think he thought that the University was a little too far to the right for him. And so I think he had some clashes with the administration. I have no details on these things. But he wasn't very happy that last year."

Long did not believe these clashes were with Wells; and Wells himself denied to me that he regarded Sanders as other than a good Dean, or that he knew of any motive for Sanders's leaving the deanship other than his desire to spend more time composing. Yet one must wonder whether Wells was entirely satisfied with Sanders. Wells was a dynamic President, highly ambitious for the University and firmly convinced of the key importance of long-range, strategic planning. But Sanders was a Dean who, when asked what was being done about postwar planning, had to confess that "we hadn't done very much about it."

Whatever the precise combination of factors that led Sanders to resign the deanship, he did, after all, occupy it for nine years. Especially by today's standards, this is a long tenure: what is surprising is not that Sanders stayed, as is often said, "only" nine years but that the other three of the School's first four Deans were willing and able to continue for nineteen, twenty-six, and twenty-four years respectively. And though Sanders did not have a grand vision of the School to guide and sustain him, he did, with the help of his faculty, effect some substantial improvements. The review he conducted in his first year was based in an objective, accurate assessment of the School's strengths and weaknesses and the differences between its pretensions and its actualities; and it resulted in a clear improvement of the undergraduate programs. Sanders was certainly right, too, in pursuing membership in NASM for the School. His success in this endeavor brought the School into much closer contact with the current state of musical education and gave it, at a stroke, much greater credibility. He also left the faculty two and a half times larger than he found it. And though he did not share Merrill's conception of the School as essentially a conservatory, his appointment of Manski prepared the ground for Bain's vigorous revival of that conception, both by creating a precedent for appointing star performers to the faculty and (an inevitable consequence of Manski's appointment) by directing more of the School's attention to the performance of opera.

The truth is that Sanders accomplished about all that a rational person would think *could* be accomplished, especially in wartime, in what was, after all, only a middling Midwestern music school. It required another dreamer—like Merrill, but with far better administrative skills—to revive the vision of a great conservatory, and it required uniquely favorable times to bring that vision to fruition. It was good that Sanders left the deanship when he did, but it was important that, between the two dreamers, someone should have come to put the School's mundane business on a sounder footing. His tenure as Dean is better regarded not as an interruption of the advance to greatness (though in a sense it was) but as a necessary pause for consolidation before the march resumed. In Sanders's deanship, Long said, "we put down musical roots": "so when Bain came along, we were *ready*."

The Bain Years (1947–1973)

I. Blitz: The First Five Years

As Herman Wells told it, he came close to missing out on Wilfred Bain. Looking for a successor to Sanders, Wells, just as he had in 1937 when seeking Merrill's successor, consulted Casey Lutton of the Clark-Brewer Teachers Agency in Chicago. He was chagrined to discover that the candidate pool had been stagnant: "I started back over the same territory and found the same names, most of whom I didn't want, . . . still available for this job. And I was astonished at how little change there had been in the music personnel situation during that period, that no new names had emerged."

Presumably Bain's was one of the old names Wells recalled: Bain had opened a dossier with Clark-Brewer as early as 1937. By 1947, though, Lutton, if not Wells, was highly impressed by Bain. Around the beginning of the year, he had suggested Bain to Wells as a strong candidate for the Indiana deanship; and, having checked to see if Bain was interested, on January 16 he sent Bain's dossier to H. T. Briscoe (the Vice President and Dean of the Faculties), to whom Wells had entrusted the paperwork of the search. The dossier is most impressive, and the endorsement in Lutton's covering letter could hardly be stronger. At North Texas State Teachers College (where he had directed the music program since 1938), Bain, "starting from scratch," had "built a remarkable School of Music." Just thirty-nine years old, but "a dynamic leader" with the "power and force that comes only from natural gifts," he seemed to Lutton one of the five best younger music administrators in the nation. (This is a plausible estimate, since Bain had already been, in 1941–44, Vice President of NASM and, since 1943, Secretary of the Music Teachers National Association.) Perhaps because he had twice noted that Bain was "a personality," Lutton felt it appropriate to close by assuring Briscoe that "he definitely has his feet on the ground and is not a long-haired, wild-eyed, wishful-thinking musician."

After receiving this package, Briscoe wrote to Bain, who confirmed that he was "definitely interested" in the Indiana job and underscored his interest by supplementing his letter with a highly detailed *curriculum vitae,* a narrative account of his activities at North Texas, and a copy of his schedule book—"to give you an idea of the activities which we have here and to give you a better picture of what goes on without your having to make a journey to Denton." He hoped, though, that Briscoe *would* visit North Texas, and he expressed his own readiness to visit Indiana. He also included a list of seven individuals who might be willing to write on his behalf. Briscoe asked all seven, and received several strongly favorable letters, stressing Bain's administrative skill and drive, his charisma, and his musicianship. Paul van Katwijk, the distinguished Dutch pianist who was Dean of Music at Southern Methodist University in Dallas, wrote that Bain combined, "in a very unusual way, . . . the academic, the artistic, and the business aspect of things"—a remark that can stand as a fair summary of the tenor of the letters.

Despite these encomia, Wells took no action on Bain, until galvanized by a further conversation with Lutton:

> Well, one day I was talking by telephone to Casey Lutton . . . , and he said, "Have you got that new dean in the School of Music yet?" And I said, "Hell no I haven't!" And he said, "Well, I told you to go down to Denton, Texas, and get Bain." "Oh," I said, "nobody in Denton, Texas, could be as good as his credentials!" You see, this was a time when Texas was largely cowboys and oil and cattle and all that kind of thing, before it became a sophisticated cultural center. "Well," he said, "damn you, go down there and look at him!"

In truth Bain was an exotic plant in Texas. He had been born in Shawville, Quebec, in 1908, the son of a Methodist minister. When he was ten, the family immigrated to the United States, settling in the small town of Cattaraugus in western New York. Bain completed high school there, and subsequently attended nearby Houghton College (a Methodist institution), graduating in 1929 with a double major in English and Music. He also earned a Diploma in Piano (extra-curricular, since Houghton did not allow credit for applied music); and he spent the summer of 1927 in studies at Eastman.

As a child Bain had aspired to be a concert pianist. His father, however, destined him for the ministry, and the son had acceded, rationalizing his collegiate musical studies in terms of their putative utility in a ministerial future: "I thought, well, there's always music in church, and so why don't I use the undergraduate [years] to learn what I need to learn and wait until seminary for a lot of other things?" In his senior year at Houghton, he had already been accepted to the Princeton Theological Seminary, when, as he sat one spring day with his sweetheart, Bain's life changed.

He had met Mary Freeman when he was waiting on tables in the

Houghton dining hall. As, carrying a tray of pies, he approached the table where Mary was seated, "she pointed at me and said, 'That's the man I'll marry.'" A courtship followed this declaration (which would more typically have come at its end), and, on a day shortly before their graduation from Houghton, Mary and Wilfred were sitting on the steps of the administration building when the President, James Luckey, came out of his office and stopped to chat. He said he supposed that Wilfred and Mary would like to marry; they confirmed this surmise. Luckey then said he thought he could get them both jobs at another Methodist school, Central Wesleyan College in South Carolina. Bain would constitute the music department; Mary would teach a variety of liberal arts and language courses. They jumped at the offer, and were married just after graduation, on July 1, 1929.

The Bains spent only one year at Central, for Luckey offered to bring Wilfred back to head the Music Department at Houghton, provided that he completed another degree in the field. The prospect was attractive, and Bain, who by this time was primarily interested in choral music, enrolled in the fall of 1930 at the Westminster Choir College (then in Ithaca, New York), where in a single academic year he completed the degree of Bachelor of Music in Voice. On his first day at Westminster, he had a transforming experience that made *a cappella* choirs his greatest musical love. In a wonderful long interview of 1983, Bain told John Wolford (a graduate student in folklore at Indiana, who conducted the interview for the University's Oral History Research Project) that

> I remember the day that Mary Bain and I walked into the Westminster Choir College office and were directed to go and listen to a rehearsal of Westminster Choir in the First Presbyterian Church next door. I must say, I never have been so thrilled in my existence as I was to hear the enormous vital [*sic*] of unaccompanied singing, where the voices really accompanied themselves, you know. This was a crowning achievement, at least to my musical ears, which had been attuned to accompanied . . . singing.

During the school year that ensued on this epiphany, he lost all thought of becoming a preacher: "the ministry faded out of existence, you see. And so I had a profession."

Back at Houghton as Head of the Music Department, Bain developed both his administrative skills and his choral technique. His Houghton choir became a celebrated ensemble, giving some 350 concerts around the eastern and middle United States and making numerous radio broadcasts, some over national networks. In 1933, Bain began spending his summers at New York University, where he earned the degree of Master of Arts in Music in 1936, and, in 1938, that of Doctor of Education in Music Education, with a dissertation on *a cappella* choirs in American colleges and universities.

It was while Bain was completing his doctorate that North Texas offered him a job. The college was seeking a director for its fledgling music program; an NYU classmate recommended Bain to the North Texas President, who interviewed him in New York, and, hedging his bet in a way that Bain would later make his own standard practice, offered him a temporary position for the summer, "to see how I worked out." At the end of the summer, Bain was offered a regular job, at three times his Houghton salary. Thus the Canadian came to Texas.

At North Texas, Bain—who by this time had, in addition to his tremendous energy and ambition, substantial experience as both a musician and a music administrator—touched down like a whirlwind. Nine years later, lamenting Bain's imminent departure for Indiana, the music critic of the *Dallas Morning News* recalled that "At the start . . . he rather took our breaths away by his energy. Not a few of us concluded that he was a young man in a hurry to create the form if not the substance of a great music school. It took us only a year or two to understand that the substance was there, too."

Indeed Bain's accomplishments at North Texas were remarkable. At the time of his arrival, the college had thirty-five music majors, all in music education. There was one practice room. By 1947, the enrollment had grown to 400, and the School's offerings encompassed the full range of academic, applied, and music-education programs, as well as courses in music appreciation. Master's degrees were offered in musicology, theory, composition, and applied music. There were ninety practice rooms, with forty more under construction. The faculty, which comprised five full-time members before Bain arrived, had grown by 1947 to twenty full-time members and twenty-one graduate student tutors; and Bain noted with pride that five of the faculty had doctorates, three of them from Harvard. Several other members of the faculty were performers of some stature: these included the tenor Myron Taylor, who had sung one role at the Met, the soprano Mary McCormic, and the pianists Silvio Scionti and Walter Robert.

Along with faculty recruitment and the rapid expansion of enrollment, the most impressive of Bain's achievements at North Texas lay in his development of a rich ensemble program. In addition to his forty-voice *a cappella* choir, there were a fifty-voice women's chorus and an eighty-voice men's choir; instrumental ensembles comprised an eighty-piece symphony orchestra, a ninety-piece concert band, a thirty-seven-piece string sinfonietta, and a harp ensemble. These ensembles performed regularly and widely. By 1947 the *a cappella* choir had given some 400 concerts throughout the Southwest; and both the Houston and Dallas Symphony Orchestras used Bain's choirs as their official choral organizations. Bain himself had evidently become a highly effective choral conductor. In his letter recommending Bain to Indiana, Antal Dorati, then conductor of the

Dallas Symphony, said that he had "not seen a better trained, better equipped, and better performing University Choir than the one under his direction." The conductor of the Houston Symphony, Ernst Hoffman, went much further, professing that "Dr. Bain is the *best* choral conductor whom I know both in this country and abroad!"

Bain had also lost no time in deploying the School's vocal and instrumental resources in the production of opera. As early as 1939, North Texas mounted the world premiere of *Cynthia Parker,* an opera by an alumna, Julia Smith. There was a great lesson in this first of Bain's operatic productions. Partly because it was a premiere, and surely in greater part because of its distinctively American and folk quality—it was based on a true story (of great melodramatic potential) about a white woman captured and adopted by Indians—the production received substantial press coverage nationally and even internationally (notices in Montreal and Toronto). In short, the School gained enormous publicity from the production, and the lesson was driven home to Bain that opera, and especially opera premieres, could serve as the best showcase of a music school's capabilities, and spread its reputation farther and faster than anything else. In the following years, the School mounted six other operatic productions of varying length and weight. The series culminated in 1947 in a production of Gounod's *Faust* that Bain took on a ten-performance tour of Texas and New Mexico. For these operas Bain, as he later said, "did everything": "I conducted, coached, supervised the principals and about everything else."

Bain was, then, thriving wonderfully in Texas. He had "loved every bit" of his time there, and the program he had created was burgeoning and exciting. There had, as he later said, been "nine years of unmixed success," and he had ridden the crest of a "wave of recognition and appreciation throughout the state of Texas." He and Mary had also grown fond of what they perceived to be "the gentle ways of the South."

Still, he was ready to move on—*had* been ready, for some time. To be sure, it would, as one of his referees (James Quarles, Head of Music at the University of Missouri) told Briscoe, take "more than mere salary" to move him. He could be tempted only by an institution that promised "a larger field of usefulness in his chosen line of work, with complete and adequate support from the administration." And indeed Bain had been on the lookout for such an opportunity ever since he arrived at Denton. Though he was working wonders at North Texas, the potential for achievement there was finally limited by the circumstance that it was not the flagship institution of the state: the University of Texas was, and that meant, as he said to Wolford, that it "got more attention, got more money," whereas North Texas was merely "on a par with several other institutions." Already by 1939—a year after he had arrived at North Texas—he had had the Dean of the College put a letter of recommendation into his Clark-Brewer dossier; and three more letters went into the file in 1940.

Before Indiana, Bain had in fact been offered positions at half a dozen other institutions. But they too, he said, all had "limitations—student body, money, objectives, and so forth." At Indiana, though, he saw what he required. The University had (thanks to Wells) "the objectives of some of the greatest universities in the country." And if it hadn't yet realized these objectives, hadn't yet actually become one of the great institutions, it had, Bain thought, the opportunity to do so.

Moreover, the Indiana School of Music *looked* like a first-rate institution, and this fact was of strikingly great significance to Bain, in a way that vindicates Merrill's claims about the symbolic importance of buildings. Like Tamino, Bain was enamored by a picture. Several years before the Indiana position opened up, he had seen the photograph of Merrill's building that was reproduced in the School of Music Bulletin (see Figure 11): he remembered "remarking to himself of the attractiveness of the building and wondering if at any time during his professional career he might be fortunate enough to be the administrative officer" in such an edifice.

In February 1947, Wells, galvanized by Lutton's imprecation, interviewed Bain over dinner in St. Louis, where he was attending the convention of the Music Teachers National Association. Wells's notes on the meeting are, since written for himself, candid: "Nice appearance—looks fit; agreeable personality and undoubtedly has a flare for administration. Was a little nervous with me and didn't do himself justice. *Is a first rate prospect* although he smells a little of his long association with a teacher's college. He obviously is keenly interested in the job."

A few weeks after this meeting, Wells finally made the trip to Texas that Lutton had urged on him. (Such trips—for the purpose of learning how candidates "measured up in the institution where they had been"—were, it will be recalled, a standard part of his thorough recruiting procedures.) While in Texas, he had a chance to experience some student performances, including the dress rehearsal for *Faust.* He was deeply impressed. Thirty years later, in the gargantuan—1,200 typescript pages—annalistic history of "The Bain Regime" at Indiana that Bain compiled after leaving the deanship, he recorded that Wells, in one of the series of interviews he had with the candidate, "had indicated his vital interest in a music performance program" in addition to a solid academic-music program. It is conceivable that Wells developed this interest only as a consequence of his visit to Texas—he was, after all, the President who had replaced Merrill with an academic musician (and who seems during that previous search to have considered seriously *only* academic musicians)—but it was an interest consistent with his personal and professional inclinations. Wells himself had been an avid performer in youth, and he remained to the very end of his life a faithful attendee of performances at Indiana. Then too, as a university president attempting to enhance the reputation of his institution, he must have been aware of the potentially large publicity value of touring performers from a music school (though he could scarcely have realized just how great that potential was, until he saw what Bain had accomplished for North Texas). And finally, Wells—who was always, and before anything else, an Indiana patriot who took seriously the mission of his state institution to serve its state—was, as is clear from many of his actions as President, constantly intent on using the University to bring culture to Indiana citizens, both in Bloomington and beyond it.

In May, Wells proceeded to the final stage of his standard recruitment procedure, bringing Bain for a visit to Bloomington. Already in love with the photograph of Merrill's building, Bain now found the campus as a whole, first seen in the beautiful Bloomington springtime, greatly appealing. Billeted in a seventh-floor room in the Memorial Union, he was "much impressed with the solidity and elegance of the building and the architecture of the nearby buildings seen from the tower window"; he was also much taken with the natural beauty of the campus. The Music Building, too, was as fair as its picture, and touring it with Sanders set Bain to fantasizing about what *he* could do with such a School, "dreaming of the possibilities of an increased student body and greater musical activities at Indiana than appeared from the Indiana School of Music statistics." (He was, as we shall see, distinctly unimpressed by the *current* musical activities at the School.)

At the conclusion of his visit, Bain was offered the deanship, together with a tenured position as Professor of Music, at a salary of $9,000. He accepted the offer on the spot, effective July 1, 1947. Recommending the appointment to the trustees for their formal approval, Wells made it clear (intentionally or not) that he had chosen Bain primarily on the expectation that he would create at Indiana a strongly performance-oriented school—would return the ordering of objectives, that is, to essentially what they had been in Merrill's time. His letter to the trustees says nothing about the academic side of Bain's program at North Texas, stressing only the school's large enrollment (which he saw as a good, in those postwar expansionary years) and, especially, Bain's performance program and its value in publicizing the college:

> His choruses, student operas, orchestras, and bands have toured all over the Southwest and have won high critical praise.
>
> I visited his School and have listened to some of his student organizations and can attest to the fact that he adheres to high standards. Notwithstanding this he has a flair for popular performances and understands the general audience. He does not hesitate to have his students appear before any gen-

> eral group. To summarize, while he has as high standards of musical performance as Dean Sanders, he is much more ready to popularize and participate in the general musical life of the University and State.

Casey Lutton was delighted with the appointment. "I am proud indeed," he wrote to Wells, "to learn that you have employed Wilfred Bain. I dare say that you have the strongest music man, certainly one of the better administrators in the United States. I look for the University of Indiana to take the leadership in the music picture in the Middle West."

Ensconced at Indiana, where he and Mary arrived in mid-July, Bain was able to get off to the same kind of flying start that had characterized his first years at North Texas, and for the same reasons: not only did he have enormous energy and drive, but he also benefited from his prior administrative experience; and if this was already true when he arrived in Denton, it was true in spades nearly a decade later. All he did in Bloomington, Bain told me, "was keep on doing what I had been doing for ten years."

In addition to the administrative skills he had honed at North Texas, the benefits of experience that Bain brought with him to Indiana inhered primarily in his having evolved a strategic plan for the development of a music school, a plan that embraced the development of both the curriculum and the reputation of the school. Where Sanders, entering upon the deanship with no previous administrative experience, felt it necessary to begin his tenure by attempting, with the help of his faculty, to formulate answers to basic questions—"What is music? What are we supposed to be doing here? What are our aims?"—Bain knew long before he arrived at Indiana what his answers were to these questions, and to most of the attendant ones. Accordingly, he was able to act with complete purposefulness from his earliest days in Bloomington, and, because he could always articulate clearly not only what he wanted to do but also why he wanted to do it, he had great powers of persuasion both with his colleagues and (what was more important) with those who controlled the University's purse strings. He had a vision, and the power to make others see and believe in it.

In his later years, when the School had become famous and his views were solicited by journalists and historians, Bain indeed liked to present himself as someone who had worked out, and had operated by, a systematic and comprehensive theory of musical education. The fullest exposition of this theory is found in the 1983 interview with Wolford. To him, Bain explained that his theory was rooted in the standard theory of liberal arts education, which holds not merely that students should acquire a broad base of knowledge in the traditional liberal studies (arts, sciences, humanities) but that the fundamental purpose of education lies not in the mastery of facts but in the development of habits of critical thought.

(Bain attributed his adherence to this theory to his having attended a small liberal arts college, "where there was a set curriculum for everyone.") Music was, of course, one of the traditional liberal arts, but in universities its place in the liberal curriculum was accorded only to academic music. Bain, however, boldly argued that applied music—for that matter, the "practice of creative and recreative art" in general—could also function as a liberal art, provided that instruction in it was oriented toward problem-solving rather than rote learning. In fact, applied music might be superior to other disciplines in teaching students to think, since it did not, like the traditional liberal arts subjects, encompass a huge body of fact, whose inculcation might preempt the fundamental goal of teaching critical thinking. Even as he explained this view, though, he candidly acknowledged the flaw in its application, which inhered in the fact that, at Indiana as elsewhere, teachers of applied music usually did not teach their students how to solve problems but instead conducted their business through "an indoctrination method." Pianists, for example, "have a tendency to teach their students to do as they were taught."

Be that as it might, music students, like all others, needed a broad grounding in the liberal arts. At the same time, they needed a comprehensive education within music itself. Bain decried the narrowness of the education commonly offered in the conservatories, where not only was there no general arts curriculum but often also no more than a superficial training in academic music, and whence students emerged as what he liked to call "one-eyed specialists." For their part, the universities regularly produced graduates whose education was deficient in the opposite way. If aspiring performers needed a good knowledge of academic music, academic musicians should also develop and maintain a relatively high level of performance skills; and this level could not be attained unless performance study was more or less continuous: performance could not "be set aside at any time during the undergraduate period without considerable future detriment." A university music school, then, was obliged to give its students—*all* its students—a thoroughly comprehensive education, comprising a solid grounding in the traditional liberal arts and a rounded diet of both academic and applied music; such a school would be, in effect, a "conservatory amalgamated into a university."

Moreover, since music education was, even in the undergraduate years, professional as well as liberal, performance experience at the university should as nearly as possible duplicate the conditions of standard professional performance. This thesis had two implications. First, students could be trained for performance careers only by faculty who were themselves professional performers: who else could really know what students would confront in professional situations? Second, students' actual experience of music-making in university should be as similar as possible to what they would later encounter as professionals; and since the great majority of graduates in applied music would, in the nature of things, work in ensembles rather than as soloists, the university was obliged to give them extensive experience in ensemble performance—and, in particular, in performing the standard literature of ensembles, as opposed to the lighter pieces often thought appropriate for student groups.

It followed that a music school should center its efforts in orchestral performance and in the production of opera. The summits of music were in the symphonic and operatic literature; the symphony orchestra and the complex operatic ensemble of orchestra, chorus, and soloists were therefore the most important ensembles for the education of professional musicians. In turn, this line of thought required that a serious music school be a *large* one. Not only would a program focusing in the performance of large-scale works require a large number of student players and singers (and for this reason, as well as for the sake of their own rounded musical education, Bain insisted that academic-music majors, too, play in ensembles), but it would also require a student body sufficiently large that one could be confident of having an adequate supply of first-rate performers for the most demanding parts. Bain's standard way of expressing this point was by an aphorism: "It takes an awful lot of milk to get the cream." According to Mary Wennerstrom, who came to the School as a piano major in 1957 and eventually became Head of its Theory Department, Bain said this "a thousand times—whenever he stood up."

It is far from clear that Bain's theory of musical education had been worked out in detail by the time he arrived at Indiana. There is no comprehensive treatment of it from this era (or, for that matter, from any time in the twenty-six years of his deanship). There is, though, no doubt that he had at least the main points of the theory in hand from his first days in Bloomington. Clearly his development of the program at North Texas had conformed to these points, in the rapid expansion of enrollment, the recruitment of professional performers to the faculty, and the focus on large ensembles. Moreover, Bain did stress to his Indiana colleagues, in his first faculty meeting, the crucial importance of ensembles in enhancing the stature of the School; and colleagues who survive from that era report that he also insisted from the very beginning that the key to building a great music school at Indiana was to build a great opera program. Further, as early as December 15, 1947, he wrote, in the context of seeking authorization for a series of additional faculty appointments, a lengthy memo to Briscoe that expounded key points of his theory.

A notable feature of this memo, which distinguishes it from the pure theorizing of the Wolford interview, is the fact that it makes clear that the steps Bain proposes were to be undertaken as much for their promotional as for their educational value; or, to put it in a way that is fairer to Bain, the memo embodies his commonsense understanding that public-relations objectives were inextricably linked to educational ones, for the reason that the School would not be able, without successful public relations, to attract the public support and the excellent faculty and students it required in order to achieve its high educational goals.

His aim, he explained to Briscoe, was to have the School "take the lead in its field in this part of the country." The prime requisite for its doing so was the creation of "a very strong instrumental, orchestral program." This was because "it is impossible to build a fine music school" without "a splendid orchestra and a good department of theory." (On other occasions, Bain added that a good library, especially of scores and recordings, was the third "great post" on which a fine music school must rest.) Indiana's theory department was already "flourishing" (the successful reconstitution of the theory program had, it will be recalled, been a central achievement of the Sanders era); but the orchestra was "not up to standard for the professional training level."

The key to building a fine orchestra was to appoint a distinguished conductor to the faculty; the reputation of such a person would attract first-rate students. If that person were the particular individual Bain recommended—Ernst Hoffman, who had, in addition to his experience in Houston, extensive European experience in conducting opera—the School could also create for itself a distinctive reputational niche: "it would not be long before we would be in a unique position in the orchestral and operatic field. . . . we would be the only state university in our part of the United States with a professional symphony conductor for the orchestra." With Hoffman, the School would be "in a position to perform opera," and would be able to offer "top-flight experience" in opera and choral music as well as orchestral music; and its reputation in these areas would attract (and would offer the *only* way to attract) "mature and distinguished student singers."

Similarly, good faculty appointees in the various orchestral instruments would attract good students in those fields. Among the recommended appointments in these instruments, Bain's memo accords the highest priority to the acquisition of individual teachers of oboe and bassoon. This recommendation, too, he justified in terms of an open niche: other schools—Illinois, Wisconsin, Eastman, Juilliard—had resident string quartets, and he was "not proposing that we go into competition with these other universities in that particular field. However, they do not have distinguished teachers for each of the woodwind instruments, nor do they have a woodwind ensemble." New Indiana appointees in oboe and bassoon could join with the present teachers of flute and clarinet to form a concert woodwind ensemble, which, touring widely in Indiana and perhaps also in neighboring states, "could function for us similarly to the functioning of the Waldron Quartet at Illinois." (The proposed ensemble —which included a French horn in addition to woodwinds—was formed in 1949, as the American Quintet.)

The idea of pursuing the ultimate goal of all-round excellence by developing and publicizing a few areas where the School might attain a competitive advantage was, in fact, fundamental to Bain's strategy (as, indeed, it was to Wells's strategy for developing the University as a whole). His most vivid articulation of this strategy took the form of a comparison from the world of retail sales. To attract the best students, he told Wolford, "you have to have a show window":

> I often say the great stores in New York like Macy's and Gimbel's, they can't put all their merchandise in their store windows for people to look at. And they must get them in the store some way or other, so that they use the store windows . . . to feature some of the unique things that are inside. And so I think every school has to have something . . . similar to this kind of thing, and I would say for instance that the operas we did occupied that . . . place.

People would, he thought, reason that "if they're good at that and can do that, why apparently they must be able to do everything well."

It was important, of course, to choose for the store window items that weren't in *other* stores' windows: "If you're going to be in business, you'd better sell something that nobody else is selling." And when I asked him why he had chosen to center the School's activities in opera, Bain replied not in terms of the high-minded rationale provided in his educational theory but in pure and candid terms of opportunism. Opera workshops were springing up in music schools all over the country in these years, but they were, in comparison with what Bain had in mind, very small-scale operations. Bain had wanted to get into a race "where it was possible to win": "You say, 'why did you do that?' Simply because competition was practically nil."

Bain—and, as it turned out, the School—were particularly fortunate in the time he arrived. The burgeoning enrollments of the postwar years made it easy to create the *large* school that his vision required, and also, since the mushrooming student body necessitated numerous additional faculty positions, allowed him to transform the nature of the faculty with a rapidity that could not have been matched in any other era.

By the time he wrote his strategic memo on appointments, he had already recruited nine new faculty members, six of whom were in place by the opening of the fall semester; and all of these appointments conformed to his plan to make the School center in the professional education of applied musicians. Here again the historical circumstances of the School were peculiarly favorable to the achievement of his aims. Bain wanted to hire applied-music faculty; but the bulk of his appointments would have had to be in applied music in any case, because there was, as we saw in the account of Sanders's deanship, a chronic shortage of faculty in this area—a consequence of the overall growth in the number of music majors, the long-term trend whereby the proportion of Music Education majors was decreasing relative to Bachelor of Music students, and the increasing demand from students in other parts of the University for applied music as an elective. Given these circumstances, and the fact that the student load of a teacher of academic music was, unlike that of an applied-music instructor, indefinitely expansible (because the former taught classes, while the latter taught primarily individuals), it was no trouble for Bain to justify doing what he wanted to do anyway. In his early years, he hired applied musicians almost exclusively.

It was presumably more difficult to justify using, as his primary criterion in applied-music appointments, performance credentials rather than standard academic ones. Shortly before leaving Texas, Bain wrote to Wells's assistant to request early meetings with the President and Briscoe, because he anticipated recommending some "unusual" appointments; these must surely have been the performing artists he wished to recruit. Professional performers were still uncommon in universities as permanent, professorial appointees (as distinguished from part-timers), not only because of reflex academic snobbery about academic credentials but because, as Bain put it, "they had the reputation of raising hell to get what they wanted," and also because in many cases they had limited experience of teaching and none of grading and other academic rituals. But here Bain could, and doubtless did, cite the precedent provided by Madame Manski (though fifty years later he still spoke with irritation of her shortcomings as an academic).

Bain won his point with Briscoe and Wells—primarily, one supposes, because Wells had been so impressed with the applied-music program at North Texas, which Bain had staffed as much as possible with performing artists. Indeed, a main source for his first cohort of performer appointees at Indiana was his former employer. Bain, whose personal qualities included not only ruthlessness but great pride and delight *in* his ruthlessness (and who surely could not have accomplished nearly so much without these qualities), makes a point of telling us, in *The Bain Regime,* that in a conversation subsequent to Bain's resignation the President of North Texas expressed his hope that the departing Dean would not raid the faculty he had assembled, reminding him in this context "of the support he had given the School of Music during the difficult times of World War II." A few pages later, Bain records that his first group of appointees at Indiana included two acquired from North Texas: Walter Robert (who, born in Trieste of Austrian parents and impressively educated in Vienna, had toured widely as a solo pianist and as the accompanist of several violinists) as Associate Professor of Piano, and Myron Taylor (whom Bain wanted to head up his opera program) as Associate Professor of Voice.

In the field of orchestral instruments, Bain's initial goal was "to find an individual teacher for each instrument"—a requisite, he thought, for attracting first-rate students of the various instruments. In the year before he arrived, the School did not have individual teachers for viola, double bass, oboe, bassoon, saxophone, tuba, or percussion. There was only a part-time teacher of French horn, and by Bain's arrival this was also true of cello: to replace von Zweygberg (who continued as a part-timer after his retirement in 1945), Sanders had, as I noted earlier, brought in Richard Clayton; but his appointment had not been renewed for 1947–48.

To fill these numerous holes in the applied-music faculty, Bain gave preference to professional performers. In his first year, he appointed, for cello, another Texas acquaintance, Sterling Hunkins, first cellist of the Dallas Symphony, and, for French horn, William Kirkpatrick, Jr., the principal horn player of the Memphis Symphony, who had also earned a Master's degree from Eastman. (When Bain appointed people with academic credentials, he strongly preferred graduates of the major American schools, above all the preeminent Eastman.) In bassoon, he appointed another Eastman graduate, Roy Houser, who had been a member of the American Broadcasting Company Symphony and other groups. Even in composition, where Sanders's position had to be filled, he chose a performer, and one who had no previous connection with academia: Anis Fuleihan, a Cyprus-born American highly regarded as a pianist and, since the mid-1930s, as a composer; appointed at the rank of Professor, he could replace both Sanders and, in part, Hoffzimmer (who was to retire in 1948, though he taught on a part-time basis until 1956).

Although his initial appointments gave him a staff somewhat more to his liking, Bain must have bitten his tongue when, at the beginning of the first faculty meeting of the fall semester, he announced that "he knew that this is a fine faculty." In truth his early months in Bloomington confirmed the low estimate of the School—students and faculty alike—that he had formed in his May visit. The student body was "modest . . . (from the standpoint of talent)." As for the faculty, during that visit Sanders had been, as *The Bain Regime* puts it, "very generous in giving verbal evaluations of the various members"—a remark capable of two different interpretations. "Most of the positive evaluations," Bain adds, "turned out to be only partially useful." To me, he made the point without benefit of irony: he thought the faculty second-rate—or third-rate. He excepted Hoffzimmer and Nettl from this condemnation (and elsewhere conceded that Manski, though she knew nothing of credit hours and such, was a very good teacher "in the production of voice"), and the judgment on the whole is too harsh: though he built, in several areas, on solid foundations created by his predecessors and their abler colleagues, Bain's later statements about the School as it existed at the time of his appointment habitually revised history in order to make his marvelous creative work there appear to have been essentially *ex nihilo*. Yet the overall assessment of the School in 1947 that he gave me nearly fifty years later coincides quite well with what we have seen of it during the last years of Sanders's comfortable but largely rudderless democracy: "It was sleepy here. Nothing much was happening. Everyone was going where he should go, but there wasn't enough of really *getting* anywhere."

Bain did not wait even until September to sound a wake-up call. He held his first regular faculty meeting on August 12, and used it to launch a series of important initiatives. Almost all of these had to do with raising the level of student performance and with developing the kind of orchestra- and opera-centered performance program that his ambitions for the School required. Thus he proposed six new courses, all in applied music: two of these created new ensembles—harp and madrigal—and there was a series of four that would constitute the basis for his opera program: "Music 325–328: Opera Workshop." To be taught by Myron Taylor, these courses would be required of all voice majors and would include "all of the aspects of the production of light and grand operas—solos, choruses, scenery, lighting, dramatic production." Bain further proposed that the rehearsal requirement for all ensembles be increased to five times a week, for at least an hour each time. This had been the rule at North Texas; at Indiana ensembles were accustomed to rehearse no more than three hours a week. Further, he secured faculty agreement to his proposal that all required recitals be recorded and archived, to provide objective evidence of performance standards in the School. (In his 1945–46 report, Sanders had announced a plan to acquire recording equipment, to be used for the same sort of purpose.)

Once the new semester was launched, and his enlarged faculty on hand, Bain held a massive—three-and-a-half-hour—meeting, at which he gained approval of still more initiatives. These included an increase in the number of credit hours required for graduation from 120 to 128 (in accordance with common practice elsewhere) and also a proposal (which considerably broadened the impact of the expansion of rehearsal time for ensembles) to expand the School's ensemble requirements for degree candidates. These requirements had been increased in Sanders's last years, so that, at the time of Bain's arrival, undergraduates were required to participate in ensembles for their first seven semesters at the School and to earn at least eight credit hours in ensemble. Bain proposed that the requirement be extended to include *all* semesters of an undergraduate program, for half again as many credit hours per semester, and be extended as well to include all graduate students (unless excused by the Dean on the recommendation of their major professor; later, doctoral candidates were specifically excepted from the requirement). Moreover, the requirement could be satisfied only by participation in one of the designated "major" ensembles: orchestra, band, and the various choirs. The expanded requirements accorded, of course, not only with Bain's theory of musical education (which emphasized the key role of ensemble experience in the development of professional musicians) but with his desire to promote the School through an extensive performance program centering in large ensembles. In December, a piano proficiency requirement was established for all music majors, and in January Bain secured agreement that students should have a jury examination in applied music each semester. He also instituted a weekly recital series (mixed recitals, involving more than one student), and enacted a requirement that students attend an average of at least one musical event a week, on penalty of losing one-half credit hour. He moved, too, to expand the summer program, with a view to creating the expectation that the School's students would attend it year-round.

These changes obviously had the effect of making life harder for the students. In his letter of recommendation, Ernst Hoffman had said that Bain "drove" the North Texas students; he immediately began to crack the whip over those at Indiana. He was more than willing to do so; here, as in many other matters, he was sustained in harshness by the pleasure he took in *being* harsh, and in advertising himself as such. Early in *The Bain Regime,* he relates with evident satisfaction that after his departure was announced at North Texas one clarinet major "fabricated a sign which he carried about the halls of the School of Music announcing the opportunity for blood donors to contribute to a blood bank for the students at Indiana University. The implication was that once the Bain regime got underway at Indiana University the students would need transfusions to keep in good health." This anecdote (which Bain liked so well that he repeated it forty pages later) is prefaced by the information that the student in question had recently won a position with the Dallas Symphony—the implication being that Bain's bloodletting was therapeutic.

Up to a point, at least, this was surely true, at Indiana as at North Texas. The primary aim of the Indiana School of Music was to train professionals in various branches of music. Except in Music Education, it was not, when Bain arrived, performing this function effectively. Before coming to Indiana, Bain had been invited to apply for the headship of the Jordan Conservatory of Indianapolis, where he says he was assured that "nothing was happening at Indiana University in music and that it was not a professional school in any sense of the word. Many of the Indiana University students were attending what they considered to be a 'suitcase school'—one in which the students went home weekends and were not very serious about studies." Within a year of his arrival, Bain had eradicated any vestiges of such an attitude—though at a cost that was, for some students, too high: by 1952, Dr. E. Bryan Quarles, the Director of the Student Health Service, thought it necessary to address the School's faculty on the unique and disturbing level of stress among music students. The students, Dr. Quarles reported, "say that they do not have time for the work that is required of them"; some of them were putting in seventy-to-eighty-hour work weeks. At the time he addressed the faculty (which occurred at an especially busy period, when an opera was in rehearsal), some ten music students—twice as many as for all the rest of the University—were under treatment for fatigue.

If the new requirements for students made their lives harder, some of these requirements also made life harder for many of the faculty. This was especially the case for directors of ensembles, who had to cope with more students and expanded rehearsal times; and the new need to test students for piano proficiency, together with the requirement for semi-annual juries, must have increased the workload for every member of the applied-music faculty. Moreover, from his first months in Bloomington Bain urged faculty members to raise their professional profiles, encouraging them to join professional societies and to "participate in music-making as much as possible." Here the example of the newly appointed performing artists could be used to turn up the heat under the faculty members he had inherited: recitals by Walter Robert and others "added encouragement," as Bain put it, "to the former faculty members to offer themselves as recitalists more frequently than they had in the past."

In the opening months of his deanship, almost all of Bain's proposals were enacted by votes of the full faculty. This was the case even though some of the changes thus approved were, as he acknowledges (or boasts), unpopular. He explains this paradox in terms of the willingness of his colleagues to let a new broom sweep as it would. The requirement, duly passed by the faculty, that all students participate in a major ensemble "was not met with any enthusiasm both on the part of the faculty and the students, but the faculty were willing to yield, so to speak, to the desires of the new leadership." (The *students,* of course, lacked even an *ostensible* choice in this and all other matters.)

Immediately, though, Bain began to move toward a reconstitution of the administrative structure of the School such that the faculty as a whole was no longer asked even to rubber-stamp most decisions. In the August meeting, he suggested that the School should have "an Administrative Council or Executive Committee[,] . . . so that it would not take the time of the entire music faculty to carry on the small business that needs to be carried on." The committee could have six members, two elected each year. He "mentioned the advisability" of such a committee again in the meeting of September 30, and in a meeting on October 14 the faculty proceeded to elect the members of what was now called the Advisory Council. No motion, however, was ever offered on the question of whether the faculty wanted a Council in the first place. Early the next month, the Council held its first meeting. Thereafter, it met with increasing frequency and the faculty as a whole with correspondingly less, and the School rapidly left behind its recent days of real and direct democracy and moved into an era in which such democracy as survived was primarily representative rather than direct.

One can see the rapid process of this change both in Bain's evolving accounts of the functions of the Council and in its progressive takeover of most of the most significant matters of School business. When he first proposed the formation of the Council, Bain explained that "it could do most of the leg work for the faculty and finally bring all the materials and recommendations which they may have to the faculty for passing." In November, he proposed establishing a regular monthly meeting of the faculty, at which "the actions of the Advisory Council would be presented," presumably for approval. By the second semester, though, the faculty was meeting only every other month. Meanwhile, the Advisory Council (which by the fall of 1948 was meeting every Saturday morning at 9 A.M.) quickly came to handle not merely the "small business" of the School but nearly *all* its business—though Bain reserved appointments and budgetary matters to himself. In the first few months of the Council's existence, some of its decisions were indeed brought to the full faculty for endorsement, but already most of them, including many important ones, were merely reported. By the fall of 1949, the Council's procedure for reporting to the faculty was simply to send copies of its minutes to all members. By 1957, Bain was describing the Council frankly as the legislative body of the School; and the full faculty's oversight had shrunk explicitly to the "right to review" Council decisions. (Bain told Wolford that the faculty exercised this right "maybe two or three times" in the course of his deanship; most of the faculty simply "aren't that much interested.")

Bain's dissolution of Sanders's direct democracy was a commonsense step that any competent dean assuming the leadership of the School in 1947 would surely have taken. As we have seen, with a rapidly growing faculty, direct democracy had, at the cost of large amounts of all faculty members' time, succeeded only in rendering the School nearly paralyzed. But Bain would have moved to take most of the School's governance out of the hands of the faculty in any case, simply on general principles. Most faculty members, he thought, knew nothing at all about administration; they did much better to spend their time in music-making or research, and in recruiting good students and teaching them.

It was not that Bain did not value, and did not solicit and sometimes defer to, the advice of members of his faculty. As he told me, it was his standard practice, while developing plans, to "try them out" in discussions with colleagues, especially with "a small circle of advisers" and with those who would be directly involved in the implementation of the plan. (He also relied heavily on the advice of his wife. Ross Allen remembers that

Bain "would always say, 'Now, Mary Bain says, Mary says. . . .'") Moreover, the Advisory Council had thorough discussions of all sorts of matters, often culminating in votes that Bain was content to treat as determinative. He was, for example, perfectly happy to have his colleagues on the Council decide the curricula for the many new degree programs introduced during his tenure. He frequently appointed ad hoc committees to develop policy recommendations, and created standing committees on such matters as promotions and academic discipline. Then too, as the faculty grew larger, it was increasingly departmentalized, and more of its routine business was handled at the departmental level.

But however much Bain consulted, however much he delegated to committees and departments, it was always clear that any cession of authority on his part was only voluntary and could be rescinded at any time. Nor did he ever lift his hand from the tiller: during the twenty-six years of his deanship, he never took a sabbatical. These were still the days when academic administrators were, constitutionally, absolute monarchs within their fiefdoms, and Bain, unlike Sanders, chose not to abdicate any of his powers. The Advisory Council "counselled" the Dean; the committees "weren't autonomous": "I wasn't forced to take their recommendation." Where Sanders had regarded the role of the Dean as one of "transmitting the collective will of the faculty to other parts of the University," Bain saw this role very clearly as one of leading, not following. He thought, as he told Wolford, that the position of the Dean in the School could be analogized to that of "the chief of staff of the armed forces, and his adviser generals, and the echelons below them." As chief of staff, the Dean was "responsible for the general master-planning." He would, if he were wise, seek out the counsel of his faculty in developing these plans, but the final decision on them was his. Important decisions were never, he told me, made outside his "small circle of advisers"—"except when I disagreed with them!"

In addition to tightening the ship, Bain's primary concern for his first year as Dean was to ratchet up the School's performance program; and of course these two projects were linked, since it would be impossible to increase the quantity and quality of performances without getting more work out of the faculty and students. As I noted earlier, he took measures to encourage faculty members to perform more often, and instituted a weekly student recital series. But his main objective was to mount more and better performances of major symphonic, choral, and operatic works, and to have these performances exposed to the widest possible audience and brought, as much as possible, to the attention of the press.

In pursuing this objective, however, Bain found himself seriously handicapped (as he indicated in his strategic memo to Briscoe) by the state of the School's orchestra. The situation was especially desperate in strings:

there weren't nearly enough student string players—Bain says that at the time of his arrival the Bachelor of Music program did not include a single violin major—and they weren't very good. To a lesser degree, the same problems obtained in the other sections of the orchestra. Because of the shortage of competent student players, throughout the history of the School it had been standard practice to reinforce them not only by faculty members but by players from outside the School: faculty wives, faculty from other parts of the University, and members of the general Bloomington community. Under Sanders, it had also become customary to bring down a few members of the Indianapolis Symphony to supplement the local players. (The Symphony was itself, in those days, far from being a fully professional orchestra. There were, Bain later said, "a few salesmen, vacuum-cleaner salesmen, and we could get them to come down and play a rehearsal and a concert for $5 and their food.") At one point, Mary Bain solicited string players in the A&P grocery store, positioning herself at the check-out counter and "questioning the customers as they were paying their bills . . . whether or not they could play an orchestral instrument or had any interest in being a member of the Indiana University Symphony Orchestra." Mary recalled having recruited five or six players this way.

Through such expedients, the orchestra managed to play its first concert of the Bain era on November 17, 1947, under the direction of Sterling Hunkins, the cello teacher. There were eight first violins, eight second violins, five violas, five cellos, and four double basses. The program consisted of Mendelssohn's Ruy Blas Overture, Haydn's "Clock" Symphony, Franck's Symphonic Variations (with a student soloist), and pieces by both the former and current Professors of Composition: Sanders's Little Symphony and Fuleihan's Two Etudes for Orchestra. Since the first chairs were occupied by faculty members (a practice that continued for several years), the solo passages were, presumably, fine. A few weeks later, on December 8 and 10, the proud history of opera at Indiana under Bain began modestly enough, with "open rehearsals" produced by Myron Taylor's Opera Workshop. The program included the third act of *Bohème* and the second of *Martha,* performed in Recital Hall with no costumes and with piano accompaniment.

At least as important, from the point of view of public relations, as these events was the inauguration, on December 14 at the Memorial Union, of the Madrigal Dinners. These simulations of Renaissance England—centered, as the name implies, in choral song and quaint fare—became one of the great traditions of the University. As the years passed, decor, entertainment, and food (stretching from Wassail Bowl to Flaming Plum Pudding) grew more elaborate, and attendance grew larger, in some years exceeding 5,000.

Bain's first personal contribution to the enhanced performance program took the ambitious form of presenting, on January 20, with the Orchestra, the Choral Union, Myron Taylor, and three outside soloists, Verdi's Manzoni Requiem. (Wells had agreed to let him hire professional singers and charge admission to the concert; Taylor was also paid for his performance as the tenor soloist.) Although Bain had conducted a number of monumental choral works during his North Texas years, the production of the Requiem was an undertaking fraught with anxiety for him, for it would constitute his Indiana debut as a conductor—on which, as he later said, "a lot of influence and future reputation were riding." For the other solo roles, he engaged Selma Kaye, Winifred Heidt (who was the following year to score a triumph at Covent Garden in *Carmen*), and the distinguished bass-baritone George London. Bain's anxiety was doubtless not allayed by the fact that Kaye fell ill and was replaced by a substitute who, proving to be unprepared, had in her turn to be replaced on very short notice by a graduate student. Moreover, London was able to arrive in Bloomington only two hours before the performance and thus sang without rehearsal. Nor was Bain, who was a highly experienced choral conductor, a very good or confident orchestral conductor. (Ross Allen reports a story in which Mary Bain, relieved that a concert her husband had conducted was over, claimed that "he had worn out five copies" of a recording in an effort to master a particular piece.) But the performance of the Verdi Requiem went well—or so, at least, Bain believed. (His choral conducting was never nearly as much admired at Indiana as it evidently had been in Texas.)

Still, Bain had concluded that his duties as Dean made it impossible for him to continue "the time-consuming, baby-sitting activities involved in choral conducting," and for the second semester he made an appointment in that field—one of two appointments in those early months of 1948 that turned out to have enormous importance in the reification of his vision of a performance-centered professional school. The appointee in choral music was George Krueger. A native of Indiana, Krueger had been a student and later a faculty member at Westminster Choir College, where he had for a number of years served as assistant to John Finley Williamson; in this role, he was responsible for the preliminary training of the Westminster Choir, which in that era performed frequently with the Philadelphia Orchestra under Stokowski and the New York Philharmonic under Toscanini. When Bain recruited him for Indiana, Krueger was director of music at a Presbyterian theological seminary in California. Arriving at Indiana on March 6, he began, as Associate Professor of Choral Music, what was to be a long and illustrious career at the School, stretching to his retirement in 1974. Bain, whose ego never prevented him from recognizing and acknowledging the contributions of others (at least if he had appointed them), praised Krueger in *The Bain Regime* as a "major asset" in the development of the School.

The other new appointee of early 1948—Ernst Hoffman—was of even greater importance to the School than Krueger, though his career at it was much shorter. Hoffman (whose appointment as conductor Bain had urged in his memo to Briscoe) was a man of substantial gifts and accomplishments. Born in Boston in 1899, he entered Harvard at fourteen and graduated at eighteen with a degree in anthropology, having also directed the university's Pierian Sodality Orchestra. Before and during his Harvard years, Hoffman had studied violin, and in 1920–21 he played violin in the Boston Symphony. (Hoffman was also a good pianist and, according to Bain, an "acceptable" violist; and he played the trombone.) He then proceeded to the Berlin Hochschule to study conducting and piano (the latter with Harold Bauer) and a year later was appointed Assistant Conductor of the Breslau Opera and Philharmonic Orchestra, becoming Conductor in 1924; over the next decade, he also appeared as guest conductor with various ensembles, including the Berlin and Vienna Philharmonic Orchestras. Hoffman left Germany to return to the United States in 1934 (that is, the year after the Nazis came to power); by that time, having conducted a wide variety of operas from Mozart to Stravinsky, he was not only a well-educated and skillful musician but also, as Ross Allen put it (according Hoffman what was probably from Allen's point of view the supreme accolade), "a practical man of the theater." In 1936, Hoffman accepted the position of Conductor of the Houston Symphony and (from 1938) Dean of that city's Southern College of Fine Arts—thereby demonstrating, as his manager Arthur Judson put it, an ability to "sense a future in almost virgin territory." When Hoffman took over the Houston orchestra, it was a semi-professional group giving six subscription concerts per season. By the time he left it, at the end of the 1946–47 season, the orchestra was giving ninety to a hundred concerts each year, and Hoffman had, according to the valedictory tribute of the Women's Committee of the Symphony, endeared himself to everyone from schoolchildren to businessmen by his lucid musicianship, his indefatigability, and "the charm of his sweet, gentle nature." He was, however, let go in 1947 and in that context suggested to Bain (with whom he had worked on numerous occasions, and admired not only as a choral director but as an academic administrator) that he appoint him orchestra conductor at North Texas. Bain had planned to do so; when he left North Texas for Indiana, he brought Hoffman to his new school instead. Hoffman was initially appointed as Visiting Conductor of the University Orchestra, but after eight months Bain made him Professor of Music.

Hoffman found his new orchestra in most respects appallingly bad. To begin with, some of the instruments owned by the School were unsuitable. As he explained in his first annual report to Bain, the trumpets and trombones were non-symphonic, the tuba "impossible," and the quality and intonation of all the A clarinets "outrageous." The string instruments were also very poor, and there was not a single five-string bass. To alleviate the situation, Hoffman loaned the School some of his own instruments and bought it a trombone and tuba, seemingly out of his own pocket. As for the players wielding these instruments, the clarinetists (taught by the Sanders appointee William Koogler, whom Bain did not rehire the next year) were unable to play in tune; and Hoffman looked forward eagerly to the addition to the faculty of oboe and bassoon specialists. In strings, the cellists and bassists (who had the benefit of instruction by the professional cellist Hunkins) played well, but the violinists and violists (with Winifred Merrill as the School's only teacher) produced an "infantile" tone, held the bow and the instrument wrong, could not play in tune, and were "unable to produce a vibrato." "Until a *first class* violin teacher is engaged," Hoffman wrote, with as strong emphasis as he could muster, "we are utterly *unfair to* and *failing in our teaching of* the violin and viola students."

In this scene of desolation, Hoffman had attempted to impose professional standards, and had accordingly increased rehearsal time still further, from the hour per day recently decreed by Bain to two hours. The extra hour was at first voluntary, but, as Bain observed, "soon became the rule." In addition, Hoffman was teaching one violin and ten piano students. His only regret, he reported to Bain, was that he could not have each of them for two hours per week instead of one.

During his first semester at Indiana, Hoffman also figured prominently in what was billed as the first annual Spring Music Festival. To be sure, the primary purpose of the festival (which had been mounted at Herman Wells's urging) was to inaugurate the organ that finally completed the University Auditorium: three of the five events were organ recitals. The instrument thus feted had been built in 1889 by Hilborne Roosevelt for the Chicago Auditorium, which was for years the city's principal opera house; at the time of its installation, it was the largest organ in the United States. When in 1942 the old theater was being converted to a USO center, the organ was sold at auction for $1,000 to William H. Barnes, who donated it to the University. Wartime shortages of building materials slowed its installation at Indiana, which was eventually completed, together with some additions to the instrument, at a cost of $50,000. At the time of Bain's arrival, the organ was in fact still inoperable, but by the spring of 1948 it was ready for display. At the festival, Barnes and Virgil Fox presented the first two recitals on it; the third was by Oswald Ragatz, the organ teacher whom Sanders had recruited in 1942. The organ was, however, disappointing. As Bain later observed, interest had been focused more on "the historical aspects of the instrument than in . . . [its] actual musical quality," and, once knowledge of its actual quality was disseminated, it proved to be nearly impossible to engage distinguished organists for performances on it. (It was not until 1969, after a complete redesign and rebuilding of the instrument, necessitated by damage from two small fires and construction debris, that the University finally had a recital organ worthy of its setting.) Happily, the Spring Festival included, in addition to the organ recitals, two other, much more auspicious, musical events, both of which featured Hoffman as conductor: a performance of Bach's St. Matthew Passion (with Bain directing the chorus) and, on May 15, the first of the full opera productions of the Bain era, a presentation of Offenbach's *Tales of Hoffmann.*

This latter production was also notable as marking the initial appearance at Indiana of the second man who was to become a mainstay of the Opera Theater, the stage director Hans Busch, whom Bain brought in on a visiting appointment. Busch was the scion of an extraordinary musical family of German anti-Nazi expatriates. His father was the conductor Fritz Busch; his uncle Adolf, a violinist, was the leader of the Busch String Quarter and a close associate of Rudolf Serkin, who became his son-in-law. Hans became an American citizen in 1942, and served in the U.S. Army. After the war, he played a role in the reestablishment of opera at Florence and the reconstruction of La Scala; by the time of his appearance in Bloomington, he had directed operas at a number of venues, including especially Stockholm, where he was the leading stage director of the Royal Opera. In 1948, he was back in the United States, teaching at Juilliard and directing a number of operas in New York.

To sing the role of Hoffmann, Busch had recruited Louis Vanelle, an opera student known to him in New York; this was one of the very few times an outsider was hired to sing a part in an opera mounted by the School (and it happened in this case only after an Indiana graduate student who had sung the role in the rehearsals was cavalierly dismissed, it having been decided that he was not good enough). Vera Scammon—a faculty wife who later became a voice teacher in the School—sang the role of Antonia; the rest of the cast were undergraduate and graduate students at Indiana (including, in the latter category, three who had followed Bain from North Texas). With a School student body of fewer than 300, it was not easy to recruit the large male chorus needed for the opera; but the presence on campus of a number of young men in a naval officers training program helped.

The production garnered rave reviews in Bloomington and Indianapolis papers. These responses were perhaps not uninfluenced by regional pride, but most of the praises ring true to anyone who knows the special excellencies of later productions of the Opera Theater. Describing the performance as "simply swell entertainment," Henry Butler in the *Indianapolis Times* was happy to declare that it left no "further" doubt "that Indiana can, in some ways, outdo the Metropolitan" (which Butler had seen in its annual visits to Bloomington). Like many observers of Indiana opera to this day, Butler was struck by the freshness and vitality, the absence of prima donna posturing, in the student singer-actors. But freshness need not imply amateurishness. The reviewer for the *Bloomington Herald-Telephone* also anticipated the response of later patrons of the Opera Theater by remarking the "almost inconceivable" level of professionalism in this student production. Finally, in the *Indianapolis Star,* Corbin Patrick noted Ernst Hoffman's contribution, commenting (as he also had in a previous review) on the "surprising results" that Hoffman had achieved with the orchestra in the few short months of his tutelage.

In the original design of the performance program for Bain's first year at Indiana, the Spring Festival was to have been the climax; and as such it would have marked, as Patrick thought it did, the culmination of "a remarkable first year of progress." As it happened, though, two midsummer events far outshone the Festival.

At a professional meeting sometime during the year, Bain had had occasion to speak with a former New York University schoolmate, Benjamin Grosso, of G. Schirmer, Inc., music publishers. Grosso suggested that Schirmer's might arrange to have the School mount the world stage premiere of Kurt Weill's folksong opera, *Down in the Valley,* which had been written originally (in 1945) for radio. Grosso would try to have Weill and his wife, Lotte Lenya, in attendance for the premiere, and to secure, for the lead, Marion Bell, who had recently starred in the Broadway hit *Brigadoon.* Bain, whose North Texas experience with *Cynthia Parker* had driven home to him the enormous publicity value of a premiere, leapt at the opportunity. The opera was duly produced at Indiana on July 15, on a twin bill (since it was not quite an hour in length) with Hindemith's brief farce *There and Back,* which Bain had also mounted at North Texas. Weill—flippantly described in the program as having arrived in the United States in 1935 with "his slender wardrobe and his slim wife"—did attend, along with that slim wife and Bell's husband, Alan Jay Lerner. Again Hoffman led the orchestra, and Busch directed. George Krueger was chorus master. This time there were reviews not merely in Bloomington and Indianapolis papers but in the *Louisville Courier-Journal,* the *Dayton Herald,* and the *Chicago Sun.* Reviewers praised Bell, naturally, but also the student cast and Hoffman's orchestra (whose excellence was all the more impressive in that, as a summer-school ensemble, it included a number of new players). Busch was praised for the economical suggestiveness of the scenery and the unaffected acting that he drew from the singers. Even better (from a publicity standpoint) than the reviews, though, was the fact that in the *New York Times* for the Sunday before the production Olin Downes had written a two-column article featuring the upcoming event.

But to Bain the sweetest of all the year's triumphs was the last one. In February, Antal Dorati, who had used Bain's North Texas chorus several times during his tenure as conductor of the Dallas Symphony, and who was now conducting the Minneapolis Symphony, informed Bain that he had been asked to conduct Chicago's Grant Park Symphony Orchestra in two concerts in the park, scheduled for July 24 and 25. He proposed that the concerts—which might be attended by as many as 100,000 people—present the Manzoni Requiem (the work that Bain had conducted at Indiana in January), with the School supplying the chorus. Bain accepted, of course, despite the difficulty of collecting a 200-voice chorus in the summer, and the expense and logistical difficulties of transporting its members to Chicago and maintaining them there. (He persuaded the University administration to cover the costs, on the ground that the event would have "tremendous advertising value.") This time Krueger trained the chorus. Thirty years later, chronicling his regime, Bain was still thrilled about the outcome of the venture, which he characterized as "the most influential in the securing of recognition" of the School. The event was a triumph, praised by reviewers for the Chicago papers (and one from Dallas). Far best of all was the review by the formidable Claudia Cassidy of the *Tribune.* Cassidy was notoriously capable of vitriol, and Bain professed to know more than one artist who would not appear in Chicago for fear of her. How gratifying, then, it must have been to him to open the *Tribune* to the headline "Grant Park Thousands Cheer Antal Dorati's Eloquent Performance of Verdi *Requiem.*" "Now and then," Cassidy wrote,

> something exciting comes along to jar you out of the deplorable routine of too much mediocre music. It came to Grant Park in two week-end performances of Verdi's Requiem, which were as free as the park itself to the tens of thousands who thronged to hear it, sat as quietly as in a concert hall to listen, and stayed when it was over to cheer themselves hoarse in its honor.
>
> If words were medals, I would be decorating those who made it possible: Antal Dorati, the director, Frances Yeend, Winifred Heidt, Gabor Carelli, and George London, the soloists; the beautifully trained chorus of 200 voices from Indiana University[; the] Grant Park Symphony Orchestra. . . .
>
> Between them they struck a spark that flamed in the night, and I am none too sure I shall hear the Requiem like that again.

Dorati and Indiana were engaged to give two additional performances of the Requiem the following summer.

Apart from Bain's own talent and drive, the most important factor contributing to his success in this first year and after was the support of Herman Wells. During most of the 1947–48 academic year, Wells was in Germany, as Acting Chief of Educational and Cultural Affairs in the U.S. Occupied Zone. An administrative committee, headed by the Chairman of the Board of Trustees—John Hastings—and including Briscoe, Joseph Franklin (the Treasurer of the University), and Wendell Wright (who was then Dean of the School of Education), was appointed to discharge the duties of the presidency. Years later, Hastings told Bain that he had asked Wells, as the latter was preparing to leave the country, "What am I going to do with this guy Bain?" Wells thought a long time and finally said: "Give him anything he wants." Although in later years Wells naturally denied having shown Bain any favoritism, the record confirms that he and his subordinates acted, within reason, in accordance with this directive. This was especially the case in respect of allowing Bain to staff the School largely with professional musicians holding few or no traditional academic credentials, in providing the financial support necessary to the rapid expansion of the School, in giving Bain unwavering (and, in at least one instance, clearly unconscionable) support in his disputes with faculty members, and in granting him unlimited and nearly unparalleled direct access to the highest officers of the University. In his first year, Bain told Wolford, he must have worn out Briscoe's patience "by calling on him so many, many times for advice"; for the following years, the President's files are littered with notes recording Bain's requests for meetings. One well-placed observer of Bain's relationships with the central administration is Dorothy Collins, an enormously shrewd and capable woman whose husband succeeded Briscoe in 1959 as Vice President and Dean of the Faculties. Collins herself, though her graduate studies had been in English, worked for the University's best-known faculty member, Alfred Kinsey, for five years in the early 1950s and, following Ralph Collins's untimely death in 1963, held positions in the Office of Institutional Research (where in 1964 she made a study of Bain's treatment of his faculty) and as a speechwriter and special assistant to a series of Wells's successors and to Wells himself when he returned as Interim President for three months in 1968, and later in his role as Chancellor of the University. According to Collins, Bain enjoyed a degree of access to Wells matched only by Kinsey. Bain's general practice was to bypass the office of the Dean of Faculties and go "straight to Wells"; for Wells, unlike (for example) Ralph Collins, would give him what he wanted.

Wells's special and invaluable support of Bain—and, in general, of the School of Music, up until his death—is explicable in terms both of his personal interests and his administrative principles. A devoted concertgoer from early youth, he recalled in *Being Lucky* the thrill he felt as a boy to have the "contact with the outside world of ideas and music" that was brought to summertime Jamestown by the Chautauqua; as I noted earlier, he was still regularly attending School of Music concerts in his nineties. Wells was also an enthusiastic amateur instrumentalist, first in the Jamestown Boys' Band, where he signed up at the age of about nine for horn lessons. Over the years, his instruments included the baritone horn, the French horn, the cello, and, in college, the harp. (This according to *Being Lucky:* Dorothy Collins, who helped him write the book, says that she "never saw a harp, never saw any *sign* that he played the harp.") While attending high school in Lebanon, Indiana, Wells actually earned money as a member—and first-chair player—of the local band, which, as he recalled, "nearly every summer evening" played concerts "at some place within driving distance of Lebanon." As an Indiana undergraduate, he took one of Jack Geiger's music appreciation courses and was, as I noted earlier, a member of the band, where he rose under Archie Warner's direction from baritone player to manager (an office whose duties were not so much musical as financial: "to finagle enough money by one means or another to get us to an out-of-town football game or so, which I did by various economies and money-raising schemes"). How could his love of music and long association with the School of Music not have caused him to look with special favor on it? As Charles Webb puts it, Wells's personal feeling for music—a feeling that needed to be "fed," that brought him to concerts "night after night after night"—"translated into a constant oversight from afar, that we must keep Music as an important part" of the University.

But in truth Wells would have accorded special treatment to Bain even if he had not had a deep personal interest in music. As President, he recognized early on that Indiana could not, given its limited financial resources as a state university, realistically aspire at this stage of its development to excellence across the board. In these circumstances, what would be far better than to accept mediocrity across it would be to single out and cultivate what he called "peaks of excellence": units where he thought a disproportionate investment of resources could create academic distinction. (Since the most the state government could be counted on for was "funds for the basic instructional work of the institution and for the basic instructional plant," the peaks could be developed only through infusions of private or federal money.) Believing as he did that the quality of the faculty was the most important ingredient in a university's success, he chose as his peaks of excellence units that had the greatest faculty strength, including especially the strongest leadership. It is not clear whether Wells regarded Music as a potential peak of excellence before he recruited Bain, but it is abundantly clear that he thought so afterward. Faculty being the key ingredient of institutional success, he spent, as we have seen, inordinate amounts of time in recruitment; but he could better afford this time because another of his fundamental administrative principles was that, having secured a strong leader for an academic unit, he should simply let that person lead it, keeping himself primarily in a responsive rather than a directive mode. This is precisely what he did, in spades, with Bain: "Give him anything he wants." Bain used every bit of this freedom, and, once he had learned the ropes, made it his practice not to tell his superiors what he was doing unless he needed something from them. "The administration," he told Wolford, "didn't know very much about what was going on. . . . I never consulted them about anything."

In the summer of 1948, though, he needed quite a lot, especially by way of additional faculty positions. He got them, making nine new appointments. Among these, his personal favorite was certainly the soprano Josephine Antoine. A member of the Met company, Antoine was also well known through her appearances, over several seasons, on a nationally broadcast radio program, the Carnation Contented Hour (Carnation Condensed Milk originating, if its slogan is to be believed, in contented cows). Antoine thus brought to the School exactly what Bain sought in his applied-music appointees: professional accomplishments and publicity value. Unfortunately, she stayed for only a year, during which she met and married Wells's chauffeur, with whom she decamped for Hollywood, where they both sought movie careers.

More than a new voice teacher, though, Bain needed, in that summer of 1948, new appointees in strings, and especially in violin. His strategic memo to Briscoe had stressed the need to appoint "a distinguished teacher of violin," not merely for the sake of the students currently in the program but, more important, as a means of attracting more and better string players and thus alleviating the dearth of competent strings that was such an impediment to the realization of his plan for an orchestra-centered school. One of Bain's central convictions was that it took distinguished teachers to attract good applied-music students: as he put it to Briscoe, "students are wise enough to want to study with someone who has proved that he or she can develop excellent performers." At the close of the academic year, Hoffman, it will be recalled, had insisted in his annual report to Bain that the School was being derelict in its duties toward violin and viola students, and he closed the report by urging that a resident string quartet be appointed to the faculty: its members would "improve our string players, assist me in rehearsals, and *attract* students. At present, string players, except cellos, avoid our University since they know that the violin teaching here is *impossible*!" (With triple underscoring for the final word.) Bain had pointed out to Briscoe that various other schools had resident string quartets, but he had said that he did not propose to go into competition with them in that field. By summer, though, he had come round to Hoffman's way of thinking.

The problem was that he could not, given the low current enrollment in strings, justify bringing in two additional violin teachers and a viola teacher. (By summer, there was room for a cellist, for Sterling Hunkins had departed for New York, under circumstances that Bain leaves unclear.) Here was one of the many instances where his *carte blanche* (which he did not at the time know he had—or else, as he told me, he would have asked for much *more*) came in handy. His superiors were, as he expressed it in *The Bain Regime,* "willing to give the School of Music the benefit of the doubt and to gamble on the future" by allowing him to make the three extra appointments. Having determined that the Berkshire Quartet—the successor to the well-known Gordon Quartet, after the death of its founder—was available, Bain traveled to Connecticut to audition the group, and then offered its members positions at the rank of Associate Professor. In the aftermath, he was disconcerted to find that the quartet "considered they had been appointed as a unit" and that consequently they themselves could determine the personnel to come to Indiana: by the effective date of the appointments, the second violinist whom Bain had heard in Connecticut had been replaced by another one.

Although the gamble on the Berkshire Quartet failed (as we shall see) to pay off nearly as well as Bain and Hoffman hoped it would, it at least did not leave the School saddled with a surplus of teachers. In consequence of the rapid expansion of enrollment—which Bain was doing everything in his power to encourage and augment—there was instead a chronic shortage, which persisted in an acute form for years, of faculty in all areas, as well as in facilities. In the fall of 1948, the number of music majors was one-fifth greater than in the previous year, having increased from 296 to 359. Moreover, Bain had decided, soon after he arrived, to declare an open-door policy with respect to students from other parts of the University who wanted to take applied music as an elective. In 1946–47, there had been, in all, 248 students taking applied music; in 1947–48 there were 435; and in 1948–49, 545, of whom 200 were elective students. Then too, the teaching burden in secondary applied music (that is, instrumental or voice training for students whose program included a proficiency requirement in some applied-music field other than their major) was heavier than it would otherwise have been because at Indiana secondary students were taught for an hour each week instead of the half hour that was the NASM standard. Even though beginning secondary students in piano were taught in classes of up to twelve, the overall teaching burden in applied music far exceeded the capacity of the regular faculty and could be managed only through the extensive use of two other categories of instructors. First, Bain like his predecessors relied on faculty wives as applied-music teachers, appointing a number of them as part-time instructors without academic rank and at low rates of pay. (Their conditions of employment became a chronic source of tension between Bain and these women and their husbands.) Second, he greatly expanded the use of graduate students as applied-music teachers. At North Texas, he had had a program of graduate student support through teaching assistantships, and he immediately secured agreement at Indiana for a like program. Thus by the fall of 1948 the School had forty faculty members, supplemented by thirty-nine graduate assistants, who taught all secondary music—except that it was necessary for Bain to recruit a dozen senior undergraduates to complete the secondary roster. By the next year, graduate assistants were also teaching 95 percent of the elective students.

The shortage of facilities was even more acute than that of teachers. Already by the last years of Sanders's tenure the Music Building was badly overcrowded. It had been designed to accommodate 200 students. By the late war years, the number of majors slightly exceeded this limit, and there was even then a substantial number of students taking applied music (as well as academic-music courses) on an elective basis. In October 1944, Sanders observed to his faculty that the School had ten applied-music studios but twenty-three full-time teaching loads in that field; this situation necessitated considerable time-sharing of studios, which increased still further as the student load continued to grow in the following years. The practice-room situation was equally bad. Shortly after Bain took office, he wrote Wells a memo listing the number of majors and elective students taking applied music, and the amount of daily practice expected of them (for majors, not less than 3½ hours per day; for elective students, 1½ hours); using these data, he made a straightforward calculation to show that the School, which had 43 practice rooms, needed 120.

By the end of the summer, the shortage of studios had been alleviated somewhat by the construction of a small annex to the Music Building that had been planned during the last days of Sanders's deanship. A wooden building that was, as Bain recalled it, "little more than a shack," the annex contained eight studios and four offices (the latter for academic-music faculty).

Much greater relief was on the way. To cope as rapidly and cheaply as possible with the mushrooming postwar enrollment, the University had contracted to buy, for conversion to collegiate uses, several surplus buildings from various military installations. One of these buildings, a frame structure that had been a movie theater for soldiers, was to be reconstructed, with the help of federal matching funds, on a site just northeast of the Music Building, as an 1100-seat classroom. In the negotiations that led to his accepting the deanship, Bain had secured a commitment that during the first year of his tenure the University would supply the School with additional practice rooms. It was in this context that a decision was made to add a number of practice rooms (and eight studios) to the converted building. Bain had the choice of thirty relatively commodious practice rooms or sixty tiny ones. He chose the latter: rooms just large enough to house a small piano. When necessary, a second instrumentalist could be shoehorned in.

In the midst of reconstruction of the building, Joseph Franklin (the Treasurer), suggested to Bain that, in view of the increasing number of School performances, the huge classroom might double as a venue for musical events. One consideration prompting this suggestion was the fact that the School was using the University Auditorium so much as to interfere with other uses of it. Bain happily acceded to the suggestion, which promised to provide the School with a third, midsize hall (between the 435 of Recital Hall and the 3,700 of the Auditorium) and also, since the new facility would not, like the Auditorium, be a union shop, to afford a great reduction in the cost of producing operas.

Bain was consulted on the design of the stage area, but for several reasons the design turned out to be less than ideal: the plans were being rapidly altered in midstream; the architect was familiar with the physical needs of spoken theater but not of opera; and Bain himself was not at the time very knowledgeable about the design of a lyric theater. The floor of the auditorium was given a mild rake (which was good), and an orchestra pit was constructed, but the stage was shallow and had a low proscenium opening of the kind suitable to the spoken theater but not to opera with its frequent tall sets. Moreover, there was practically no side-stage space, and thus a very limited capacity for housing scenery when it was not actually on stage. Under the stage there were a few dressing rooms—later only one long dressing table, because the rooms had been expropriated for offices, studios, and storage—and a workshop. But the workshop was not sufficiently roomy to allow the construction of large sets; and there was no door of sufficient size to allow large flats to be constructed elsewhere and brought into the building in one piece. Until 1954, the building was also, though ventilated, not air-conditioned, to the great discomfort on many occasions of performers and patrons alike; performers and stage crews were also discomfited by the cramped quarters under the stage: in large-scale productions, which might involve well over one hundred people, Bain said a couple of years later, "the jam of human traffic is unbelievable." With all its faults, though, the converted structure enormously facilitated the development of Bain's opera program, and thus of the School as a whole. Although the building was not at first designated solely for School of Music use, Bain proposed that it be named the University Opera House; but the suggestion was rejected, and it was given a more prosaic name, East Hall.

The School began using the new building in the fall of 1948, but the stage area was not completed until the beginning of 1950; thus for 1948–49 Bain had again to produce opera in the Auditorium. In the event, this was just as well, for the sole opera produced in his second year at Indiana needed the grandeur of the larger, infinitely more elegant hall.

As we have seen, Ernst Hoffman was a man of unusual energy, both mental and physical, and he was, moreover, accustomed to the constant work of a symphony conductor obliged both to prepare a program each week and to fulfill all the attendant duties of such a position. In Bloomington, therefore, although he threw himself into his work with what Bain characterized as "Germanic thoroughness," and accomplished wonders with the orchestra in a few short months, he had time on his hands. This was especially the case because his wife remained for a considerable period in Houston, so that she could be with their son, an undergraduate student at Rice.

In these circumstances, Hoffman, especially lonely and at loose ends on the weekends, used often to tag along with the Bains on Sundays. First he would accompany them to the early morning communion service at Trinity Episcopal Church (the Bains having left their humble Methodist origins behind), and then, after a light breakfast, the three would proceed to the Bloomington Country Club, where Bain was, with Mary, engaged in what he later called "the preliminaries of learning to play golf." Hoffman, though not at all athletically inclined, saw in these occasions an opportunity for extensive shoptalk, and followed the Bains around the course, dressed, as Bain many years later fondly recalled, "in his full length overcoat, with a bowler hat." On these perambulations, Hoffman, as Bain remembered it, did "most of the talking, constantly suggesting plans, personnel, and opportunities for the betterment of the school"; he walked "along beside us chattering like a magpie." Later Bain regretted that he had not accepted more of Hoffman's proposals, which would, it seemed to him in nostalgic retrospect, have been highly advantageous to the growth of the School.

Among the proposals he did accept, though, was a particularly bold one. During one of the Sunday golf excursions, Hoffman asked Bain what he thought of the idea of the School's presenting Wagner's Grail opera, *Parsifal.* Surely Bain's first thought must have been that the idea was absurd. *Parsifal,* five hours long and massive as well in every other way, was hardly an undertaking for amateurs; though relatively undemanding as Wagner operas go, it had been the exclusive property of Bayreuth and a few of the world's major companies. (The Met traditionally staged an Easter-week *Parsifal.*) But Hoffman listed the student singers who could, he believed, perform the various roles; and for the important part of Gurnemanz, the sturdy senior Grail Knight, George Krueger (who was not merely a fine bass-baritone but, at 6'10", the tallest professor at Indiana) was eminently suitable. Hans Busch could perhaps be brought in again to direct. In other ways, too, *Parsifal* was an especially shrewd choice. The orchestral forces required are distinctly smaller than for most Wagner operas. Winds are prominent in the score, and, as Ross Allen recalls, winds were—because of the strong tradition of high school bands in Indiana—the strongest section in the School's orchestra. (In the following years, as the wind faculty grew in size and distinction, more and more of the best high school wind players chose to attend Indiana. Within a few years, Allen says, visitors—especially those from countries lacking the secondary school band tradition—were simply amazed by the excellence of the brass and woodwind sections in the orchestra.) Similarly, for the two choruses that figure in *Parsifal,* Hoffman would have the advantage provided by the School's strong tradition of choral singing. Despite such considerations, which made Hoffman's proposal seem less outrageous, it was still, as Bain later recalled, "almost staggering." But since he had great faith in Hoffman's ability to do what he said he could, and since a successful performance of *Parsifal* could scarcely be bettered as the kind of conspicuous and unique achievement that he sought, above all, for the promotion of the School, he accepted the proposal: "I thought, well, for heaven's sake, if he thinks we can do it, let's see what he can do."

Charles Webb regards the ease with which Bain made decisions as one of his greatest strengths as an administrator; and this particular decision, before which most would have quailed, was one of the best and most important of his life. The performance was scheduled for April 10, 1949—Palm Sunday—in the Auditorium. Act I would be given at 4:00 P.M.; in accordance with Bayreuth tradition, Acts II and III would follow after a break for dinner. Busch accepted a second visiting appointment to the School. Hoffman, in addition to conducting, made the English translation of the libretto. Krueger was featured, but in the off-stage role of Titurel, the aged former king of the knights, rather than as Gurnemanz. All the other parts were sung by students, with the very difficult soprano role of Kundry being, at Hoffman's suggestion, divided between two of them. The demanding male roles were sung by some of the mature-voiced students who, thanks to the GI Bill (which financed veterans returning to school), abounded in the postwar period. Parsifal was sung by Guy Owen Baker, a graduate student in the School; King Amfortas was David Aiken, a graduate student in English who had been a fighter pilot (and who later became a professional singer). The flower maiden dancers came from the modern dance workshop of the School of Health, Physical Education, and Recreation. The task of mounting (and viewing) the opera was made somewhat less onerous by heavy cuts, totaling more than an hour. Hoffman was always ready to cut; it was an aspect of his practicality. (One story, perhaps apocryphal, has him cutting the entry of the third voice in an orchestral fugue, on the ground that the theme had already been heard twice.) And if a student player couldn't manage a phrase, he would rescore it.

The production of *Parsifal* was received, in the Bloomington and Indianapolis papers, with the hoped-for incredulity and enthusiasm, and it was decided to present the opera again a month later. Far more important, Bain—evidently having concluded that the opera's promotional potential was more or less unlimited, and that it could indeed become the School's signature offering, the main item for the store window—determined to make *Parsifal* an annual Lenten event. (The suggestion that he do so is attributed to Elsie Sweeney of nearby Columbus, a fine amateur pianist who had studied with Josef Lhévinne and with faculty members of the School, and who, as I noted earlier, became one of its most important financial supporters.)

The wisdom of this decision was confirmed the following year, when Cecil Smith, the editor of *Musical America* and music editor of *The New Republic,* wrote about the 1950 production of *Parsifal* in the latter journal. Like other observers, Smith said, he had been skeptical when Bain first announced that the School would mount *Parsifal:* "It sounded suspiciously like a bid for publicity rather than an honest artistic enterprise." (Of course it was both.) Wagner's last opera requires a level of skill "which even a professional company like the Metropolitan achieves only occasionally." But at Bloomington in that second year of *Parsifal* and the third of Bain's deanship, Smith witnessed what was "beyond all comparison . . . the most remarkable operatic production I have seen in an American school." Busch and Hoffman held their student charges to "standards of first-rate performance":

> On the ample stage of the university auditorium . . . the visual aspects of the opera were considerably more satisfying than they are at the Metropolitan. Simply mounted, with only a few token suggestions of realism, the scenes were given illusion by expert, appropriate, and flexible lighting and by continuous ensemble acting that spared us the traditional semaphoric gestures and pseudo-spiritual deadpan delivery. The devotional qualities of the first and third acts were humanized to a degree I had not supposed possible. . . .
>
> The adequacy of the vocalism was one of the chief surprises of this grassroots *Parsifal.* Not only was the singing unexceptionable in style; the voices were well trained for operatic projection, and nearly everyone sang with real expressiveness. . . . The whole time, Hoffman's student orchestra maintained an excellent balance with the voices, and played eloquently, zealously—and in tune.
>
> The audience was deeply moved by the genuineness of the occasion, and so was I. . . . [The production] is a distinguished achievement.

The following year, both *Time* and *Newsweek* sent reviewers to Bloomington for *Parsifal,* and published highly favorable accounts. The 1952 production was praised highly in *Opera News,* which stressed the professionalism of Hoffman's orchestra and the "well-trained and talented singers" directed by Busch. Hoffman's translation of the libretto was "completely convincing," and in general "viewers from other parts of the country, as well as from Europe, felt that the performance not only reached a considerable level of skill, but showed a real understanding of Wagner's art. The large auditorium was filled to capacity with an audience that was deeply moved and impressed by what it saw and heard." Spreading the fame of the 1953 production to a national popular audience, a photojournalism piece in *Life* noted that the production had "majestic settings and dynamic staging which beat hands down the *Parsifal* given by New York's Metropolitan."

By 1950, then, and indeed to a considerable extent even as early as 1949, the School's opera program had already achieved much of its current distinction. In great part, this astonishingly rapid flowering is attributable to the fact that the historical moment was uniquely favorable to the development of a collegiate opera program: it was largely owing to the rich supply of mature student voices, unequaled before or since, that the Indiana program "shot up," as Bain later put it, "just like that"; and the rising tide of émigré European musicians, including many who had worked in opera, crested in the same postwar years. Opera programs were, in fact, springing up all over the country. But no other program achieved the startling rise of that at Indiana, and the difference must be attributed primarily to Bain: to the fact that he got into the opera business a little sooner than many of his counterparts and, more important, drove the development of it with unmatched clarity of vision, sureness of touch, and ambition—in all of which he was abetted, and sometimes led, by his key appointee, Hoffman.

For the rest of the Bain era, it was essentially only the *scale* of the opera program that changed. In support of this claim, one can cite a draft brochure on the Opera Department—written, evidently, in the summer of 1949—in which the essential features and the rationale of the program as it exists even today are spelled out with remarkable completeness.

The brochure is prefaced by an overview of the School as a whole, one that makes clear that the niche that Bain wanted Indiana to fill was already sharply delineated. The School was "attempting to furnish" the "most extensive course offerings . . . and musical experiences . . . for . . . pre-professional training" of any school in the country; its students were afforded "an excellent opportunity for performing music in large musical organizations" and "for participation in the performance of great music." In this context, the Opera Department could be seen as "a natural outgrowth of the aims and ideals" of the School as a whole, in that it furnished "complete facilities for the training of singers, conductors, stage directors, coaches etc. for a professional career." In its production style, the Department's aim was to take "a fresh and modern approach. . . . Special emphasis is given to the integration of musical and dramatic expression": the School trained "singing actors who behave like human beings on the stage rather than like automatons. Meaningless 'operatic' gesticulations are replaced by natural poise and grace." (In this respect, the youthfulness of the singers—who were, after all, usually portraying youthful people, especially lovers—was a great advantage.) The fact that productions were presented in English was explained in terms of the Department's "fresh and modern" approach. America was, the brochure noted, the only place where opera was not normally presented in the language of the audience (this was true); the only way to make it popular with large American audiences was to present it in intelligible English translations—a perfectly sensible argument in the days before projected translations. The physical aspects of production were also in line with modern trends, eschewing the stereotypically operatic. Sets, lighting, and costumes were

> governed by the musical and dramatic character of the particular work. Their functions are to create the appropriate atmosphere and to *serve* the action in coordination with all the other elements . . . of [the] opera. . . . the Opera Department has successfully experimented with simple and somewhat stylized sets. Three-dimensional units, mobile and versatile, combined with effective lighting, have proved more efficient and dramatic than many a lavish set in traditional operatic productions.

In sum, the program aimed to offer, in all aspects of opera and in the most up-to-date way, "a training functioning with professional performance standards. Indiana University believes that it offers a unique opportunity in this respect."

Clearly Wells had chosen Bain in the expectation that he would create at Indiana the same kind of opera program that he had developed at North Texas. By the time Wells set out to look for a new Dean, after all, it was apparent that Indiana was in several ways particularly well suited to develop a program in this field. As Sanders had pointed out, in the Auditorium the University had an enviable facility for the presentation of opera; it had a well-known operatic soprano on faculty; and it had, through the Met visits, a conspicuous association with opera and a local and regional audience that had been trained up to it.

Nonetheless, Bain's superiors were initially leery of his evident intention to move strongly into the expensive business of operatic production. Even after the success of the Weill premiere, Joseph Franklin was sufficiently perturbed at having heard Bain mention his plans for developing an opera program that in October 1948 he wrote the Dean a rather formal note cautioning him not to proceed in this direction without explicit authorization from Wells: "I am sure you are aware of the various financial arrangements that seem to be involved with such a course, but I do feel it important that we have an early meeting with President Wells before you commit the University to any definite program that there might be some danger of lack of financial ability to carry out." But when the public success of the first *Parsifal* performance was added to that of the Weill production and the other early ones, resistance dissipated, and the School was, as Bain said, "assured . . . of continued financial support" for staffing the Opera Theater—and this despite the fact that *Parsifal* had been a substantial money-loser. In view of the relatively high cost of the production, it had been decided to charge admission. (The decision established a precedent honored to this day, when, apart from certain Summer Festival events, the operas are the only School of Music events to which admission is charged.) But the box office receipts of $2,500 were considerably exceeded by the production costs of $7,000. (Thus the first *Parsifal* production established another precedent still in effect: that the Opera Theater runs at a deficit, which has been covered by the University administration, presumably in recognition of the enormous promotional value of the program for the University as a whole.)

At the same time that the acclaim of the early productions made the opera program more attractive to Bain's superiors in the University, it made the program known, and attractive, to prospective faculty and students. Recognizing the opportunity afforded by this combination of circumstances, Bain moved rapidly to consolidate the position. In the fall of 1949, Hans Busch was appointed to a regular position as Associate Professor (though he served on a part-time basis until 1966); and the mezzo-contralto Anna Kaskas, a member of the Met company, was appointed as Assistant Professor to replace Josephine Antoine. At North Texas, Bain had worked with Kaskas in a Houston production of Bach's B-minor Mass. The Met soprano Agnes Davis had also been a soloist in that production, and in 1950 Bain appointed her as Assistant Professor. In 1949, Helmuth Wolfes was appointed as opera coach. (Previously Hoffman had, in addition to everything else, done most of the coaching.) Wolfes was not reappointed the following year, and was replaced, on the recommendation of Kaskas and Davis, by Archie Black, a professional accompanist to concert singers.

Early on, Bain's superiors had hoped that his opera program would be able to share production resources with the Department of Speech (which included theater), and Vice President Briscoe had directed him to talk with Lee Norvelle, the head of that department. But, though the two units did collaborate in a 1949–50 production of *The Merry Widow,* Norvelle "very courteously indicated" (as Bain later put it) "that not a saw, hammer, nail, piece of wood, or a foot of floor space for the preparation of scenery for opera could be made available and that their own program of theater productions consumed all of their working space and full use of their equipment." In retrospect, Bain regarded this as "one of the most fortunate decisions to be made for music and opera at Indiana University, for it meant that it was necessary for the School to find its own theater, its own work spaces, the equipment for the designing, painting and construction of scenery and the designing, construction and storage of costumes." This necessity figured in the modified plans for East Hall; it also led Bain to begin, by 1949, to recruit technical staff for the opera program. In the fall of that year, Walter S. Russell was appointed as the first of a series of Technical Directors for the Opera Theater.

Little more than a month earlier, Ross Allen had appeared on campus.

Recently discharged from the army, Allen, who held a bachelor's degree from a teachers college in Missouri, was looking for a place to do graduate work. Here the power of *Parsifal* as a recruiting tool is evident. Allen had heard about "a legendary performance that seemed absolutely unthinkable. . . . I had heard that there was here in southern Indiana a performance of this work that hadn't been heard . . . except in a few places that you could count on the fingers of one hand." He came to talk to Bain around the beginning of August, but the Dean was in Chicago for the second year's Grant Park performances. So Allen went instead to a rehearsal of *The Merry Widow.* The first Parsifal, Guy Owen Baker, was Prince Danilo; and the flower maidens had metamorphosed into can-can girls. The production struck Allen as "amazingly good." He decided to enroll in the School, and in the first production in East Hall—March 2–4, 1950, *La Bohème*—he is listed as Chief Property Man. He intended to get a doctorate in musicology and leave, but he found himself staying on; in 1952, he was stage director for a production of two chamber operas composed by students; and in 1953 he was appointed to the faculty as Stage Director and Instructor in Music, thus becoming the second director to hold a regular faculty position at the School.

In these early years of the Opera Theater, there was no formal committee for repertory or casting. Both matters were left primarily to the conductor and director, advised by the voice teachers and by Bain, who kept close tabs on the whole operation and obviously could have his way whenever he chose to. Indeed he exercised tight control over the opera program throughout his deanship and, as he told Wolford, regarded his willingness to exercise his authority as key to the program's success. Whereas at another school the head of the voice department, wanting to stage an opera, might have trouble securing the cooperation of the orchestra conductor, Bain could and did say simply, "We are going to do this": "See, . . . I don't come to you and say, 'Will you be willing to let us do this?' I'd say, 'Plan on accompanying the opera on such and such a time, and the number of rehearsals necessary to get it done.' . . . The basic thing is that I had control. . . . That's why it went."

As the number of good voice students increased, the practice of double-casting—that is, having partly or entirely different casts for different performances of a work—became standard. Since the quality of the production was Bain's overriding concern, he also felt free (as he did throughout his tenure) to cast faculty members in roles to which he thought no available student could do full justice. In accordance with operatic tradition—and often as a way of scouting potential appointees—guest professionals were frequently engaged to assist in staging individual productions. Thus for the spring 1951 production of *Rigoletto* (the School's inaugural Verdi), for the first time a professional—H. M. Crayon of the Met and the NBC Television Opera Theater—was engaged to design the scenery; Bain was highly satisfied with the results.

Bain saw to it that the repertory continued to mix standard operatic fare, light opera or musical comedy, and the premieres that would gain the attention of the press and those interested in being associated with a cutting-edge opera theater. (Busch was also keen to stage premieres.) Thus it was, as Bain later said, "in keeping with the general desire to attract the attention of the press, and the musical world," that he scheduled for May 1950 two more world premieres: *The Veil,* a one-act opera (a gothic tale of tragic love in a nineteenth-century madhouse) by Bernard Rogers of the Eastman faculty, and *The Jumping Frog of Calaveras County,* a comic work (based on Mark Twain's tall tale) by Lukas Foss. (In the first of its ventures into televised opera, the School mounted a very cramped broadcast performance of Foss's work from the local station.) Indeed the double bill did attract attention. Virgil Thomson, in his capacity as music critic of the *New York Herald Tribune,* attended rehearsals and the opening performance and was impressed both by the works and by the "excellent Indiana productions." The event was also reviewed, twice, in *Musical America,* by Cecil Smith and by Paul Nettl, as well as in the *St. Louis Post-Dispatch,* the *Louisville Courier-Journal,* and papers nearer to home. In February 1952, the School mounted another double bill, the world premiere of *A Parfait for Irene* by Walter Kaufmann (who later joined the faculty) and the first stage performance of an opera that was to become extremely popular on television (for which it had been written and produced the previous Christmas Eve), Gian Carlo Menotti's *Amahl and the Night Visitors.* As Corbin Patrick said in the *Indianapolis Star,* the School was developing a reputation as "a main experimental station in the world of opera."

By 1949–50, it had become School policy to restrict the presentation of opera to the regular academic year and devote the summer to musical comedy. That summer, the extremely ambitious program of musicals comprised Romberg's *The New Moon,* Friml's *The Firefly,* and Weill's *Street Scene.* (By 1957 it was recognized that this rigid division of activities gave summer students only a very limited taste of lyric theater, and the School began mounting an opera each summer along with the lighter fare.)

By 1951, the only element missing from the comprehensive, self-sufficient opera program that Bain envisaged was ballet. He had little familiarity with dance, and it was and is difficult to build a good ballet program in a university setting, simply because the most talented dancers are normally trained, from an early age, in the residential ballet schools. But Hoffman had pointed out to Bain early on that operatic production on the grand scale they had in mind would frequently involve ballet, and for this reason had urged him to create a ballet department. In retrospect,

Bain wished he had acted on this advice at the time, but he did not; so *Parsifal* had to find its flower maiden dancers in Physical Education, and in general the element of dance in the School's operas was conspicuously inferior to the other components. Bain soon came round to thinking he should hire a dance teacher, but it was not until 1951 that he found the money to do so—money for which he thanked Mary Maurer, the only female member of the Board of Trustees, who told her colleagues and members of the University administration that this weakness in the opera program must be addressed. Having secured the money, Bain made his first move toward a ballet department by appointing Marguerite de Anguera, who ran a ballet school in Indianapolis, to a part-time position at Indiana.

There was, across the campus, general approbation of the opera program and of other developments in Music that improved the quality of local life. The appointment of the Berkshire Quartet, whose contract stipulated six Bloomington concerts each year, was particularly well received. Still, the rapid expansion and transformation of the School occasioned considerable alarm and opposition. On the part of the administrators of other academic units, opposition appears to have stemmed mostly from a jealous concern about the growing prominence of the School within the University, and the implications of the increasing size and importance of Music for the allocation of limited University financial resources. According to Bain, such opposition centered in the College of Arts and Sciences, a circumstance that he attributed, fairly or not, to fear (entirely justified, as it turned out) "that the Music School was going to be the prominent thing in the University, that they would be left behind. I appointed the Berkshire Quartet the second year I was here, and they thought that was great: 'Now we'll hear some chamber music. . . . Oh yes, I'm fond of music.' But if it began to encroach on something *they* were doing . . ."

There was also, even at this late date, still opposition to the idea of music as an academic discipline, opposition that came to light especially when Bain set out, soon after arriving, to reinstate the degree of Doctor of Philosophy in Music. "I had a time getting that through," he told Wolford, "because there were an awful lot of diehards that looked at music and said, 'This isn't worthy, this is afternoon games.'" Still, in 1948 Bain succeeded in having the degree reinstated, with specializations in theory, musicology, and music education; he was also able to establish the degree of Doctor of Education in Music Education. Here as elsewhere in the early years, his success was attributable to the fact that Music had some important friends in other fields (not to mention its best friend, in the President's Office). Among these, Bain numbered especially Stith Thompson (once principal cellist in Merrill's orchestra), who was, at the time Bain applied for reinstatement of the doctorate, Dean of the Graduate School.

If Bain encountered opposition from other quarters of the University, he also met it, in these early years, in very substantial amounts within the School itself, and from both students and faculty. Though his innovations resulted in a rapid improvement in the quality and repute of a musical education at Indiana, the School's students were, as I indicated earlier, much less cognizant of these long-term gains than of their short-term pains. The ensemble requirement was (as it remains) burdensome, and its unpleasantness was increased by the fact that Bain, with a view to the common good, made it the rule that students were assigned not necessarily to the ensemble they preferred but to the one where they were most needed. Orchestra members, too, began to chafe at the requirement to play *Parsifal* every year. Such students frequently protested, reasonably enough, that these repeat performances wasted their time. Their complaint in fact brings to light a fundamental problem with Bain's theory of education, a conflict between its central purpose and one of the collective activities necessary to achieve that purpose: the education was supposed to be broadly professional; but devoting a large chunk of time each year to the same opera clearly did not tend to inculcate breadth. On the other hand, these repeat performances had enormous public-relations and advertising value, and good public relations and advertising were fundamentally important in attracting both financial support and first-rate students.

Students also grumbled about the requirement for attendance at concerts, on penalty—sternly enforced—of loss of academic credit; and in 1950 Bain instituted practice-room checks (the possibility of which he had mooted in his very first faculty meeting in 1947). Years later, Dorothy Collins was still bemused by this extreme example of the School *in loco parentis:* "He had a woman who checked every room that was supposed to have practice people in it, and every day of the world he got attendance reports. I couldn't believe that, and I saw her book; there was no question she did that." To be sure, practice-room checks had a long history in the School. In the Merrill regime there had been penalties for unexcused absences from practice, and in 1941 Sanders's faculty, having canceled the penalties in 1938 with evidently unsatisfactory results, instituted "drop-in checks." But the checking had apparently been discontinued by the time Bain arrived, and the return to this disused form of control provoked, as he recalled, "considerable resistance" on the part of the students, who were understandably unhappy at no longer being able to employ "their own judgments as to when and where to practice"; this was doubtless especially the case with the many veterans, who were grownups, often with families. In general, as it seemed to Bain, he had had "a rough time with the students; I don't think they liked me very much when I first came." But these were still the days before student power, and resistance was effectively limited to such gestures as sneaking out of recitals: early in 1949,

Bain briefed the Advisory Council on the report of "Miss Seagroatt, recital proctor," that "20 students left a student recital as soon as she turned her back, . . . after the first number."

More substantial resistance was offered by some of the faculty. For the most part, this resistance was located among those members whom Bain had inherited from Sanders, and he attributed it, in the main, to their disapproval of the greatly increased emphasis on performance. Retrospectively, though, he did acknowledge that some of the resistance might have been attributable not to the substance of the changes but to the pace he insisted on for their implementation: to his impatience and his expectation that changes should be accomplished "in record time." We may surmise, too, that his imperiousness offended faculty members, who might, after all, have been partial to democracy even if they had not grown personally accustomed to it with Sanders; and probably some members—and not just those directly affected—were offended by Bain's harsh treatment of members of whom he disapproved. Faculty in music education had an extra reason for discontent. Bain's emphasis on performance, and the fact that his early appointments did not include any in music education, suggested to them that, as Bain put it (without disputing the accuracy of the formulation), under the new regime music education "might occupy a secondary place and that the students majoring in that area might be considered as second class academic citizens."

According to Charles Webb, who doubtless had his information on the matter directly from his predecessor, as a result of this internal resistance Bain's early days at Indiana were as rough with the faculty as with the students. Some of the opposition he faced "seemingly was not very nice. So that it would have daunted a less formidable person." By 1950, Bain was ready to attempt to (as he put it) "bridge the gap" between himself and the disaffected faculty members by appointing one of the inherited faculty to a position as Assistant to the Dean; his reluctance to delegate, let alone cede, any of his authority was overcome not only by his desire to make a show of good will but also by the fact that it had become difficult for him to find time even for such choral conducting as he had reserved to himself after Krueger's arrival. The obvious choice for the Assistant job was the agreeable and generally popular Newell Long (who was also a member of the music education unit), and Bain offered him the position. Long held out for the title of Assistant Dean; if Bain were not satisfied with his performance in that role after one year, he would voluntarily resign the position. Bain accepted this proposal, though not happily.

From his point of view, the experiment proved disastrous. Far from dissipating the resistance, Long's deanship provided it with a clear center around which to coalesce. "All the faculty who had a problem came to *him,* not to me"; and Long began to represent himself as the leader of the "loyal opposition" (a phrase that, off the record, Bain regarded as merely a contemptible oxymoron).

In one of his earliest faculty meetings, Bain had stressed the importance of the faculty's presenting a unified front. "If at any time we have any occasion to differ with one another," he hoped that "we will present a solid front to the townspeople, faculty and students all the way through." Bain himself abided by this precept, and, for example, habitually eschewed criticism of his colleagues (including those he was on the point of firing) in his annual reports to the President. Even years later, in *The Bain Regime,* he went out of his way to avoid faulting Long's conduct as Assistant Dean: "It must be understood that at no time did Professor Long commit any acts of disloyalty or administrative unfriendliness." But this appears to have been a liberal construction, for what Long did do was pass on to Wells some sort of written critique of Bain's performance, which argued that he should not, for various reasons, be continued in the deanship. What the "loyal opposition" had not reckoned with, though, was the completeness of Wells's loyalty to Bain. For the President's response to this critique was to call Bain in, give him the critique, and tell him to get rid of Long. Bain couldn't really get rid of him, because he was tenured; nor is there any indication that he wanted to do so. What he did do was exercise his option to remove Long from the assistant deanship at the end of the first year—an outcome that he described in bland terms in his annual report: "The arrangement did not succeed and Mr. Long requested to be returned to a full-time teaching schedule."

Long was tenured, but some others were not, and the next year Bain provided his colleagues with a chilling object lesson in what that fact could mean. Not all the opposition to Bain came from the inherited faculty. One of his first bold moves had been to appoint Anis Fuleihan to the professorship of composition. Since Fuleihan was also a well-known pianist, and was more interested in and capable of teaching piano than composition, he began, as Bain later said, "to acquire the influence and reputation usually assigned to the principal teacher of piano." This influence was effective on Bain himself, who appointed several junior members to the piano faculty on Fuleihan's recommendation. The upshot was (at least as Bain saw it) that Fuleihan gathered "a small coterie" of pianists around him, a fact said to illustrate "the possibility of the developing of pockets of interest and blocks of voting power." *The Bain Regime* (from which these phrases are quoted) says no more about the coterie or how Bain acted to counter it; to me, decades later, he said only that he made Fuleihan "toe the line."

Other things being equal, perhaps he would have been willing to leave it at that: since he had (as the outcome of the recent insurrection had made even clearer) absolute control over the School, Bain could afford to tolerate faculty who did not approve of him. But he was also dissatisfied with Fuleihan's professional performance in the School. As early as his 1949–50 report to Wells, Bain had expressed his concern that the composers on faculty were not attracting the sizable numbers of talented composition students he hoped for: for this to happen, he suspected "that it will be finally necessary to bring to the campus a composer who is chiefly interested in composition and who is [a] distinguished active composer." (The only other composition teacher was Bernhard Heiden; though he later became well known, his reputation at that time was evidently not yet sufficient to draw in students.) Nor was Fuleihan entirely satisfactory in his *de facto* role as the principal teacher of piano. As Bain told Wolford, although Fuleihan was "an enormously gifted musician," "I did not consider him as great a pianist as I wanted for the head of the piano department."

In 1951 Fuleihan was awarded a Fulbright Research Fellowship for a year's study in Egypt. This was a signal honor for a member of the faculty, and both Bain and his superiors in the University administration were happy to have him accept the fellowship. Although Fuleihan was not tenured, Bain gave him firm assurances (or so Fuleihan later said, and why would he have accepted the award if this were not the case?) that his position was secure. He was, after all, a key member of the School's faculty, one of only seven full professors. Moreover, the University administration appeared to confirm the assurances by granting him a leave of absence, and he was duly listed in the School's official Bulletin as "Professor of Composition (on leave of absence, 1951–52)." Further, at some point during his leave, Fuleihan was asked by the government of Lebanon to serve as Director of the National Conservatory of Beirut for a few months after the termination of his Fulbright year: but Bain told him that he could not be spared for more than one year, and Fuleihan declined the offer. During his absence, he had carried on a bantering, friendly correspondence with Bain, even suggesting that he and Mary might like to share a house with him in Lebanon the coming summer.

Fuleihan was, then, understandably astonished to receive, on March 21, 1952, in Cairo, a letter from Bain informing him that he would not be reappointed for 1952–53. Bain's excuse lay in the fact that, as a result of the downturn in University enrollment that marked the end of the postwar boom, he had been required, like other heads of units, to cut 8 percent from his budget.

The injury to Fuleihan was considerably compounded, as he explained in letters of protest to Wells and Briscoe, by the timing of the notification. He had declined the position in Lebanon, and it was also too late to apply for a renewal of his Fulbright for a second year (which he might well have obtained); nor was he, several thousand miles from his adoptive country, favorably positioned to seek alternative employment in North America for the coming year. Moreover, the timing of Bain's letter did not clearly conform to the University's own rules for notification of non-renewal of appointment, which required that such notification be made not less than three months before the end of the final semester of the current contract. Bain's letter was dated March 15; the University calendar listed the end of the second semester as occurring on June 10. Bain later claimed that in his understanding the semester ended on Commencement day, June 16; but even with this interpretation Fuleihan did not receive the letter the required three months in advance. But these were only quibbles. As Bain's superiors, if not Bain himself, surely knew, standard American practice required a full year's notice of non-renewal for a person with several years' service in a regular position.

Wells, however, and with him Briscoe, conceded nothing to Fuleihan, not even a decent sympathy. The President's reply to Fuleihan's letter was drafted by his assistant, Peter Fraenkel, who showed it to Bain for his approval before mailing it. Curtly legalistic, the letter does not address the particulars of Fuleihan's case at all but rather takes the form of brief general remarks on the budgetary necessity of reducing staff and the fact that, by University policy, dismissals of non-tenured faculty can always be made "by the mere act of giving timely notice of the desire to terminate." The letter (which Bain deemed "excellent") might just as well be a form letter, with Fuleihan's name filling in the blank at the beginning. Briscoe's reply to Fuleihan is no lengthier, but at least it does address him as an individual, reminding him that he had signed a statement certifying that he had read the University's tenure policy and understood how it applied to his own position, and that it appeared "that Dean Bain has fulfilled the requirements of our policy in just the same manner that other deans have handled similar situations." (Fuleihan, having had before his initial appointment no experience of academe, was innocent of its ways; he claimed that Bain had assured him—orally—that tenure was a mere formality that would come in the fullness of time.) Indeed, only one officer of the University—Ralph Cleland, the Dean of the Graduate School—treated Fuleihan with candor and decent human feeling. At the end of the summer, Fuleihan instituted formal grievance proceedings. After a detailed investigation, a Board of Review found that he had not been given proper notice of non-renewal, and awarded him a year's salary as severance pay (to be reduced by the amount of any salary he might earn elsewhere in the 1952–53 academic year). To Wolford, Bain chortled over this outcome, for the money, incredibly, came not out of the Music School's budget but, with the approval of the University Librarian (whose wife had studied with Fuleihan), out of the library budget. In 1953, Fuleihan did assume the leadership of the Beirut Conservatory, where he remained for seven years before returning to the United States.

The shameful treatment of Fuleihan is instructive in showing both how far Bain would go to get what he wanted (not that there is any reason to think he would not have gone farther still) and how far Herman Wells would go to give his Dean "anything he wants." Yet it is also instructive in a third way. For there is no question that Bain's ruthlessness and Wells's unconditional support were, in this instance as in others, of net benefit to the School: inexcusable in terms of personal morality, the shabby treatment of Fuleihan conformed perfectly to the "higher morality" of *raison d'état.* Room having been made on the piano faculty by the death of Associate Professor Adolph Weiser in October and the departure of two of the junior piano faculty Bain identifies as members of Fuleihan's coterie, the Dean was able to appoint Sidney Foster, in the second semester, as Resident Concert Pianist. It seems likely that the acquisition of Foster, and an early favorable impression of him as a faculty member, were what prompted Bain's sudden move to dismiss Fuleihan. Though he was clearly not satisfied with his composer-pianist, Bain had just as clearly expected (even demanded) to have him back on faculty after a single year abroad; but Foster, a well-known young concertizing artist—he had been, in 1940, the first winner of the Leventritt Award—who had been teaching at Florida State University, could evidently replace him in the role of primary piano teacher. Foster turned out to be a superb appointee. Despite his temporary-sounding initial title, he stayed on to become Professor of Piano (eventually Distinguished Professor, a title the University bestows on very few) and in fact became one of the mainstays of the School, exerting the drawing power both for students and for other piano faculty that Fuleihan had lacked, and proving to be a master teacher. As for the professorship in composition, Bain left it vacant. He did not appoint another composer until the second semester of the 1956–57 academic year, when Walter Kaufmann joined the faculty—but as Lecturer in Music Literature.

Looking back over his deanship in the act of writing its history, Bain saw 1951–52 as the watershed, and this assessment was surely accurate. At the beginning of that year, the School had 483 undergraduate and graduate students (not counting several students in the Bachelor of Arts in Music program), so that it had more or less reached the enrollment of 500 that Bain often cited, in these early years, as his target. The regular faculty now numbered just over fifty, and they were supplemented by sixty-nine graduate and six undergraduate Assistants. The goal of having an individual instructor for each orchestral instrument was also attained that year, by the appointment of a percussionist, Richard Johnson—who, with a Bachelor of Arts from Indiana and a diploma from the Paris Conservatory, was the first African-American appointed to the faculty of the School and to that of the University as a whole. (By one report, Johnson was hired only at the insistence of Ernst Hoffman.) The orchestral and operatic programs were flourishing, and, thanks especially to the latter, the School had achieved a reputation as one of the most innovative and intriguing of American music schools. Bain's own summary of the School's condition by the end of his fifth year as Dean was that it had "reached a plateau of activity": its future growth would take place "within the framework of already established educational patterns." This formulation is accurate in the sense that by 1952 the School had been committed to occupying the particular niche that Bain had chosen for it: Indiana University was to have (as he had meant North Texas to have) the *big* music school, the supermarket or department store among schools, offering programs in every branch of the art and showcasing especially the performance of those large-scale works that only a very large school could effectively mount. Yet the term "plateau" is also misleading, for there was no pause, no leveling off, in 1952 in the development of the School. For the remaining twenty-one years of his deanship, Bain worked continuously on improving the quality (and, until the last years, on increasing the quantity) of the School's faculty and students and on expanding the range of its activities in every conceivable way.

By the end of the first five years, internal resistance to him had faded away, for several reasons. First, as the fates of the "loyal opposition" and Fuleihan's "coterie" convincingly showed, it was both futile and dangerous. Second, resistance was inevitably eroded by the rapid increase in the quality and reputation of the School, which was obviously owed to Bain and his policies—and which of course rendered even stronger the support he enjoyed from the central administration. And finally, by this time there were few or no students left who remembered the old, easier days, and the faculty was dominated by people whom Bain had hired, and who had come precisely because they were enticed by his vision of the School's development: in the summer of 1952, there were only seventeen faculty members remaining from the Sanders era.

A vivid picture of the School in this period, from the special standpoint of one of the dozen or so black students then enrolled in it, was given me by David Baker. Having graduated from Crispus Attucks High School in Indianapolis—an inner-city school famous for producing nationally known basketball players and jazz musicians—Baker matriculated at the University in 1949, two years after Bain's arrival. Small-town southern Indiana was at that time still essentially an apartheid society. "You couldn't get a haircut; you sat in the balcony of the movie theaters." The University had a scattering of black students, but it too was generally segregated. There were no dormitories for blacks, and "we had special places we had to sit in the eating halls." In sharp contrast, music-making in the School was thoroughly integrated: blacks with whites and students with faculty (and all, in the earliest Bain days, with a few players from outside). Baker, a brilliant and staggeringly creative man who joined the faculty of the School a dozen years after leaving it with a master's degree in 1954, remembers the early Bain years with considerable fondness. The classes were dispersed (as we shall see) into various buildings, "so we were fragmented in that way, but we were solidified in a lot of other ways, simply because . . . when you have so few students and so few faculty, everybody knows everybody, and there's a kind of camaraderie that inevitably does exist." His own main musical interest, jazz, did *not* exist in the School: "you didn't play jazz in the practice rooms." But in the orchestra "we played opera, we played ballet, we played whatever. . . . it was a good situation musically because there was a lot going on. . . . we had a very good conductor in Ernst Hoffman." And in sum, "we got a very, very good education."

The Bain Years

II. Building the Mega-School

Through nearly all of his tenure, Bain was steadily intent on increasing the School's enrollment—a large student body (and, he evidently thought, the larger the better) being the prime requisite for implementing his vision. In a 1948 faculty meeting, he had enunciated to his colleagues a profound truth of academic administration: "you have," the minutes record him saying, "only what you create and that's all." Nothing comes to those who merely wait. In the matter of enrollment, the implication of this doctrine was that he and his associates should constantly do everything in their power to attract more students.

The key to success in the endeavor lay, Bain knew, in advertising and public relations, and throughout his deanship he employed a variety of methods to bring the School to favorable attention. In his early days in Bloomington, he was pleased to learn that the University had a "field man" for music (Lawrence Kingsbury) making the rounds of the high schools, and he was of course happy to continue the Music School's long tradition of reaching out to high school students by hosting a variety of clinics and contests for them, as well as workshops for their teachers. He was also eager to raise the public profile of his faculty. As I noted earlier, he urged all members of the faculty to join professional organizations, and to attend such affairs as the annual meeting of the Indiana Music Educators Association, where they could cultivate the elementary and secondary school music teachers upon whose "good will and friendship" the recruitment of students heavily depended. Applied-music faculty were strongly encouraged to perform more, especially off-campus. In a December 1947 meeting of the Advisory Council, Bain noted that Juilliard had a booking officer; later that month, in his strategic memo to Briscoe, he recommended that Indiana also appoint such an officer, and committed the School to paying half the salary for the position. In 1949, Herbert Petrie became the University's first Manager of Musical Organizations (latterly "Musical Attractions"), a position subsequently occupied by many others, including, in the early 1960s, the young Charles Webb.

Radio was another important vehicle for showing what the School's faculty (and students) could do. In his first semester at Indiana, Bain was able to have the occasional broadcasts of School performances expanded into a weekly series, "Music from Indiana." In early 1952, a series of thirteen programs from the School was carried on forty-seven stations, in Louisville and Cincinnati as well as throughout Indiana; later that year, the faculty acceded to the request of the University's Director of Radio and Television Communications that the School produce five fifteen-minute programs each week; and by the mid-1950s it was also offering weekly programs on the campus television station.

Furthermore, like Merrill, Bain was convinced of the value for the School of traditional paper advertising. Also in his first semester at Indiana, he proposed that the School produce a set of six yearly bulletins, two for alumni, two "pictorial" ones for high schools, and two that would include general information and course descriptions: "Constant advertising," he explained, "is the purpose of these." The following year he announced plans to send bound copies of the previous year's recital programs "to the music schools over the country," and to send 4,200 postcards to patrons of the Auditorium Series, advertising the School's programs for the current year. In 1949 he took out a full-page advertisement in *Musical America,* which cost all faculty members 2.5 percent of a month's salary. The purpose of the advertisement, as he told its sponsors, was "to attract undergraduate material." Again like Merrill, Bain was fond of characterizing the School as a business—in his case, a manufacturing concern that processed raw materials into a salable product. (Thus the oft-heard claim that the School is a "factory" is perfectly consistent with the intentions of its great entrepreneur.)

Once recruited, the students themselves were obliged—like it or not—to do their part to recruit their successors and raise the profile of the School, by participating in outside performances. As Bain had said in his first faculty meeting, the large student ensembles were of the utmost importance in public relations: it was from hearing these groups that the public would "award to us a fine reputation." Accordingly, he began forthwith not only to cultivate opportunities for one-time performances but to develop (as he had at North Texas) an extensive program of tours. The orchestra, he told his colleagues in November 1948, "ought to be on tour for one week each semester, in order to interest the type of player we need here." Immediately upon arriving, he had taken personal charge of the mixed-voice University Singers, which he intended to make "the prime concert touring organization" of the School, to represent it "as ambassadors in public relations and recruitment." Like the orchestra, the group did make a number of tours—including a twenty-performance one as early as 1948—but Bain met a good deal of resistance from its members, who, as he grumpily recorded in *The Bain Regime,* appeared to have "more interest in making music in Bloomington than under the inconvenient circumstances of missing classes and having to make up studies." So the group did not in fact play the role he had planned for it. Not everything that had worked at North Texas worked at Indiana: it was because he had had such success in touring his singers in Texas that Bain had placed such high hopes in the Indiana group. He had also had great success at North Texas with touring opera productions. But though he announced to his Indiana faculty in October 1948 that an opera tour was in the works, he drew back, and in fact he did not manage to take any operas on the road during his early years in Bloomington.

Indeed the most successful touring groups were—as had always been the case—those whose stock-in-trade was popular rather than classical. Bain had small personal interest in this kind of music, but he had no trouble recognizing the key role that it could play in the School's public relations. As he pointed out to Wolford in 1983 (that is, at a time when the School was, as it is now, mounting more performances of classical music than any other music school in North America), the Marching Hundred "will play to more people in one season at the home games here than all of the concerts we do in a whole year. . . . it's a different kind of music, . . . but . . . if you're talking about representation to the general public, you can't forget the marching bands." The University had of course long been represented by the Marching Hundred, and even longer by the Glee Club. But the latter organization had ceased regular touring in 1940, and at the time of Bain's arrival the Indiana university that was making hay with its popular music ensembles was rival Purdue. "Many people think Purdue has a Music School and I.U. has not," Bain told his Advisory Council in November 1948, "because they take whatever groups they have out for performance"; in particular the Purdue Glee Club was an enormous public-relations engine. To meet this challenge, Bain in 1950 commissioned George Krueger to re-create the Men's Concert Choir as the Singing Hoosiers, thus launching what Bain liked to refer to as the School's "show business." In 1952, he asked a new member of the choral faculty, Eugene Bayless, to establish a female group, the Belles of Indiana. Both groups succeeded, and the Belles succeeded wildly: within a year it was the most-booked of the University ensembles, with thirty-four off-campus appearances in 1953–54. In the same year, the Singing Hoosiers made thirteen off-campus appearances, as did the Symphony Band, which also made six joint appearances with the Marching Hundred. All in all, student soloists and ensembles performed off-campus 147 times that year (compared to fourteen off-campus performances by faculty members).

Within the next few years, the School's tours became both a national operation and, thanks especially to the USO, which booked tours to

American military installations abroad, an international one. Moreover, the School's major classical ensembles began to do substantial touring, if scarcely on the scale of the popular music groups. In 1954–55, the University Singers, together with the orchestra (which had since 1950 been dubbed the Indiana University Philharmonic Orchestra), made both a two-week domestic tour, which included an appearance at Carnegie Hall, and a two-week tour of American bases in Japan and Korea. The following year, the Belles made their own Far Eastern tour, of two *months'* duration. In the next few years, the same path was traced by the Singing Hoosiers, supplemented by the Hoosier Queens (originally a quartet; from this start, the Singing Hoosiers evolved into a mixed choir); and both that group and the Belles made USO-sponsored excursions to Europe.

In time, Bain was also able to realize his ambition of touring the School's operatic productions. Most of these tours were fairly modest, in-state affairs. Beginning in 1955, it became customary to tour the summer musicals to the Ohio River city of Evansville. There were numerous performances in Indianapolis; for several years, starting in December 1961, the Opera Theater took nearly all of its productions (other than *Parsifal*) for performances at an Indianapolis high school. There were occasional presentations elsewhere in the state, especially at the University's branch campuses and at Purdue. A few of the School's productions were also exposed to more distant audiences. The earlier of the two most important out-of-state presentations occurred in April 1956, when *Parsifal* was performed at the annual meeting of the Music Educators National Association in St. Louis. The reviewer for the *Post-Dispatch* judged the performance excellent "by any standard": "imaginatively staged, well sung, effective in its decor and carried through on a steadily sustained dramatic line," and supported by "a finely disciplined orchestra." Far better (from a public-relations point of view), a small part of the performance—about eight minutes—was televised nationally by NBC. The event as a whole was, of course, extremely gratifying to Bain and his colleagues.

Eight years later, in the summer of 1964, the School mounted *Turandot* at the New York World's Fair, where it was (in consequence of a suggestion Bain had made to the Governor) the official entry of the State of Indiana. In the background of this venture was a series of bold recent experiments in offering an especially grand opera each summer. It may be recalled that in 1957 the policy of restricting the summer operatic fare to light opera and Broadway musicals had been abandoned. By 1961 Bain and his colleagues in the Opera Theater felt ready to go to the opposite extreme, mounting *The Mastersingers of Nuremberg*. The following summer the Theater presented another Wagner opera, *The Flying Dutchman*. (Ross Allen says the School's ambitious programming was sometimes a subject of mirth in New York operatic circles. "They'd say, 'Well, I hear you are going to do *Götterdämmerung* this week, ha ha ha.' Make us feel like such fools, you know. But this never bothered Bain. He'd say, 'If they can do better, let 'em.'")

For the summer of 1963 it was decided to create a different—in scenic terms, even bolder—spectacle, by presenting *Aida* in the University's football stadium. The cast of nearly 400 included a 143-voice chorus and 179 extras (among them, in the final performance, Bain, garbed as a slave). The key figure in this production was the scenic designer Mario Cristini (a permanent faculty member since 1961), who had staged similar spectacles at the Baths of Caracalla in Rome and the Arena in Verona. The audience for the four presentations totaled about 14,000; according to Bain, they came from ten states.

The success of this production prompted the even larger one of *Turandot,* which was presented four times in the stadium and twice in the Singer Bowl at the World's Fair, where it supposedly drew the largest crowds ever to see opera in New York. Margaret Harshaw (on faculty since 1962) played the cruel princess. The first day at the fair was a great success, though the roar of the airplanes taking off from nearby LaGuardia did not help; the second day's performance was rained out halfway through. Rain or not, the World's Fair appearance was a huge public-relations coup. It was complemented, with the cognoscenti, by one that had shortly preceded it: *Musical America* had made "Music at Indiana U." its cover story for April.

The success of the School's tours primarily depended on the caliber of the student performers' musicianship; and this in turn depended on the caliber of the instruction they received at the School. For this and other reasons, the ultimate key to the steady increase in enrollment that Bain wanted lay (after the postwar boom ended in the early 1950s) in the quality of the faculty. Moreover, increasing the number of *excellent* students—the "cream"—depended more directly on the quality and reputation of the faculty, for these were especially the students who, as he had put it to Briscoe in 1947, "are wise enough to want to study with someone who has proved that he or she can develop excellent performers." Faculty recruitment was thus the most important of Bain's tasks—as, indeed, it is for any academic administrator, except in those periods when money is too scarce to allow it. As we have seen, the automatically burgeoning enrollments of the postwar years, which necessitated a rapid enlargement of faculties everywhere, enabled him to make a flying start in recruitment; and then the process became self-sustaining, as the growing reputation of the School led to further increased enrollment, which in turn led to still more additional faculty positions.

Bain was, then, constantly occupied with faculty recruitment and with the associated tasks of retaining those faculty members who performed to his satisfaction and weeding out those who did not—or, when their tenured status prevented his dismissing them, making their lives as uncomfortable as possible in the hope of driving them to resign. Faculty management (as we may designate this congeries of tasks) is both the area of leadership in which he was most brilliantly successful and, as the Fuleihan case suggests, the one in which his pattern of action was most disturbing. When he arrived in Bloomington, the School had a faculty middling in both size and distinction; when he left the deanship in 1973, the School had the largest music faculty in the world and surely the most distinguished. The costs of building this monumental edifice had included a good deal of human misery, inflicted by practices on the part of the Dean that were callous and even cruel; but though his cruelty was perhaps sometimes gratuitous—answering more to Bain's internal needs than to the real needs of the School—in general there is no doubt that, as I have said of the Fuleihan affair, his practices made perfect sense in terms of *raison d'état.*

To a remarkable degree, Bain kept the entire process of faculty recruitment in his own hands. This was less true toward the end of his tenure, by which time the faculty was so good, and so huge, and embraced so many diverse specialties, that he made it his standard practice, as he put it, to leave it to the individual departments to do "the preliminary work in the searching and screening" of prospective faculty in their fields. But even as late as 1968, Bain, in response to the growing faculty ambition for self-government that was a facet of the revolutionary fervor of the times, put on record his determination to continue to reserve to himself all appointments decisions. Noting that "the extent of rights and responsibilities of the faculty in identification, selection, recommendation, appointment, and retention of new faculty members has recently been questioned," the Dean reminded his colleagues that the policy of having the "administration" take "primary responsibility in these matters is the result of many years['] experience. Never has a department of the School of Music had the right to choose, appoint, or dismiss one of its faculty members." He justified this policy in terms of efficient division of labor. Like Menenius Agrippa lecturing the uppish plebs, he explained that the body politic functioned best when all its members stuck to their assigned tasks: "the faculty is, and should be, primarily concerned with their professional activities—teaching, writing, and performing." By assuming responsibility for recruitment, he was "relieving the faculty of a time-consuming chore that we feel can best be handled by the administration. While we are all fellow faculty members, we do not all share the same duties."

But he also had another reason, which he politely declined to mention, for keeping recruitment in his own hands: early on, bitter experience had convinced him that faculty members in a particular field could not be trusted to recommend the best people for appointment in it. When, as he told Wolford, he asked someone, "Now, who . . . would you suggest?" the respondent "never came up with the top person. . . . And that's the reason why we have some . . . mediocre people" (hired, presumably, before Bain learned his lesson). The root of the problem lay in the fact that "people are not going to try to find somebody who is superior to them in reputation or performance. . . . that's just human nature." But if the faculty is continuously to improve, it is obviously necessary that new appointees *be* superior to those already on staff. To avoid, then, ending up "with a whole lot of persons you fundamentally don't want," Bain thought he must do "a lot of the spadework" himself.

There was, of course, much less of a problem for entry-level appointees than for more senior ones: it was presumably easier to get disinterested advice about them (since they would be less likely to be perceived as threats); and in any case mistakes at the entry level were easily remedied by dismissal. Moreover, Bain had, throughout his deanship, good sources of entry-level appointees of whom he had personal knowledge, first from North Texas and then from Indiana. To cite the prime example of those in the former category, in 1949 he appointed Ralph Daniel as Assistant Professor of Musicology. Daniel, a brilliant student who had completed a series of degrees at North Texas during Bain's tenure there, had proceeded to Harvard for further studies. (He completed his doctorate in 1955.) Daniel became a key member of Bain's faculty, entrusted with most of the responsibility for developing the School's doctoral program in academic music. Early on, too, Bain firmly established a policy—for which the School became and remains notorious—of appointing its own Graduate Assistants to a great many of its entry-level positions. He would, as Mary Wennerstrom recalls, "just take people who seemed to be doing a good job and . . . say, 'well, you'll be on the faculty.'" In *Regime,* Bain says that these appointees had "their undergraduate and master's degree training at other institutions," as if this had been his general requirement; but many of them had only their undergraduate training elsewhere, and some of them —like Wennerstrom—had all their degrees from Indiana. "Inbreeding," as it's called, is universally regarded by academics as an unhealthful appointments practice; but in fact the School was greatly strengthened by a number of these appointments (such as that of Wennerstrom—and that of Charles Webb), which suggests that Bain generally made good, objective judgments in this area. He argued with some plausibility that, after all, one knew much more about one's own graduate students, who could be observed over a considerable period of time, than about candidates from other schools, whom one knew, as a rule, only from a review of their dossiers and the acquaintance afforded by the brief campus visit that was part of the recruitment process.

In choosing candidates for more senior appointments—which were, obviously, far more important than those at the entry level—Bain consulted widely. He may not have generally *trusted* his faculty's advice, but he nonetheless *solicited* it (though only at his pleasure), both on the matter of what fields he should make appointments in and for names of possible candidates. Menahem Pressler remembers that the Dean "had a little black book, and if someone on the faculty would mention another name he would write it in that," and sometimes "he would hear it a second time mentioned, and slowly he would make his decision." On performers, he also consulted well-regarded music critics for newspapers in the major cities. And during the Met's annual visits, as well as on trips to hear opera in New York, he became, as he put it, "a hunter for voice teachers and opera production personnel." The Met visits, especially, afforded "much opportunity to converse with the singers, the orchestral players, and the backstage personnel, as well as the Metropolitan administration."

Once having decided on a candidate, Bain proceeded to the courtship stage; and though he was not, in the early years, recruiting for a famous school, he had from the beginning certain advantages. First, his operation was streamlined (like his predecessors') by his near-autonomy: he involved his colleagues in recruiting only as much as he chose to, and as the dean of a faculty—and, moreover, the dean of all deans who had the most direct link to Wells, and his unreserved backing—Bain's movements were largely unimpeded by the senior administration. Charles Webb says that, after a while, Bain was in a position to say to candidates, "What do you need? I can provide it." In recruiting performers, he also had, in the early years, the advantage of having relatively little competition from other schools; and, for those who had reached a point where they were tiring of the road, or at least a point where they were beginning to think about what would happen when the day came—who could say how far in the future?—when they could no longer earn a living as touring performers, Bain was able to hold out the prospect of job security (which was, to be sure, often more apparent than real) and of retirement years supported by a university pension.

Singers, whose careers generally do not extend beyond middle age, were particularly susceptible to these inducements. One of Bain's great coups was the recruitment of the distinguished Met tenor Charles Kullman, whom he first approached, during a Met visit to Bloomington in the mid-1950s, in the foyer of the Memorial Union. Bain correctly judged the time was ripe, because he "realized that Mr. Kullman's career at the Metropolitan, while by no means over, was in a decline." Kullman joined the faculty in 1956 (and remained until he retired, in 1971). For such a person, the presence of other notable performers on the School's faculty made the prospect of taking up residence in the wilds of Indiana more palatable. In Kullman's case, Bain was sure, the presence at Indiana of others formerly associated with the Met made him receptive to his overtures.

In addition to the recruiting advantages just enumerated, Bain had those that derived from his clear and inspiring vision of the School's destiny and from several facets of his personality. He had, first, unlimited chutzpa. No one was too august to be approached. During his very first weeks at Indiana, he tried to interest Benjamin Britten in the composition professorship vacated by Sanders. Pressler confirms that Bain "was not embarrassed to ask anyone, even Rubinstein (in my presence), if he would join the faculty." He also had considerable charm, and unlimited patience and persistence. Pressler had never heard of Bain when (in 1955) the Dean first called him: "But he was persistent. He called back, he didn't take 'no' for an answer."

Bain's charm and persistence, and the increasing attractions of the School and the University, would not, though, have been sufficient to recruit and retain active performers and operatic production personnel without the addition of one other ingredient: he had to make it possible for such individuals to continue their performance careers—which were, after all, important to them for both artistic and financial reasons. This was the case even with those whose careers, though in decline, had yet some life in them, and it was overwhelmingly the case with those who were in the ascendant. Nor would Bain have *wanted* performers to abandon their touring careers, even if he could have gotten them to do so, for he would then have forgone the great public-relations and recruiting benefits of having the names of his faculty members before the public: performers advertised the School whenever a program or a review included the information that they taught there.

But while it was common practice in conservatories to allow faculty members to accommodate their teaching to their performance schedules, the normal expectation within the University was that its faculty would, during the teaching term, stay on campus and teach. In this regard, too, the geographical situation of the School was highly disadvantageous: it was and is much easier for a musician living in a major city, where there are good travel connections to other major centers, to combine a teaching career with a performance schedule than it is for a musician living fifty miles south of Indianapolis.

For this problem, Bain persuaded his superiors to accept a solution that has been of the utmost importance to the development of the School. The Dean of the Business School had successfully made the case that, given the private-sector opportunities for people in his field, he could not hire and retain good faculty members unless they were allowed to supplement their academic salaries via non-academic business activities such as consulting. The same was true, of course, for faculty in others of the University's professional schools, including Medicine and Law. Pressing the analogy between performing musicians and professionals in these other fields, Bain was able to secure permission for the performers on his faculty to be sporadically absent from campus during the teaching term, provided they rescheduled whatever lessons they might miss during these absences. (The arrangement was feasible only because performers, unlike faculty in academic music, normally taught individual lessons rather than classes meeting on a fixed schedule.) In time, it became University policy that any faculty member might devote one day of each teaching week to non-academic business. Bain construed this rule as meaning that these days could accumulate, and thus concluded that a performer might be absent from campus for as long as three consecutive weeks of each fifteen-week semester. (And faculty members might choose not to teach at all during the summer term.) The prototype of such arrangements in Music was worked out in the negotiations that led to Sidney Foster joining the faculty in early 1952, and was indeed crucial to his appointment, since Foster had no intention of giving up his concert career. To be sure, some of those already on faculty played off-campus engagements, but Foster was, as Bain later recalled with pleasure, "perhaps the first genuinely concertizing artist, with the intent of carrying on extensive concert activities," to be appointed to the School. If he had not been able to proffer the kind of arrangement pioneered with Foster, Bain could not have recruited the highly distinguished performance faculty that he collected. When he was courting the rising star Pressler, he enlisted (as he often did) the aid of a faculty member who might have influence with the candidate: he had Foster call Pressler. "Come, you'll love it," Pressler recalls Foster saying: "You're free. If you do your work, you are free to do your concerts."

For many performers and opera production personnel, it was truly the best of both worlds. Ross Allen told me that Bain let him go "three times a year to keep my union card, in staging various places." Adding these outside engagements to the regular round of School productions, Allen was able to stage, in the course of his career, over 160 works—whereas "the gentlemen working in the best houses are lucky if in a career they get as many as thirty works to do." For instrumentalists who had a concert career but also required a steady income, the School could provide a better base than an orchestral position, because such positions required a great commitment of time, on an inflexibly scheduled basis. This consideration figured, for example, in Janos Starker's decision, in 1958, to leave the Chicago Symphony (where he was principal cellist) for a position at Indiana. To him and others, Bain could say (as he told Wolford), "Here are the people you're supposed to teach. They're supposed to have so many hours of instruction during the semester. They're supposed to go over a certain amount of material. It's all written and spelled out, and that's your job. How you *do* it is [also] your job."

To be sure, this flextime policy has been a source of resentment on the part of academic-music faculty, and it has sometimes been abused. In 1954 Bain recommended that Hans Busch have his salary docked for showing up late for the fall semester, and by 1967 faculty (and student) absences for performances elsewhere had become so numerous as to interfere seriously with the School's ensemble program. Bain's way of dealing with those who "jumped over the traces too many times" was, he told Wolford, to say to them, "All right, if you're going to be gone more than three weeks in a row, we're going to get a substitute in here for you during that time. You're not going to pay the substitute, we're going to take the salary away from your check and pay the person." (This arrangement prevented faculty from subcontracting their teaching at the lowest possible rate.) But despite its problems, the flextime system has remained one of the cornerstones of the School's operation.

As the years passed, it became increasingly easy for Bain to attract distinguished faculty, owing to a snowball effect. Pressler was influenced by Foster's presence on faculty. Having reversed Sanders's dismissal of Nettl, Bain presumably found it easier to present Indiana as a plausible academic home to Willi Apel (the author of *The Harvard Dictionary of Music* and other distinguished publications). He joined the faculty at Indiana in 1950, which then, with both Apel and Nettl there, became a plausible home for *any* musicologist. In 1953, Bain, already having much to offer anyone in opera, was able to recruit Frank St. Leger, who, as artistic administrator of the Met under Edward Johnson, had largely run the company. Dismissed by Johnson's successor, Rudolf Bing, who saw him as an all-too-potent symbol of the *ancien régime,* St. Leger proceeded to Hollywood as an adviser to Twentieth Century–Fox on making movies of operas. By 1953 he was very happy to accept Bain's offer of appointment at Indiana as a coach-accompanist. (The two had become acquainted during the Met visits to Bloomington.) St. Leger had, naturally, a tremendous knowledge of opera and of singers. He went on to become one of the School's most important conductors and, among his colleagues, one of the most respected and influential members of the faculty. Moreover, he was of tremendous help in faculty recruitment, in two ways: since, as Bain said, "he knew every important musician in New York, if not in the United States," he proved to be invaluable for his assessments of candidates; and the very presence at Indiana of such an illustrious person rendered the School more attractive to prospective appointees. Other first-rate appointments had the same effect, and by the latter years of Bain's deanship, it was, he said, "not necessary . . . very often to go searching for faculty since the interests and intentions of various artists to be on the faculty" were usually made known to him "either through formal application or by word of mouth of friendly colleagues."

Even though the number of the School's faculty positions (and its salary budget) constantly grew, in order to take maximum advantage of these mushrooming recruitment opportunities Bain needed both to spread his salary dollars as thinly as possible and to maximize what one might call the liquidity of his faculty assets. His strategy was continuous incremental improvement of the faculty. At first, he told Wolford, "I didn't have the greatest faculty, . . . because I didn't have the money to buy them. But as I replaced them, I always replaced them with better people, . . . and finally we tried to replace them with the absolute best." To implement this strategy, his tactics were to spend as little as possible on each faculty member and to keep as many as possible of the faculty untenured (so that he could fire them whenever better people came along).

By the early 1960s, various aspects of Bain's treatment of his faculty were of sufficient concern to the central administration that, as I noted above, Dorothy Collins, then employed in the Office of Institutional Research, was commissioned to make a detailed study of these matters. It is a pity, though perhaps not entirely surprising, that the explosive document that resulted is not to be found among the other reports, duly archived, of the Bureau, or anywhere else. (Bain told Collins "a hundred times" he wished she could find the report—no doubt he would have read it with not shame but pride.) Collins, though, easily recalls the main findings of the study—which she succinctly summarizes in the judgment that Bain was "a devil"—and she is, along with Charles Webb, the best source of information on these matters.

In salaries, Bain's policy was simply to be as stingy as he could without jeopardizing what he wanted to do. At the bottom of the faculty hierarchy, the Graduate Assistants were paid poorly even by the standards of this academic proletariat: worse than those at other music schools and worse—often by a factor of two—than those in other segments of the University. For those Assistants whom, at the conclusion of their graduate program, Bain wanted to advance to regular faculty status, but also for prospective faculty from elsewhere, his practice—which is, to be sure, a common one—was to offer as low a salary as would suffice to recruit them; in subsequent years, he raised their salaries not at all, or as little as would suffice to retain them (provided he *wanted* to retain them): "he starved them," Collins says.

The cumulative effect of this policy was that, in the same years that the School was becoming the best and most celebrated unit of the University, average salaries in it were sinking to the bottom echelon of University salaries. In 1971, a faculty union was established; in the spring of 1973—Bain's final year as Dean—it published all faculty salaries. The School of Music ranked dead last among academic units (the professional schools and the College of Arts and Sciences) in terms of average salary. The full professors, as a group, fared worst of all, with an average salary conspicuously lower than those of their peers in other units—a consequence of the fact that most of them had had especially long-term experience of the effects of Bain's policy of minimal raises. Adding fuel to the firestorm that ensued the publication of the salary data was the fact that they also revealed striking inequities among salaries *within* the School. Bain managed to deflect much of the indignation to the University administration (which, to be sure, had a fair claim to some of it), but in truth the salary pattern in the School was primarily attributable to his money-stretching policies. Up to the present, though some progress has been made, average salaries in Music continue to lie near the bottom of the salary distribution at Indiana, and this fact—astounding to anyone who knows the School's reputation and its dominating stature within the University—was a constant theme in the annual budget requests of Charles Webb.

Apart from the shortage of salary money, the main impediment Bain faced in achieving the rapid incremental improvement of his faculty was the institution of tenure: once tenured, a faculty member cannot be replaced at the pleasure of a dean when one that looks better comes in sight. For Bain, this was primarily a problem with respect to faculty he had inherited from Sanders, for most of whom, as we have seen, he did not have a high regard. Those who *weren't* tenured he fired; with those who were, his practice was to treat them as badly as he could, presumably in the hope of persuading them to seek employment elsewhere. It is, though, difficult to dislodge tenured faculty members, in part because those targeted for dislodgment are, as a rule, just the ones who have the hardest time finding other employment. Thus Bain's policy with respect to these members served, as far as I can tell, in the main only to make their professional (and probably also personal) lives miserable, by giving them as little remuneration and as bad teaching assignments as he could manage: these are the two principal weapons that administrators can turn on tenured faculty. Collins cites especially the example of William Ross, the voice teacher who was one of Sanders's initial appointees. Bain would "give him one assignment in this building way over here and then one clear over on the other side, and you'd see Bill just trudging over the campus." "It was amusing what he did, really," Collins told me, "if you weren't the victim"—a remark that recalls Will Rogers's observation that "everything's funny, as long as it's happening to somebody else." But presumably some modest benefits accrued to the School from this shabby treatment of the disapproved: by giving Ross and others wretched assignments Bain was able to give better ones to some of those people whom he wanted to attract or retain.

If Bain thought his predecessors had made egregious mistakes with regard to tenure, though, he also candidly and ruefully confessed that he made some of his own. In a couple of instances, he succumbed, with open eyes and against his better judgment, to public pressure in the granting of tenure. Sanders had highly touted Margaret White, whom he had hired in 1945 to teach piano and harp. Though White was "a very nice person," Bain regarded her accomplishments on both instruments as modest; yet he gave her tenure because of her popularity with the faculty and the community. A decision to dismiss her "would have been questioned very much," and Bain, who evidently was, in these early days at Indiana, not yet ready to go against public opinion in such a matter, gave in. "I should have had a little bit more backbone," he told Wolford, "and a little more of the dictator that they accuse me of, and said, 'No, we're not going to have you.'"

He made a far costlier mistake about the Berkshire Quartet. Bain had persuaded the central administration to allow him to appoint the quartet in the hope that the presence of this well-known ensemble on the faculty would both improve the quality of instruction in strings and serve as a recruiting draw for good string students. From the beginning, though, the quartet had not worked out. As I noted earlier, Bain was disconcerted to find, when the group arrived in Indiana in the fall of 1948, that it included a different second violinist from the one he had auditioned; and he was dismayed by various aspects of the quartet's collective behavior. They immediately began to protest their assignment as first-desk players in the orchestra; they were always absent in the summer. They did not even play well. Two members were excellent musicians: Fritz Magg had been the solo cellist of the Vienna Symphony at the age of twenty; David Dawson, who had entered Juilliard at fifteen, had for five years been the principal violist of the Minneapolis Symphony. But the replacement second violinist was (or so Bain told Wolford) "a big zero," and the first violinist, Urico Rossi, "was about that, too." Rossi was "a very fleet-fingered man," Bain said to me, but he didn't practice enough. As a result, and also as a result of the demoralizing effect of this on the other members, the quartet "played out of tune a lot," despite the fact that Bain "raised hell with it all the time they were here." Worse yet, it was difficult to get students to study with the two violinists, and the presence of the quartet did not at all exert the drawing power for new students that had been Bain's main object in bringing it to campus. Still, Bain let all four members of the group have tenure, for the same kind of reason as with White. Faculty members at Indiana as elsewhere greatly liked the idea of a resident quartet. "The academic faculty are," as Bain said to Wolford, with the condescension of the professional toward dilettantes, "people who enjoy listening to chamber music, and so, as a consequence, they like to go to the main auditorium on Sunday afternoons and spend a quiet, contemplative two hours, or an hour and a half, listening to pleasant sounds and being entertained. Well, this was part of gentility and the like." Thus the general response to the appointment of the Berkshire Quartet had been highly positive, and Bain accordingly feared the public reaction if he did not give all its members tenure. So again, against his better judgment, he "put up with mediocrity."

Bain was nothing if not a quick study, though, and he soon mastered the art of deferring or denying tenure. He had, from the beginning, the habit of bringing people in for short-term appointments, so he could have a "look-see" at them. Early on, too, he discovered that he could secure performing artists for look-sees that might actually extend to years of microscopic examination, because performers themselves knew little about tenure. "Most of them," Bain said to me, "didn't know the ways of getting a permanent job. So I didn't enlighten them." Though it is scarcely credible, Hoffman himself was not granted tenure until 1955, his ninth year at Indiana.

Many performers, too, were actually leery of those categories of appointment that led to tenure, feeling that professorial titles attached to their names worsened their competitive position as concertizing artists, by evoking the familiar distinction between those who teach and those who do. Foster, when Bain courted him to replace Fuleihan (one of those who understood too little about getting a permanent job), preferred to be appointed to Indiana as Resident Concert Pianist; and, following the precedent established by this designation, Bain regularly appointed performing artists with titles of this sort. He also appointed many faculty (including even some performers) as "Lecturers," because years spent as "Lecturer," like those spent in "Resident" or "Visiting" appointments, did not count toward tenure. "Lecturer" was and is common as a designation for non-tenure-track teachers in American universities (and particularly their music schools), but Bain came to use the title so frequently for relatively senior (and thus relatively well-paid) people that, as Dorothy Collins discovered in compiling Indiana data for the comparative salary statistics published by the American Association of University Professors, Lecturers at the University were paid, on average, better than anywhere else in the country. (Once assured of the desirability of holding on to such people permanently, Bain was happy to convert their appointments to regular academic ones: this occurred with Foster in 1954, despite his leeriness of academic titles.) As for those appointed initially to tenure-track positions, the Dean, schooled by his youthful mistakes, became notoriously willing to fire them up until the last moment before they would have achieved tenure, replacing them either with better people or simply with comparable ones who were, since appointed at the entry level, cheaper.

For a variety of reasons, then, Bain's strategy of rapid enlargement and steady incremental improvement of the faculty succeeded brilliantly; just how brilliantly becomes apparent when one surveys the growth, over the course of his deanship, of the various departments. The following summary, far from being exhaustive, includes for the most part only those appointees who were of particular importance to the School in either or both of two ways: because of their substantive contribution to its work, or because of the luster their reputations lent to it. I have omitted some distinguished performers who came only for a short period and other individuals who, though appointed by Bain, achieved distinction only after he left the deanship. Even so, the survey occupies a good many pages: we are, after all, talking about a music faculty that became, under Bain, the world's largest. (For a complete list of faculty for the period 1910–99, see Appendix 2.)

Having inherited Manski and brought Taylor with him from North Texas, Bain went on, as we have seen, to strengthen the voice faculty by recruiting Josephine Antoine, Anna Kaskas (who, replacing Antoine, stayed until 1957), and Agnes Davis. Davis arrived in 1950 and remained on faculty until her death in 1967; over the next few years, Bain added Ralph Appelman (1952), who, recruited as a graduate student, spent his full career at Indiana; the baritones Charles William Shriner (1954) and Marko Rothmuller (1955); and, in 1956, Charles Kullman. The following year he recruited the bass-baritone Paul Matthen, who had toured extensively and been for a time a leading baritone of the Stuttgart State Opera. In 1957 and 1960, respectively, he added two more Met singers, the soprano Virginia MacWatters and the great mezzo-soprano Martha Lipton, and in 1962 still another, Margaret Harshaw, who had been (as Bain put it) one of the reigning divas of the Met's Wagner wing. In the Ring alone, she had sung fifteen different roles—more than any other artist. Harshaw became one of the most important faculty members in the history of the School, in terms not only of her pedagogy but also of the contribution her presence made to the reputation of the School and its drawing power for excellent voice students. In 1966 Bain achieved what briefly appeared to be another great coup, in the appointment of the extremely distinguished Met soprano Zinka Milanov. (In his early years at the Met, Rudolf Bing thought Tebaldi's the only soprano voice of comparable quality.) Milanov's career was essentially over, though, and most students had no knowledge of her august name; unhappy at Indiana, she left after a single year. The appointments of Jean Deis (1967) and Gianna d'Angelo (1970) worked out much better. Deis, who had sung leading tenor roles at a number of European and American opera houses, including the New York City Opera and the Los Angeles Opera, remained on faculty not only through the rest of Bain's deanship but through most of Webb's; so too did d'Angelo (who in consequence of injuries sustained in a car accident had had to retire after a half-dozen years at the Met). And finally, in 1971, after years of assiduous courtship, Bain succeeded in recruiting one of the best-known singers in the world, Eileen Farrell—who, however, grew unhappy after several years at the School, and resigned in 1980.

As Bain clearly understood, his recruitment of members of the Met could succeed only with those who had passed the zenith of their careers, and the fact that he appointed so many such people (including directors, instrumentalists, and other personnel in addition to singers, so that for a while he had over fifteen former members of the company on faculty) gave rise to the pleasantry that the School was "the graveyard of the Met."

By the early 1960s, though, Bain was also making a practice of recruiting singers near the *beginning* of their careers. This development was a consequence of the gradual drying up of the pool of returning veterans (of World War II and then the Korean conflict) who had, owing to their vocal maturity, been stalwarts of Bain's opera program from the beginning. Since he regarded it as vital, from the standpoint of public relations and the reputation of the School, to have demanding roles well sung, he began to recruit a special category of junior faculty consisting of singers who were "old enough to sing the mature roles and at the same time not so vocally attractive that the siphoning of them off to local and major opera companies became a problem"; in addition to singing the mature roles, they taught lesser voice students: music education majors and those studying voice as an elective. Some of these junior faculty—like Roger Havranek and Roy Samuelsen, both of whom eventually became full professors—were culled from the ranks of Indiana graduate students. Others came from elsewhere; these included Frederick Gersten, who had been a leading baritone in German opera houses, and Polyna Savridi, who had been a member of the Met's National Company (a short-lived touring company of young artists).

As we have seen, Bain was also eager to build up the choral program at Indiana, and in this endeavor George Krueger played the key role, not only as a conductor but as chairman of the choral department from 1948 until two years before his 1974 retirement. Eugene Bayless, it will be recalled, joined the department in the 1952–53 academic year, while still a graduate student. In 1963, another graduate student, Robert Stoll, was appointed; he later became director of the Singing Hoosiers. The following year, Bain made a major appointment in the choral field: Julius Herford, who had been a professor at the Westminster Choir College and Juilliard, among other institutions (and was notable, *inter alia,* as Robert Shaw's teacher), joined the faculty as Visiting Lecturer and then, after a year, as Professor. His appointment substantially enhanced the reputation of the department, and large numbers of graduate students came to Indiana to study with him.

Among instrumentalists, Bain inevitably had to recruit more pianists than anything else. Piano majors were numerous, and all other students had to complete a piano proficiency requirement; and there were also students from other parts of the University studying piano as an elective. The piano students thus formed a hierarchy, and so did the piano faculty: many of them were journeymen hired to teach the teeming masses (often in groups); and then there were those recruited because of their musical distinction and assigned to teach the most promising students.

Pianists were, like singers, a category in which Bain's recruitment effort over the years was enormously successful, and one in which the importance of the snowball effect was particularly evident. Ernest Hoffzimmer, who was still on the faculty when Bain arrived, had established that it was possible for a reputable pianist—even a European one—to accept employment at Indiana, and this fact was further confirmed by the appointments of Walter Robert and Anis Fuleihan. It was, though, Fuleihan's replacement, Sidney Foster, who became the major catalyst in the creation of a piano faculty that was, by the time Bain left the deanship, extraordinarily distinguished. Bruno Eisner (presumably invited for a "look-see") spent the second semester of the 1952–53 year as Visiting Pianist at the School; he continued in this capacity for the next two academic years. In 1953 two other concertizing artists, Ozan Marsh and Béla Boszorményi-Nagy, were appointed as Resident Pianists. Marsh stayed until 1957, Nagy until 1962. Two more Resident Pianists were added in 1955. One of them, the young American artist William Masselos, stayed only a single year, to Bain's regret; the other, Pressler, talked into coming to Indiana by Foster, remained to become one of the very greatest of the School's teachers and, especially with his colleagues in the Beaux Arts Trio (founded the year he arrived at Indiana), one of its greatest concertizing artists. Joseph Battista and Ray Dudley were appointed Resident Pianists in 1957. Dudley remained until 1963; Battista became Professor of Piano in 1961 and remained until his untimely death in 1968 at the age of fifty. In 1960, Charles Webb—one of Walter Robert's doctoral students—was given a faculty appointment. Two additional Europeans were appointed in 1962: Vlado Perlemuter, highly regarded especially as an interpreter of Chopin and Ravel, did not take to American ways and returned to France after a single semester; the prize-winning Hungarian pianist Gyorgy Sebok (having frequently played with Starker, he was brought in at the cellist's request) proved, like Pressler, to be one of the most durable and greatest of the piano teachers in the history of the School. Also in 1962, Bain appointed the brilliant American pianist Abbey Simon (a close friend of Foster), who remained at Indiana until 1977.

In 1963 Bain recruited the pianist and composer Walter Bricht. Before emigrating to New York in 1938, Bricht had taught in Vienna, at both the Horák Schule and the Volksconservatorium; he had also concertized widely in both Europe and America. He spent the last years of his life at Indiana, dying in 1970. The same year Bricht arrived, Bain appointed the young Chilean pianist Alfonso Montecino, known especially as a Bach and Beethoven player; he remained on the faculty until retirement. Karen Shaw, who as a graduate student had served as Pressler's assistant, was elevated to the ranks of the faculty in 1965 and eventually became a mainstay of the Piano Department. In 1968, the dazzling pianist Jorge Bolet was appointed. That Bolet was at the time experiencing an ebb in his concert career made it easier to recruit him; to his and the School's good fortune, his reputation soon soared to new heights. (He resigned in 1977.) Another 1968 appointee, Pietro Spada, was let go after a single year, but must be mentioned because he innocently became the occasion of one of the most famous School stories. Departing abruptly and in a chafe after his appeal of Bain's decision to dismiss him had failed, Spada was discovered to have left behind, on the floor of his emptied studio, an attaché case. It was only after the University police had gingerly transported the case to the football stadium, where they attempted to detonate or deactivate its contents with shotgun slugs, that it was found to contain a student's scores.

As we have seen, the greatest weakness in the faculty at the time of Bain's arrival was in strings. Since the 1945 retirement of von Zweygberg, Richard Clayton (with a bachelor's degree from Michigan State College) had been the only non-emeritus member of the Cello Department; and the only teacher of violin and viola was Winifred Merrill. The situation in cello had been substantially improved by the appointment of Sterling Hunkins in place of Clayton. Hunkins's departure after a year coincided with the arrival of the Berkshire Quartet. But their appointment did not, as I noted earlier, work out well, and the expected legion of string students was not lured in by their presence. Moreover, having appointed the quartet and, against his better judgment, given all its members tenure, Bain was not for several years in a position to make additional appointments in strings. In consequence of these circumstances (and doubtless also of the fact that secondary-school training was directed much more to winds than to strings), the dearth of string players among the School's students continued for years: it was Bain's constant lament as late as 1958.

By that time, however, the School had grown so large that he had begun to be able to make further appointments in strings. The bassist Murray Grodner was appointed in 1955; he had formerly been principal in the Houston Symphony and assistant principal at Pittsburgh. In 1957–58, when the members of the quartet were on sabbatical, Bain brought in four string players on one-year contracts to replace them. One of these appointees was a man of great stature: Ede Zathureczky, who had been for fifteen years head of the Franz Liszt Academy in Budapest; an excellent violinist, he had concertized extensively with Bartok. Zathureczky was available as a result of the Soviet suppression of the Hungarian uprising of 1956, in the aftermath of which he had fled to Vienna. Other distinguished Hungarian musicians were similarly eager to leave their homeland, and, over the next few years, enough of them ended up at Indiana (where they joined Boszorményi-Nagy), and figured so importantly at the School, that it became customary in local parlance to refer to them collectively as "the Hungarian contingent." The story of Zathureczky, however, ended unhappily. Despite the violinist's distinction, Bain characteristically declined to offer him a tenured position not only in his first year but in the second to which his appointment was extended, and he "worried considerably," as Bain later recalled, about his lack of security at Indiana;

meanwhile, the Communist authorities in Hungary had made it clear that he would be welcome to return to his former position. Zathureczky was thus kept in a constant state of indecision, and, especially since he was hypertensive, it was not very surprising that in May of 1959 he suffered a cerebral hemorrhage and died, at the age of fifty-six.

The preceding year, Bain had recruited the individual who became the most distinguished member of the Hungarian contingent, Janos Starker. As it happened, Starker had been in Bain's debt since 1947, when the Dean was asked to participate in a subterfuge on his behalf. Starker, displaced by the war, was living in Paris. Antal Dorati—like Starker, a graduate of the Franz Liszt Academy—wanted to recruit him as principal cellist for the Dallas Symphony. Starker could not, however, gain admission to the United States without the guarantee of a job there, and Dorati could not make that guarantee, because the Dallas Symphony was a union shop and Starker was not a member of the union. It was suggested to Bain that he could write a letter to Starker indicating an interest in appointing him to the faculty at Indiana; Bain (and the trustees of the University) agreed, and the resulting letter was enough to secure Starker's entry to the country—following which he joined the union and the symphony.

By the late 1950s, Starker was principal cellist of the Chicago Symphony; but the obligations of this prestigious position had come to interfere seriously with the realization of his goals as a soloist and chamber player. He was thus willing to leave the orchestra for an appointment at Indiana, where Bain's flextime policy made it possible to combine the financial security of an academic appointment with the relatively unimpeded pursuit of a concert career. (Bain had thought—rightly, of course—that a faculty where Starker was added to Fritz Magg would become a "Mecca" for cello students. But he had a moment of doubt in the summer of 1958, by which point only one student had indicated an interest in coming to the School to study with Starker. Writing Starker to convey this news, Bain urged him to do whatever he could to stir up more students, adding darkly that a shortage of them "would immediately raise the question of whether or not it would be advisable to reappoint you for the academic year 1959–60.")

As the appointment of Starker demonstrated, Bain had now reached a level in the incremental improvement of his faculty where he could plausibly aspire to raid major orchestras for their key players; and a number of other such appointments over the next dozen years resulted in further dramatic improvements in the quality and reputation of the School. Of all the appointments of this kind, the one that Bain regarded as most important—indeed as probably the best of his appointments in any category—came in 1960, two years after he recruited Starker.

Searching that year for a "master musician" to replace the deceased Zathureczky, Bain ventured to call Josef Gingold, the concertmaster of the Cleveland Orchestra under George Szell. Born in the Belorussian city of Brest-Litovsk in 1909, Gingold had come to the United States shortly after World War I (during which he and his family had been in a German internment camp). Having played the violin since early childhood, he studied in New York in the 1920s with Vladimir Graffman and, in 1927–29, in Belgium with Eugène Ysaÿe. Returning to New York in the midst of the Depression, he supported his family by playing on Broadway and in other commercial venues. He would, he later said, "take any job, one that would pay $5 or $10. I chose to be a professional musician and wanted to stay one. I had no false pride." In 1937 he became a charter member of Toscanini's NBC Symphony, and in the following years also played, with three other members of the orchestra (William Primrose, Oscar Shumsky, and Harvey Shapiro), in the Primrose String Quartet. In 1944 he left New York to become concertmaster of the Detroit Symphony, whence he removed in 1947 to Cleveland. During his time there, he also taught at Western Reserve University and the Cleveland Music School Settlement (he himself had been a settlement-house student in New York), and had a number of notable pupils, including Jaime Laredo.

Gingold responded positively to Bain's approach, and, after a visit to Bloomington, accepted his offer of appointment—a turn of events distressing to Szell, who tried to persuade Bain to take his assistant concertmaster instead. For Gingold, the principal attraction of an academic appointment was evidently not that it would afford greater opportunity to concertize but that it would enable him to spend most of his time doing what he loved best, which was teaching. (Indeed his absences from Indiana were primarily for the sake of teaching elsewhere: for thirty summers, he directed the chamber music program of Ivan Galamian's Meadowmount School in Westport, New York.) At Indiana, it became his standard practice to carry a student load more than twice the normal one—a practice he continued for sixteen years after he reached retirement age, until a few weeks before his death in January 1995. He became perhaps the most celebrated, and surely the most beloved, violin pedagogue of the late twentieth century, having taught, among many others, three winners of the Queen Elisabeth of Belgium Competition (Miriam Fried and Nai-Yuan Hu in addition to Laredo), Eugene Fodor, Yuval Yaron, Joshua Bell, and Corey Cerovsek. Bain said he had "never worked with a truly more wonderful human being" than Gingold: a view that seems to have been universal among his colleagues.

If Gingold did not take full advantage of the flextime policy, Starker certainly did, with the result that most of Bain's subsequent appointees in cello were hired as assistants to Starker, to teach his students during his absences. The first of these assistants was Leopold Teraspulsky, who was lured away, in 1960, from his position as first cellist of the NBC Radio Orchestra in Chicago. According to Bain, Teraspulsky did not prove nearly as popular with students as either Starker or Magg, did not like the role of assistant, and had a generally unhappy time at Indiana, which he left in 1971. For several years in the late 1960s, Tsuyoshi Tsutsumi, who had come from Japan to study with Starker, served as his assistant; years later, he returned to Indiana as Professor of Cello. In Bain's final year as Dean, the distinguished cellist Eva Czako Janzer, who had known Starker since their childhood in Budapest, joined the faculty with duties that included assisting her old acquaintance. With her violist husband Georges Janzer, who was appointed at the same time, she had been a member of both the Grumiaux Trio and the Vegh Quartet. (After her death in 1978—in her early fifties—Starker established the Eva Janzer Memorial Cello Center in her honor; it continues to sponsor scholarships, and visits by eminent cellists for master classes at the School.)

The final decade of Bain's tenure also saw a number of notable appointments in violin and viola. Since its foundation in 1955, the Beaux Arts Trio had been in residence at Indiana during the summers, and for this reason its violinist, Daniel Guilet, had been a member of the summer faculty. Guilet was a fine player, who had managed his own quartet and had been Toscanini's last concertmaster at the NBC Symphony, and Bain was pleased to be able to recruit him to a year-round position in 1963; he remained until his retirement in 1969. (The Beaux Arts cellist, Bernard Greenhouse, though solicited for the School by both Bain and, later, Webb, was simply not interested in a full-time teaching position.)

In 1964, Albert Lazan, the second violinist of the Berkshire Quartet, resigned his position in the group. Since he retained his position on the faculty—where there was no shortage of violinists but only one violist—Bain decided to replace him in the quartet with a violist who was also an excellent violinist: Irving Ilmer, of the Fine Arts Quartet. Though Ilmer was a brilliant musician, this ingenious solution failed to work out. He did not prove popular with students, and, not having been granted tenure, left the School in 1971. Perhaps the decision on his tenure was influenced by the fact that in 1965 Bain had recruited an absolutely ideal appointee in viola, William Primrose, who, not surprisingly, turned out to be an enormous draw for viola students and thus solved, for Indiana, the problem of the shortage of violists that generally besets music school orchestras.

In 1966, Bain appointed, as Visiting Professor of Violin, Tadeusz Wronski, a former dean of the Warsaw School of Music and a splendid teacher—a fact that had been confirmed in a series of summer appointments at Indiana. He returned to Warsaw in 1967, but came back to Indiana for a three-year stint in 1969; and in 1975 he came back for good. In the meantime, Bain had capped his remarkable series of string appointments with the recruitment of three more violinists. In one of his astounding feats, he in 1971 persuaded Ruggiero Ricci—whom he had been courting for some time—to accept a position at the School; Ricci stayed, though, only until 1974. Also in 1971, at Gingold's suggestion, Bain appointed the Italian violinist Franco Gulli to a summer position; by 1972 he was Professor of Music. His wife, the pianist Enrica Cavallo-Gulli, who had taught at the Milan Conservatory, joined the faculty as Lecturer in 1973, and eventually also attained the rank of Professor. Finally, in 1972, Bain expanded the Hungarian contingent by appointing Michael Kuttner as Professor of Violin and, replacing Ilmer, as second violinist of the Berkshire Quartet; unfortunately, Kuttner died of a heart attack in 1975, at the age of fifty-seven; his memory is preserved in the Kuttner String Quartet, a student ensemble chosen annually by competition. In twenty-six years, then, Bain brought the String Department from the abyss to such eminence that, looking back in 1983, he could say to Wolford that in his judgment strings had "contributed more to the excellence of the School of Music than any other single department."

Bain was also highly successful in the recruitment of wind players. At the time of his arrival, the School had no particularly distinguished teachers in this area. For his first three appointees in it, he chose, characteristically, Eastman graduates: William Kirkpatrick and Roy Houser (both of whom had substantial orchestral experience), and the oboist Darrel Stubbs; they joined with two survivors from the Sanders era—Lawrence Kingsbury and Charles Keen—to form the resident wind quintet that Bain intended as a vehicle for publicizing the School's new strength in the field. When the flutist Kingsbury resigned in 1950, he was replaced by another Eastman graduate, Edward McGough. In 1954, Kirkpatrick fell victim to the policy of incremental improvement, and was replaced by Verne Reynolds; and the next year Stubbs was replaced by a fifth Eastman graduate, Keith Kummer. (Bain later regretted firing Stubbs, since he was, as Bain told Wolford, "a very nice person, a real gentleman," who "would have been an excellent member of this faculty." But he thought Kummer "slightly better," and even the slimmest of margins was always enough for him.) Four years earlier Bain had appointed the trombonist Thomas Beversdorf (also an Eastman graduate), who had come to Indiana for doctoral studies. Elevated to the faculty, he eventually became Professor of Trombone and Composition.

In 1958, Bain—who was by then in a position, in winds as in other fields, to recruit top-flight orchestral players—appointed James Pellerite, the first flutist of the Detroit Symphony, to replace McGough. Pellerite left in 1960 to become first flutist of the Philadelphia Orchestra, and was replaced by Harry Houdeshel, the solo flutist of the U.S. Navy Band. Indeed the year 1960, which had also seen the arrival of Josef Gingold (and Martha Lipton), was an *annus mirabilis*. Bain successfully raided the Chicago Symphony for its principal horn player, Philip Francis Farkas, one of the world's leading hornists. "Fresh in my mind," Farkas later recalled, "was the fact that some of the great artists of my youth had gradually deteriorated in their playing ability until younger players no longer viewed them with respect. I realized that I would rather quit at my peak, even if it were five years too soon, than to play five minutes too long." He accepted Bain's offer of a position with salary equal to, and benefits superior to, what he received in his orchestral position, and stayed on at Indiana until retirement, becoming as distinguished a pedagogue as he had been a player. Also in 1960, Bain deprived the New York Philharmonic of its first clarinetist, Robert McGinnis—though, unlike Farkas, he turned out not to function well in an academic setting, and remained at Indiana only three years. In 1961, Bain made two more major appointments in winds: Jerry Sirucek, the second oboist of the Chicago Symphony; and, from the New York Philharmonic, William Bell, the world's preeminent tuba player: at eighteen, he had been chosen by John Philip Sousa to be principal tubist in his band; when he was later a member of Toscanini's NBC Symphony, the Maestro had declared him the finest tuba player he had ever heard. In the same year, Pellerite returned to the School.

In 1963, Earl Bates, principal clarinetist of the St. Louis Symphony, joined the faculty, as did Louis Davidson, the former first trumpet of the Cleveland Orchestra, Lewis Van Haney, the second trombonist of the New York Philharmonic, and Leonard Sharrow, first bassoonist of the Chicago Symphony. The following year the appointment of the saxophonist Eugene Rousseau finally allowed Bain to say that the School had individual teachers for every band instrument as well as every orchestral one. Rousseau, who spent the rest of his career at Indiana, played a major part in gaining acceptance for the saxophone in the classical music world: he gave the first solo recitals on the instrument in Amsterdam, Berlin, London, and Paris, and was the first saxophonist invited to teach at the Mozarteum Summer Academy in Salzburg. In 1968, another first-desk player of the Philadelphia Orchestra, Henry Charles Smith, joined the faculty as a teacher of trombone, though he stayed only until 1971, when he resigned to become Associate Conductor of the Minneapolis Orchestra; he was replaced by Keith Brown, who had been the trombonist of the New York Brass Quintet, and principal with the Metropolitan Opera Orchestra and the Casals Festival Orchestra; he remained at Indiana to have a long and distinguished career, retiring in 1997. And in the same year Bain made another of his great appointments, recruiting Harvey Phillips to replace the retiring William Bell.

The youngest of ten children of a Depression-era Missouri farm family, Phillips had dropped out of the state university in his freshman year to join the Ringling Brothers and Barnum & Bailey Circus Band—which was staffed, in those days, largely by people who had played in Sousa's band. Phillips loved the circus, but his career there ended when Bell, who became his patron, teacher, and hero (and who had also in youth played in a circus), wired to inform him that Juilliard was prepared to offer him a full scholarship. After Juilliard, in 1967, Phillips went to Boston to serve as assistant to Gunther Schuller, who had just been appointed President of the New England Conservatory; four years later he left for Bloomington, where he assumed not only Bell's faculty position but his mantle as the world's greatest tubist. Throughout his long career at Indiana, Phillips devoted himself to promoting the tuba and its literature, often using flamboyant methods that recalled his circus days. In 1973 he established the annual Octubafest—a week of nightly tuba recitals by various players culminating in a "Fest" at his Tubaranch south of town. In 1974, he established TubaChristmas—in honor of Bell, who had been born on Christmas Day. After a trial run in Bloomington, with Phillips and other tubists playing carols while dressed as TubaSantas, TubaChristmas made its New York debut, with 250 tubists—in later years, twice that number—playing beside the great Christmas tree in Rockefeller Plaza. In the subsequent years, both Octubafests and TubaChristmases have multiplied across the United States and beyond. To enrich the tuba literature, Phillips has commissioned more than a hundred works. "Any time I meet a composer I admire," he told Whitney Balliett, "I don't let up on him about writing a piece for the instrument until I get a positive answer." Sometimes the commission fees have been characteristically unconventional. A Vincent Persichetti serenade cost Phillips two cases of Beefeater gin.

Two other appointments rounded out the cadre of orchestral teachers. In 1960, finding that there were more percussion students than could be taught by Richard Johnson (and Harry Huxol, whom he had appointed as Assistant Director of Bands in 1957), Bain recruited George Gaber, who had for a time been a member of the Pittsburgh Symphony under Fritz Reiner and had also played under a number of other first-rank conductors. This appointment proved to be an excellent one: the School became highly attractive to percussion students, and Gaber was eventually elevated to the rank of Distinguished Professor. By 1965, Bain had concluded that he also needed to recruit an additional harpist. As we have seen, he was not impressed with Margaret White (inherited from Sanders), and he found that the School did not get many good harp students. His remedy for this problem was to appoint, on the advice of the former members of the Chicago Symphony on faculty, Peter Eagle, a free-lance harpist who had played with the CBS Symphony in Chicago and the Chicago Philharmonic. Like Gaber, Eagle remained at Indiana until retirement.

In 1954–55, the size of the student body permitted the creation of a second orchestra, which was assigned to accompany the operas. Until the end of 1955, almost all the performances of both the Philharmonic and the new orchestra were conducted by the tireless Hoffman, and Bain had no need to recruit any more conductors. This was especially the case because Frank St. Leger, though hired as a coach-accompanist, was also an excellent conductor. (He had originally been appointed to the Met, in 1939, as an Assistant Conductor.) When Hoffman was on sabbatical leave in the fall of 1954, St. Leger took over the Philharmonic, and, though he was in his sixties, shouldered the responsibility of taking it on tour. This was the tour, with the University Singers under Bain, that included a performance at Carnegie Hall: St. Leger told Bain that the last time he had appeared there was at Nellie Melba's farewell performance, for which he was the accompanist.

Still another conductor was available in the person of Wolfgang Vacano, who, like St. Leger, had been hired (in 1951) as a coach-accompanist, though his credentials qualified him for a more elevated position. Vacano's case was one of many in which Bain benefited from the dislocations caused by the rise of Nazism. Having graduated from the Berlin Hochschule with a major in conducting, Vacano had been coach and conductor in various German opera houses. With the advent of the Nazis, he fled to Buenos Aires, where he became a conductor of the Teatro Colón. In 1951, he came to the United States, taking up residence in Chicago, and, having been recommended to Bain by Hans Busch and the Met stage director Herbert Graf, was interviewed and hired. At the time, Bain had no idea that Vacano would become a part of the conductorial staff (or, still less, that he would turn out to be one of his most important appointees), but by 1953 he was conducting performances of the Opera Workshop, and during Hoffman's sabbatical he conducted the regular operatic productions. Even after Hoffman returned, Vacano conducted one of the summer musicals and, in the fall of 1955, *Faust* and a double bill consisting of Ravel's *The Bewitched Child* and Puccini's *The Cloak.* For the first and third of these, Vacano also supplied the English translation of the libretto.

Over the Christmas holidays that year, Hoffman and his wife Annemarie visited their son in Houston, where he was by that time attending medical school. Early on the foggy morning of January 3, 1956, near Meridian, Mississippi, they collided head-on with a pick-up truck that had veered into their lane, and were killed instantly. Hoffman was fifty-six. The Hoffmans had continued to think of Texas as their home; both Wells and Bain made a winter journey there for the funeral.

In the aftermath of this bitter blow, St. Leger took over as the regular conductor of the Philharmonic, while Vacano assumed responsibility for conducting the rest of the operatic productions for the school year. It was obvious, though, that the two could not indefinitely perform Hoffman's duties in addition to their own, and Bain launched a search for a new conductor. His method was the sensible one of bringing a series of three candidates for one-month stays. The third of these, Tibor Kozma, got the job. A further addition to the Hungarian contingent, Kozma had graduated from the Franz Liszt Academy with a degree in piano and had subsequently studied both piano and conducting in Dresden. In 1939, with war breaking out, he gave up the conducting career he had developed in Germany and Czechoslovakia and emigrated to Ecuador, where he became director of a radio station, organized the country's first radio orchestra, and taught at the National Conservatory. In 1941, he came to the United States, and, after a period of conducting Broadway shows, in 1948 joined the Met as an Associate Conductor. (He conducted *La Bohème* in the Met's 1955 visit to Bloomington.) As Vacano's service as opera conductor in the fall of 1955 indicates, Bain had been moving toward a system in which there would be two different operatic production teams; after Kozma's appointment as Professor in the fall of 1957, this system was formally instituted, with Vacano as the other musical director.

Over the years, however, Bain and Kozma grew to dislike each other intensely. (Ross Allen tells the story of a casting meeting in which Bain's secretary announced that the Dean had phoned to say he would not attend due to illness. "Oh?" said Kozma. "Nothing trivial, I hope?") At base, their conflict probably derived from the fact that both had strong and blunt characters, so that they could scarcely avoid frequent collisions; Kozma was also famously choleric. Artistic differences exacerbated—and, after a time, were inextricable from—the personal ones. Among other things, they disagreed about repertory, Kozma on one occasion going so far as to deprecate in print an opera—Boito's *Mefistofele*—that Bain had assigned him to conduct. Then too, Kozma's approach to operatic performance differed in some key ways from that of Hoffman, which Bain evidently regarded as ideal for the School. In sharp contrast to his predecessor, Kozma was opposed to cuts (and even wanted, though he never quite achieved it, to present *Parsifal* with absolutely no cuts); he also felt strongly that the orchestra should always be heard—which meant, from Bain's point of view, that he drowned the singers. Hoffman (like Bain) had thought it vitally important that the audience catch the words—which were, of course, always in English—and he was even willing to slow the tempo to attain this end. Allen recalls the School's 1951 performance of *Rigoletto,* in which Hoffman made sure that the audience understood Sparafucile's plan to substitute another's body for the Duke's: "One . . . man . . . in . . . a . . . sack . . . is . . . as . . . good . . . as . . . another." The tempo caused eyebrows to raise "clear across the theater." Doubtless Bain's growing difficulties with Kozma sharpened his nostalgia for the lost co-adjutor of the heroic age of his deanship—a nostalgia that would have been great in any case and that, like his gratitude, shows in Bain's every later reference to Hoffman.

As the School grew larger, it became apparent that yet another principal conductor was needed, and this role eventually fell to Harry Farbman. Farbman, who had studied with Leopold Auer and Alexander Bloch and had concertized widely as soloist and chamber player, had been recommended by Gingold as someone who could handle part of the flood of violin students that inundated the School after Gingold's arrival. But at the time of his appointment in 1961, Farbman had been for many years not only concertmaster of the St. Louis Orchestra but also its Associate Conductor, and though he was hired by Bain as a violin teacher and not as a conductor, in the course of time he was given more and more conducting assignments, and was eventually named a principal conductor. Not surprisingly, he worked especially well with string players, and was in general very popular with the students, who became "infected," Bain said, by "the love of music [that] permeated his entire musical concept."

On the opera production team, Hans Busch remained a principal stage director throughout Bain's deanship and beyond; this was also true of the School's other great director, Ross Allen. In the later 1950s, Bain was able to appoint two excellent set designers. Andreas Nomikos (recommended, like Vacano, by Herbert Graf) had his first stint as a visiting faculty member in 1957, and in 1960 became a regular member. The truly stellar appointment in this field had a similar history: as I noted earlier, Mario Cristini was first a visitor in 1959 (when he came as a Fulbright Scholar), and became a permanent member in 1961. Though his background was in the professional theater rather than academics, he proved to be, for the School's opera program, not only a great designer but a great teacher; and both Bain and Webb speak of him as the single most important person in the development of the opera program. After Cristini's death, in 1970, Bain was not immediately able to find a replacement that satisfied him. Nomikos was appointed Acting Director of Stage Design and Technical Production, but did not succeed to the regular position, and left the School. The permanent replacement, Antonin Dimitrov, was, especially by comparison with Cristini, a disappointment. He was let go in 1973, when Bain at last found the successor he wanted: Max Röthlisberger, who had long been the principal designer for the Zurich State Opera. In the meantime, in 1971, Charles David Higgins, a pupil of Cristini with a new Bachelor of Science degree in Theater, had been appointed as Master Painter; under Bain's successor, he eventually rose to be a full professor of scenic design, and became one of the regular designers for the Opera Theater.

Ballet was an especially difficult field to staff. As I noted earlier, Bain wanted a ballet program frankly as an adjunct to the opera program, and this fact, together with the fact that most of the most promising ballet students are to be found not at universities but at residential ballet schools, whence they proceed directly to ballet companies, made it hard to attract and hold good teachers. In 1954, Bain's initial appointee in ballet, Marguerite de Anguera, resigned and was replaced by Patricia Sparrow. Bain had somehow failed to recognize, though, that Sparrow's background in modern dance did not suit her to teaching classical ballet (which was what he mainly needed taught), and her appointment continued only until 1956, when she was replaced, on the recommendation of the head of the Metropolitan Opera Ballet School, by Gilbert Reed. Reed, who had danced with the Ballet Russe de Monte Carlo as well as the Met, seemed an ideal choice, especially since he was married to a talented young dancer—Nancy Reed—who could, Bain saw, dance the female leads at Bloomington. Gilbert Reed developed the curriculum for a ballet major, and was, in Bain's view, the best choreographer he ever recruited. In 1959 he inaugurated the annual productions of *The Nutcracker*, which, with local children and guest artists supplementing the members of the School, have become a pleasant Bloomington tradition. Reed was not, however, very successful in recruiting students to the program; enrollment remained small, and the Department was consequently unable to perform much of the standard repertory.

Finally, in 1969, Bain gave up on Reed and replaced him as department head with Marina Svetlova, who had been prima ballerina of the Met company (and had danced in some of its Bloomington productions). Latterly, she had directed a summer ballet school for high school students, and Bain correctly surmised that a significant number of the students of this school would, if Svetlova joined the faculty at Indiana, come there as ballet majors. Her appointment, though, precipitated the resignation both of Reed and of Richard Stowell, who had become the last of a series of ballet teachers brought in, seriatim, to assist Reed. Their departure allowed Bain to recruit, on Svetlova's recommendation, the famous Anton Dolin, who had been the principal partner of Alicia Markova and later the founding Artistic Director of London's Festival Ballet. Dolin was appointed Professor of Ballet and co-chair of the Department. He remained only until 1972, but while he was in Bloomington he proved, like Svetlova, to have substantial drawing power for students, and the increased enrollment allowed the appointment of three additional teachers: Kenneth Melville, Jurgen Pagels, and John Kriza. (Male teachers were preferred to females because of the chronic scarcity—endemic in ballet schools—of male students: *someone* had to dance the male roles in the Department's productions.) In the last years of Bain's deanship, then, the Ballet Department was substantially improved, though it was still by no means one of the School's strong departments.

If it took Bain a while to find a satisfactory head for the Ballet Department, the same was true of the Band Department. As I noted earlier, Bain was well aware that the School's public reputation depended heavily on the response to its large ensembles, including the Marching Hundred. At the time of his arrival, the band was still under the jurisdiction of the Department of Military Science and Tactics, but in the summer of 1948 an agreement was reached whereby an independent Band Department was created, under the general advisement of an interdisciplinary committee.

At the same time, Bain replaced the band director—Gerald Doty, a string player by training—with Daniel Martino, who had been band director at the Universities of Minnesota and Ohio. Under Martino, the quality of the Hundred improved; and the general situation of the Band Department improved, to Bain's mind, in 1951, when he succeeded in having it become a department of the School of Music.

Bain eventually decided, though, that Martino had not been a good choice for the directorship. The basic difficulty for the Band Department, once under the aegis of the School, was that it had to satisfy two very different constituencies: the large one that wanted stirring renditions of popular music of the kind associated especially with marching bands, and the much smaller but very influential one—consisting, as it did, of almost all of the School's faculty and its classically oriented wind students—that was interested in the more serious music associated with symphonic bands. Martino, whose previous experience had been primarily in directing marching bands at other sports-oriented Midwestern schools, was able to satisfy the first constituency but not the second, and in 1954 Bain fired him and replaced him with Michael Bowles, who, having been both the head of the Irish Military Band School and the conductor of the New Zealand National Orchestra, seemed unusually well qualified to satisfy both constituencies. Since he had no experience of American-style marching bands, though, a high school band director, Logan Turrentine, was hired at the same time, as Director of Marching Bands. Proving unsatisfactory in this role, he was replaced after two years by Ronald Gregory, who was appointed as Bowles's co-director, and, when Bowles left the next year, as Director of Bands. By this time, as Bain later said, he had tried "nearly every combination of talents and individuals." However, Gregory was also unable to satisfy the second of the band's constituencies. (There developed, Bain says, a widespread view that John Philip Sousa himself could not have created a band that would satisfy this constituency.) By 1967 the criticism of Gregory by the wind and percussion faculty had become so insistent that Bain replaced him in the directorship by Frederick Ebbs, who had previously been director at the University of Iowa, where he had led both a typical Big Ten marching band and a particularly fine symphonic band. With this appointment, the problem of the directorship was solved: Ebbs went on to have a distinguished career at Indiana.

In addition to the marching band and the vocal ensembles, Bain's other concern in the area of popular music was the development of a jazz program. He had started such a program (which went on to achieve national prominence) at North Texas, and by 1959 was ready to launch one at Indiana. In that year he appointed Edwin ("Buddy") Baker, a trombonist who was an alumnus of the School, to establish jazz ensembles, and in 1961 added Roger Max Pemberton, who had just completed a Master's degree in woodwinds at the School, and whom Bain regarded as an excellent jazz arranger. Pemberton left in 1964 and Baker the following year, when he was replaced by Jerry Coker. Coker himself stayed only a year; in leaving, he recommended as his replacement David Baker. Although Bain was (according to Baker) not inclined to accept that advice—he wanted a "name"—he eventually did so. Bain never admitted to any reluctance in the matter, and in later years, Baker says, frequently told him, "that's the best decision I ever made." And indeed it *was* one of the best. Baker himself has achieved great distinction, and the School's pioneering undergraduate and graduate degree programs in jazz, which he designed, have served as models for similar programs elsewhere.

A large majority of Bain's appointments were in applied music, and by the time he left the deanship only about a fifth of the over 150 faculty members of the School were academics—a proportion that reflects both the fact that the School had become overwhelmingly performance-centered and the fact that academic music is taught in classes, not one-on-one. Bain was, however, just as committed to making the best possible appointments in academic music as in applied. He sincerely believed in a rounded musical education, and in particular, as he had said in his strategic memo to Vice President Briscoe, thought that it was "impossible to build a fine music school" without having "an A-No. 1 theory department." And of course he also wanted a distinguished academic-music faculty simply because he wanted the School to be the best in everything.

His policy of incremental improvement of the faculty could not, though, reach the same heights in academic music as it eventually did in applied, for several reasons. Those Eastern universities where music had always meant more or less exclusively academic music had an insurmountable head start on Indiana in this area; and the fact that the School rapidly became known as one strongly focused on performance did not help in closing the gap. Then too, Bain did not have the same level of personal interest in or knowledge of academic musicians as of performers, nor was he ever able to achieve the kind of snowball effect in academic music that he achieved in applied: there were relatively few first-rate academic musicians on faculty to attract others, whether by personally assisting in the recruitment process or simply by being known to teach at Indiana. Not surprisingly, he did best in musicology, where he did have (in addition to his former North Texas student Ralph Daniel) Paul Nettl and, from 1950, Willi Apel to attract not only first-rate musicologists from elsewhere but also excellent students who might subsequently be recruited to the faculty.

Although Bain's interests in musicology were restricted to music in the European classical tradition, without any effort on his part, or any expense, from early in his tenure members of the School were able to participate in a pioneering effort in ethnomusicology. In 1948, the Department of Anthropology acquired George Herzog, a Hungarian-born scholar who was the foremost authority in America on what was then called comparative musicology. From 1948–49, Herzog offered a course (later a pair of one-semester courses) on Folk and Primitive Music; this was also listed among School of Music courses. Those who took the course included Paul Nettl's son Bruno (who completed all his degrees at the School, culminating in his 1953 doctorate in musicology). Indeed, Herzog, though not a member of the School's faculty, supervised Nettl's dissertation. With its strong Anthropology Department and emerging programs in folklore and linguistics—both of which assumed departmental status in the early 1950s—the University in fact afforded a rich nexus for ethnological studies in general: Nettl also took courses from Stith Thompson and C. F. Voegelin, as well as from Apel.

Herzog had brought with him from his previous position at Columbia an archive of ethnomusicological materials; during one of his several lengthy hospitalizations, in the summer of 1954, his recent student Nettl was appointed to put the archive (which Herzog had evidently treated as his private collection) on a more formal footing. Shortly after this appointment, though, Nettl was offered a teaching position, which he prudently accepted, at Wayne State University, and the curatorship of the archive went instead to another recent graduate of the doctoral program in musicology, George List. Thus List became in 1954 the first supervisor of the Archives of Folk and Primitive Music (now the Archives of Traditional Music), a position he retained until his retirement in 1976; he also had an academic appointment, first in Anthropology and later in Folklore. Herzog's paired folk-music courses (not always taught by Herzog himself) continued to be eligible for credit in the School of Music until 1966, when they were replaced in the Bulletin by two new Anthropology courses, Seminar in Ethnomusicology I and II. From 1960 through 1964, List appeared in the Bulletin as Lecturer in Music—at no cost to the School, as Bain smugly observed. The School also benefited, indirectly, from the 1962 appointment of Alan P. Merriam to the Department of Anthropology. A leading authority on African music, he played a key role in making the University a center of ethnomusicology rivaled in size only by UCLA.

During this same period, Bain made five regular appointments in musicology. John White, who as a doctoral candidate in the early 1950s had performed brilliantly as both teacher and researcher, was appointed to the faculty in 1961. To Bain's chagrin, however, he came and went very considerably, leaving in 1967 to become director of the early music ensemble Pro Musica, returning in 1970, and leaving again and finally a year later to accept a position at Hunter College. A far more durable appointment was made in 1962, when the Director of the University's Russian and East European Institute, Robert Burns, approached Bain with the proposal that he appoint a young scholar of Russian music, Malcolm Brown.

Burns's institute was, in those Cold War and post-Sputnik days, very well funded, and he offered to pay all of Brown's salary for the first year, and half of it the next. Some members of the Department had met Brown at conferences and endorsed the proposal, and so the young scholar, who was completing his doctorate at Florida State, was hired. He stayed throughout his career—declining offers from other universities largely because he knew they could not match Indiana's musical life—and became not only an important scholar of twentieth-century Russian music but a key member of the School, serving as chair of the Musicology Department for many years.

The first great luminary of the Department, Paul Nettl, had reached the mandatory retirement age of seventy in 1959, but had been reappointed on a year-to-year, part-time basis for several years thereafter. When, in 1964, he finally went into full retirement, Bain, who thought it necessary to replace him with another eminent figure, still had not secured one. In 1965, however, he was able to appoint Hans Tischler, a senior scholar who had completed his doctorate at Yale in 1942. When he came to Indiana, Tischler had already long been engaged on his great edition of the medieval motets. Bain's recruitment in this field was effectively completed the following year, when he brought in two Assistant Professors, Thomas Noblitt, a recent doctoral graduate of the University of Texas, and Austin Caswell, a product of the University of Minnesota. Both remained at Indiana throughout their careers.

Whereas Bain almost always went outside for his appointees in musicology, music theory rapidly became (and has remained) by far the most striking example of the "inbreeding" of the School's faculty. His first two appointees in the field—Roy Will (brought in as Associate Professor in 1949, to head the Department) and Preston Stedman (appointed in 1953)—had both done their graduate work at Eastman, as had Charles Kent (appointed in 1955) and Lewis Rowell (1959), but most other appointees in the field, beginning in the middle 1950s, had Indiana doctorates. William Christ, who had completed his doctorate in 1952 and then taught at the University of Cincinnati, returned to the School as Assistant Professor in 1955. Allen Winold was appointed in 1957, while still a graduate student, as Assistant to the Dean and Instructor in Music; when he completed his doctorate in 1963, he was elevated to the rank of Assistant Professor. Richard Pierre ("Pete") DeLone had been a Graduate Assistant in theory while working on a doctorate in composition. He completed his studies in 1958 and, after two years as an Assistant Professor at Washington State University, returned to Indiana as a regular member of the theory faculty. (He served as chairman of the Department from 1968 to 1977.) Vernon Kliewer completed his doctorate in theory in 1961 and was appointed Instructor. (He had previously taught at Arizona State College, Flagstaff.) The same year, William Thomson joined the faculty as Assistant Professor: he had been an undergraduate at North Texas during the 1940s, had earned an Indiana doctorate in 1952, and had subsequently been head of music at a Texas teachers college. Mary Wennerstrom, who had been at the School since her undergraduate days as a piano major and had remained as a graduate student in theory, impressed the members of the Department so greatly that she was appointed as Lecturer in 1964, only a year after completing her master's degree. In the latter part of Bain's tenure, though, four outsiders were appointed: Horace Reisberg and Gary Wittlich in 1966, Robert Shallenberg in 1969, and Bruno Amato in 1971. But Bain's final appointee in the field was another local product, John Nagosky, who had taken his doctorate at the School in 1962 and was appointed as Assistant Professor in 1972.

To at least some extent, the Department's heavy reliance on Indiana graduates resulted from its having evolved its own system for teaching theory (eventually embodied in over a dozen textbooks authored by members of the Department in various combinations). This was the so-called "lecture-drill session plan," in which, as in the physical-science model of lectures plus laboratories, students were lectured to in large groups twice a week and then divided, for the other three days, into classes of ten or twelve for drill and additional instruction. Almost the only people who could, it was thought, function effectively as instructors in this system were those who had cut their teeth on it as Graduate Assistants in the drill sections. But surely the Department also suffered from a competitive disadvantage in recruiting good theorists from outside. For them, the general disincentive to academic musicians inherent in the School's well-known domination by applied music was reinforced by the need, if one took a position there, of coping with the huge lecture classes that increasingly typified the Department's operations.

If a good Theory Department was high among Bain's priorities, the Music Education Department was not a priority at all. As he said to me, in the early years he "neglected music education very specifically," so that he could use the available faculty positions "to get in people who could really blossom"—by which he meant, at least primarily, good applied musicians. As I noted earlier, this focus not only conformed to his personal interests but was a necessary response to the trend in enrollment away from music education into applied music, and the consequent chronic shortage of applied-music teachers: in comparison with other fields, music education was, at the time of Bain's arrival, very fully staffed. Nor was he, in this field, in a position to apply his policy of incremental improvement by firing people and replacing them with better ones. The people on the music education faculty, he told Wolford, "were on tenure, and we had to live with them until they matured to seventy, or left this world sooner."

Still, enrollment in music education, though gradually falling in proportion to that in applied music, continued through most of Bain's deanship to grow in absolute numbers, and by 1953 it was necessary to add another member to the Department. Demonstrating at this juncture that his concern for quality extended even to the bottom of his list of priorities, he did not make a junior appointment but brought in, at the rank of Professor, Jack Watson, who had been on the faculty of the University of Southern California. Watson was a scholar of some standing, and Bain assigned him primarily graduate courses, including those in research methods.

In 1963, however, Watson, who had risen to become not only Chairman of Music Education but Director of Graduate Studies for the School, left to take the position of Dean of his alma mater, the College-Conservatory of Music of Cincinnati. At the same time, Bain let go another member of the Music Education Department, Ross Ekstrom, an Instructor who had served as Watson's assistant. He replaced the two men with William Sears, a good researcher who specialized in music therapy, and Miriam Gelvin, a specialist in elementary education. In 1966, he added Charles Hoffer, and three years later brought in both Robert Klotman (recruited as department head) and Leon Fosha. His final appointment in music education came in 1972, when he hired Grace Kirkwood.

If Bain was relatively little interested in music education, composition was, like theory, among his high priorities: he hoped that it would assume a "central place" in the School. Moreover, again in contrast to the situation in music education, he had, from the beginning, room to make appointments. Sanders's resignation left one vacancy—which reopened in 1952, when Bain dismissed Fuleihan. In the aftermath, the composition faculty consisted of Bernhard Heiden and a fraction of the trombonist Thomas Beversdorf, who taught composition in addition to his instrument.

As I noted earlier, however, Bain did not appoint another composer until 1957—when he named not one but two. The first of these, Walter Kaufmann, represented a splendid addition not only in composition but in musicology. A Bohemian who had studied in Berlin and Prague, Kaufmann was a brilliant, multi-talented musician, a prolific composer who was also an accomplished pianist, a conductor, and a noted authority on the music of India. His opera *A Parfait for Irene* had, it will be recalled, been given its premiere at Bloomington in 1952. Kaufmann arrived in the winter semester of the 1956–57 academic year; the following autumn, Bain brought in Roy Harris (who had lost out to Sanders for the deanship) as Visiting Professor. He stayed on for two additional years as Resident Composer. But Bain was disappointed that Harris did not prove to be a strong attractant to first-rate composition students; and Harris, always restless anyway, moved on after the third year.

In the remaining years of his deanship, Bain was able to make three other notable appointments in composition. In 1961 he acquired Juan

Orrego-Salas, a distinguished Chilean composer who had been forced out of his position as head of the Conservatorio Nacional of the University of Chile by a shift in the country's political topography. He came to the School as the result of an overture made to Bain by the Rockefeller Foundation, which was interested in funding the start-up phase of a program in Latin-American Music; the Center that Orrego-Salas developed—the largest of its kind—became one of the ornaments of the School.

In 1967, still bothered by the School's continuing relative weakness in contemporary music, and especially electronic music, Bain brought in the remarkable Iannis Xenakis. Born in Romania of Greek parents in 1922, Xenakis had taken a degree in civil engineering in Athens and achieved some distinction as an architect; he had also become prominent as a theorist and composer of electronic music. At Indiana, he took over the electronic music laboratory that had been established in 1966 (and that evolved under him into the Center for Mathematical and Automated Music). From the first, though, the relationship between Xenakis and most of the rest of the School was not entirely happy. His early lectures on new approaches to composition aroused substantial interest, not just in the School but among avant-garde thinkers across the campus. But his mathematically based theories proved extremely difficult to grasp, and interest in the lectures rapidly waned. Moreover, Xenakis's music turned out to be not much played at Indiana—perhaps, as Bain thought, because other members of the School were not sufficiently interested in it to make the "heroic effort" that adequate performance of it required.

By the time Xenakis resigned from the School in 1973, he had virtually no students: those interested in electronic music found Bain's last appointee in composition, John Eaton, much more attractive. Eaton's connection with the School began in the 1969–70 academic year, when he was brought to campus to assist in the preparation of a production of his opera *Heracles,* which was to be performed at the dedication of the new opera house then under construction. The following year he joined the faculty.

In general, there was a reciprocal relation between the size and quality of the faculty and that of the student body. As Bain had seen clearly from the outset, improving the faculty in a particular field was the best way of attracting more students (and a larger number of first-rate ones) in it; in turn, enrollment growth allowed him to enlarge the size of the faculty. And as he enlarged it, he improved it still further, both in the areas in which student numbers were most rapidly expanding and in those where he hoped to *stimulate* expansion. Taken together, these areas embraced the full range of musical education for budding professionals and for amateurs; thus both the faculty and the student body expanded rapidly. By 1952 total enrollment had reached 500; ten years later it had doubled to

1,000; in 1971 it peaked at 1,701 (859 women, 842 men), while the masthead listed a faculty of 154. The orchestra- and opera-centered school now had four orchestras, and mounted from seven to nine different operas each year; the School could boast that it offered opera every Saturday night during the fall and winter semesters. Among American cities, only New York had an opera season as long.

By the end of Bain's deanship, the School had in fact been for some years the largest one anywhere—the huge supermarket or Macy's of music, with courses and degree programs in every area, that he had envisioned from the beginning. The Bachelor of Music was offered in piano (and piano accompanying), harpsichord, organ, all the orchestral instruments, voice, composition, theory, and jazz studies. The Bachelor of Music Education was offered with specialties in either choral or instrumental music or a combination of both. There were three different Bachelor of Science programs: in Music and an Outside Field, in Ballet, and in Opera Scenic Technique; the Bachelor of Arts in Music continued to be offered through the College of Arts and Sciences. There were also (since 1971) two programs in stage technology, a one-year program leading to a Certificate in Stage Technology and a two-year one leading to the degree of Associate in Science. At the graduate level, the degree of Master of Music, Applied Music Major, was offered in the same fields as the Bachelor of Music (minus accompanying and plus voice pedagogy). There were also Master of Music programs with a major in either strings or woodwinds (for those who wanted proficiency in a range of instruments in one of these families), in Organ and Church Music, in Electronic and Computer Music, and in Choral Conducting, Instrumental Conducting, and Musicology. Then there was the Master of Music Education, the Master of Science—offered in Music Theater Scenic Techniques, Stage Direction for Opera, and Ballet—and the Master of Arts in Music, Music Education, and Arts Administration. The Doctor of Philosophy degree was offered in Music Education, Musicology, and Theory; there was also a Doctor of Music Education. The Doctor of Music was offered in a variety of fields: Music Literature and Performance (in orchestral instruments, voice, or piano); Music Literature and Pedagogy (in voice, piano, or brass); Voice Pedagogy; Composition; Coaching, Conducting, Performance, and Literature of Opera; and in Instrumental or Choral Conducting. There were also Specialist Certificate programs, open to those with master's degrees, in Multiple Arts (arts, humanities, and education) and School Music Administration and Supervision; and there was the Artist Diploma program, for elite performers—often foreigners—who had, or thought they had, no use for an academic degree. (There had been such a program on the books in Merrill's day, but at that time it represented merely wishful thinking.) Finally, studies in several special areas were facilitated by a series of research and performance centers. At the end of Bain's deanship there were four of these: the Latin-American Music Center, the Center for Electronic and Computer Music (which succeeded Xenakis's Center for Mathematical and Automated Music), the Black Music Center (established in 1971 with the support of the National Endowment for the Humanities but discontinued after 1975), and the Institute for Vocal Research (designed to foster the development of better, scientifically based methods for the teaching of voice).

Another dean might have thought there should be some limit to the growth of the School, or at least that the rate of growth should be proportioned to the rate at which the physical facilities needed to accommodate the swelling ranks of students and faculty could be provided. But until the last years of his tenure Bain never really had an upper limit for enrollment in mind, and his idea of the optimum growth rate for the School was that it should grow as fast as possible. To be sure, in the first half of his deanship he frequently referred to a goal of 500 undergraduate music majors plus 150—later 200—graduate students. But when in 1960 total enrollment surpassed 700—with 482 undergraduates and 315 graduates—he simply continued beyond it, without pause. The growth of the School consistently outpaced that of the University as a whole; in 1950, for example, when the end of the postwar enrollment surge resulted in a decrease in enrollment of 4–5 percent for the University overall, the number of music majors increased by 13–14 percent. Nonetheless, in faculty meetings Bain frequently stressed the need to push the enrollment higher. In his 1957–58 report to Wells, he lamented that "the undergraduate enrollment is making no spectacular gains"—as if spectacular gains were only what he had a right to expect, and without any consideration as to why such gains might be a desideratum.

In the central administration, though, the concern was not with a temporary absence of spectacular gains but with the general mushrooming trend of the School's enrollment. Bain knew this; he told Wolford that he thought "there were many times when the administration were dismayed at the growth, and didn't know what to do with it." (This was doubtless especially the case because the instructional cost per student in Music, though still offset by an applied-music fee, continued to be, as it had been since Merrill's time, among the highest of any unit of the University.) Desperate to find out what enrollment goal Bain really had in mind, Wells on one occasion asked Mary, who told him she thought he might be aiming for about 1,500. Asking Bain directly, Wells got the same answer: a student body of 1,500 would, he said, "contain a sufficient number of students of all kinds of majors and skills to guarantee that the music production program . . . would be of strong assistance in the students' educating one another"; that is, there would be enough students "to perform the great monumental works of music history." But when enrollment did reach 1,500, in 1968, Bain let it expand still further (though, as we will see, in the final years of his deanship he took a different tack). Like the number 500, the number 1,500 didn't actually mean much to him; he had given it, he recalled in *The Bain Regime,* only because "the answer to President Wells' question seemed to lie in the announcement of a specific figure"; to me, he freely acknowledged that he never had any particular maximum enrollment in mind: the School "just grew." He was, moreover, deeply concerned when, after 1965, the enrollment in music education began to decline. It did so, clearly, because the School had acquired the reputation of not being interested in music education students, and of not treating them well. Although this situation was a direct and probably inevitable consequence of Bain's having focused the School so intently on the training of elite performers, he was genuinely distressed by it, and in the last several years of his deanship devoted much time in meetings of the Academic Council (the committee of department chairs, which, formed in 1961, absorbed the Advisory Council two years later) to the development of ways both to increase the number of music education students and to assure that, once enrolled, they were treated equitably.

As for the idea that increases in enrollment should not be allowed to outpace the School's ability to provide physical facilities for its students and faculty, Bain was convinced that adherence to this principle would simply preclude the School's achieving the size he thought it needed. As he assured his colleagues, new facilities would come if and only if the School were clearly overcrowded. In 1951, speaking about his enrollment goal of "at least" 500 undergraduates and 200 graduate students, he observed that "if there were that many students the buildings would not be adequate, but if the need were there, we would get more buildings."

This theory—an application of the general principle that "you have only what you create and that's all"—was surely correct. Additional facilities could only *follow* increased enrollment, never precede it. But unfortunately there must always be a substantial time lag between the recognition of the need and the satisfaction of it. This being the case, when one drove expansion as hard and unremittingly as Bain did, the shortage of facilities was bound to be chronic and extreme.

As we have seen, already in the late Sanders years the Music Building was badly overcrowded. In Bain's first summer at Indiana, the construction of the small annex brought some relief, as did, a year later, the provision of classroom space and an additional sixty practice rooms in East Hall. Nonetheless, with the rapid expansion of enrollment and faculty size, the School continued to be overcrowded—and was, after a while, grotesquely so. In his 1948–49 report, Bain observed that in the Music Building "every tiny room, such as the projection booth, the organ chamber, the organ blower rooms . . . is converted into studio and office space." The following year's report noted that the men's and women's locker rooms had "been cut up into studios and the lockers placed in the halls";

the lounge, too, had been partitioned into small offices. Even with the conversion of the locker rooms into studios, by 1951 twenty-five studios were being shared, either between two faculty members or between a faculty member and a Graduate Assistant. The rule was that anyone who taught less than a full load had to share. Manski and Kaskas were among those reduced to this indignity.

The administration's preferred response to the overcrowding was to grant the School tenancy of various buildings scattered around the campus. By 1953, the School's activities were spread over seven buildings, some of them as much as half a mile apart: the Music Building and its annex; East Hall; and (as Bain enumerated them in his 1952–53 report), "Lincoln House on Forest Place for offices, studios and classrooms; the former Paint Shop on Jordan Field for Ballet instruction; South Hoosier Hall for choral rehearsal and for classes." There were also band rehearsal quarters in the University Auditorium. As time passed, some of these buildings were lost, to different uses or to demolition, and were replaced by others: the 1955–56 report, for example, notes that Graduate Assistants were teaching applied music in the former School of Religion Building and in Hight House and Crane House. In 1959–60 the School's activities were spread over a total of eight buildings.

There were two problems with this response to Music's crowded condition. First, it dispersed the School's business all over campus (enabling Bain to set Bill Ross trudging great distances between classes). Second, it meant that the School was using a number of buildings that were not always well suited to its specialized activities and not, in general, the newest or nicest buildings on campus. Bain was bitter about the slights he perceived in this aspect of the administration's treatment of the School. Years later, he grumbled to Wolford that its development had been inhibited by the administration's unwillingness to "get us quality practice rooms. . . . we got the flimsiest, we used old buildings of all kinds that were ready for demolition."

These unsatisfactory arrangements were, as I observed earlier, at least in part an unavoidable result of the tremendous rate of expansion that Bain imposed on the School. He himself, however, did not see it that way, and indeed regarded the stopgap measures in housing as simply one example of a general niggardliness that, he thought, characterized the attitude of the central administration toward the School. Thus despite the enormous number of appointments he was allowed to make, he felt hard done by in that the rate of appointments did not keep pace with the enrollment growth; and despite having been provided with enough money to have built a faculty that was surely unsurpassed in overall quality by any in the world, he felt, looking back, that "the administration really did very, very little to help from the standpoint of using money to get the very best teachers." In fact, with a splendid irony, this most favored of the deans concluded that he was, in terms of financial support, the *least* favored. He placed the blame on Wells. Though in public pronouncements he constantly lauded the President for his generous support of Music, in private he used to say to Charles Webb (in low but pungent style) that Wells "always had us sucking off the hind tit." In *Being Lucky,* Wells did in fact acknowledge that Bain "was allocated much less money than he could have expected on the basis of the School of Music's rapidly rising enrollment." But of course no amount of support would have seemed enough to Bain.

While the School could get by, if inconveniently and unhappily, with various temporary supplements to the Music Building and East Hall, there was no question, from the early years of Bain's deanship, that it needed another large permanent building. By the 1955–56 academic year, the central administration was ready to respond to this need; in July 1956, Bain was able to report to his faculty that a new building was in the final stage of architect's drawings. The structure, which would cost $3,000,000, was to be an annex to the Music Building; during the following academic year, the small existing annex was torn down to make room for the new one. It was not, however, until June 1958 that ground was broken for the building, which was finally opened for use in the summer of 1960; at the same time, the scattered temporary accommodations were relinquished.

Seldom in the annals of architecture can a building so unattractive have been grafted onto one so handsome. At 100,000 square feet, the Music Annex is two and a half times as large as the parent building. Unlike that building, though, it does not have its area disposed in the usual rectangular shape with the usual windows. A five-story, limestone-clad cylinder, the structure is joined to the main building by a four-story bridge. Inside, each floor has two concentric circular hallways. These are lined variously with studios and offices (totaling 95), practice rooms (105), rehearsal rooms (5), and classrooms (3); in the original configuration, there were also a ballet studio and a sheet-music library. A cylindrical core contains lounges, lockers, and washrooms; straight hallways, leading to the bridge on one side and the back staircase on the other, bisect the circles (though not the core). The effect is labyrinthine, and the ease of losing one's bearings in the building is increased by the circumstance that its corridors are windowless. Indeed the building as a whole is windowless except for the first two floors. If the effect from inside is of a maze, that from outside is of something like a very tall cyclotron. One is not surprised to learn that when the faculty was first presented with a model of the building there was some complaint that there had not been enough faculty participation in the planning, and (as the minutes of a faculty meeting of September 1956 delicately put it) "some question about the appearance." Bain explained that the third and fourth floors were given over to practice rooms, "in which windows are not desired; fifth floor is rehearsal rooms which are generally without windows."

The "Round Building" (as it is commonly called) did not have its dedication until April 15, 1962, when it was celebrated with a program preceded by a concert of the Symphonic Band and followed by the annual presentation of *Parsifal.* The principal speaker for the occasion was Paul Hume, the music critic of the *Washington Post* (who had achieved popular celebrity when Harry Truman threatened to beat him up for criticizing his daughter's singing).

Unfortunately, by the time the building opened, the School, whose enrollment reached 797 in the fall of 1960, had already more or less outgrown the capacity of the fused buildings plus East Hall. Moreover, the inadequacies of East Hall were ever more glaring, and the discrepancy between the quality of the School's opera program and the quality of its theater was ever more galling to Bain and doubtless to others. By 1960, when the Music Annex was completed, the central administration had conceded that a new opera theater should be built, and at that time drawings were prepared for a square annex (including an opera theater) to the round annex; Wells mentioned the plans for a new building to replace East Hall in his remarks at the dedication of the Annex. But the sixties were a period of rapid growth in the University as a whole, and it was impossible to keep up with the need for new buildings; trailers were scattered around the campus. Thus for several years the plans for an additional music building stalled.

In 1967, however, Eggers and Higgins of New York (the University architects and, in that capacity, the firm responsible for the Round Building) were asked to draw up plans for a Musical Arts Center that would be built on or near the site of East Hall. In order to clear the way for the eventual razing of the old building (and in an attempt to keep the need for a new one literally before the administration's eyes), Bain secured permission to transplant the opera productions, as of fall 1967, to the auditorium of the University School (a laboratory school that had recently moved to a new building). Though a handsome facility, the auditorium seated only 600, and was inconvenient for the staging of opera in various ways. Essential modifications were made to the auditorium; lighting, curtains, and other items were moved from East Hall, which continued to be used for recitals and classes.

In a meeting of March 1949, Bain had reminded his colleagues on the Advisory Council that smoking was prohibited in East Hall, since "it is a fire trap." On January 24, 1968, the building burned to the ground. The scene was operatic; Ross Allen recalls Fritz Magg saying how Wagnerian it looked: the conflagration of Valhalla. More prosaically, the Bloomington newspaper noted that forty-six pianos were destroyed; when the fire was out, spectators "could clearly see in the ashes the locations of each of the pianos in the practice rooms."

Wells recalled that he was in Indianapolis on the day of the fire, and saw the smoke cloud on his way back. When he heard that it was East Hall that was burning, he said, "Oh, Bain gets his new building." Bain himself enjoyed recounting that "many friends and acquaintances" jokingly accused him of starting the fire, or at least arranging it, as a way of guaranteeing that he would get his opera theater. Certainly the destruction of East Hall made the provision of a new building more urgent (and helped to clear its site); and contracts for it were awarded in April. While the new building rose, the School was again granted some temporary accommodations, in several former dormitories: Sycamore Hall (a handsome limestone building adjacent to the Annex) and three buildings in the ramshackle "Trees Center" complex not far from the School. (The School had also used Trees Center buildings in the 1950s.) For some of the School's purposes these buildings served well enough, though, not being soundproofed, very poorly for practice rooms; and fluctuations of temperature and humidity made them disastrous for the pianos that had been bought to replace those destroyed in the fire. (The School has retained Sycamore Hall ever since, using it for offices, classrooms, and, until the opening of the Simon Center, the Music Library; most of this space will finally be relinquished once the remaining phases of construction of the Center are complete.)

The late 1960s and early 1970s were a time of revolutionary fervor, nowhere more than in the universities. The activist idealism displayed by many American students in the Civil Rights Movement of the middle of the decade of the sixties turned, by its late years, into massive, overtly revolutionary, sometimes violent student protests against the Vietnam War. At Indiana, the protest movement was not less intense than elsewhere. In 1968, Elvis J. Stahr, who had succeeded Wells as President in 1962, resigned, citing "presidental fatigue" as his reason. He was replaced by Joseph L. Sutton, whose tough-guy approach to the protestors proved so disastrous that he was relieved of office in the spring of 1971.

Within the Music School, protests were comparatively subdued, probably, as Bain thought, because most of the students, as aspiring professionals committed to an arduous and unrelenting discipline, knew they had little time to spare for politics. Nonetheless, by the spring of 1970 (the time of the American invasion of Cambodia), enough music students were heavily involved in political activity that the Academic Council felt it appropriate to issue a statement recommending that faculty "sympathetically consider flexible grading procedures whereby grades of 'Incomplete' or grades earned to date may be awarded whenever feasible to afford opportunity to those students desiring to cease attending all courses as of this date in order to devote their energies to activities related to current issues."

Activism was, however, not limited to national issues but spilled over, at the School as elsewhere, into a general rebellion against authority, including in particular traditional academic authority. The music students, Bain recalled, "protested practically every procedure offered for their education by the faculty." The ensemble requirement was a special focus of discontent. Students had always resented the requirement, but it now chafed even more than in the past, especially as a result, in two ways, of the fact that some of them played in professional orchestras in nearby cities such as Terre Haute, Fort Wayne, Evansville, and Owensboro, Kentucky. The mandatory (and unpaid) rehearsals and performances entailed in the ensemble requirement conflicted with the students' professional engagements; moreover, playing in unionized orchestras they learned union ways, and began to bargain with the School for strict limitations on their obligation to its ensembles; and indeed a formal agreement was worked out whereby students could be required to devote no more than ninety hours each semester to ensemble duties. Students also wanted to play more solos, and the School's programming practices were altered somewhat in response to this demand. Even the operatic programming may have been touched by the ferment of the times. In 1969 the School presented Handel's *Deidamia,* perhaps in part because it was, as the opening sentence of the program note proclaimed, "an opera about a draft dodger named Achilles."

From students the spirit of insurrection passed, if in muted form, to faculty. As I noted earlier, Bain's autocratic appointments procedures became a subject of discontent. In the University as a whole, new, much more elaborate policies, involving committees at various levels, were enacted to govern decisions on promotion, tenure, and dismissal. Student evaluations of faculty members' teaching began to play a role in these decisions, and student input began to be solicited on candidates for appointment. Bain, of course, greeted these developments with dismay and contempt. The idea that students knew enough to make worthwhile evaluations of their teachers offended him. As for the faculty committees on promotion and tenure, they were "not a complete waste of time," but they did "slow the decision-making process by many hours and much effort on the part of uninitiated, unknowing and sometimes unsophisticated faculty who had been appointed to the review committees." The times were aptly characterized, he thought, as the "Era of Documentation and Paper." He doubted (as the general) that "a successful war could be waged if consultation on every move were in the hands of a committee or if approval of committees had to be secured before action could prevail." In truth, his style of leadership had fallen out of fashion.

In these stressful years, Bain, in consultation with his colleagues, reversed course on two matters dear to him. First, he decided that the annual productions of *Parsifal* would be discontinued. These had long been unpopular with students who played in the orchestra for them, on the ground that playing the same work year after year wasted their time. Moreover, *Parsifal* required such a large outlay of the School's human and material resources that the rest of the second-semester opera series was necessarily more modest than many would have liked: the other productions had to be relatively small, and it was difficult to create *new* productions. The possibility of dropping the annual *Parsifal* had indeed been discussed as long ago as the middle 1950s: Ross Allen recalls a meeting when someone asked whether there were another Wagner opera that the School could do instead. (St. Leger, who disapproved of Hoffman's heavy use of the scissors, suggested that the answer might be to "do the cuts of *Parsifal*.") The question of whether the annual production should be discontinued had become more pressing by the late 1960s, because the audience was declining (and fell below 2,000 in 1969), so that the opera, which had paid its way for years, was in danger of becoming a money-loser. In this context, Bain in November 1969 raised with the Academic Council the question of whether the presentations should be halted. Various opinions were expressed. Toward the end of the discussion, Allen Winold made the telling point that the annual *Parsifal* no longer really functioned as the School's signature event. "Twenty years ago" the School's operatic reputation "rested on its production of *Parsifal*." Now, though, "it is known as the School with opera every Saturday night. If we are concerned about discarding a tradition, shouldn't we simply recognize that one tradition has been replaced by a better one?" A straw vote indicated that a majority of the Council agreed with this position, and in the aftermath of the meeting Bain canceled the 1970 production (which would have been the twenty-second one), opting to present *The Valkyrie* instead. In 1970–71, there was, for the first time since 1949, no Wagner opera. *The Valkyrie* was reprised in 1972, and *Parsifal* was played two more times: in 1973 (Bain's final year as Dean), with a dedication to the memory of Ernst Hoffman, to whom Bain, speaking from the stage, paid a full and moving tribute, and in 1976. In retrospect, though, Bain thought he had made a mistake in canceling the annual production. He took full responsibility for the decision (faculty assertiveness or no, he was still dictator), but looking back twenty years later, he pronounced it "a very sad, inappropriate thing to happen to a . . . truly noble and esteemed tradition."

By the 1969–70 academic year (when the School had 1,565 students), Bain had also begun to second-guess his policy of unlimited expansion of enrollment. At the beginning of the next academic year (when the enrollment dropped to 1,504), he discussed with the Academic Council the fact that there were "too many" undergraduates, which rendered it impossible to provide anyone other than graduate students to teach many of them applied music. There was also the distressing shortage of facilities, especially practice rooms; even instrumental majors could now be assigned a practice room for only two hours a day.

For the remainder of Bain's deanship, the question of how to limit enrollment was a constant theme; it gained more urgency from the circumstance that the recession of the early 1970s had brought the School to what Bain characterized in a March 1971 meeting as "the lowest financial ebb we have been [at] in a number of years." The problem posed by the financial difficulty was, he added, exacerbated by the fact that the School was competing for the best students with some institutions whose budgets had not been so drastically curtailed. (Presumably these were the more affluent private universities and conservatories—for example, Curtis, whose endowment has always allowed it not to charge tuition.) The Dean was now happy to attribute to someone else the idea—for which he had taken full credit in the past—that facilities would always track enrollment: he referred to "a previous high administrator of the University whose theory was that a flood of students would solve any problem faced by the University." Bain had "reservations about that theory now, however, because there is always a 'lag in the hardware.'" In the fall of his last year, enrollment, which had reached its all-time high of 1,701 the preceding year, dropped to 1,516 (a number that Bain now professed to think "ideal"). His final report to the President recorded the unsurprising fact that "it has become apparent that our enrollment cut-back has led to an increase in quality of the students in general."

Though Bain's last years in office were marked by increasing student and faculty discontent, and by revisionism and retrenchment, they were also marked by the great culminating event of his career, the completion of the Musical Arts Center. He had not had sufficient opportunity or knowledge to shape adequately his first Indiana opera theater, and, in truth, had he had these in unlimited abundance, no great masterpiece could have been made of the converted recreation center. But the second time around he had both the necessary knowledge and the clout, and he took care to get the new theater right.

As I noted earlier, by 1960 the University administration was on record as intending to erect a building to replace East Hall. In the early stage of formulating plans for the new structure, Bain brought a series of theater designers to campus to share their expertise. But by this time the School's own faculty included members with a detailed knowledge of various opera theaters, especially Mario Cristini and Ted Jones. Cristini, having come to Indiana after thirty years as stage designer for the San Carlo Opera in Naples, and having also created sets for La Scala, the Paris Opera, Covent Garden, the Met, and other theaters, was, Bain found, as knowledgeable as most of the external consultants. Jones, a member of the technical staff, had formerly managed a touring repertory theater and the symphony orchestra of the U.S. Seventh Army in occupied Germany, and while there had seen a number of the celebrated new German opera houses in construction. He returned to Germany in 1961 on a Fulbright Grant to make a formal study of the technical facilities of these houses.

In this as in all other matters, though, Bain wanted to maintain personal oversight, and so in late October of 1962 he and Mary, their trip partially financed by the University, embarked on the SS *Rotterdam* for a month-long tour—clearly one of the high points of their lives—that took them, accompanied by Jones, to more than twenty European theaters. Stopping in New York on the return journey, Bain met with representatives of Eggers and Higgins to distill his newly gained knowledge into suggestions for changes to the drawings the firm had previously prepared: the European trip had radically altered his concept of the Indiana theater.

At some point, the then-new University President, Elvis Stahr, asked Bain whether he would object to replacing Eggers and Higgins (evidently for political reasons) with an Indiana architect. Bain agreed, which was surely fortunate, given, on the one hand, the New York firm's design for the Music Annex and, on the other, the result achieved in the new theater by the Hoosier architect, Evans Woollen of Indianapolis. Woollen committed himself fully and thoughtfully to the project. In late 1964, he accompanied Jones, who had by that time been formally named Building Coordinator for the Opera Theater, on a whirlwind tour of German houses; he also made a close study of the Met's new Lincoln Center theater (which opened in 1966).

Within the next few years, plans for the Indiana theater were finalized, and construction began (after East Hall burned) in 1968. The building was completed by early 1972, at a cost of $11.2 million. Of this sum, $2.4 million came from federal grants and $300,000 from the insurance on East Hall. The remainder was raised by the University through a combination of a bond issue and private gifts, which were solicited as a major objective of the sesquicentennial capital appeal. The key gifts came from Mr. and Mrs. Herman Krannert of Indianapolis and from the School's long-time benefactress, Elsie Sweeney. Hoagy Carmichael also made a major contribution, underwriting the building's large foyer, which bears his name. Herman Wells and the Bains were among those contributing $25,000 or more. By the time the financing arrangements had to be given definite form, the actual cash in hand from donations totaled a relatively modest $1.5 million of the $5.1 million the University was hoping to collect, so the bond issue was set at $6.9 million, with the provision that later-materializing pledges would be used to accelerate the retirement of the bonds.

The building is a marvel. A four-story rectangular structure of concrete, 213 feet by 280, with a volume of 4.4 million cubic feet and 192,000 square feet of floor space, the Center dominates its part of the campus. Though unmistakably modern, it recalls, when viewed from the side or back, with its circular turrets near the corners, a castle or fortress. Viewed head on, its real function is more readily apparent, through the broad expanse of glass that fronts the Carmichael Foyer. On the lawn, a forty-foot-high Calder stabile, a massive steel-plate structure painted red-orange and puckishly named "Peau Rouge Indiana," provides a dramatic foil to the building.

The foyer, which stretches nearly the building's width, is bounded on the back by the rough, board-formed concrete wall of the auditorium. At the sides, suspended ramps and spiral staircases lead to the upper levels. The auditorium itself is relatively small, as befits both the immature student voices that have to fill it and the size of the town. With only 80 feet from curtain to back wall, the wide, shallow hall has just nineteen rows of main-floor seating, with a capacity of 910. The second-, third-, and fourth-floor terraces add another 550 seats, for an overall capacity of 1,460. The color scheme of the auditorium, as one outside observer put it, "appears to have been designed by a color blind person": particularly striking is the relation between the plum-colored seats and the red textured plaster walls, which may produce in audience members the impression of being enveloped in a large womb or, more prosaically, in a room whose walls have been covered in shag carpet.

What most strikes one on entering the hall, though, is the huge expanse of the purple velvet curtain at its front. Eighty-six feet by sixty-six, the curtain provides the first indication that this theater of modest seating capacity houses operatic production facilities to which, in North America, only those of the Met were, at the time the Center opened, comparable. The main stage is 90 feet wide by 60 feet deep. The adjustable proscenium is, at its largest, 69 feet wide by 39 feet high—lower but substantially wider than the Met's 54 feet square. As at the Met, two side stages and a rear stage, each with a motorized movable floor ("wagon"), flank the main stage and allow for rapid shifting of complete sets. The rear stage, which also includes a motorized turntable 48 feet in diameter, can be combined with the main stage to create a performance area 120 feet deep (surpassed among American theaters only by the Met's 146 feet). Both side and rear stages are equipped with soundproof doors, permitting simultaneous rehearsals on different stages. The backstage area also includes scenery storage rooms as large as the side stages; the huge stage house in fact occupies more than half the volume of the building. The orchestra pit (which is larger than, for example, that at Washington's Kennedy Center) is divided lengthwise into two sections, each of which can be elevated independently to form an extension or apron to the stage.

The remainder of the building is given over to a miscellany of activities related to the Center's theatrical and instructional purposes. There are dressing rooms (which double as practice rooms) and chorus rooms, workshops where sets and costumes are created, a design library, classrooms, rehearsal rooms, meeting rooms, offices, storage rooms, and laundry facilities. The Ballet Department has found a permanent home on the third floor, where there are three studios and a suite of faculty offices.

The Center—which in its early days students liked to call Fort Bain or the "Salle de Bain" (a term first applied to the Round Building, whose architectural footprint resembles that of a commode)—was opened on January 29, 1972, with a performance of *Don Giovanni,* but it was not dedicated until April: Bain wanted to prepare carefully for this occasion, which he clearly intended to be the greatest public-relations event in the history of the School. In order to achieve this result, he needed to ensure that the dedication attracted a host of music critics from around the country. He had not forgotten the lesson, learned long before in Texas, that operatic premieres provided the best way of luring critics. There was some discussion of commissioning a new work for the dedication, but that course proved to be prohibitively expensive, and in the end Bain settled for a nearly virgin one, John Eaton's *Heracles.* Completed in 1965, the work had been performed only on Italian radio, in 1969. Among its attractions was the fact that Bain could get a bargain price on it from the publisher, and that its epic scope and demands seemed appropriate to such an epic moment and would showcase a large number of the School's singers and instrumentalists; indeed, some three hundred members of the School took part in the performance. One critic suggested that there might also be veiled self-referentiality in Bain's choice—his labors to achieve the Center having been those of a modern Hercules, mastering bureaucrats and paper instead of hydra and Augean stables. Not content to have merely one musical event for the occasion, Bain extended the festivities into a full Dedication Week Festival (April 15–21), which featured two performances of the Philharmonic under the direction of Louis Lane (Resident Conductor of the Cleveland Orchestra), two carillon recitals displaying the recently donated Arthur R. Metz Memorial Carillon, a faculty chamber concert featuring, among other items, a Mendelssohn trio performed by Gingold, Starker, and Sebok, and two pieces by faculty members: one by Orrego-Salas, performed by Eugene Rousseau and Hans Graf (a Visiting Professor from the Vienna Academy), and another by Thomas Beversdorf, performed by James Pellerite and Charles Webb. There was also a ballet gala and a long program of student soloists and ensembles. At one point in this event, Eugene Fodor (who won the Paganini Competition the same year and was to share top prize in the Tchaikovsky Competition in 1974) played Paganini and Wieniawski.

In all but one respect, the festival was just the kind of huge public-relations success that Bain had envisioned. Twenty-two music critics were on hand, including Harold C. Schonberg of the *New York Times,* Michael Steinberg of the *Boston Globe,* Paul Hume of the *Washington Post,* and Thomas Willis of the *Chicago Tribune.* Everyone was duly overwhelmed by the size and sophistication of the production facilities, which, it was recognized, were rivaled—not necessarily surpassed—only by those at Lincoln Center. There was general agreement that the acoustics were superb, and that the building was physically impressive, though a few of the critics commented unflatteringly on the auditorium's color scheme—but after all, as one of them noted, the hall could "always be repainted tastefully in the future." (It hasn't been.) In sum, there was general agreement that, as John Ardoin of the *Dallas Morning News* put it, "a small town tucked away in a corner of Indiana now boasts one of the major performing arts facilities to be found in the United States."

Moreover, everyone was deeply impressed by the professional standards attained in the production of *Heracles.* Schonberg wrote that the performance was "marvelous." In phrases that have decorated Opera Theater brochures ever since, he said that the singing and acting of the cast (which included three faculty members and, at Eaton's request, Olivia Stapp of the Vienna State Opera) "cannot be overpraised," and pronounced the orchestra "as good as most professional groups in the country." Willis said the orchestra performed "with a consistently professional standard of which any opera house in the world could be proud."

Only the opera itself was a failure—and that on a scale befitting its epic pretensions. Eaton's score, which the composer modestly said (in his program notes) "completely exhausts every traditional technique of contemporary music," was in fact, Willis observed, "a narrow catalog of historical Austro-Germanisms" derived from Schoenberg, Berg, and Sessions. (Others added Strauss's *Elektra* to the recipe.) The libretto—by Eaton's friend Michael Fried, an art history professor at Harvard who probably should have stuck to his last—was perceived as interminably expository and repetitious, as well as high-flown. Steinberg said it lived "at a dreadful crossing of the windy with the prosy." The work as a whole, he added, "wanders shapelessly on and on"; Willis pronounced it "one of the most self-indulgent, overworked, repetitious, and tedious" works he had ever sat through. Most other critics expressed similar views. Imagine, then, how sweetly for critics and regular audience members alike relief turned into delighted surprise when the curtain, having descended for ostensibly the last time, rose again and, as Steinberg remembered the scene,

> the stage filled up with prop girls and crew, the cyclorama rose and other things moved about and disappeared, the center wagon complete with turntable and temple of Zeus moved back (about halfway to Indianapolis, it seemed), the tracks were filled in and the pit covered, and then, as the climax of this animated, delightful, and tautly-paced show, the wagon stage

> from the right rolled on front and center, bearing buffet tables, student waitresses, and beef stroganoff and quiche lorraine for 2000. [See Figure 41.]

In the paean of praise for everyone except Eaton, Fried, and the colorist of the auditorium, there was only one discordant note. This was sounded by Willis, who, though impressed like all the other critics by the accomplishment of the singers and players and by the facilities (which were, he observed, "far superior to anything in Chicago"), also took the occasion of his review to read the massive and, as he not unfairly said, "gaudy" Center as the epitome and symbol of Bain's approach to the deanship. "After 25 years," Willis wrote, "Dean Bain is known as an extraordinary master of the university expansion game." As his culminating work, the Center—"the house that *Parsifal* built"—"replicates and freezes the present philosophy of the institution it houses." What Willis meant by "philosophy" was not Bain's elaborate philosophy of musical education but the purely pragmatic considerations that complemented it. These considerations, as they applied to the decision to make opera the centerpiece of the School, Willis understood perfectly:

> Opera was the key that unlocked one door after another here. Sung in English from the beginning, it was communicative theater as well as "a cultural goal for an entire region," to borrow a favorite Bain phrase. As a high-visibility product with built in snob appeal, it could attract money from both political and private sectors. With the aid of a sympathetic top university echelon who understood opera's potential public relations value, Indiana built a national reputation with its splashy, professional productions.

Willis did not say what he would have had Bain and Indiana do instead: how it would have been preferable *not* to have created what he acknowledged to be "an all but unequalled opportunity to learn the arts and crafts of the operatic world," or how this opportunity—and the comparable ones the School supplied its students in other fields—could have been established without what Bain himself called the School's "show business." Fundamentally, Willis's objection was not to Bain's school but to what, in its grandiosity and flash, it so potently embodied: the troubling eternal dependence of musical culture on money, and thus on those (whether governments, corporations, or individuals) who have it; a dependence that renders many musicians and, ineluctably, all directors of musical institutions, if they are to succeed in the world, in some part hucksters and showmen. Bain was entirely clear-eyed and unsentimental about this dependence, which he exploited to the benefit of his institution with a degree of success that cannot often have been matched in the history of musical education.

The Musical Arts Center and the other material and cultural assets of the School as they existed when, on June 30, 1973, he relinquished the helm constitute the most meaningful evidence of that success. But another piece of evidence arrived a year and a half later, when *Change* magazine published an updated version of a 1973 survey of the reputations of American professional schools. Unlike the first version, this one included music schools. Its rankings derived from the tabulated responses of the deans of the surveyed institutions to the question "What in your opinion are the top five schools in your profession?" On the objective value of such tabulations, Samuel Johnson long ago made the definitive remark: "A compendium of gossip is still gossip." Nonetheless, the tabulations lent great added credence to an opinion that had, as far as one can make out, been fairly widespread for a decade or so, namely, that Bain and his colleagues, with the support of Wells and others in the University administration, had turned an average Midwestern music school into the best music school in the nation. Indiana stood first in the *Change* survey, followed closely by mighty Eastman, and then, at a somewhat greater distance, by Michigan and Juilliard. Illinois, Curtis, Southern California, and Oberlin rounded out the list.

6

The Webb Years (1973–1997)

I. You Can Make It Anywhere

Following his unhappy experience with Newell Long in 1950–51, Bain had not been in a hurry to appoint another Assistant Dean. Although the rapid growth of the School rendered him increasingly in need of administrative aid, for the next several years he made do with a series of individuals appointed with the title "Assistant to the Dean" (which was also what he had wanted to call Long), none of whom, with the exception of one transient Instructor, held faculty positions. In 1955, though, Bain took a long step back toward the institution of the assistant deanship, appointing two relatively senior faculty members to the position of "Administrative Assistant to the Dean": George Krueger would play this role with respect to the undergraduate program, and Roy Will with respect to the graduate program. In 1960, Will, having left the School to become Chairman of Music at Wayne State University, was replaced in the graduate program (and as chairman of the Theory Department) by William Christ, a forty-year-old veteran who had been an Assistant Professor since 1955; and in 1962, eleven years after the Long debacle, Christ became the third person (after Nye and Long) to hold the rank of Assistant Dean in the School.

This was not the only sign, in the early 1960s, of Bain's increased willingness to broaden the administrative base of the School. As I noted earlier, in 1961 he created an important new standing committee—the Academic Council, consisting of the Dean (from 1962, Deans) and the department chairs—and in 1963 was content to let this larger council absorb the Advisory Council. As of that date, members of the old council became members of the new one; as their terms expired, they were not replaced. From that date, too, the Academic Council played essentially the same role in the School's administration as its predecessor had, processing all the routine business and reporting its decisions to the faculty as a whole, and occasionally discussing some less-routine matter; though initially restricted (as its name implied) to academic matters, the Council gradually encroached on other areas. It should not, though, be imagined that the creation of this larger council (which grew continually larger still, as the number of departments increased) betokened a move on Bain's part toward greater democracy in the School. The Advisory Council had been elective; by contrast, all the members of the new council—Christ and the other department heads (Christ continued as head of theory for two years after becoming a dean)—had not been elected to their positions but appointed by Bain. And Bain continued to make all the most important decisions within (or, if he disagreed with them, without) his "small circle of advisers."

In 1964, with Christ on leave, Bain appointed his final Assistant Dean, Charles Webb. Perhaps he initially meant for Webb to serve only in an interim capacity; in any case, the appointment is rather stunning, since Webb had completed his doctorate only that year: it cannot often have happened, as it did in this case, that an individual has been simultaneously made Assistant Professor and Assistant Dean. But the surprise is less with Bain than it would be with another dean, because he clearly regarded "Assistant Dean" as not functionally much different from "Assistant to the Dean." In either rank, what he required was loyal and energetic executants rather than framers of policy (these he could find in his "small circle"). Moreover, by 1964 Webb, then thirty-one, had actually had substantial experience as a music administrator.

Born in Dallas in 1933, Webb had evinced musical gifts early. Like Bain a scion of devout Methodists, at the age of four he began picking out on the family piano songs he had heard at church; at six he began his first "job" as a musician, playing on Sunday afternoons at a mausoleum outside the city. By age nine, his keyboard accomplishments were such that he was accepted as a pupil by the Dean of the Music School at the local Southern Methodist University, Paul van Katwijk (one of the music administrators who had written to H. T. Briscoe on Bain's behalf in 1947).

After Webb finished high school in 1951, he enrolled, like his parents before him, at SMU as an undergraduate. At first, though, he did not intend to major in music. His father, like Bain's, hoped his son would follow in his own professional footsteps; but this father was a banker, not a minister. There had been no musicians in the family, and Charles Webb, Sr., had a hard time conceiving of music as a profession. "You can play the piano *any*time," his son recalls him saying, "but you've got to make a *living*."

Charles Jr. accordingly began his undergraduate career with the idea of majoring in business, but from the first he did not enjoy his courses in that field. After his freshman year, he obtained a summer job as accompanist in the touring choral-music workshops established by Fred Waring. The tour ended in Boulder, Colorado, where Webb ventured to ask Waring whether he thought he could make a living as a musician. Waring said he did think so, and Webb then asked him if perhaps he would be willing to say that to Webb senior—who, as it happened, was vacationing with his wife and other child (a daughter, Nancy) in the area. Waring undertook this mission, and, perhaps partly because his example showed that a musician could be successful even by the standards of a banker, Charles Sr. was convinced, and suggested to his son that it might, after all, be a good idea for him to major in music. Indeed Webb returned to SMU to complete, in three and a half more years, a double major (like Bain) in music and English, as well as, in 1955, a master's degree in music. In the summers, he worked for Waring; the rest of the year, he was organist and choir director at his home church.

After graduation, Webb spent two years in the Air Force, as a Personnel Services Officer, in which capacity he organized a glee club of pilots that gave concerts throughout the country and won second prize in a competition of Air Force choral groups worldwide. Discharged from the Air Force in 1957, he returned to SMU as assistant to Orville Borchers, who had succeeded van Katwijk as Dean of Music. Borchers pointed out that if Webb liked university work and wanted to continue in it, he should acquire a doctorate; the place to go, especially in piano, was Indiana. Borchers had known Bain from his Texas days, and telephoned to recommend Webb to him.

Doctoral studies were not the only thing on Webb's mind in that summer of 1958. In December 1955, while stationed at an Air Force base in southwest Texas, he had met another musician in neighboring Big Spring. Kenda McGibbon, still in high school at the time, was the organist in a local church. The minister, who knew Webb from Dallas, thought it would be a good idea for the church to have some duets. "So we got together to practice," as Kenda recalled in 1996, "and that's how it all started." They were married on June 21, 1958, and in the fall set off for Bloomington, where he enrolled in the doctoral program in piano and she undertook to complete the bachelor's degree in harp that she had begun at SMU.

Borchers had told Bain about Webb's experience with choirs, and had suggested that the Dean install him as accompanist for the Choral Union. Bain took the suggestion, and, as Borchers had predicted, found that he liked Webb very well both as a musician and as a person. (He had actually met him years earlier, when Webb had played at North Texas as a six-year-old prodigy.) He must have felt a special kinship with a young Methodist pianist and choral director; but it's easy for *anyone* to like Webb, whose great musical gifts are equaled by his affability, industriousness, and general intelligence. Since Webb had also had substantial experience with a touring musical group, one can see, too, why early in 1960 Bain telephoned to offer him appointment as Manager of Musical Organizations and Instructor in Music—a double offer that Webb readily accepted.

By 1964, then, Bain had had four years to assess Webb's administrative skills and potential; thus, given that he did not require seniority in an Assistant Dean (nor was there anyone in a position to gainsay him on the matter), it is not really so surprising that he tapped Webb for the role.

The role itself proved, also not surprisingly, to be more that of an Assistant than of an Assistant Dean. Though Christ and Webb held the same rank, there was, for the next several years after Webb's elevation, always the sense that the older, more experienced Christ was higher in the hierarchy than Webb. This was so much the case that colleagues from the period typically have the false memory that Christ was Associate Dean and Webb Assistant Dean. Webb himself, telling me of his 1964 appointment, added that he thought "that is when he appointed William Christ Associate Dean." But in reality both were Assistant Deans until 1969, when both were promoted to Associate Dean.

With Webb, Bain shared information—even about the budget, which was not open to anyone else in the School, even Christ—without reservation. Webb told me that when he later became Dean, he encountered absolutely no surprises. To at least some extent, this openness on Bain's part stemmed from his regarding Webb as essentially an extension of himself, to whom, handily, he could transfer some tasks for which the rest of him had little time or aptitude. Bain did not, for example, like to write, and did not write well—a fact that is evident (paradoxically) from his massive history of the "Bain Regime," which he dictated, and which he appears to have revised either very poorly or not at all. By contrast, Webb wrote easily and gracefully. Bain was, Webb told me, "not terribly good extemporaneously, and so every morning I came in early, looked at all the correspondence, and took everything that I thought that I could and dictated something, had the thing on his desk." The arrangement in this area typified the relationship. Recognizing what was called for, Webb was willing, in the Dean's Office, entirely to submerge himself in Bain: "I served him well; that is, I tried to think in every situation what would *he* do."

It was undoubtedly the fact that Bain thought of Webb as entirely loyal that primarily moved him, when his long tenure was finally nearing its end, to back Webb as his successor. By Bain's time at Indiana, though the University retirement age was seventy, there was a rule that no one could hold an administrative position beyond the age of sixty-five. Bain had no desire to step down—"I never got tired of being Dean," he told me—but step down he must, in the summer of 1973. As this juncture approached, he decided that the next best thing to being Dean would be to have an extension of himself as Dean, and so he began to let it be known that Webb was his preferred heir.

As it happened, this succession was not hard to arrange. It seems to have been generally assumed by the faculty that the successor would be an inside candidate (this is the normal preference of faculties, and it is also the normal preference of central administrators when there is a sense that all is going well in the unit). It would, then, be either Christ or Webb. For the first few years of their deanships, it was generally assumed, insomuch as people thought about the matter that far in advance, that Christ would get the nod. He was senior to Webb in years and experience, he was thought to want the job, and he had rendered the School excellent service in a number of areas in addition to the deanship: as Director of Graduate Studies, Chairman of the Theory Department, and principal author of the series of theory textbooks that emerged from the Department. He did, though, have the great handicap of being an academic musician in a school dominated by performers; and as time passed his star began to wane, both by comparison with Webb's rising one and because some of his ideas for the School were not widely applauded—one of these, generally regarded as quixotic, was to build a sort of gothic cathedral to foster the School's graduate program in Organ and Church Music.

As Bain's term neared its end, the University undertook a full national search for his successor, conducted by a university-wide faculty-student committee. The committee spent a year in the search and let it be known that they had considered more than sixty possible candidates. Reportedly, there was some concern expressed, in representations to the committee and within the group itself, that if Webb were the successor Bain might continue to be powerfully involved in the administration of the School—precisely what Bain hoped would be the case. But Webb had strong support from the performance faculty; he was, moreover, well regarded by the central administration, having been appointed Associate Dean of the Faculties in 1969—a position that he held simultaneously with the associate deanship of Music, spending mornings in the one office and afternoons in the other. Finally, despite any misgivings about Bain's role in a Webb administration, it would surely have been impossible for the University to have gone against the wishes of the nonpareil outgoing Dean; so the outcome was not really in doubt. Recalling the juncture, Dorothy Collins told me, "I don't think any of us thought there'd be anybody but Charles." Webb's appointment was announced in December; Bain let it be known how pleased he was (according to the *Indianapolis Star*, he viewed the appointment "with undisguised glee"); and on July 1, 1973, there was, after twenty-six years, a new Dean of the School of Music.

To be sure, the old Dean did everything he could to retain his authority, laboring to make Webb, who had been so dutiful as Assistant and Associate Dean, merely his surrogate. The first clear sign of what he had in mind was his decision not only not to retire (which he probably should have done, since after so many years as an administrator he was not suited to return to teaching) but not even to take the sabbatical leave that customarily ensues on the conclusion of a university administrator's term of office. Naturally, most administrators are more than happy, at such a moment, to vanish for a year, often in part because of their recognition that the successor will find it easier to establish himself or herself if the predecessor is not on the scene. And one might think that Bain, who had not had a sabbatical in his entire academic career, would be especially eager to take one. This was not, however, the case: he wanted to remain in town precisely because he thought he could in this way prevent Webb from taking his own course—or it may have been that he thought that Webb, whom he had known only as his creature, had no course of his own to take.

After Webb and his family had moved to the home they have occupied since 1968, Bain, who lived nearby, had established the practice of rendezvousing with the younger man every morning and walking to the School—a distance of a little over a mile—with him. When Webb became Dean, Bain continued this practice, as indeed he did until he retired in 1978. Thus for the first five years of his deanship, Webb had, willy-nilly, the pleasure of his predecessor's company every morning on his way to work, with Bain "commenting very freely," as Webb recalls, on School matters and Webb's conduct of them, and especially "on what he didn't like."

What Bain wanted, of course, was for the School to continue straight along the path he had set it on. And indeed for the most part it appeared, in the early days of Webb's deanship, as if this would be the case. Webb had, after all, little incentive to make great changes in the School: what would be the point of radically altering a course that had brought the School charging to the forefront of musical education? Then too, the beginning of his tenure came at a time of great financial stringency in the School, when the main aim of the Dean had to be simply to avoid, or at least minimize, contraction of its activities. The stringencies attendant on the recession that had clouded the final years of Bain's deanship continued, and from October of Webb's first year were exacerbated by the sharp increases in oil prices decreed by the Organization of Petroleum Exporting Countries, then first flexing its muscles.

In an Academic Council meeting of November 1, Webb informed his colleagues that the School's budgetary situation had, over the past few months, greatly worsened. As always, Music was an expensive unit to run. The 1973–74 budget had projected a gap of $400,000 between revenues (from tuition and fees) and expenditures, which was to be covered by the central administration. A revised projection, though, indicated the shortfall would be at least half again as large as originally anticipated, and in consequence the administration wanted the School to cut, in midstream, $25,000 from the budgeted expenditures for 1973–74. Moreover, Webb had been instructed to prepare a 1974–75 budget that reduced expenditures by $90,000 from the previous year.

As a general rule, the only place an academic unit can effect large budget savings is in faculty salaries. To realize the required savings for 1974–75, Webb had really only two choices: to reduce salary increments for continuing faculty or to reduce the number of faculty positions. Given that the level of faculty salaries had been, since the publication of University salary data in the spring, an especially sore point with School faculty, he was doubtless right to choose the second course; in that same dour meeting of November 1, he announced a freeze on all positions that would come vacant for the following year. (In the event, the freeze was lifted, and the School did have a number of new appointees the following fall.) He also instituted a three-year plan to improve the salary situation in the School, though the means by which he intended to attain this goal are not clear, and in fact the plan achieved relatively little: the poor salary position of the School, compared both to other important music schools and to other units of the University, continued, as we will see, to be a major problem not merely for the next three years but throughout Webb's tenure.

Other initiatives of his first year, having only a modest cost, were more easily brought to fruition. For the summer session, he created a new orchestra, which, like the School orchestra of the old days, mixed faculty and student players; a quarter-century later, this Festival Orchestra still exists, each summer performing, as in the original conception, under a series of guest conductors. Always aware, like his predecessor, of the importance of good public relations, Webb immediately launched an "Indiana University Artist Recording Series" (which, beginning auspiciously with four records featuring Starker, Pressler, Gingold, and others, continued on an occasional basis over the years) and a twice-yearly publication, *Music Alumni Notes,* which not only reported alumni news but surveyed such matters as faculty appointments and achievements, notable events in the life of the School, and testimonies to its excellence and eminence. He also appointed a committee to revise the undergraduate core requirement in music theory and music literature, with a view to integrating the teaching of these subjects more closely with each other and with performance.

Webb was fortunate in having to make only small adjustments to the administrative team. Christ graciously agreed to continue as Associate Dean (as he did until his retirement in 1985), and the extremely able Ralph Daniel continued as Director of Graduate Studies (a role he had assumed in 1963). Allan Ross, a doctoral graduate of the School and a member of the choral faculty who had latterly been Director of Undergraduate Studies, became Assistant to the Dean, making room for one of Webb's close friends, Henry Upper, in the vacated position. A fellow Texan, Upper had met Webb when they were piano students at SMU, and had come, like him, to Indiana for a doctorate. In 1970, at Webb's urging, Bain had appointed him Instructor; when he completed his doctorate in 1972, he became an Assistant Professor. Webb also attempted to bring order to the complex and vitally important matter of student admissions by creating the position of Director of Admissions, to which he appointed, in what would turn out to be a fateful move, John Nagosky of the Theory Department.

There was not much, even for Bain, to object to in any of these necessarily modest initiatives; and he was very pleased with the creation of the Festival Orchestra, a move that he was still applauding twenty-five years later. It soon became clear, though, that his effort to retain control of the School was not succeeding. Indeed it was doomed to fail, for two reasons. First, though Webb had quite properly been deferential to Bain when he was merely a member of his administrative team, brought in expressly to execute Bain's policies rather than to set policies of his own, when he became Dean he naturally wanted to establish himself in his own right—which he could do only by deviating, at least to some extent, from the course set by his predecessor. Second, Webb had much more incentive to try to satisfy the generality of his colleagues than to satisfy his predecessor; in fact this was his *duty,* however much he was indebted to Bain. And most of his colleagues were, at the time when he became Dean, dissatisfied—not particularly with the nature of the School (since it had been so overwhelmingly successful), but very much with the autocratic way in which Bain had run it.

This discontent was exacerbated by the fact that Bain, in forgoing his sabbatical and staying at Webb's side (literally, every weekday morning), appeared so clearly to confirm the suspicion that he did not mean to relinquish power, and that the danger in making Webb his successor was that Bain would be able to influence him unduly. Bain, as Ross Allen puts it, "just stayed on after he had had his farewell and everything"; and this was a huge tactical error. "Everybody said, 'Is he still here?' instead of saying, 'Oh, don't you miss Wilfred?' If he had gone away for a year and then come back, I think he would have been received with great joy—'Oh, Wilfred, come back and do something about this'—and he would have loved that."

What made matters much worse for Bain was that he did not merely stay around but managed to stay in an administrative capacity—in a way that clearly violated the University rule against administrators above the age of sixty-five. He desperately wanted to retain control of the Opera Theater, which was both his favorite part of the School and its most celebrated part, and Webb acceded to his passionate plea to create for him the position of Artistic Director of the Opera Theater, where his principal duty would be to chair the casting committee—as he had chaired it during his deanship.

His tenure in the newly created directorship (which was abolished at his retirement) was disastrous. Not only did his securing it confirm the worst suspicions about his desire to retain power and Webb's willingness to let him do so, but he simply could not (since he no longer had real power) successfully govern the Theater. Installed in the manager's office at the Musical Arts Center, he tried to carry on in his old style, but found that no one of consequence paid much attention to him.

This was the case both within the School and in the University administration. On August 21, 1973—less than two months after he ceased to be the dean of deans, the all-powerful director of the University's golden School—he applied, in his new capacity as Artistic Director, for travel money ($442.82) to attend the Metropolitan Opera Auditions on the district, regional, and national levels. But now it was *his* turn to be treated shabbily. His letter was shunted from one office to another, lost a while in the shuffle, and finally answered, in a letter from Lynne Merritt, Jr. (Vice President and Dean of Research), on April 2—a month after the auditions had concluded. No doubt the fatal delay was, as Merritt profusely averred, accidental. But it was an accident that would not, could not have happened while Bain was Dean. How far the mighty had fallen from the twenty-six years of "give him anything he wants," and how fast.

Within the Opera Theater itself, Bain's problems came especially from the two men who thought, with some justification, that *they* should be running it, Busch and Kozma. (St. Leger had reached retirement age in 1960, though he continued to teach part-time until a little over a year before his death in 1969.) Kozma had long been at bitter odds with Bain, and the relationship between the Dean and his first stage director had also soured over the years. As long as Bain was the School's absolute monarch, no one in it, of course, could win fights with him. But now it appeared to be payback time, and Busch and Kozma had, moreover, right on their side, in the form of University policy. In November 1973, the two wrote a letter to President John Ryan, protesting in the strongest and nastiest terms, and clearly not for the first time, "the continued presence of Mr. Wilfred C. Bain" (not "Dr." or "Prof.," though he was both)

> in an administrative function ("Artistic Director of the I.U. Opera Theatre") [, which] constitutes disregard of assurances repeatedly given to the Search and Screen Committee and also in violation of the rules of the University. . . .
>
> As responsible academic citizens and artistic executives of the Opera Theatre, we consider this situation detrimental to the operation of the Opera Theatre and to the governance of the School of Music, since it threatens to degenerate into dual leadership.
>
> Since the customary channels seem to have been exhausted, we now have

> no other choice but to bring this situation to the attention of the Board of Trustees.
>
> We would therefore appreciate your arranging a meeting between the Board and the undersigned at earliest mutual convenience.

Three weeks later, in response to Ryan's letter promising to look into the matter, the complainants made it clearer that they blamed Webb for the situation as much as Bain: "Our day-by-day experience is that Mr. Bain consistently exercises administrative functions, the very thing about which the Search and Screen Committee and ourselves warned the central administration prior to the appointment of the present Dean." (Kozma had, however, recommended Webb as the successor in a memo to the Chancellor of the Bloomington campus during the search for a new Dean.)

Ryan declined to bring the complainants before the trustees. Instead, he briefed Webb on the matter, who made a personal plea to Kozma and Busch to cease their efforts to dislodge Bain; they acceded, though they doubtless also continued to make Bain's final years at the School considerably unhappier than they would otherwise have been. But in truth Bain was probably less upset by Kozma and Busch's hostility than by two heresies (as he regarded them) that Webb himself committed, in the early years of his deanship, in respect to longstanding policies of the opera program.

First, Webb moved away from Bain's policy of casting faculty members in the most demanding roles. Bain thought it vital to the reputation of the Opera Theater, and of the School as a whole, that all roles in its productions be well sung; unless there was a fully adequate student for a given role, he put a faculty member into it. But over the years it had come to seem to key faculty in the opera program, and to Webb, that in order to recruit the best students to the program, and to pacify those already in it (many of whom greatly resented Bain's policy), it was necessary to let students sing the leads as well as the lesser roles; and as Dean he instituted a policy to this effect. Since the early years of his deanship, faculty members have been cast in the operas only occasionally.

At that stage in the School's development, this was surely the right course to take. To Bain, though, it seemed disastrously wrong. "He wasn't," Webb says, "very happy about that, and was on me quite a bit. 'Where are the good singers?' 'The tenors can't sing high notes,' and things like that." He continued to make these complaints for the rest of his life.

The second of Webb's operatic heresies was a move—albeit extremely hesitant—away from Bain's policy of having all operas sung in English. This policy made perfect sense in the days before the advent of projected titles, and when the students were all North Americans themselves, and aiming for cisatlantic careers. But in the 1970s, more and more of the graduates of the program were going on to careers in European houses, so that it became, as various members of the voice faculty and others pointed out to Webb, increasingly desirable for the School to produce at least a few of its operas in the original languages. Webb agreed, and on April 5, 1975, for the first time ever, the Opera Theater staged an opera—*Rigoletto*—in a language other than English. To Bain, as Webb says, "it was as if I had committed a mortal sin. . . . he ranted and raved against it, . . . told me the whole thing was going to go down the drain." He insisted that "the public is not accepting this," and claimed to be getting letters from distraught and angry patrons; he would bring one such letter to show Webb:

> So he brought me a letter from a woman from Indianapolis, . . . and it was a diatribe, . . . pretty damning for what we were doing. But he left in the envelope, because he didn't see it, a little note from this woman, who said, "Dear Dean Bain, will this letter be strong enough?" So here I have this thing, and I never said a word, let on like I had it. . . . Because he was going to make his point or die.

(As it turned out, the position was far from being entirely lost: Bain was not the only faculty member who strongly preferred to have the operas sung in English, and up to the present a large majority of them have continued to be so, despite the fact that in the era of projected titles the general tide is strongly in the opposite direction.)

Added to the frustrations of his artificial role in the Opera Theater and what he perceived as the disloyalty and ingratitude of some of his colleagues, the changes that Webb made rendered Bain alienated from the School and deeply ambivalent toward his successor. In letters to Webb over the years, written from Bloomington or from the Bains' winter home in Palm Beach, he frequently evinced affection for both Charles and Kenda, and lauded Webb's accomplishments as Dean. Yet to Wolford, ten years after the end of his own deanship, he said that his successor was an "enigma" to him—by which he meant that he could not understand how Webb, who had been so "obedient" as "my assistant," had as Dean done things of which his former master disapproved—and he expressed generally similar views to me in the summer of 1996, twenty-three years after leaving office (and seven months before he died). Dorothy Collins, who knew Bain well for decades, told me that same summer that he, who "built this school, . . . has nothing good to say about it now."

To a considerable extent, his alienation poisoned the final quarter-century of his life. I do not mean to suggest that his late years were empty. He had, during and after his deanship, the satisfaction of numerous honors—a series of honorary doctorates, medals from the Eugène Ysaÿe Foundation of Belgium and the National Society of Arts and Letters, and, in 1988, the Peabody Medal for Outstanding Contributions to Music in

America. He regularly turned out for musical events at the School (if only, it sometimes seemed, to be in a position to denigrate them). He had Mary almost until the end, and after her death in 1993, surprised and pleased those who knew him by marrying, the next year, Elizabeth Myers, a widow and a fellow resident of the attractive University-owned retirement community where in his last years he had his primary circle of friends. (The new couple retained their neighboring but separate apartments.)

But in the great School for whose marvelous rise he was primarily responsible, it is impossible not to think of him as having been, for the twenty-four years of his life after the deanship, a lonely man. "Nobody asks me anything," he told Webb; "nobody comes to me." He always retained an office in the MAC, though after he retired it was not the manager's office but a small one just off the mezzanine lobby, next door to the rest rooms. Until the late summer of 1998, when the office was cleared for its next occupant, one could still find there, among other items grown poignant with time, yellowed notes for the course he taught, in his early years at Indiana and again after he left the deanship, "The Administration of Music in Higher Education." There were also piles of materials pertaining to his second annalistic work, a documentary history of the Opera Theater, which he appears to have completed in 1990. (Comparable in size to its massive predecessor, this second work was, like it, not printed but only photocopied and bound, in the fashion of a doctoral dissertation. Scarcely anyone seems ever to have read it or even to know it exists.) In the year before Bain's death, Webb spoke wistfully of the long last act of his predecessor's life: the "sadness" is that he "hasn't enjoyed some of the relationships that he could have had with the School, with people, by relaxing just a little bit, and not still wanting to be in the driver's seat." Perhaps he did relax a bit in that last year. Although to me he was still making, at eighty-eight, his customary unflattering remarks about Webb and what the School had become under him, he also said: "I don't disapprove, generally speaking, of the whole thing. Besides that, I'm tired."

Though Webb had trouble with Bain, he appears to have enjoyed, in the early years of his deanship, the strong approval of a large majority of his other colleagues. In an interview with the *Daily Student* a year and a half after Webb's installation, Josef Gingold in fact claimed that the new Dean was "extremely well liked by the entire faculty": "We admire him tremendously. I, for one, feel privileged to know he's running the school." If there were some (in addition to Kozma and Busch) whose admiration was not as unreserved as Gingold thought, either their numbers were small or their views unrecorded.

In part, this early enthusiasm for Webb was (as later events retrospectively confirm) only the honeymoon that most new officeholders enjoy for a time, irrespective of their actual merits. But Webb did in fact have great merits that rendered him an impressive and charismatic figure and in several respects a highly effective Dean. Naturally these qualities had been apparent before he was Dean, and they had contributed to his becoming the favorite candidate for the job; but they could be displayed and appreciated to the full only after he was installed in it.

He had (and still has) incredible energy. Beginning his day at 6 A.M. with seventy-five minutes of piano practice—necessary because he took every possible opportunity to play in public—he set off for the School at 7:35, walking as fast as Bain's legs would carry him. (Left to himself, he is the fastest walker anyone has ever seen.) Arrived at the Music Building, he put in a full day, with a break for swimming at noon. On Sundays, starting in 1959, he served as choir director and then, since 1968 and continuing to the present, as organist of the First Methodist Church, taking his duties in this realm as seriously as those of the deanship. He traveled a great deal; yet if he got back to town anytime Saturday night or Sunday morning before church started, he would be there. (Moreover, he kept this arduous professional and private schedule year after year in unbroken succession: like Bain, in the entire course of his deanship Webb never took a sabbatical; nor did he ever appear to need one. In his twenty-fourth year as Dean, he was as fresh and cheery as he had been in the first.)

There were also his humanity and unabashed aspirations to virtue. A genuinely religious man, he openly set high moral standards for himself; and he openly insisted that his colleagues also exhibit high standards, because they were inevitably role models for their students, to whom they would transmit whatever values they embodied. This stance may well have seemed quaint to some of these colleagues, but generally it appears to have inspired admiration and trust. He was, as Menahem Pressler put it, "a *good* man, in the true sense of the word," who would always "be there" if one needed "support or advice or help."

Then there was Kenda, whom everybody loved, and whom one would call Webb's greatest personal and professional asset, if "asset" did not have the wrong, proprietary flavor. Warm, compassionate, and outgoing, her humanity was at least a match for his. Religious like him, and with the same ethic of duty and self-discipline, she regarded his elevation to the deanship as having made her, too, a "public servant," the First Lady and perennial hostess of the School. She played this role to perfection, and indefatigably. At the time of Webb's retirement, Kenda reckoned she had served meals to 30,000 people during her years as the Dean's consort. As the couple's four children—all boys—appeared on the scene and sequentially reached something like the age of reason, they also played an important part in the social service of the deanship, acting regularly as co-hosts and sometimes even taking the place of their absent parents. When Thomas Beversdorf died, with Charles and Kenda out of town the boys on their own initiative prepared a full meal and took it to the widow. (They were all too young to drive, so the babysitter chauffeured them.)

Finally, Webb was a tremendous performer both as a public speaker and as a musician, and his accomplishment in these areas worked powerfully in gaining him respect and influence. On occasions formal and informal, he spoke eloquently and sometimes movingly, and always without notes. He was equally fluent and versatile as a musical performer. In his early years at Indiana, he was, like Bain, primarily associated with choral music, a field in which his summers with Fred Waring had given him great experience. (These summer stints continued for several years after Webb came to Indiana; eventually Waring made him dean of the workshops.) From his initial role as accompanist to Bain's Choral Union, he had risen by 1961 to be conductor of the University Singers, the group that Bain in 1947 had claimed for his own. In 1967, Webb became conductor of the Indianapolis Symphonic Choir, a position he held until 1981 (as if he were short of things to do in Bloomington). Like Bain too, but evidently with much greater success, he also became an orchestral conductor, and in the 1960–61 academic year was charged with forming a small concerto orchestra, to accompany student soloists. During his assistant and associate deanships, he actually chaired the Department of Instrumental Conducting.

Unlike Bain, though, Webb was also a highly accomplished solo and chamber performer on the piano, and an organist; and this fact turned out to be of tremendous importance for his relations both with colleagues and students and with people outside the School. A well-trained and experienced keyboard player before he arrived at Indiana, he had studied at the School principally with Walter Robert. Years later, Robert recalled that Webb had never been his student in the normal sense: "Charles was a colleague whom you were privileged to teach a little." Above all, he was, as a member of the performance faculty described him in 1988, "an incredibly gifted accompanist." This was a dean who could and did play with Starker and Gingold. Marilyn Keiser, a Professor of Organ who often heard him perform at First Methodist, regards him as one of the finest service players she has ever encountered; Sylvia McNair, who was for two years the soprano soloist with the church choir, calls his performing talent "extraordinary": "It just lifted us all into a new level of participation, both in music and in worship." He was also a splendid duo-pianist. In the summer of 1952, he had met William Wallace Hornibrook, a fellow member of Waring's staff. The two discovered that they could play together well, and even improvise together. Thus began a partnership that became much more convenient when Hornibrook joined the faculty in 1966; it has lasted to the present and taken them all over the world.

The fact that the Dean was a performing musician of such stature naturally did much to win him the respect of the performance faculty—who, it will be remembered, made up about four-fifths of the faculty as a whole. It surely also had a considerable effect on most of the academic-music faculty, whose interest in music was not, of course, purely theoretical. Moreover, as was clear to all his colleagues, the Dean's personal stature contributed significantly to his effectiveness in dealing with prospective faculty and students. Outside the School, he could be an emissary for it in a way that none of his predecessors could—given that, as the Presidents of the University had long been aware, in music the only thing that really matters for public relations is performance.

As far as the faculty were concerned, though, probably the *most* attractive qualities of the new Dean were his independence from his predecessor and his interest in their views. He did not automatically defer to Bain's advice; and he was refreshingly eager to hear the advice of *others*. When one asks faculty members who were present at the time what especially marked the transition from Bain to Webb, they invariably cite the "openness" that Webb brought to the administration of the School. "Charles was more responsive," as Malcolm Brown says, "and sought more input": "when Charles came into that office, he opened the door more readily, . . . and . . . certainly made an effort to change the character of the Dean's office." His openness extended to the students, too. In his first year, Webb reconstituted the Student Advisory Committee (which had been established in the tumultuous years of the late sixties) as the Student Representative Committee, with its size doubled to twenty-four; and he met with this group every Saturday morning. (Twenty-four years later, he was still having these meetings, though on weekdays.)

Indeed Webb made attentive listening the central tenet of his philosophy of administration. For, quite apart from the useful advice about the School that one might acquire in this fashion, the Dean's listening to its members was important to their morale, and thus, he thought, to the general well-being of the institution, in two ways. First, it was important for each member of the School, from whatever position in its hierarchy, to know that his or her views would be heard, would be received with respect, at the School's highest level, even if they did not in the end prevail. "I'm trying to allow people to have the opportunity to have their say," Webb told the *Daily Student* in 1978: "I do believe it's important for people to be able to say, 'I was at least heard.'" Second, there was the importance of understanding and, as much as might be, satisfying his faculty colleagues' personal needs and aspirations. Webb recalls Walter Robert saying that "one of the great things about the Bain administration was that nobody liked it, but they didn't dislike it bad enough to leave." For Bain's successor, though, the goal was not merely to keep faculty from leaving but to keep them in a frame of mind in which they would, as he expressed it to me, "really want to produce at the highest possible level and are excited by what they do." To accomplish this, it was necessary to know, for each member, what really mattered to him or her:

> Because the needs are very different from individual to individual. To some, salary is the most important thing; to others, believe it or not, it's relatively unimportant: the location of the studio, with two windows, is absolutely vital. Well, you can't always *give* everybody a studio with two windows. But you can listen and try to see what motivates this person and that person, because if you *can* provide, then you can expect a high rate of return, and generally *get* it.

Webb's openness was also good for faculty morale because it was perceived, in these early years, as part of a move toward the democratization of the School. This was, as we will see, substantially a misunderstanding, but in truth Webb was happy to have the faculty participate more fully and, what was at least as important, more coherently—and thus more effectively—in the School's administration. The obstacle to coherence lay in the fact that the administrative structure had, in the Bain years, grown on an ad hoc, as-needed basis, with the Dean expanding the administrative team here or adding a committee there, as he saw fit. There was no written "constitution"—nothing, that is, like a faculty handbook—and, as far as I can tell, not even any reporting-line charts: the only clarifications of the administrative structure came orally from the Dean at meetings of the faculty or the Academic Council, whenever he saw the need (as when new members were added to the Council), or when a specific question arose about relations between committees.

For the first few years of Webb's deanship, matters continued in the same fashion. Thus in an Academic Council meeting of September 1974, when that body was exercised about a scheduling decision of the Ensemble Committee, the question arose whether the former had authority to review and reverse a decision of the latter. There being no constitution to refer to, and the Dean being absent, Sidney Foster asked Bain (present as Artistic Director of the Opera Theater) "to explain the responsibilities" of the two committees, "since he created both of them." Bain's response was that "any item which generates serious disagreement should be referred to the faculty [as a whole]." Foster was evidently unhappy with this answer, saying that he saw no point in discussing the disputed decision at all if the Council had no authority to reverse it; yet "if the Council is a legislative body, then we ought to do something about this issue." Christ, chairing the meeting, then made three points, all of them valid but not, taken together, very helpful: "1) it was originally conceived that this group should concern itself [only] with academic matters; 2) it was the first group formed with other groups being added later without a clear line of authority; 3) it is the governing body and representative of the faculty." The ensuing discussion led to the introduction of a motion intended to reverse the Ensemble Committee's decision, but having an utterly farcical opening clause: "IF THE ACADEMIC COUNCIL HAS THE POWER TO DO SO . . ." Fortunately for the honor of the School, the motion was defeated.

At the following week's meeting, Webb, back on campus, admirably clarified the situation. There were, he was careful to say, some matters—that is, those he reserved to himself, such as the determination of salaries—that were not within the purview of the Council. But in other respects the Council "represents the School of Music and speaks for the faculty. . . . If a conflict occurs between the various bodies, then the Academic Council has the final action." He thus conferred legality, by decanal imprimatur, on the gradual encroachment, over the years, of the Academic Council on matters that were not strictly academic. Christ approvingly observed that "we now know the governing body of the School of Music"—without any suggestion that it was odd that no one (other than the Dean) had known this basic fact sooner.

The question of the Council's scope arose again a little over two years later, when, in December 1976, Bernhard Heiden lamented the fact that the group seemed to concern itself only with quotidian business and never with broad policy matters. In response, the very able David Fenske—who had been appointed Associate Music Librarian in 1971 and, having completed his Wisconsin doctorate in musicology, succeeded Daniel as Secretary of the Council in 1973 and became Music Librarian the following year—proposed the formation of a standing committee on educational policy. Webb endorsed the idea, and the committee, chaired by Christ and including Webb and Upper as well as Heiden and four other faculty members (two academic musicians and two performers), began meeting in February. What it discussed, however, was not educational policy but administrative structure, on the ground that a main impediment to the development of educational policy lay in the unclear mandate and relations of some of the School's committees. In October, the committee issued an interim report proposing that the thirty-member Council replace itself by a smaller School of Music Council. This would unambiguously be the legislative body of the School—though, in conformity with the sweeping powers accorded deans by the University, it would be merely advisory to the Dean, in whom the ultimate authority in all matters, to whatever extent he chose to exercise it, would perforce still lie. The new council would, however, have undisputed authority over the three committees that, in the new structure, would report to it: undergraduate and graduate curriculum committees, and an ensemble committee (which would in turn have three subcommittees, for instrumental and choral music, opera and ballet, and chamber music); all the committees would have their members appointed by the Dean. (There were a number of committees that did not appear on the neat organizational chart that formed part of the report: a summary compiled in 1979–80 listed seventeen additional ones.)

This reorganization would give the School a coherent and more efficient governmental structure and would presumably leave the new council more time for strategic discussions of broad policy and planning issues. The Academic Council debated the report for several months, and in February 1978 approved a revised version of it; in this version the membership of the new council was fixed at sixteen elected faculty members representing the various fields (only four of them from academic music—a proportion slightly higher, though, than that of academic musicians in the faculty as a whole), one from the technical staff of the MAC, two students (one undergraduate and one graduate), and, *ex officio,* the deans and the Directors of Undergraduate and Graduate Studies. Thus was inaugurated the administrative structure that, though expanded over time by the addition of more Council members and more committees, has governed the School ever since. The first meeting of the School of Music Council took place on September 7, 1978; Henry Upper was acclaimed as Secretary.

If the enactment of this new administrative structure gave a boost to faculty morale by fulfilling some at least of the recurrent dreams of self-governance, the *students'* morale must have been enormously improved by the great event of the following year, the opening of the Music Practice Building. As we have seen, the School was short, often desperately short, of practice rooms throughout Bain's deanship; nor did the opening of the MAC (albeit it contained a few dressing rooms that could double as practice rooms) contribute significantly to the solution of the problem. Moreover, many of the existing practice rooms were in Linden Hall, the last of the Trees Center buildings retained by the School—a structure not suited to this purpose nor, in its dilapidated condition, to any other. The rooms, about six feet by nine, had paper-thin walls; opera costumes were stored in alternate rooms to baffle the sound, and at one point students were asked to collect egg cartons for insulation. (They turned out to work quite well.)

Bain had lobbied for a practice building in his annual reports and doubtless elsewhere, and discussions of the matter were under way between the School and the Chancellor's Office (that is, Wells's office) during his last year as Dean. Finally, in 1974, the central administration made a new practice building its top priority for construction on the Bloomington campus.

It was not, though, until 1977, after what Webb calls a "Do You Really Need This?" visitation from members of the legislature, that the approval of state funding made it possible to erect a new building. Webb gives much of the credit for the approval to Helen Clouse, who had been since

1959 the practice-room supervisor (and was still in this role, at the age of ninety-three, in 2000). During the inspection of termite-ridden Linden Hall, one of the legislators moved to enter a particular room, whereupon Mrs. Clouse "yelled out, 'Don't open that door, you'll fall right through the floor!' And he went and opened it, and, sure enough, you could see the *ground* underneath this thing, where the floor had just fallen to pieces. So he said, 'I see that you *do* need this building.'"

Mrs. Clouse, who, Webb says, over the years had "not only handled assignments, but provided, usually at her own expense, an endless supply of Kleenex, candy, aspirin, change," turned the first shovel at the ground-breaking ceremony on October 18. The compact and handsome two-story building, erected at a cost of $1.4 million on a site across the street and just to the west of the Music Building, has an exterior of limestone and large mirrored-glass panels; inside, surrounding a central lounge on each floor (the lower one including Mrs. Clouse's "central control desk"), there are eighty prefabricated soundproof practice-room modules. Opened in 1979, the building was dedicated on October 13, with, as the musical component of the occasion, over 150 students performing simultaneous concerts in the eighty modules, thus providing, as Webb noted in his annual report, "a live demonstration of the superb sound-proofing of the new building." Sylvia McNair was one of the performers in Room 137.

Nine months previously, in January 1979, the *Chronicle of Higher Education*, a monthly that serves as the paper of record in its field, published a set of rankings of the faculties, in the central academic disciplines, of American universities and professional schools. These rankings, based on a 1977 survey of faculty in the various fields, in the case of music generally confirmed the results of the *Change* report: Indiana was again ranked number one, followed in order this time by Eastman, Juilliard, Michigan, Illinois, Yale, Southern California, Oberlin, and Northwestern. The School was thus two-for-two in survey-based national rankings.

Given this and the other gratifying developments of the first six years of Webb's deanship, one would expect there to have been a continuing high level of satisfaction, on the part of faculty and students, with the School and its presiding spirit. But by the late 1970s the Dean was in fact getting mixed reviews.

In April 1978, the *Daily Student* published an article sampling the views of members of the School of Music on their Dean. Half a dozen faculty members were quoted by name (along with Webb himself); and there were three quotations from graduate students, who were content to remain anonymous. Webb was praised highly by the voice teacher Ralph Appelman (by this time a full professor nearing retirement), who claimed that the School had changed from a "benevolent monarchy" under Bain to a "democracy" under Webb. The Dean had "been wise in not causing faculty unrest through overriding decisions" (presumably those of the Academic Council) and as a result had "built a very peaceful and happy faculty." But no one else, other than Bill Christ, had anything particularly flattering to say (or if they did it wasn't quoted). Appelman himself had mixed feelings about the new form of government. Whereas "action was almost immediate under Bain," the proliferating committee structure under Webb meant that "it takes more time to decide issues"; it was "a much more peaceable way than it is expedient." And indeed what Appelman saw as peace, some viewed as stasis—at best. Elmar Burrows, an opera coach since 1969, said the School was "either standing still or regressing"; Christ's fellow theorist Pete DeLone lamented that there had not been much growth; he and John Eaton singled out contemporary music as an undergrown field.

These were the views of only a few, not necessarily representative, faculty members and students. But similar views were expressed late the next year to a committee that had made an officially sanctioned and conscientious effort to gather opinions of Webb's performance from as many members of the School as possible.

Until recently, deans at Indiana served *sine die,* at the pleasure of the President and Trustees. In the late 1970s, though, a system of administrative reviews was established, which would generate periodic reports for the central administration. As it happened, Webb was the first dean to be reviewed. For this purpose, a committee was struck in October 1979, consisting of five faculty members of the School, one student, and two members of other academic units; one of the outsiders served as chairman. The committee invited submissions, either written or oral, from all faculty, students, and non-academic staff not merely of the School but of the University as a whole, and in response received thirty-two letters and interviewed twenty-nine faculty members and administrators; they also met with the Student Representative Committee and with Webb himself.

The committee reported, and endorsed, a litany of highly complimentary remarks about the Dean. Webb enjoyed "excellent relations with his faculty on a personal level and . . . all, in spite of some disagreements, look to him for leadership." Several tributes were quoted—including phrases such as "this wonderful man," "a superior human being," "a resourceful, sensitive, and human [*sic*] leader"—and the report noted that "comments of this kind appeared many times in letters and in the interviews."

While this was doubtless true, it was perhaps stressed so strongly by way of balance or (for Webb) consolation for the substantial number of criticisms that the committee also reported. Faculty salaries were at or near the top of the faculty's collective mind. Though the committee—citing the continuing hard times for the University and the unresponsiveness of the central administration—did not particularly blame the Dean for the lack of progress on this front, it is nonetheless evident that the three-year plan for the improvement of salaries that Webb had announced in his first year had not succeeded; in the period since 1976, at least, the relative position of music faculty had actually worsened. (The salaries of the graduate student Associate Instructors remained "embarrassingly low," though in this matter, too, the committee recognized that there was little the Dean could do on his own.)

There was also some grumbling about abuses of the flextime policy, as well as about the heavy teaching loads and thus about the enrollment and the steadily declining faculty:student ratio. The School numbered 1,732 students in the fall of 1979: over the past fifteen years, the size of the faculty had remained constant, while enrollment had grown by more than 50 percent. (The number of graduate students had nearly doubled.) Though the Music Practice Building had just opened, students averred that there was still a shortage of available rooms.

In what would prove to be an ominous note, the committee reported some special dissatisfaction with Webb among the academic-music faculty. Naturally, this group had, in 1973, not been as happy about the appointment of the performer Webb as their colleagues in applied music had been. At the beginning of Webb's term, they were, Mary Wennerstrom told me, "just sort of lukewarm and waiting to see how this would play." By the end of the decade, there was a significant division of opinion among them on the matter. Some members of the group had expressed themselves generally satisfied with Webb's performance; but the committee had also received "forcefully given evidence . . . that teaching loads [in academic music] remain extremely heavy, that some worthy research projects are not given satisfactory administrative and financial encouragement, and that [there is] an inadequate awareness by the Dean of a proper and necessary balance between academic and performance matters."

The report also recorded a perception, both by some students and by some faculty members, that the Dean's much-applauded openness was not necessarily linked to action on the matters brought to his attention, and that his willingness to rationalize and enlarge the administrative structure of the School did not mean that he was committed to democratizing its operations. The revision of the committee structure, which both Webb and the faculty had endorsed largely on the ground that it would streamline the School's government, had not had that effect. At least some faculty members blamed the Dean: "His attempt to work through committees is time consuming and leads faculty to comment that he is indecisive in making hard decisions." Here a quality that had formerly been construed as a virtue was relabeled as a fault; and something similar was happening with respect to Webb's heavy schedule of musical performances. The committee recognized that his conspicuousness as a performer was valuable to the School but, citing the "majority opinion" expressed to it, noted that "the time involved in these activities may cut into the time available for administrative duties," and urged the Dean to "re-evaluate" the size of his commitment to performance.

The greatest worry embodied in the report, though (as also in the 1978 *IDS* article), was the fear that the School was drifting—that Webb was merely shepherding it along paths established by Bain, without developing a creative response to the changing conditions that it faced. In this regard, the report stressed especially the need to reevaluate the balance in the curriculum between academic music and applied; the need for greater attention to contemporary music; the need for better publicity and public relations (especially the desirability of using the School's students and faculty "to spread its reputation throughout the city, state, and nation"); and the problem posed by an aging faculty and the difficulty, in an era of financial restraint, of replacing retirees with people of comparable stature. In general, there was a "concerted interest" in "the formulation of a policy that articulates the artistic thrust and image of the School."

There had, in fact, recently appeared a document that purported to address just such strategic concerns. Carrying out another dictate of the central administration, the School had just submitted a ten-year plan for 1979–89. But the review committee found this report, written by Webb and Christ with the benefit of such consultation as they deemed appropriate, to be the opposite of reassuring. The report was, as the committee quite accurately stated, for the most part "not a visionary study of the future but a laudatory glance at the School's accomplishments." The need for long-range planning, and the worry that it was not getting done, had, it will be recalled, been an explicit concern in the School since at least the end of 1976, when Bernhard Heiden had initiated the drive for reorganization of the administrative structure by lamenting the fact that the Academic Council, though supposedly the policy-making body of the School, was in practice almost entirely given over to the micro-management of quotidian business. But the School of Music Council was turning out not to discuss strategic issues any more than its predecessor had.

Webb does not claim, even in retrospect, that at the time he became Dean he had a strategic plan encompassing all or even most of the issues raised by the review. Asked about his early vision for the School, he cites two goals (for neither of which he attempts to take sole credit: they derived from ideas being bruited about by the faculty in the period).

The first was a plan to expand the School's activities in the areas of early music and contemporary music (two extremes of relatively little interest to Bain); that Webb had this plan from the beginning is confirmed by an *Indianapolis Star* interview just after his appointment was announced in December 1972, in which he spoke of his intention to improve the School's offerings in both these areas, as well as in jazz (where there was already an undergraduate degree program) and classical guitar (where he had to wait for a degree program until 1989). In the fall of 1974, the School paid to have an elaborate publicity supplement published in *Music Journal;* in it one reads that plans were already being made for an Early Music Institute. In contemporary music, though the review committee felt that not enough had been done, one significant step had occurred as early as 1975, in the establishment of the New Music Ensemble under the direction of Frederick Fox. Fox had received his doctorate in composition from the School in 1959; in 1974 he returned as Visiting Professor, and the following year became Professor. Two years after its founding, the ensemble performed at the Inter-American Music Festival in Washington. For early music, the key move was made in 1979, when Webb brought in Thomas Binkley as Professor of Music. Educated at Illinois, Binkley, a lutenist, had proceeded for further studies to Munich, where in 1959 he founded the Studio der frühen Musik, a quartet which over the next eighteen years toured worldwide and made numerous celebrated recordings. A major figure in early music, he was, at the time of his appointment to Indiana, teaching at Stanford—where Webb's successful raid produced, he says, "livid rage." Within a year of his arrival in Bloomington he had become the founding Director of the Early Music Institute, which quickly became a major center in its field, continuing under Binkley's direction until his death in 1995.

The second part of Webb's early vision for the School, as he recalled in the 1990s, had been one of "moving it up a notch"—by which he meant turning a major national school into a major *inter*national one, famous worldwide and thus attracting first-rate students from around the world. The primary means for effecting this change would be to take the School's best student performances to the great world cultural centers. (This was something different from sending the Indiana Belles and Singing Hoosiers on tours of American military bases abroad.) There is, though, no mention of the plan to move to an international stage in the *Star* interview or anywhere else (as far as I can determine) in the first years of Webb's tenure, and one wonders whether perhaps the idea crystallized as the overriding priority for him only over time. If so, one of the seeds was probably a German excursion made, in the spring of 1976, by a choral group from the School. The impetus came from a Visiting Professor, Helmuth Rilling, conductor of the Gächinger Kantorei of Stuttgart, who invited the School to send a thirty-member chorus to Germany to take part in his series of recordings of all the Bach cantatas. While in Germany, the chorus also toured for three weeks, to enthusiastic reviews.

In the summer of the same year, Webb was approached by Harry Kraut,

Personal Manager for Leonard Bernstein, about the possibility of the School's touring Bernstein's one-act opera *Trouble in Tahiti* to Israel, where it would form part of a festival being sponsored the following spring by the Israel Philharmonic to mark the thirtieth anniversary of the Maestro's first concerts there. The opera had been written with a youthful cast in mind; and Kraut knew the reputation of the opera program at Indiana. Naturally Webb leapt at the chance. After trying out the opera in Bloomington, the student troupe went to Israel for the two weeks of the festival, where they appeared in nine of its fifteen programs; seven times they presented a double bill consisting of *Trouble in Tahiti* and a revue of Bernstein's Broadway music, and twice they performed with the Israel Philharmonic in a suite from *Candide.*

In addition to these international tours, student groups made, in the early Webb years, two especially notable domestic appearances. The first was the School's participation in the "Haydnfest" at Washington's Kennedy Center, where for a two-week period in September 1975 scholars and musicians from around the world gathered to discuss Haydn and listen to his music. The musical director of the festival was Bain's old collaborator Antal Dorati, who invited the School to present Haydn's *The World on the Moon*—the festival's only opera and its only student performance. Kozma conducted and Ross Allen directed. The reviews were highly favorable; Michael Donaldson, writing in the *Washington Star,* called the production "quite simply a brilliant achievement[,] . . . one of the highlights of the Haydnfest so far." A year later, Juan Orrego-Salas's oratorio *The Days of God,* commissioned by Dorati for the National Symphony Orchestra as one of its American Bicentennial programs, premiered in the Kennedy Center with a 144-voice School chorus. While in Washington, Orrego-Salas heard a PBS commentator say that if he couldn't continue to live there he would want to live in another city with a splendid cultural climate, such as "San Francisco, Seattle or Bloomington, Indiana."

All these events underscore the oddity of the review committee's recommendation that Webb use the School's students and faculty "to spread its reputation throughout the city, state, and nation." How much more did they expect? In any case, asking Charles Webb to encourage more tours was like asking Br'er Rabbit to spend more time in the briar patch: he was very happy to oblige.

In November 1978—a year before the review committee began meeting—Webb reported to his colleagues in the new School of Music Council that, at a recent meeting of the National Endowment for the Arts he had attended in New York, several people had suggested the School establish a performance series in that city. Asking for his colleagues' views on this proposition, he found them generally enthusiastic. Harvey Phillips linked it tantalizingly to the increasing need of the School (like all other educational institutions) to attract outside funding: performances in New

York would provide a way to bring the School to the attention of more of those with money to give.

Endorsing the plan was easy; bringing it to fruition would be a long and complex matter. First of all, to have any hope of making money from such a venture, or even of covering its expenses, the School would need sophisticated financial advice. Fortunately, this was available through the Indiana University Foundation.

The IUF, which coordinates all serious fundraising at the University, was established in 1936 by a group of individuals spearheaded by John Hastings, who had just concluded a term as President of the Alumni Council. Constituted as a not-for-profit corporation legally separate from the University, the foundation was set up to "receive, hold, manage, use and dispose of" gifts to the University. Herman Wells assumed office the following year; and it quickly became apparent how conformable the IUF was to his recognition that Indiana simply could not become a major educational institution unless it succeeded in cultivating sources of major funding other than the parsimonious state legislature. The foundation has proved to be of enormous value to the University.

For the New York venture, the IUF played a vital role. Thanks to its president, William Armstrong, who had great faith in Webb, and who understood the tremendous publicity potential of a New York series, the foundation not only offered professional counsel on the fundraising aspects of the venture but agreed to underwrite whatever expenses were not covered by donations and revenues from ticket sales. With this support, the School was by early 1981 able to develop a plan for a blockbuster—multiple-event, multiple-venue—inauguration for the series. In the elaboration of this complex plan, Leonard Phillips, a doctoral graduate of the School's Musicology Department who had recently become the first IUF liaison officer for Music, played a key role; in the boldest stroke of the plan, it occurred to him to ask whether the School might rent the Metropolitan Opera House for an evening. By February, Phillips was in a position to lay out in a memo to the President of the University the details of the economics and publicity for the trip, which was scheduled for late April. A New York firm had been hired to handle publicity and public relations, and the memo outlines elaborate plans in this area. The projected cost of the venture was $291,000. Of this amount Mead Johnson and Bristol Myers had each donated $5,000; the School would contribute $30,000 from its own budget; and the IUF would contribute $50,000. The projected income from ticket sales was $44,000—and it was hoped that the sale of thirty-five Met boxes at $10,000 each (with 50 percent of the revenue going, as with all the Met seats, to the house) would net an additional $175,000. Summing all these items, the projected income was $309,000.

While these arrangements were being made, the School's faculty was determining the actual offerings. In the end, it was decided to present Martinů's last opera, *The Greek Passion,* at the Met, an orchestral concert at Avery Fisher Hall, an evening of chamber music at Carnegie Recital Hall, and, at the Abraham Goodman House, concerts by the Chamber Choir and the New Music Ensemble. Two hundred and fifty students would be involved; four truckloads of sets and equipment would also make the trip.

Musically, and in terms of publicity and public relations, the venture was an overwhelming success. For *The New Yorker,* Nicholas Kenyon attended three of the five events and reported that "several times during the three . . . , I had to remind myself that these were student forces, not professional groups." Not surprisingly, the opera—which was the first and remains the only student production ever staged at the Met—made the biggest impression. This was the New York premiere of *The Greek Passion* (the trial run in Bloomington having been the American premiere). The work itself failed to generate much enthusiasm, but the production, directed by faculty members but sung and played entirely by students, had an enormous impact. Like other reviewers, Peter G. Davis in the *Times* was drawn to the production partly by a desire to see whether the long-standing reputation of the Opera Theater was deserved:

> As much interest centered on the Opera Theater as on Martinu. Many good things have been heard about the productions given in Bloomington since 1948—the annual presentations of Wagner's "Parsifal," the many premieres of important operas and the high quality of the performances—and here was opportunity for New York to see first-hand how the group would come to terms with a large-scale piece.

New York had not been disappointed: "As matters turned out, whatever could be done for 'The Greek Passion' the Opera Theater did with assured professional skill and respect for the material. . . . The orchestra played impressively. . . . The large cast performed with ease and security." Harriet Johnson of the *Post* began her review by affirming that "The Indiana University Opera Theater, ever bold, adventurous and professional, lived up to its reputation," and ended by observing that "We would be far richer artistically in this country if there were more companies like this." Mary Campbell's Associated Press review anticipated *The New Yorker* by saying that the Opera Theater "performed so well one could hardly believe the stage was full of students." She added that "Daniel Brewer, who sang the leading role, is the best-sounding new tenor we've heard on the Met stage in a long time." The Met itself, though it had merely rented the house and was not officially "presenting" the opera, nonetheless had, as *Opera News* noted, "vested concerns in the abilities of whoever might be using its stage." The production was permitted on the stage, a spokeswoman for the company explained, "because, in our considered opinion, it was most worthy of being seen": "It held the stage very well. It did *not* look like a school production in any way."

In planning for the excursion, Webb had stressed the importance of having it present an essentially typical sample of the School's student productions. Undertaking a large project, many schools, he noted, "start in August and finally put it on in May. It is important for us that we have not stopped school, but what we are taking is a flowering" of "our normal educational process." He must have been gratified at the way Nicholas Kenyon took the point: one had to remind oneself, the critic said, not only that these were student groups but that "they represented only a sampling of the regular musical activities on the Indiana campus: while two hundred and fifty students were in New York there were still well over a thousand students at the School of Music; forty concerts took place there during the same week."

When the receipts were counted, it turned out that the costs were $328,000 ($37,000 over the projection) and the income from ticket sales $164,000 ($55,000 under the projection). Thus the IUF, which had agreed to make good any shortfall, ended up paying more than twice the $50,000 it had originally budgeted. The Foundation's officers were, though, Webb reported to the Council in June, happy with the results: "They have said that they could not have bought even for $1,000,000 the advertising that came to the university and the School of Music."

Given this sensational beginning, the School naturally continued the New York series, though with only a single major event each year. The second year's venture, however, was not altogether a public-relations triumph. The venue this time was The Cloisters (the medieval branch of the Metropolitan Museum of Art), and in this apt setting the School's Early Music Institute on three days in March gave four performances of the reconstruction by Thomas Binkley and the medievalist Clifford Flanigan (a faculty member in Indiana's Comparative Literature Program) of the "Greater Passion Play" included in the thirteenth-century manuscript compilation known as the Carmina Burana—seemingly the first time the play had been produced in some seven hundred years. Artistically, the production was if anything even more successful than the preceding year's performance at the Met. In an utterly splendid review—learned, incisive, beautifully written—in *The New Yorker,* Andrew Porter noted the complex problems involved in presenting the work and lauded the solutions that Binkley and his colleagues (especially Ross Allen as stage director) had developed, as "carefully judged, precise, and convincing." But those are, he added, "cool epithets":

> What we heard and saw was a drama that [as another medieval text said a passion play might] "truly aroused the bystanders to genuine tears and compassion." It was passionate, piercing, overwhelming—one of those perfor-

> mances not often encountered that pour the past into the present, that leave listeners for hours afterward all but speechless and make hard the return to mundane life.

"Not even the Met's 'Parsifal,'" he said (comparing the School's offering to another Lenten event, which he had previously reviewed in glowing terms) "was a drama more gripping or more moving."

This was exactly the kind of publicity, confirmation of the School's (and not just the Opera Theater's) stature, that the New York series was intended to generate; but unfortunately the event also generated severe criticism of the School for producing a work that, like other medieval representations of Christ's passion, can scarcely not be found in part anti-Semitic. The production in fact provoked a firestorm of complaint from the Anti-Defamation League and others. In consequence of this reaction, the Metropolitan Museum agreed never to stage the play again; at Indiana, the level of concern or anxiety over the matter may be judged by the thickness of the file of internal memos and draft letters inspired by it. The School had already committed to three additional performances of the play in the spring of 1983; in the end, the production went ahead, but only after the University agreed to modify the text and to include a disclaimer in the program in any and all future performances.

No such controversy clouded the success of subsequent years of the New York series. In 1983, the Chamber Choir and Chamber Orchestra performed Bach's B-minor Mass in Lincoln Center's Alice Tully Hall. In 1984, a fortunate conjunction of events allowed the School to be conspicuous in three New York venues within three days. On March 18, the unmatched eminence of the School's opera program was apparent in the fact that, of the twenty-six semi-finalists competing that day in the Metropolitan Opera National Council Auditions, six were current or former students of the School, as were two of the eleven winners. The same evening, at the Roosevelt Hotel in midtown, the School's Jazz Ensemble was the featured group in a "Salute to Maynard Ferguson." And two days later, the School and the Metropolitan New York Chapter of the IU Alumni Association sponsored a concert featuring eighteen students—eight soloists and two chamber groups—at Carnegie Recital Hall (the idea being to showcase the breadth of individual talent at the School). In 1985, the New Music Ensemble represented the School, presenting, in two concerts at Symphony Space, works by five School faculty members and four New York composers. The next year, David Baker took the Indiana University Jazz Ensemble to perform at the same venue; two weeks later, the eleven winners of that year's Met Auditions appeared in concert at the Lincoln Center house: this time, four of the eleven were current or former Indiana students, a record unmatched by any school before or since. In 1987, the School was again represented by its early-music program, this time in the form of the Baroque Orchestra, a period-instruments ensemble established in 1983 under the direction of the great baroque violinist Stanley Ritchie, who had joined the faculty in 1982. The orchestra was led, in baroque fashion, not by a conductor but by Ritchie as principal violinist; sometimes other faculty members supplemented the students. For the New York trip, the ensemble was enlarged by three of these, all of whom had come to Indiana within the past few years: the harpsichordist Elisabeth Wright, who had been appointed as Assistant Professor in 1982 (and who is married to Ritchie, with whom she also forms the Duo Geminiani); the superb British tenor Paul Elliott, a founding member of the Hilliard Ensemble; and the eminent Dutch recorder player Eva Legêne, who, like Elliott, had joined the faculty in 1985. The orchestra played to a capacity audience in Merkin Concert Hall.

Although in almost every subsequent year there has been at least one important performance in New York by a School group, this appearance of the Baroque Orchestra was the last of the regularly scheduled events of the annual series. Undertaken as a way of publicizing the School in the musical capital of America, the series had come to seem less necessary. The School had become well known throughout the musical world, and its reputation was constantly refreshed and enlarged by appearances—taking place without the need for School sponsorship—of the many notable performers among its faculty and graduates, and even among its students, increasing numbers of whom brought glory to it as competition winners. Moreover, the cost of the New York series was high, in terms both of money and of the time given over to it by its organizers. And as the fame of the School grew, there was also an ever-growing number of *other* attractive performance activities on which these scarce resources could be expended.

A few months after the Baroque Orchestra's descent on New York, for example, the Philharmonic Orchestra played at the Kennedy Center, with Lukas Foss conducting. The occasion was a concert in memory of Arthur M. Sackler, coinciding with the opening of the Smithsonian Museum of Asian Art that bears his name. Starker also appeared in this concert, playing a Bach suite, and the pianist Byron Janis. Sherrill Milnes and Paul Plishka sang, accompanied by the orchestra. The event was a great success. Joseph McLellan, writing in the *Post,* characterized the orchestra's playing as "fresh, vital, and rich in sonority" and Starker's performance as "flawless," and observed that "at its best . . . the concert reached the highest levels of performing art." Two months later, on December 10, the New Music Ensemble performed in San Francisco as part of the San Francisco Symphony's New and Unusual Music series. The reviewer for the *Examiner* wrote of the "inherent splendors" of the Indiana ensemble, whose playing represented, he thought, "a miraculous combination of commitment and clarity."

There were also an increasing number of opportunities for the kind of performances that Webb thought most important in raising the School's international profile, those that took student ensembles to great world cultural centers. In 1984, at the invitation of the executive committee of the American Bandmasters Association, the School's Symphonic Band went to Tokyo to play at the first joint meeting of the association and its Japanese counterpart. The eighty-two-member ensemble also gave five other concerts during a two-week tour of Japan. In the summer of 1988, not one but two of the School's orchestras enjoyed residencies at major music festivals in France. In May, the Philharmonic appeared at the Festival International d'Évian. The ensemble played five concerts, two led by faculty members of the School and the other three by guest conductors: Michael Stern, Emmanuel Krivine, and Mstislav Rostropovich (who ten years previously had told the *Washington Star* that "maybe the most powerful musical impression of my life" was a 1975 visit to the School). During the same European excursion, the orchestra traveled to Geneva to present an all-Russian concert, conducted by Rostropovich and Maxim Shostakovich; Rostropovich also soloed, in Tchaikovsky's Rococo Variations. The Queen of Spain and Princess Irene of Greece were included in the packed house, and the concert was broadcast on radio and television. In August, the School's second-ranking large ensemble, the Symphony Orchestra, was orchestra-in-residence at the piano-music festival at La Roque d'Antheron, where it accompanied, among others, Paul Badura-Skoda, Rudolf Firkušný, and Pressler. The following summer, the Philharmonic returned to France—this time Paris, where it participated with three other youth orchestras from around the world, chosen from a list of six drawn up by Leonard Bernstein, in a week-long gala celebration of the opening of the Bastille Opera House. Gingold's pupil Corey Cerovsek soloed, and the program included the European premiere of a piece by graduate student David Dzubay (who later joined the faculty).

The broadcast media offered another means of publicizing the School (or, to put it idealistically, of sharing its musical wealth with the public outside Bloomington), and this means was especially attractive because it could bring performances to a much larger audience than could ever attend them in person. Moreover, it could do so at a fraction of the cost of touring, and without its complex logistics. The School had, of course, a long tradition of broadcasts, stretching back as far as 1938, but by the 1980s several factors made this electronic packaging of its wares substantially more appealing than had earlier been the case. First, the product the School had to offer was by now truly first-rate. Second, it had become a name-brand product, easy to market. Third, the technical resources for producing high-quality recordings were now available in Bloomington, in the expanded facilities of WFIU (the University's NPR station) and, especially after David Pickett arrived in 1983, in the School's own facilities.

Before joining the faculty, the British-born Pickett had worked on recording projects as important and diverse as Klemperer's *Die Walküre* and the Beatles' *Let It Be* (and had also been conductor of the Bushey Symphony Orchestra); brought to Indiana as Associate Professor, he became the School's first Director of Recording Arts.

In 1980, the School launched a weekly radio chamber music series called (as one of its predecessors had also been) "Music from Indiana," produced and distributed by WFIU. That year the series, which featured both faculty and student performers, was broadcast on six Indiana stations. By 1983, it had already achieved national syndication on American Public Radio. Fifty-four stations carried the program; within a few more years over a hundred had aired it. By 1987, the weekly audience was estimated at 115,000 in the continental United States and Hawaii. Excerpts were also featured on NPR's widely distributed "Performance Today" program. The Opera Theater achieved broad national exposure when, in 1987, NPR's "World of Opera" series (the off-season fill-in for Saturday afternoons at the Met) broadcast the School's production of Rimsky-Korsakov's *The Legend of Tsar Saltan.* (This was in fact the School's second national broadcast of a Rimsky-Korsakov opera: in December 1978, PBS had televised its production—the American premiere—of *The Night Before Christmas.*)

From the early Bain years, the remarkable quality of some of the School's musical performances had, as we have seen, recurrently inspired press attention that went beyond reviews to reports on the educational system that produced such astonishing results. The dedication of the MAC, which brought many notable observers of the American musical scene to Bloomington, had been a major occasion for expositions of this kind, and they continued afterward. Harold Schonberg of the *New York Times,* who had written so gratifyingly about the MAC and its dedicatory performance, was lured back to Bloomington in 1974 by an especially intriguing operatic offering, Busoni's *Doctor Faust.* In addition to a review —in which he praised the production as "not only handsome and imaginative . . . [but] brilliant as well"—he wrote a second article lauding both the production and the School itself, especially (as he had before) for its opera house and its splendid faculty. More substantial pieces occasionally appeared in magazines, and in the 1980s a remarkable series of these both testified to and enhanced the enormous reputation that the School by this time enjoyed in America and Europe.

In 1982, the music monthly *Ovation* published a detailed survey of the educational opportunities afforded by twenty-five of the best American music schools. Twenty-four of them were treated in alphabetical order; Indiana was singled out for "a more in-depth look" at the beginning of the article. Though citing the "oft-heard statement that the school is a big factory in which students can get lost" (Pressler, stressing the individual relationships with teachers, is quoted in rebuttal), the treatment of the School is highly laudatory, and, while the point is not directly made, the clear implication is that it is foremost among the schools surveyed. In 1983, a French music magazine, *Diapason,* devoted three pages to the virtues of the School, praising its simultaneous emphasis on practical professionalism and on giving its students a well-rounded education, and holding it up as a model for musical education. A similar article appeared the following year in the British string magazine *The Strad.* Also in 1984, *Opera News* published a four-page article on Indiana, surveying in the most flattering terms the past and present of the Opera Theater. Two years later, the *Smithsonian* published a long and interesting—and highly laudatory—article on the School, complete with a dozen photographs.

By far the most important press relationship in the history of the School, though, was that with Andrew Porter, who, in his capacity as principal music critic of *The New Yorker* from 1972 to 1992, was surely the most respected and widely read reviewer in the nation. Porter's sustained and increasingly intimate connection with the School began in 1974, when, like Schonberg, he came to Bloomington in December to review the production of *Doctor Faust.* He quite liked what he saw and heard. Kozma's conducting was "precise and persuasive," the orchestra played well, Röthlisberger's sets "caught the mood of each episode," the choirs were strong, the soloists generally good.

Porter did not return to Bloomington until three years later, when he reviewed *The Night Before Christmas* for both *The New Yorker* and the *Financial Times* (whose first music critic he had become in 1955). He attended performances on two successive evenings, and found himself, as he said in the *Times,* bewitched. The opera was conducted by a Visiting Professor (who, as it turned out, stayed on as a regular faculty member), Bryan Balkwill; he "did not miss the brilliance" of the work, Porter wrote, "but he caught, too, the tenderness and humanity" of it. The student cast played comedy with "stock staginess. . . . But that—a failing not limited to student stages!—was the only weakness in a delightful presentation which any professional company might envy."

Porter returned the following April to review the premiere of John Eaton's *Danton and Robespierre,* a visit that reinforced his enamorment. Monumental like its predecessor *Heracles, Danton* was generally far better received. Writing in *The New Yorker,* Porter called it a "large, exciting, adventurous, and vividly theatrical piece." Again he had attended two performances, and afterward listened to tapes of both "with a kind of amazement at the sustained level of accomplishment." Again he loved the work of the conductor—Thomas Baldner, another Visiting Professor who was appointed Professor the following year. "It would," he wrote, "be hard to overpraise the work of . . . Baldner, . . . the Bloomington student cast, the

Bloomington student players, and all who prepared them." He urged the public broadcasting networks to secure a copy of one of the tapes, so the entire nation could at least *hear* "this remarkable work." The production was, simply, the opera event of the season.

In the spring of 1980, he came back for productions of *Porgy and Bess* and, the following week, a double bill consisting of Busoni's *Arlecchino* and another Eaton opera, *The Cry of Clytaemnestra.* He thought Indiana's *Porgy and Bess* "the most enjoyable and persuasive production" of it he'd ever seen. The performance of *Arlecchino* was "enchanting." *Clytaemnestra,* like *Danton,* he found admirably composed and admirably performed. (Five years later, Porter became Eaton's collaborator, preparing a reduction of Shakespeare's *Tempest* for the composer's operatic version of it, premiered by the Santa Fe Opera in 1985.) His review of *Clytaemnestra* also praised the MAC as "a match for the best German opera houses and so far as I know unrivalled in this country," and, in a phrase that has echoed endlessly through subsequent School publicity, observed that the Opera Theater "has struck me as just about the most serious and consistently satisfying of all American opera companies."

In November 1980, Porter came to Bloomington once again, to review the production of Borodin's *Prince Igor,* which he generally admired, though he found the singers not as well prepared as on previous occasions. There was, however, abundant vocal talent on display, the orchestra was "bright," and Röthlisberger's sets were "big and handsome": "If the Met wishes to mount an 'Igor' in borrowed décor, it could well use them." He also returned twice in 1981, to review the American premiere of Wolfgang Rihm's chamber opera *Jakob Lenz* and the American stage premiere of Janáček's *The Excursions of Mr. Brouček.*

By early 1982, he was ready to move in. In addition to being a celebrated critic, Porter had achieved distinction as a translator of operatic libretti; he was also greatly interested in stage direction. In view of these facts, some members of the School's Opera Planning Committee suggested to Webb, who was happy to agree, that Porter be invited to Bloomington for several weeks to direct a production of *The Abduction from the Seraglio* that would use his new translation of the text. He accepted, and performed to general satisfaction. Sylvia McNair was Constanza (though only in the second cast: Clarissa Behr sang the role in the first cast).

Following this venture (which was replicated in 1985 with Handel's *Tamerlane* and in early 1992 with *The Rake's Progress*), Porter—who endorses Peter Brook's view that "the more the critic becomes an insider, the better"—fortunately did not feel obliged to recuse himself from further reviews of School performances. Within a few months, he reviewed the New York production of the Carmina Burana passion play, comparing it on equal terms, as I noted earlier, with the Met's *Parsifal.* In 1984, he returned to Bloomington to review the School's production (he didn't like it) of Philidor's *Tom Jones.* The following year, he lauded the New Music Ensemble's New York concerts. In 1987 he was again in Bloomington, to review the School's production of its third Rimsky-Korsakov opera, *The Legend of Tsar Saltan,* which held him "spellbound." As usual, he found Röthlisberger's design distinguished, and he observed that the Met (where Zeffirelli's *Turandot* had recently debuted) could find the Indiana production "a model for décor that is romantic, colorful, richly inventive, amusing, and not vulgarly ostentatious—décor that matches and enhances the music, doesn't seek to drown it." In 1988, he came to review the School's production of Luigi Rossi's *Orfeo,* prepared and led by Thomas Binkley. Affirming that "Bloomington is an important American company," he summed up his view of this particular production by saying that "the show was not ideal but was a big second step—the first was . . . the Passion Play . . . —toward bringing early-music university enterprise before contemporary audiences." The publicity afforded the School by this long series of reviews was, it hardly needs saying, invaluable; and it was a sad day for the School (as for many readers of *The New Yorker*) when in 1992 Porter returned to England, where he became the music critic of the *Observer.*

The 1980s also witnessed the efflorescence of the School's other most important relationship with an individual, that with the most famous American musician of his time, Leonard Bernstein. The romance with Bernstein had its prehistory in 1976, when he and Webb had met to discuss the School's possible contribution to the Bernstein festival in Israel. Reporting to his colleagues on this meeting, Webb noted that there had also been some discussion of Bernstein's making a guest appearance at Indiana at some point in the future. Nothing came of this idea until 1981, when the University created an Institute for Advanced Study. The Institute would have Visiting Fellows, and it was decided that Bernstein would be invited to be the first of these.

Bernstein was then sixty-three, nearing the end of his creative life, and the invitation arrived at a bad time for him. As Harry Kraut, his Personal Manager, recalled, "Lenny was pretty depressed, and he was having real compositional problems, . . . a block. And he was sitting here in New York, and he had just about decided to give up. . . . and he kept on saying [with regard to the invitation to the heartland], 'Well, I don't know, I'm so depressed, I don't know whether all that Midwestern enthusiasm, that I'll be able to stand that.'" Kraut, though, persuaded him that precisely what he needed was to get away from New York, and finally Bernstein "sort of reluctantly agreed."

Understanding the situation, Webb secured for him—"in a matter of seconds," as it seemed to Kraut—a retreat away from Bloomington and the University, in the form of a condominium on Lake Monroe, a large and scenic reservoir about twenty minutes south of town by car. The School picked up the tab—$400 a month, which came to $600, since Bernstein stayed nearly six weeks—and this was the only cost to it of a visit that turned out to be priceless.

Bernstein holed up at the lake for the first few days of his visit, trying to work on what was to be his last opera, a sequel to *Trouble in Tahiti* called *A Quiet Place.* But, as Kraut recalls, before long "the lure of all those young performers just a few miles north got him out." Once the ice had been broken, he immersed himself in the life of the School, and especially in that of its composition and conducting students, attending workshops and critiquing rehearsals. Most important from his point of view and doubtless most exciting from that of the students, he began to take sections of the opera-in-progress—as it now genuinely was—to the School for them to play for him; sometimes these sections were only a few hours old. On one occasion, he had fifteen singers and five pianists prepare a trio from the work, so that he could test different interpretations and voice combinations. One witness recalled him sitting in the middle of a rehearsal room in the MAC, "clad in a yellow turtleneck, a pink sweater, jeans, and cowboy boots, with that sculptured aureole of white hair and intense smile so familiar from hundreds of hours on television—beating time, asking the singer to give more, to quietly float a high note." Often he took the baton himself.

In Kraut's view, Bloomington was a "lifesaver" to Bernstein's composing career. "This is my composing time," Bernstein explained to the students at one point, "and I guard it very jealously. I am working well here; we have accomplished a lot. It's extraordinary to have so many talented people in one place. I'm honored that such beautifully prepared students have taken the time from their studies . . . to prepare my opera. . . . It's very exciting." Early in the visit, heart characteristically on sleeve, he confided in a public address that "just as a result of the couple of visits I've made, the few hours I've had of contact with the students and faculty, I have to report, albeit a bit reluctantly, that I've fallen in love with the School." Privately, he told Webb "I hope you know what you have in your school." He had, he said, been all over the world on numerous campuses, but there was no place that could match the School's depth in so many areas.

Bernstein was never, of course, all work and no play, nor did either his work or his play usually take place at the times of day most people regard as appropriate. As much as possible, he recreated his big-city social life in the sticks. If he had always been the last to leave a party in the world's capitals, so was he in Bloomington. One Indiana dawn found him pounding out Gilbert and Sullivan on a faculty member's parlor piano.

Though he had urged Bernstein to make the trip, Kraut had in fact had trepidations about the cultural dissonances that it (like the Met visits of old) would surely produce. In particular, he was worried about how the party animal Bernstein might get along with the clean-living Webb: "Because here is this Methodist church organist who is the dean of a school of music, who gets up at five o'clock in the morning, meeting this man who's traveling around the world, who's never sleeping when he's supposed to be sleeping, getting up at four o'clock in the afternoon and going to bed at four o'clock in the morning and drinking and swearing and carrying on a good deal." But when "they laid eyes on one another—love at first sight."

But this was not all that surprising for two charismatic figures, one of whom also had a charismatic family on hand, and a beautiful home. Bernstein "spent a considerable amount of time at our house," Webb says. Presumably part of the attraction was that of an excursion into an opposite life, the apotheosis of the Protestant ethic. Who, though, could not like spending time with this family? How the experience worked on Bernstein's thoughts and feelings is evident in the fact that, as Webb recalls, "one evening he came for dinner and surprised us by presenting us a manuscript, which was entitled 'Blessed Are the Webbs'" (a chorale). Moreover, his affection for the Webbs proved durable. Almost at the end of his life, he sent them another manuscript, this one from the last composition he completed, *Arias and Barcarolles.* The gift was a song entitled "Mr. and Mrs. Webb Say Goodnight," a vignette of bedtime at the Webbs' house from the era of Bernstein's visit, when, with the four boys still at home, bedtimes were lively.

In fact Bernstein's fondness for the School was in substantial part a fondness for the Webbs, and here—as, really, in many other instances—Webb performed a service to the School simply by his and Kenda's being who they are. Just how great the service was in this case cannot be accurately measured. We know, for example, that it was on Bernstein's recommendation that the Philharmonic Orchestra was later invited to participate in the opening of the Bastille Opera; but how many other times did a word from him raise the School in someone's estimation, or lead to an invitation for one of its individuals or ensembles to perform somewhere?

One such incident, though, is fully documented. In 1987, with Bernstein's seventieth birthday a year away, the Boston Symphony undertook to mount a four-day celebration of the event, to be held at Tanglewood the following August. In addition to concerts by the Symphony and Pops, the gala would encompass an astonishing array of guest performers, including Beverly Sills, Lauren Bacall, Rostropovich, Yo-Yo Ma, Midori, Hildegard Behrens, and Christa Ludwig; Seiji Ozawa, John Williams, and Michael Tilson Thomas would conduct. Asked which of his works he would especially like to have performed for the event, Bernstein immediately requested *Mass* ("A Theater Piece for Singers, Players, and Dancers"). When the organizers told him they could not muster the huge and diverse forces the work required, he suggested that Indiana be invited to present it.

As it happened, this suggestion followed on one he had made eight years previously, when, remembering the success of the Israel tour, he had hoped that the School would be able to present the mass at the upcoming tenth-anniversary celebration of the Kennedy Center. (The controversial work had been premiered there in 1971.) But the Center wanted a thoroughgoing rock version of the piece, which as Bernstein wrote it included substantial rock elements, and this the School declined to offer. There was no such condition on the Tanglewood offer, however, and the School accepted, though the lead time was minimally adequate. *Mass* was presented in Bloomington in April 1988; afterward, the set had to be modified to fit the Tanglewood shell, and the logistics worked out for transporting to western Massachusetts a cast of 250 students—including orchestra, choir, the University Children's Choir, dancers, rock bands, and singing/dancing "street people." (The School was able to amass these forces despite the fact that this was also the summer when two of its orchestras were at festivals in France.)

An audience of ten thousand witnessed the performance. Though the critics in attendance maintained the reservations about the work itself that had dogged it since its premiere, they praised the production. The audience was highly responsive; Bernstein himself was ecstatic. Joining the cast on stage, he told the audience that "my gratitude is endless": "This is one of the finest performances I've ever seen. I don't mean only of *Mass:* I mean of anything." Speaking to the press afterward, he said:

> I don't know how, short of a miracle, this all took place, and on such a level. I think it's all Charlie Webb, it's the spirit of Dean Webb and everything he stands for—somehow [it] gets into the corpuscles of everybody in that school. God bless him.

The Webb Years

II. Quo Vadis?

As the seventies and eighties passed, key figures of the Bain era gradually dropped off the School's roster, lost to retirement or death. Julius Herford retired in 1973, William Primrose the following year. As I noted earlier, Michael Kuttner died in 1975; so also did a second member of the Berkshire Quartet, the violist David Dawson. The same year, Harry Farbman, Walter Robert, and Newell Long retired. In his forty-year career, Long had taught thirty-six different courses (including one in physics). Robert took early retirement, to clear the way, he said, for younger teachers and to go back to school himself. Already a polymath when he came with Bain from North Texas, he had over the years taken various courses in classical languages, and after retirement completed a master's degree in Greek.

In March 1976, Bain's nemesis Tibor Kozma was killed in a car wreck, as his predecessor Ernst Hoffman had been; he was sixty-six. Frederick Baldwin, a pianist who had joined the faculty as a lowly Instructor in 1950 but had risen to be chairman of the Department for the period 1960 to 1972, retired in 1976. Sidney Foster died in 1977 at the age of fifty-nine; Wolfgang Vacano retired that year, as did Walter Kaufmann, though he continued teaching, part-time, until his death in 1984. (It remained common—as it had been in Nettl's day—for outstanding faculty members to be asked to teach after retirement on a year-to-year basis.) Bain himself, it will be recalled, retired in 1978, as did Ralph Appelman. Marko Rothmuller retired the following year, and Ralph Daniel took early retirement in 1980; he died in 1985 at the age of sixty-three. Margaret Harshaw also retired in 1980, though she taught part-time until 1993. Hans Busch, too, retired in 1980; afterward he continued the distinguished Verdi scholarship in which he had long been engaged.

Bernhard Heiden, appointed by Sanders in 1946, retired in 1981, as did Peter Eagle. The next year, Louis Davidson, Philip Farkas, Virginia MacWatters, and Urico Rossi all retired; Oswald Ragatz, the organist appointed by Sanders, retired in 1983, after forty-one years at the School. Martha Lipton retired the same year, though she continued teaching on a part-time basis throughout the remainder of Webb's deanship and beyond. Richard Johnson died that August, at sixty-one, and Pete DeLone the following March, of a heart attack at fifty-five. That summer, Vera Scammon and Fritz Magg retired; he had served as chairman of the String Department for all but the first two of his thirty-six years at Indiana.

Frederick Ebbs—the band director who had succeeded where so many others had not—retired in 1984 and died suddenly a few months later. Harry Houdeshel and Eugene Bayless also retired in 1984. Hans Tischler, Georges Janzer, and (as I noted earlier) William Christ retired in 1985, George Gaber and Murray Grodner in 1986, Juan Orrego-Salas and Max Röthlisberger the following year. Jerry Sirucek retired in 1988, Earl Bates in 1989.

In 1980, the deanship review committee had worried that it would be difficult to replace the departing luminaries from Bain's faculty with people of comparable stature, and in this connection had also been perturbed by the School's lack of "consistently applied appointment procedures in which appropriate faculty are involved"; that is, by the fact that Webb, like Bain, kept appointments largely in his own hands. It is of course impossible to measure reputations (or, still more, collective reputations) precisely or objectively, but, surveying the additions made to the faculty in the years whose major losses are catalogued above, one does not find any clear diminution in quality. As in the preceding chapter, though, one is overwhelmed by the sheer numbers of appointees—sometimes a dozen or more in a single year, though the faculty was now not growing, but simply being maintained at a steady state—and I can mention only the most notable additions.

In the Voice Department, the tradition of recruiting opera stars at or near the end of their careers continued. Walter Cassel, a leading baritone at the Met from 1943, came to Indiana in 1974, and Camilla Williams was recruited in 1977. Like Cassel's, her singing career had spanned thirty years, including the barrier-breaking moment in 1946 when, as Butterfly in a New York City Center Opera production, she became the first black woman ever to be put under contract by a major American company. In 1980, the celebrated Russian-Italian bass Nicola Rossi-Lemeni joined the faculty; his wife, the soprano Virginia Zeani, was appointed at the same time. Eventually both she and her husband attained the rank of Distinguished Professor, making them the only such married couple in the history of the University.

The soprano Reri Grist, who, though American, had made her notable career primarily in Europe, taught at the School from 1981 through 1983. The Italian soprano Gabriella Tucci, who had enjoyed a fine career at the Met, was appointed as Visiting Professor in 1983 and stayed on for two additional years in a regular position. The dramatic tenor James King joined the faculty in 1984, as did Lynn Luciano and Carol Smith. Gloria Davy, who had sung the title role of *Aida* at both the Met and the Vienna State Opera, was appointed in 1985. As I noted earlier, Paul Elliott joined the faculty in 1985 as a member of the Early Music Institute. In 1986, both the tenor Carlos Montané (who had been the first Cuban to appear as a leading soloist with the Met) and Norman Phillips (a leading baritone for the Vienna State Opera) were appointed; Klara Barlow, a leading soprano with the Met from 1971 to 1980, came the following year.

The 1970s and 1980s also witnessed several excellent appointments in operatic production and various species of conducting. James Lucas had been a guest stage director at the School on several occasions (including a 1985 production of Bellini's *La Sonnambula* that marked the School's first use of projected supertitles); in 1987 he was appointed to the regular faculty. In 1988 (Max Röthlisberger having retired the previous year), the scenic designer Robert O'Hearn was brought in; he had designed productions for the Met, the Santa Fe Opera, and the Vienna Volksoper, as well as for ballet companies and Broadway shows. As I noted earlier, the orchestral conductors Thomas Baldner and Bryan Balkwill both came, initially on visiting appointments, in 1977. In choral conducting, Jan Harrington had been appointed Assistant Professor in 1973, while still a graduate student, and in 1980 Robert Porco was recruited at the rank of Professor. Harrington has remained on faculty up to the present; Porco, who over the years took on increasingly heavy outside commitments (as choral director of the renowned Cincinnati May Festival and conductor of the choruses of the Cincinnati Symphony and, latterly, the Cleveland Orchestra), resigned in 1999.

In the keyboard departments, the mid-1970s witnessed a series of spectacular appointments. The Naumburg Competition winner Zadel Skolovsky joined the faculty in 1975, and the following year the superb British pianist John Ogdon was added. (He remained, however, only through 1980.) In 1977, the brilliant young American James Tocco arrived; he had won eight major competitions. The same year, Anthony Newman, whom *Time* had called, fairly enough, the "high priest of the harpsichord," came as a Visiting Professor. Appointed to the regular faculty the following year, he remained until 1982. In 1978, Michel Block, who had won the Leventritt Award, was recruited, as was Balint Vazsonyi, a Hungarian pianist who had made concert history in 1976–77 by playing all thirty-two Beethoven sonatas in chronological order over two-day periods in New York, Boston, and London. As I noted earlier, the harpsichordist Elisabeth Wright was appointed in 1982. The pianist Shigeo Neriki joined the School in 1980, and in 1983 Edward Auer came, as did the organist Marilyn Keiser. In 1984, Leonard Hokanson arrived. Born on a tiny island off the coast of Maine (where he began his keyboard studies on the accordion), he had gone on to become a pupil of Schnabel and had subsequently made a performing career in Europe as both soloist and chamber player, and as accompanist of the great German baritone Hermann Prey.

In strings, the first notable appointment of the Webb era was that of the violinist James Buswell in 1974. At Indiana, where he remained until 1986, he branched out into conducting, and became the founding conductor of the Chamber Orchestra. As I noted earlier, the Polish violinist Tadeusz Wronski, who had previously held visiting appointments, returned to the School as a permanent faculty member in 1975. The same year, Henryk Kowalski, who had been Gingold's student in the Artist Diploma program, joined the faculty as Visiting Lecturer; he remained to rise through the ranks. In 1976, both Laurence Shapiro (former concertmaster of a chamber orchestra, the New York Philharmonia) and Abraham Skernik (principal violist of the Cleveland Orchestra) joined the faculty; they replaced Kuttner and Dawson in the Berkshire Quartet. The violinist and violist Paul Biss, formerly a Gingold pupil, returned to the School as a faculty member (first on a visiting appointment) in 1977.

The same year saw the advent of two remarkable string players. The cellist Gary Hoffman, having completed bachelor's and master's degrees and gained an Artist Diploma at the School, became, at twenty-two, the youngest faculty appointee in its history. He remained until 1987, the year after he became the first North American to win the Rostropovich Competition. The Gingold pupil Yuval Yaron had comparable early achievements. In 1972, the Israeli-born violinist had won second prize in the Paganini Competition; three years later, at the age of twenty-two, he took first prize in the Sibelius Competition and shared first prize in the Montreal Competition. Having earned the Artist Diploma in 1977, he joined the faculty two years later, and has continued at the School to the present.

In 1980, the violist Mimi Zweig was appointed as Assistant Professor; she has remained at the School ever since. At the same time, the Russian violinist Rostislav Dubinsky was appointed at the rank of Professor. His wife Luba Edlina, a pianist, was appointed Visiting Lecturer; she eventually rose to the rank of Professor. Together with Yuli Turovsky they formed the Borodin Trio. A passionate exponent of Shostakovich and a dedicated teacher, Dubinsky became a beloved figure among string students. His MAC Chamber Music Festival, held at noon for a week in the fall and again in the spring, with, in each concert, several student ensembles playing in the lobby before a few dozen delighted spectators, was perhaps the single most engaging event in the School's yearly schedule. His death from lung cancer in the fall of 1997 took from the institution one of its most admirable citizens.

As I noted earlier, the supreme baroque violinist Stanley Ritchie, an Australian by birth, joined the faculty in 1982, three years after the appointment of the founding Director of the Early Music Institute, Thomas

Binkley. In 1985 the Institute was further strengthened by the appointment of Eva Legêne and that of Wendy Gillespie, a viola da gamba player who had been a member of the Waverly Consort.

Three first-rate string players were added in 1986: the violinist Miriam Fried (one of Gingold's Queen Elisabeth of Belgium winners), and two more bassists, Bruce Bransby and Lawrence Hurst. Hurst had been on faculty at the University of Michigan since 1962. Bransby came, like so many of his predecessors in the String Department, directly from a position in a major orchestra, having been principal bass with the Los Angeles Philharmonic since 1978. Two years later, Tsuyoshi Tsutsumi, Janos Starker's former student and assistant, and the first graduate of the Artist Diploma program (in 1965), returned as Professor.

There were also, in these years, strong appointments in the other orchestral instruments. Robert Elworthy came to the School in 1977 after seventeen summers as principal horn with the Santa Fe Opera; Sidney Rosenberg, appointed the following year, had been principal bassoonist of the Israel Philharmonic and co-principal of the Montreal Symphony. In 1981, Webb made a spectacularly good appointment in harp, raiding Susann McDonald from Juilliard, where she had for ten years chaired the Harp Department. The first American to receive the Premier Prix in harp at the Paris Conservatory, she had made, at the age of twenty-three, a celebrated three-concert debut in Carnegie Hall, and had, over the years, gained a reputation as one of the foremost performers and teachers of the harp. By 1989 she had been elevated to the rank of Distinguished Professor; the following year she established the USA International Harp Competition, which is held at the School triennially.

In 1984, the hornist Michael Hatfield, an alumnus of the school who had for over twenty years been principal horn of the Cincinnati Symphony, returned to Indiana as Professor. The percussionist William Roberts was appointed the same year. Like many other percussionists, he had had extensive experience not only in classical music but in jazz and other popular musics. In 1985, the trombonist Edwin Anderson joined the faculty, after more than twenty years in the Cleveland Orchestra (where he had participated in over two hundred recordings). Myron Bloom, appointed the same year, had also played with the Cleveland Orchestra, as principal horn for more than fifteen years; subsequently he had been first horn of the Orchestre de Paris. In 1986, Gerald Carlyss, who had been principal timpanist with the Philadelphia Orchestra since 1967 and had taught at Curtis, joined the School, as did the flutist Carol Wincenc, noted both as performer and educator; the very next year the highly distinguished British flutist Peter Lloyd joined the faculty, after twenty years as solo flute of the London Symphony. Formerly head of the Flute Department at the Guildhall School, he had also been a member of the Tuckwell Wind Quintet and the English Taskin Players. (Neither Wincenc nor Lloyd, however, remained at Indiana for long: she left in 1991 to pursue her burgeoning concert career, and he departed in 1993 to return to London.)

The superb Canadian clarinetist James Campbell also joined the faculty in 1987. A renowned soloist and sought-after chamber music player, he had collaborated with Starker and Pressler, as well as with such artists as Glenn Gould and Elly Ameling. His fellow clarinetist Howard Klug was appointed in 1988, as was Edmund Cord, a graduate of the School who had been principal trumpet with the Israel Philharmonic, the Santa Fe Opera, and the Utah Symphony.

In 1977, the School had finally made a second regular appointment in jazz, bringing in Dominic Spera as Associate Professor. A bachelor's and master's graduate of the School, he had had a wide range of experience as a trumpeter not only in jazz bands but in classical, Broadway, and popular-music ensembles. In 1989, Webb, being at last on the brink of achieving his goal of establishing a degree program in classical guitar, brought in Ernesto Bitetti. Born in Argentina, he had made more than twenty recordings, had had pieces written for him by Rodrigo and Castelnuovo-Tedesco, and had performed as soloist with orchestras including the English Chamber Orchestra, the Prague Chamber Orchestra, L'Orchestre de la Suisse Romande, and the BBC Symphony.

No doubt the department in which the appointments of the 1970s and 1980s made the greatest difference was Ballet. After Anton Dolin's departure in 1972, the upward momentum that had been achieved following his and Marina Svetlova's arrival had begun to dissipate. Temporary appointees came and went at an alarming pace. Svetlova ceased chairing the Department in 1975, at which point it was placed in receivership, with Allan Ross (Webb's Assistant, and a choral musician) acting as chairman for two years. He was succeeded by a Visiting Professor, Nicolas Beriozoff, who also held the position for two years, and then by Dudley Davies, an Assistant Professor brought in specially for this purpose. The faculty was strife-riven. Department meetings were rarely held; in a 1980 meeting between students and faculty called to discuss the Department's situation, the faculty, according to a letter written to Webb by one of the students present, "instead of communicating with the students, insisted on arguing among themselves and wandering off the points being discussed."

The situation of the Department did not significantly improve until 1985, when Jean-Pierre Bonnefoux was brought in as Professor and Chairman. Bonnefoux had been, at twenty-one, a principal dancer with the Paris Opera Ballet and, later, with Balanchine's New York City Ballet; he had also choreographed for the Munich, Pittsburgh, and Louisville Ballets. This excellent appointment was followed the next year by two others, of the husband-and-wife team of Jacques and Virginia Cesbron. Jacques had danced with the Met Opera Company, and had been a soloist with the Harkness Ballet and a principal dancer with the Pennsylvania Ballet, where Virginia had also danced. The spectacularly changed fortunes of the Department under Bonnefoux were also evinced, in 1989, by the appointment of his wife, Patricia McBride. In 1961 she had become the youngest principal dancer of the New York City Ballet, and in the following years, when she and Suzanne Farrell were the company's prima ballerinas, danced numerous leading roles, many of them choreographed expressly for her by Balanchine, Jerome Robbins, Peter Martins, and others. When she retired from the company to join Bonnefoux at Indiana, the event was marked by a gala; as she took her final bows, over 13,000 roses were showered on the stage.

As a result of these appointments, ballet at Indiana was transformed. The number and quality of students increased, and the Department not only became much more capable of making substantial contributions to Opera Theater productions but was also, with the resumption of the fall ballet (which had been allowed to lapse), able again to mount two full programs each year in addition to the annual *Nutcracker.*

In his final year as Dean, Bain had arranged the appointment of Carol MacClintock as Professor in musicology, thus getting off his successor's era to what appeared to be a good start in appointments in academic music. MacClintock, who had completed her doctorate at the School in 1955 and had most recently been teaching at the Cincinnati College-Conservatory, had achieved a distinguished record of scholarship in early music. The appointment, however, failed egregiously, according to Bain because the other five members of the musicology faculty, feeling (doubtless with cause) that they had not been properly consulted about the matter, were not especially welcoming. MacClintock resigned after a year to return to Cincinnati. The vacancy she left was filled, the following year, by Peter Brown, who was not only a Haydn scholar but an excellent hornist, having studied with Farkas in Chicago and played with the Chicago Brass Quintet and the Milwaukee Symphony. Also in 1974 (as I noted in the preceding chapter), the composer Frederick Fox joined the faculty; like Brown, he remained at the School for the rest of his career.

Equally durable were four other academic-music appointments of the late 1970s. In 1975, Michael Gordon, who had previously been District Supervisor of Music for the New York City Board of Education, was appointed Associate Professor in music education; a key member of the Black Music Caucus of the Music Educators National Association, he also achieved notable success within the University, becoming Dean of Students in 1981. In 1977, George Buelow, a well-known scholar of baroque music, was appointed as Professor in musicology. In 1978, both Marianne Kielian (later Kielian-Gilbert) and David Neumeyer joined the Theory Department. Kielian was still a graduate student, completing a doctorate at Michigan; Neumeyer, who had attained his doctorate at Yale, was already establishing himself as an authority on Hindemith. In later years he became a major personage in the School, both as a scholar and, in the 1990s, as Director of Graduate Studies.

The year 1983 witnessed a number of significant appointments. The composer Harvey Sollberger was appointed at the rank of Professor. Previously located in New York, he had taught at Stony Brook, CUNY, and Columbia. At Indiana, where he remained until 1992, he succeeded Fox as director of the New Music Ensemble. Jane Fulcher, a specialist in nineteenth-century French music, joined the Musicology Department as an Associate Professor, and Charles Schmidt, who had just completed his Indiana doctorate, was appointed in music education. The most portentous appointment of 1983, though (signaling as it did a new level of attention to electronic technology in the School), was that of David Pickett, who, as I noted earlier, was the School's first professorial-level appointee in recording arts; by 1990 he had developed a degree program in Audio Recording.

A series of strong appointments from the second half of the 1980s completes this survey. In 1985, Benito Rivera, an early-music scholar who had taught at CUNY, Richmond, and North Texas, was recruited in music theory, at the rank of Associate Professor. In 1986, Estelle Jorgensen, previously at McGill, came to Indiana as Professor in music education; another senior appointment in the same department came in 1989, when Stanley Schleuter, a prolific scholar formerly at Kent State, was recruited. Three composers were added. In 1987, Eugene O'Brien, whose compositions had won a number of awards and who had been a Bellagio Fellow of the Rockefeller Foundation, was named Associate Professor. The same year, Jeffery Hass, a doctoral student in the School who had previously studied and taught at Rutgers, and who since 1983–84 had held an appointment as Lecturer at Indiana, was made Instructor, and Director of the Center for Electronic and Computer Music. In 1988, Claude Baker arrived. Previously a faculty member at the University of Louisville and at Eastman, he had won a number of awards; the year after his appointment, Leonard Slatkin, the conductor of the St. Louis Symphony, called him one of the three "best young symphonic composers in America." Two musicologists were also appointed in 1988. J. Peter Burkholder, recruited as Associate Professor, had, while teaching at Wisconsin, done seminal work on Charles Ives; and Thomas Mathiesen, recruited at the rank of Professor, was a major addition to the School. He had previously taught at Brigham Young University, where he had become the nation's foremost authority on ancient Greek and medieval Latin music theory texts. At Indiana, where he directs the Center for the History of Music Theory and Literature, he immediately became, as his colleague Malcolm Brown (who was to retire in 1993) had long been, a key figure not just in his department but in the School as a whole. In 1996, he was elevated to the rank of Distinguished Professor; the only other academic musician to achieve this status had been Walter Kaufmann.

Despite the many excellent appointments, and the School's many triumphs of the 1980s (which had included yet another number-one ranking, this one in a 1983 survey of performance programs by the National Association of Music Executives of State Universities), there continued to be, through this decade and into the 1990s, a significant amount of faculty discontent with the Dean. Indeed discontent, at least as measured by the three subsequent deanship reviews in the quadrennial series inaugurated in 1980, increased.

In May 1984 the second of the review reports was issued. As before, the findings included much that was glowingly positive. The committee noted that the School's excellence had been maintained, especially in the area of performance, where the high standards of the Bain era had perhaps even been surpassed. Much of the credit for this sustained excellence was accorded to Webb, who was also praised for developing the new program in early music and programs in audio, keyboard, and opera costume technology, and for appointments that had revitalized the Harp and Organ Departments. In the area of public relations (where the 1980 report had somewhat bewilderingly found the Dean lacking), the new committee thought he was performing extremely well; moreover, its members recognized that public relations—which academics often high-mindedly disdain—was not mere window dressing but was vitally important in the effort to attract superior faculty and students and to secure adequate financial support for the School. More generally, the report acknowledged that many observers both inside and outside the School (the committee had solicited views from officers of other leading music schools) regarded Webb as an outstanding administrator, who was "managing to control an extremely complex school with a faculty of widely diverse talents and personalities."

In comparison with its predecessor, though, the new report was noticeably less flattering. The high workloads of faculty, and the low salaries both of the regular faculty and of the graduate Associate Instructors were again, for example, cited as major foci of discontent; but now, in contrast to the 1980 report, the committee recorded a widespread tendency to blame the salary situation on the Dean (though no hint was offered as to how he might, given the budgetary constraints under which he was bound to operate, increase salaries without simultaneously decreasing the number of their recipients and increasing still further the workload of the survivors).

The committee also reported widespread discontent with Webb's reluctance to let decisions out of his own hands. Though other members of the administrative team had nominal authority in various areas, the general perception was that in practice every significant decision made either by them or by committees charged with responsibility in particular areas was "re-decided" by the Dean. The result was a tendency for members of faculty (at least those whose standing allowed it) to ignore the rest of the administrative structure and go directly to Webb.

As in 1980, but now more strongly marked, there was also discontent about the paucity of formal procedures in key areas. While the structures for faculty consultation and decision-making had certainly been improved since Bain's day, some faculty members, at least, still felt that they were "insufficiently consulted and informed." This was the case in decisions on tenure, promotions, and especially appointments.

The most common complaint, though, and the perceived problem that most concerned the committee—like its predecessor—had to do with what was seen as Webb's failure to articulate a clear and persuasive vision of the goals of the School. A number of faculty were concerned as to whether there was sufficient planning for the School to retain, in the coming years, its leading position.

The 1984 report is fiercer than its predecessor both because there was evidently more discontent to record than there had been four years earlier and because the gentler remonstrances of the previous report had failed, as the committee members and a number of their colleagues thought, to get the Dean's attention. At least at first, there were signs that this rougher one had accomplished that purpose. In successive July meetings of the School of Music Council, Webb addressed the two major areas of concern in the report, by undertaking to appoint a committee to review the School's administrative structure, and, the following week, by opening the floor to a discussion of long-range plans.

The results of these initiatives, though, were modest. Various themes relating to planning were discussed—including especially the need for studies of changing student demographics and enrollment patterns, and of the appropriate evolution of the curriculum—but the executive body to which the Council's views were forwarded was only the Administrative Committee. This was the group, consisting of the administrative officers (five by this time), into which Bain in his latter years had formalized his "small circle of advisers." As far as one can tell, the committee took no particular action on the matters thus brought to its attention.

The ad hoc committee appointed to review the School's administrative structure was chaired by Henry Upper, who was by this time an Assistant Dean. When it completed its deliberations in March 1985, it announced (as a fiat, not subject to review by the Council) what appeared to be a substantial administrative reorganization. Instead of two subordinate deans—a general purpose Associate Dean and an Assistant Dean who was also Director of Undergraduate Studies—there would now be three, with clearly differentiated functions: an Associate Dean "having direct responsibility for a number of general administrative committees and duties," an Assistant Dean for Academic Affairs, and an Assistant Dean for Administrative Affairs. In presenting this new model to the Council, Upper and Webb naturally touted it as a fitting response to the concerns embodied in the 1984 report, whose phraseology they echoed. "With the assignment of specific areas to either Associate or Assistant Dean levels," Upper noted, "many items will no longer need to go directly to the Dean for final approval." This relief would allow the Dean "to give more time and attention to strategic planning and those matters for which he is solely responsible." Webb noted that the reorganization responded to the committee's recommendation that an additional administrative officer be added.

But in fact the number of administrators did not change at all, and their identities changed only insomuch as was necessitated by Bill Christ's retirement at the end of June. On June 30, the administrative team consisted of Webb, Christ as Associate Dean, Upper as Assistant Dean, John Nagosky as Director of Admissions, and Vernon Kliewer as Director of Graduate Studies. The next morning, when the reorganization went into effect, the team consisted of the same people, except that Christ had been replaced on it by yet another theorist, Allen Winold; and everyone had either changed chairs or had his chair renamed: Upper became Associate Dean, Kliewer and Nagosky became Assistant Deans for, respectively, Academic Affairs and Administrative Affairs (Kliewer retained the title of Director of Graduate Studies, and Nagosky was still Director of Admissions), and Winold became Director of Undergraduate Studies (the other part of Upper's former portmanteau position). Moreover, it did not appear, over the next few years, that the new structure resulted in any real difference in the way decisions were made in the School: Webb himself still made all the ones that mattered.

In truth, among the main foci of discontent in the 1984 report, it was only in the area of salaries that clear progress was made in its aftermath; and even there progress was rather modest. In 1984, the average salary of full professors in Music placed the School twelfth among a comparison group of thirteen academic units that included, in addition to Music, ten Arts and Sciences departments and the Schools of Education and Health, Physical Education, and Recreation. By the next year, the School had moved to ninth place, and the following year to sixth—after which, in 1987, it dropped again to ninth. But even an improvement from twelfth to ninth was clearly better than no improvement at all, and in these years Webb also managed to reduce greatly the inequities that appeared when the salaries of academic-music faculty were compared with those of performance faculty of the same academic rank and years of service. As for the impoverished Associate Instructors, by the 1987–88 academic year their stipend, which was $1,750 when the 1984 report appeared, had risen to $2,500—though it was not until 1989–90 that the stipend reached the University minimum standard. (And this in a university where the average stipend for graduate-student teachers put it at the bottom of the Big Ten.)

Gratitude was felt and expressed for these financial improvements, but academics do not live by bread alone. (No one who did would become one.) It was thus not surprising, given the small progress on other fronts, that when the report of the third deanship review appeared in October 1988, the level of faculty discontent had increased still further.

Half the members of the faculty made their views known to the committee. All but a tiny number of these supported Webb's continuation as Dean, and about a third of them praised him uncritically, in the familiar terms: he was open, supportive, humane, constantly espousing and exemplifying high standards in both professional and personal conduct; a "Renaissance Man," as one letter put it, whom the "faculty is indeed fortunate to have . . . for a role model." (He also again received strong support from respondents outside the School, in whose perspective all that was apparent was that the School had, under Webb's leadership, not merely sustained its eminence but even enhanced it.) The remaining two-thirds of the faculty respondents, though, were "selectively critical"; and among the academic-music faculty (who, to be sure, constituted only a fifth of the faculty as a whole) sharp discontent seems to have become essentially universal.

Although the criticisms included a good many of those voiced in the earlier reports, this time they were even more highly concentrated on problems with the structure and style of Webb's administration, and with his "perceived insensitivity" to academic music and its practitioners within the School. Indeed, complaints about these two matters so greatly outweighed all others in frequency and intensity that the committee took the remarkable step of focusing its report exclusively on them.

The criticisms of the Dean's attitude toward academic music were mainly confined to the academic musicians themselves, but the criticisms gained force from their ubiquity within that group, and by being so passionately felt and so eloquently expressed. (This group consisted largely of people who were, as scholars, in effect professional writers.) What comes across most strongly in the extensive excerpts the report quotes from their submissions is a deep sense of hurt, rooted in a perception that the Dean neither knew much about what they were doing nor much valued it.

To be sure, Webb had not been deaf to previous complaints of this kind, and the collective report submitted (in addition, that is, to the individual responses) to the committee by the academic faculty acknowledged that he had demonstrated his concern for academic music in various ways, such as by taking steps to reduce the teaching load in the academic departments, by adding a new position in musicology, and by following the advice of academic-area Search and Screen Committees in making several first-rate appointments; and of course Webb, with his humanities background, unequivocally shared with his predecessor the view that musicians required a rounded education. But what this view primarily meant to him was, at least according to the academics, that performers needed a good knowledge of academic music in order to be good performers; and so, as it seemed to the academics, he regarded their function in the School as fundamentally one of providing "service courses" ("preferably with huge enrollments"). Correspondingly, the Dean was perceived as having no real understanding or appreciation of the research mission of the academics.

If these criticisms were mainly confined to the academics themselves, the complaints about administration were nearly as prevalent among the performers as among the scholars. By the time the 1988 report was in preparation, the faculty had had three years to see the effects of the administrative reorganization prompted by its predecessor, and the general opinion, which the committee shared, was that they had made no real difference. This was the case because the Dean was "unwilling or unable" to delegate decision-making authority. As one respondent said, Webb continued to run the School "essentially in the same way Bain ran it," which meant that he felt "absolutely and *personally* responsible for attending to every detail of its operation, whether the matter at hand be routine or far-reaching": "To get a broken classroom record player repaired, one must complain to Charles, because complaints to Nagosky get nowhere. An outstanding graduate student needs $125 in travel support, . . . but only Charles, not Kliewer, is empowered to grant the funds." These were, the writer averred, authentic examples.

Accordingly, it remained the case, as the 1984 report had said, that everyone who could manage it bypassed the lesser administrators and went directly to Webb; and again the fact that the Dean was eternally caught up in quotidian matters was linked, rightly or wrongly, with his failure to articulate a clear vision of the School's long-range goals: when would he have had time to reflect on such matters?

The committee also endorsed criticisms of the make-up of the administrative team (a theme first raised in the 1980 report). Consisting of two pianists and three theorists, this group was scarcely representative of the faculty. (In view of the small number and relatively low status of academics on the faculty, it will surely seem remarkable that three of the five administrators were drawn from their thin ranks: we will return to this matter.) Moreover, all five had their terminal degrees from Indiana—a fact that could plausibly be related to the group's perceived disinclination to do anything other than keep the School moving along straight rails. The need for an additional high-ranking administrator—recommended by the previous committee and only spuriously satisfied by the 1985 restructuring—was "continually" brought to the attention of the new committee; indeed some members of the academic faculty nursed the chimera of dual leadership for the School, an arrangement that would leave Webb all the glamorous tasks at which he was so good, but turn over to a second Dean the mundane operation of the School. The review committee endorsed the more modest proposal, by which another Assistant or Associate Dean would be added. But this move would be helpful, they thought it necessary to say, "if, *and only if,*" Webb were genuinely willing to delegate responsibility to such an officer.

The skepticism apparent in this remark pervades the report as a whole, and had been, the committee pointed out, common in the submissions it had received: after two previous reviews that were felt to have had little effect, there was small hope that a third one would make much difference. Indeed the committee reported itself "not at all sanguine about the prospects for any meaningful change in administrative practice at the School."

In retrospect, this pessimism appears greatly excessive, since in fact the committee's report marked—to whatever extent it may have *caused*—a watershed in the governance of the School. Even before the report appeared, Webb's attention was focused on some of the matters raised in it. In a postscript, the committee explained that most of its work had been completed by February; by the time the report was issued in October, there had been "what many faculty members perceive to be an important and positive change in Dean Webb's public acknowledgment of academics and the academic area within the program of the School." (Why the committee did not, in the light of this new information, revise the body of its report is not clear.) Moreover, Webb had decided by September 25—four days after the committee met with him to discuss their draft report—that the successor to the expiring 1979 ten-year plan would be developed not, like that one, by the deans but by a broad group encompassing every sector of the faculty. He appointed a five-person umbrella committee (which included only one administrator, Kliewer, though Allen Winold was later added) and allowed it in turn both to choose its own chair and to establish a series of five subcommittees, which would prepare reports in the various relevant areas; and in October it was agreed in a meeting of the School of Music Council that the Council would have veto power over all recommendations included in the reports.

This was the largest-scale exercise in democracy at the School since Sanders's day, and, by the powerful precedent it established, it more or less guaranteed that the process of (re)democratizing the School's governance would continue. Furthermore, it imparted great additional momentum to the drive toward decentralization and rationalization of governmental procedures that had had its main manifestation in the deanship reviews. The report of the subcommittee on "Structural Organization" reiterated a number of the recommendations of these reviews: "Each administrator should be given full authority to carry out assigned duties"; the Dean should "provide philosophical, educational, and artistic leadership"; the subordinate deanships should be resliced, with (as the 1988 review had recommended) an "Associate Dean, Academic" and an "Associate Dean, Performance"; and so on. Once the Council had approved the new ten-year plan—as it did, unanimously, in August 1990—these recommendations acquired the force of something like law. So too did the other recommendations contained in the plan, above all one that called for the establishment of "a procedure for formal review of each associate and assistant dean, and [of] appointed directors of areas such as undergraduate and graduate studies, admissions, etc."

This latter recommendation gained urgency from the findings of two other subcommittees, those on "Curriculum" and "Recruitment, Admissions, and Financial Aid." In superb reports—thorough, beautifully reasoned, and clearly and attractively written—these subcommittees drove home the point that the performance of at least one of the administrators was in desperate need of review. While doing so, the subcommittees also provided the School with by far the most serious attempts at strategic planning it had yet seen and, in executing this work so well, strikingly underscored the fact that one of the greatest justifications for increased faculty governance in the School lay in the tremendous resource that a faculty of this caliber represented.

Both subcommittees were alarmed by certain enrollment trends in the School. Whereas the 1979 ten-year plan had anticipated that the ratio of undergraduate to graduate students would remain constant at about 3:2, this ratio had in fact changed dramatically, so that by 1989 slightly more than half the School's enrollees were graduate students. This circumstance had serious financial implications, for the graduate programs—most of which involved high-level individual performance instruction—were the School's least cost-effective ones. Concern about this aspect of the performance program (undergraduate as well as graduate) dated back to Merrill's time, but the problem now mattered more than ever, for the University was, under its new President, Thomas Ehrlich, in the process of moving to "Responsibility Center Management," which meant essentially that each school-sized unit of the University would be responsible for generating its own revenues.

The situation was exacerbated by the fact that about a third of the graduate performance students were foreigners. This statistic represented the culmination of Webb's plan to make the School an international institution, and it undoubtedly meant that the general level of performance was higher than ever (since admission was more competitive), but it had proved to have some disturbing consequences, societal and academic as well as financial. Was it appropriate for an American state university to allocate a substantial proportion of its resources to the training of students the great majority of whom would leave the country once their training was complete? Furthermore, many of the foreign students did not have good enough English to allow them to function satisfactorily in the academic component of their programs; and to avoid this problem (and also because they often had minimal interest and preparation in academic music), many of them enrolled in non-degree programs having little or no academic component. The Artist Diploma program, in particular, was frankly intended primarily for foreign students. But this and the other non-degree programs were even less cost-effective than the graduate degree programs.

To this congeries of problems, the subcommittee on Curriculum proposed a set of entirely plausible solutions. The School should work to restore (in a total student body that would remain the same size) the 3:2 ratio of undergraduates to graduates, and within both groups should take measures to shift enrollment from less cost-effective programs to more cost-effective ones, and to increase the number of non-music majors taking highly cost-effective music appreciation courses. The subcommittee recommended that the number of non-degree students not be allowed to exceed 5 percent, nor that of foreign students 8 percent. Simultaneously, the problem of students—not just foreign ones—who were unable to function satisfactorily in academic courses should be addressed by modifying the School's admissions criteria. Over the course of time, it had become the case that the only thing that really mattered for admission was the performance audition; the subcommittee urged that such factors as high-school class standing (for undergraduates), scores on standardized tests, and degree objective should also be taken into account. The degree program that the subcommittee wanted especially to favor was the Bachelor of Music Education: this was both the most cost-effective program and the one that had the most obvious relevance to the School's situation in a public university. Yet the steady decline in the proportion of music education students, which had already begun in Sanders's day and had been increasingly lamented by Bain and others, had continued. At the time of the 1979 ten-year plan, 22 percent of the School's undergraduates were in music education; ten years later, the proportion had dropped to 17 percent.

There was, however, a great obstacle to increasing the number of music education students, in the long-established and well-deserved reputation of the School as a place where these students were second-class citizens. Indiana was known to be essentially a performance school; and there were performance faculty who simply refused to accept music education students into their studios. (Like all the other undergraduate curricula, music education included a substantial applied-music component.)

Worse yet, the shockingly bad overall condition of the School's recruitment and admissions operation posed a massive obstacle to increasing either the quantity or the quality of students in *all* categories: this was the burden of the report of the subcommittee on Recruitment, Admissions, and Financial Aid. Enrollment in the School had been declining for several years, from close to 1,700 to just over 1,500 in the fall of 1988. There had been a drop in undergraduate enrollment in general (not just in music education), which had been offset only partially by increased graduate enrollment. To some extent, the downward trend could be explained by demographics: the baby boomers had already passed through the system, and falling enrollments were a nationwide phenomenon. But the School was also suffering from the fact that there had been a great expansion in the number of schools offering programs like its own, and from the fact that it was, in comparison with many of these competitors, doing a spectacularly poor job of recruiting.

This was true in a number of respects. First, the Admissions Office was essentially passive. Whereas some schools were vigorous in soliciting students, Indiana simply relied on its reputation to bring good ones knocking on its doors. Thanks to the School's eminence, this policy was reasonably successful. But once students showed up at those doors (at the audition weekends), they were routinely treated in ways that might almost have been consciously designed to send them packing.

There were many horror stories about the audition weekends, several of them authenticated by the letters of outraged parents. Students were not told what to expect in the weekend; when they arrived, there were no signs directing them to the bulletin board where audition times and places (sometimes changed without notice) were posted, to practice rooms, to any central gathering place, or to some place where they might obtain information. Faculty conducting the auditions were often, the subcommittee noted, "rude and inattentive, failed to introduce themselves to the students, and talked, smoked, and ate while students played."

Financial aid—both the size and nature of offers and their timing—was another disaster area. As a unit of a state university, the School had never been able to be fully competitive in financial aid; again its reputation had allowed it to attract many excellent students anyway. But now, with increasing competition—especially at the graduate level—from other fine schools that offered not only more money per year but also multiyear guarantees (which Indiana seldom did), this way of doing business was less and less successful. The School aggravated its problems by making financial-aid offers very late. An inter-university agreement stipulated that the acceptance date for aid offers be April 15; but the School often made its offers so near that deadline as to preclude adequate comparative consideration of them. Frequently it was as much as a month or two behind its chief competitors.

While many individuals had earned a share of the blame for the wretched situation in an area of activity that was, after all, along with faculty recruitment the one most vital to the welfare of the School, clearly the primary responsibility had to be laid at the feet of the person who, as Director of Admissions, was formally responsible for it. The subcommittee, however, politely declined to mention Nagosky. Instead, it offered, among a series of recommendations that under the circumstances more or less wrote themselves, one for a reorganized Office for Recruitment and Admissions that would be overseen by a Recruitment Committee and would be under the direction of an officer who, "as the servant of the faculty, . . . should be chosen by the faculty, and should report to the faculty through the Recruitment Committee and the Admissions Committee."

In June 1991, nine months after the approval of the ten-year plan, Webb instigated the administrative-review process mandated by it, appointing a small committee chaired by the musicologist Malcolm Brown and dubbed the Administrative Review Committee (henceforth ARC). The committee was originally charged with reviewing only one of the administrators—Kliewer—but at its own request was subsequently authorized to review as well the performance of the other two major administrators, Upper and Nagosky. The following April, having consulted widely, it issued a long, thoughtful, and frank report, which, the document repeatedly affirmed, embodied the consensus views of the faculty.

For Kliewer and Upper, the reviews included some criticisms but were generally positive. Kliewer was faulted for his authoritarian style and "dour" manner but was praised as conscientious and hard-working. Upper was criticized for dilatoriness but praised for constantly soliciting advice and opinions from faculty and students alike; the report is pervaded by respect for his great knowledge of the School and his hard work, and by fondness for his personal qualities. In the case of Nagosky, the findings were only what one would have expected: the committee recommended that he be relieved of responsibility as soon as a replacement could be secured.

For a student of the operation of the School, though, and especially of the drive toward democratization and administrative decentralization that constituted the major concern of the faculty in the 1990s, the most interesting part of the report is that where the committee appears to be acting *ultra vires:* not content to review the three administrators, Brown and his colleagues interpreted their mandate as allowing them to make general comments, and enunciate general principles, about the governance of the School; and they prefaced their reports on the deans with a set of recommendations on these larger matters that, together with the rationales for them, constitute nearly half of the composite report.

The recommendations—which, though more detailed than those of the ten-year plan and the deanship reviews, are in general wholly consonant with them—begin with a series addressed to the most urgent problems, those of recruitment and admissions. Arguing that in the current competitive climate the School needed a proactive recruitment policy, the committee sensibly suggested that the shortest and best way to achieve one would be to bring in a professional recruiter; that is, to make the directorship of admissions and recruiting a full-time *staff* position, and to launch a national search for an experienced person to fill it.

A second set of recommendations was designed to cure the problem, long a source of concern, of administrative inbreeding in the School. Not only the admissions directorship but *all* major administrative positions should be advertised; administrative appointments should never be open-ended but should instead be for terms of at most five years, with performance reviews in the penultimate year and reappointment contingent on a favorable review.

Moreover, the School should do away with portmanteau administrative jobs and titles: no one should be—as all three of the administrators under review were—"charged with the responsibilities of more than one major administrative office or designated by more than one title." The present system of intense concentration of powers resulted, on the one hand, in administrative inefficiency (the committee suggested that both Kliewer's dourness and Upper's dilatoriness might result from overwork) and, on the other, in conflicts of interest. Upper, in particular, was both Associate Dean for Administration and chairman of one of the departments he administered (Piano).

The committee also recommended yet another reslicing of the associate deanships. In the immediate aftermath of the approval of the ten-year plan, Webb had implemented, though only in his musical-chairs fashion, its recommendation—based on one in the report of the 1988 review committee—that there be an Associate Dean, Academic, and an Associate Dean, Performance: Kliewer was redesignated as the first (and continued as Director of Graduate Studies) and Upper as the second. (At the same time, Allen Winold, who was retiring, was replaced as Director of Undergraduate Studies by Eugenia Sinor, an Associate Professor of Music Education, who thus became the first female member of the School's central administrative team—like all the others, though, she had her doctorate from Indiana.) A scant two years later, however, the ARC was endorsing the view of a "conclusive majority" of those interviewed by it, who "voiced regret at the decision to separate implicitly the mission of the . . . [School] into 'academic' and 'performance' areas." (There is no hint in the report that this separation had occurred as a direct result of the recommendation of a previous report that had been approved unanimously by the School of Music Council.) Now it was seen—as perhaps it should have been foreseen—that this division tended to exacerbate the tensions between performers and academics; and the new committee recommended that there be an Assistant/Associate Dean for Administration and another for Instruction.

Throughout these series of recommendations, the pervasive, interrelated themes are the need for greater faculty governance and for the abolition of ad hoc procedures in the decanal administration. The committee noted that it had been handicapped in its (assigned) work by the absence of job descriptions for the subdeans; there were "no comprehensive lists of duties and responsibilities or precisely established lines of authority against which to measure an individual dean's performance." (Kliewer and Upper provided partial remedies for this problem by preparing detailed statements of the duties and responsibilities of their respective offices "as they understood them to have evolved over the years"; Nagosky declined to provide such an outline.) Formal job descriptions should, the committee reasonably thought, be drawn up for all these positions, and they should be approved by the Council; once administrative jobs had been advertised, applicants for them should be reviewed and ranked by a faculty advisory committee. The revised admissions policy whose development would be an initial assignment of Nagosky's replacement should be formally presented to the Council for ratification. Administrators should stop "chairing and *de facto* dominating a majority of the most influential committees in the school." In general, the ARC, "reflecting a conviction expressed by numerous senior faculty members," affirmed its "belief in the principle of faculty governance."

But in truth a very substantial degree of faculty governance had already been achieved. The new ten-year plan—developed by a broadly representative faculty committee and approved by the School of Music Council—set the basic agenda for the School in the 1990s (as of course such a plan *should* do); in this role it was importantly supplemented by the ARC report, whose key recommendations were also duly approved by the Council. The Dean continued to be by far the most powerful individual in the School; but by 1992 the Council and its various committees, together, surely constituted a force as great. Although the Dean remained constitutionally empowered with full responsibility for the School and full authority over it, the School had become, in practice, no longer a dictatorship but a limited monarchy, in which the Council continued to probe for further inroads into the Dean's prerogatives.

Moreover, the power of the Council had come to be largely vested in the academic musicians—a stunningly ironic result for a group that constituted a small minority of the faculty and regarded itself as contemned and oppressed. Academics had in fact long played a disproportionately large role in the administration of the School, both because they had a natural or acquired affinity for some major parts of administrative work —serving on committees, reading and writing reports, endlessly talking and even listening—and because performers (especially the most active ones) were regarded as having better things to do (and were too often away from the School doing them). As we have seen, most of the members of Bain's and Webb's administrative teams were academics; and all but one secretary of the Academic Council and its successor the School of Music Council has been an academic. (The exception was the technologist David Pickett.) It was, though, only in the aftermath of the report of the 1988 deanship review, in which the sense of injured merit of the academics was given its most plangent expression, that their disproportionate representation in the School's administrative bodies increased to a truly startling level. Evidently Webb and the Council had concluded that justice to the academics required that this small fraction of the faculty be granted something approaching—and sometimes greatly exceeding—parity on the School's key committees. The Ten-Year Planning Committee comprised three performers, two academics, and a composer; on its five subcommittees, though, taken collectively, academics outnumbered performers nearly two to one. Given a faculty where performers outnumbered academics four to one, this is an astonishing figure. Having digested this surprise, though, one is less surprised to find that the planning committee's recommendations for the composition of the Council's standing committees call for parity between academics and performers. The composition of the five-member ARC is also striking, consisting as it did of two academics (one of them its chair), a staff member, a composer, and a single performer.

Even as the ARC was reviewing the performance of the subdeans, another committee (whose School faculty contingent comprised two academics, two performers, and a composer) was conducting the fourth and final review of their boss's performance: the first group reported in April 1992, the second in November. The review took place, then, in the context of a series of recent actions on Webb's part that appeared to confirm that he had taken to heart much of the advice of the 1988 review. He had been bestowing signal marks of esteem on the academics. He had established a democratic process for the development of the ten-year plan and had subsequently implemented a number of the recommendations offered in it and in the ARC report. These included the recommendation that Nagosky be replaced as Director of Admissions by a new staff member secured through a national search. Webb had acted expeditiously on this recommendation, and the search had turned out very well. By the time the deanship review committee had completed its work, Nagosky had already been replaced—seven months after the appearance of the ARC report—by the able and experienced Gwyn Richards, a graduate, in music education and conducting, of Michigan and, at the time of his appointment, an associate dean of the eminent music school of the University of Southern California. (Richards was also accorded a part-time position in choral conducting.)

Nonetheless, the review committee's report, though certainly milder than the 1988 one, was still not especially flattering. To some extent the continuing reservations stemmed from the perception that even when Webb had complied with recommendations of the previous deanship review committees and the ARC, he had often done so in ways that seemed half-hearted or that involved cosmetic rather than substantive changes. There was, moreover, still discontent—which had indeed intensified—about the Dean's perceived failure to develop, or to create a satisfactory mechanism for the development of, a clear and persuasive vision of the best course for the School over the next decades. The basic question was that of how (if at all) the School should change in order to adapt itself to what the committee called "the changing musical milieu." In a world where the audience for classical music appeared to be shrinking steadily, and the musical scene increasingly permeated by various electronic technologies, did it make sense for the School to continue to focus its efforts so nearly exclusively—and on such a huge scale—on the traditional training of classical musicians? Perhaps it did, but in any case the rapidly shifting musical tide seemed to make it imperative that the School, as the committee said, "affirm and articulate" its reasons for either continuing on course or altering course. It was only in the context of such a carefully formulated and articulated vision that sensible decisions could be made about such matters as curriculum, the optimal size of the School, and the appropriate relative size of various segments of the student population—especially graduate students (who still made up more than half the student body) and music education majors (whose numbers had, despite efforts inspired by previous reports, fallen further, so that they now comprised only 15 percent of the School's students).

These arguments are compelling—as indeed the similar ones in the earlier deanship reviews had been—and it is not difficult to understand the frustration of the committee and its predecessors at the fact that Webb seemed never fully to come to grips with the need for comprehensive strategic planning. The development of the new ten-year plan had offered an especially obvious opportunity for doing so, but it had been missed—though in truth the blame for this failure lay as much with the planning committee and the School of Music Council as with Webb. Surely the committee's report should have included not just the subcommittee reports on problems and solutions in particular areas of the School's activities but a strategic overview as well—a point that David Pickett raised when, in March 1990, the report was submitted to the Council. Webb agreed, and Kliewer, as chairman of the planning committee, undertook to supply such a preface, which would, he said, be based on responses to the draft report when it was submitted to the faculty as a whole. This was of course not a way to get anything done. Five months later, Kliewer proposed that the Council was at the point where it should vote to accept the report in principle, despite the fact that it was still not entirely complete. Among the missing pieces was the "philosophical projection for the coming years," which "was to have been written by faculty members who had suggestions to put forward, but nothing has been received to date." The Council voted unanimously—but ill-advisedly, one may think—to approve the document in its incomplete form. As far as I can ascertain, the philosophical statement never materialized. Indeed the most serious attempt at comprehensive strategic planning in the Webb era did not come until four years later (in 1994), when the Agenda Committee of the Council proposed that that body devote several meetings to what Mary Wennerstrom (by then Secretary of the Council) characterized as "open discussion . . . aimed at giving our standing committees specific direction for their work and at providing guidance on the 'global issues' that are so frequently mentioned." One of the instigators of this proceeding was Gwyn Richards, who explained (as the 1992 deanship review committee's report also had) that sensible decisions about admissions could not be made in the absence of such a global framework. Long and interesting discussions followed, which were doubtless of use to Richards and the others guiding the School; but no one would, I think, claim that a series of Council minutes constitutes a wholly satisfactory strategic plan.

If we ask why Webb never led the School through a full planning exercise, the answers would seem to lie mainly in his personality and administrative style. He was so busy with other things—especially since he was so reluctant to delegate—that he scarcely had time to engage with a large, sprawling, intractable problem that was, moreover, in its very nature not, or not very often, immediately pressing: like most other administrators, he doubtless found that immediate demands are so numerous that long-term concerns are constantly pushed to the horizon. Then too, he was, by nature and long habit, a man much more comfortable dealing with the present than with the future. He was not merely, as Bain called him, a "ready musician"—a marvelously quick study, and capable of sophisticated improvisation—but a ready *man,* with a presence of mind and an ability to think on his feet most obviously manifested in his remarkable ability as an extempore speaker. He was a splendid crisis manager; and if his colleagues wished that he managed with sufficient foresight that crises occurred less often, his failure to do so may have reflected not only the fact that he had from childhood been a ready person rather than a long-range planner but also, perhaps, the fact that he gained a kind of Kiplingesque satisfaction from his ability to master crises: "If you can keep your head when all about you / Are losing theirs . . ."

Some of his other problems with his colleagues also seem traceable to aspects of his personality. Doubtless he should not have relied so heavily for so long on the views of a small, nearly static group of subordinate administrators who, as was repeatedly pointed out to him, represented too narrow a segment of the School's spectrum of activities and too uniform an educational background. But he was intensely loyal to subordinates; and, presumably, like other administrators he was reluctant, excessively but understandably, to dismiss people who were loyal to *him,* and with whom he knew he was able to work, in order to replace them with others who were in this connection (however well they might play an instrument or do research) unknown quantities. He should have delegated more, but, again like many other administrators, he obviously found it difficult to loosen his hands on the reins that had been entrusted to him (which is also why he, like Bain, never took a sabbatical). One may think that he should have twigged sooner than he did to the injured feelings of the academic faculty, which could have been assuaged to some extent (as in fact they latterly were) simply by his taking the trouble to learn more about what academics do and demonstrating that he valued these activities. But Webb, though extremely intelligent, is not a scholar by temperament or training, and his praises of scholarship never seem rooted in the genuine understanding and appreciation necessary to making them altogether satisfactory.

At the same time, Webb's problems were to a considerable extent not a function of his personality but of the length of his deanship and the nature of the era in which it fell. In part, the gathering discontent with him is to be explained simply as a typical example of the natural history of relationships between academics and their administrators. For reasons that have more to do with the individual and collective psychology of the faculty than with any merits or demerits of the administrator, these relationships normally begin (except in those horrible cases where an administrator is forced upon a faculty against its will) with a honeymoon, in which faculty perceive the new administrator, especially in contrast with his or her predecessor, of whom they had wearied, as scarcely able to do anything wrong; over time, this perception gradually changes, almost irrespective of the administrator's actual performance, to one in which he or she is perceived as scarcely able to do anything right. This is a phenomenon all too familiar in human relationships generally; with university faculty (as perhaps with other professional groups) its effect is exacerbated by the conviction of many or most of them that they themselves could do a better job in the administrative position than its occupant is doing—a conviction that, though of course sometimes correct, is facilitated by inescapable ignorance, on the part of other faculty members, of the constraints under which administrators labor.

Additionally, in Webb's case as in that of myriad other administrators of his generation, disenchantment was strengthened and accelerated by the growing aspirations for faculty self-governance that have been a continuing legacy of the 1960s at Indiana and everywhere else. Bain himself, who had been both willing and easily able to crush any such aspirations in his early years as Dean, had increasing difficulty controlling them toward the end of his tenure. His successor, though legally in exactly the same position—that is, serving at the pleasure of the President and Trustees (whose pleasure was, naturally, unallayable as long as the School retained its preeminence) and with constitutional responsibility for, and thus authority over, every aspect of the School's activities—found these aspirations, and the discontent resulting from their partial frustration, growing steadily on him. Even when, in the late 1980s, he began to yield large expanses of ground, he could not satisfy a good many of his colleagues, simply because no amount of ground, short of the entire domain, would have been enough. It was his fortune to be Dean through all but the opening years of an extended period when the administration of academic units was undergoing a profound and necessarily stressful change from autocracy to democracy. He presided over the School—with remarkably steady grace, aplomb, and patience—in a revolutionary era when it was the fate of administrators (even more than usual) to have harsh things said about them.

At Indiana as at nearly all other colleges and universities, appointments procedures had over the years become, like nearly all other procedures, increasingly formalized and complex. In the School of Music as elsewhere, they were, by the 1990s, consuming, in the doubtless commendable attempt to achieve complete equity with respect to all applicants and full representation of the views of all faculty and students, enormous amounts of time and paper. In accordance with University regulations, Search and Screen Committees, appointed by the Dean on the basis of recommendations from the concerned department, were required for every position to be filled. To be sure, the recommendations of these committees were not binding on the Dean, who in this area as in all others retained the legal authority to do as he chose. But it had become the case that, as Webb says, the Dean could not go counter to these recommendations very often and still hope to have "a successful administration." There is no reason to think, though, that he found this particular constraint distasteful or burdensome. He did on occasion exercise his prerogative to disregard committee recommendations, but his approach to appointments from the beginning of his tenure had been fundamentally consultative, and he was generally happy to accept the recommendations.

Bain had found that faculty members could not be trusted to name the strongest potential appointees in their field. Though he never renounced that rule, presumably it does not apply—or not, at least, with the same force—to a faculty heavily stocked with individuals so eminent that they could scarcely feel threatened by any newcomer. Be that as it may, it is not apparent that the gradual shift in responsibility for appointments in the School has had any deleterious effect. It is in general harder than in former days to recruit top-flight instrumentalists, because their engagement fees or orchestral salaries are now greatly in excess of what the School (or any school) can pay. But a survey of the more significant appointments of the years from 1990 through 1997—that is, the final years of Webb's deanship—suggests that the School continues to do at least as well in this regard as its competitors.

The most dramatic faculty changes in these years occurred in the Voice Department. Camilla Williams retired in 1990, though she continued to teach part-time. Nicola Rossi-Lemeni died the next year, at the age of seventy. In the period from 1991 through 1997, Jean Deis, Gloria Davy, Gianna d'Angelo, Carol Smith, and Roy Samuelson all retired, and Lynn Luciano succumbed to breast cancer, at the age of fifty-five. Accordingly, the pace of hiring to the voice faculty in the 1990s was furious, with eleven appointees by 1997. These included the soprano Teresa Kubiak, who joined the Department in 1990 after fourteen years at the Met, and the extremely distinguished bass Giorgio Tozzi, who came in 1991, as well as five other senior appointees: Martina Arroyo (for many years a leading soprano with the Met), Costanza Cuccaro (who had been a leading lyric-coloratura at the Deutsche Oper Berlin), and Patricia Wise (who had for fifteen years been a leading soprano with the Vienna State Opera) were appointed at the rank of Professor, as were the tenor James McDonald and the bass Paul Kiesgen. Two fine young tenors, Michael Belnap and Alan Bennett, joined the faculty as Visiting Lecturers in 1995 and were subsequently appointed to regular positions. But the most striking appointment of a singer was not to the Voice Department but to the Early Music Institute, where the untimely death of Thomas Binkley—in April 1995, at the age of sixty-three—necessitated the recruitment of a new Director for the illustrious unit he had headed. His replacement, who arrived in 1996, was Paul Hillier, the preeminent choral director of the early music movement. A native of England, he had co-founded and been musical director of the Hilliard Ensemble, and later the Theatre of Voices, a group whose repertory ranges from early music to Arvo Pärt and Steve Reich. At the time of his appointment to the School, he was on the faculty of the University of California, Davis.

On the opera production team, the director James Lucas, who left the School in 1994, was replaced by Vincent Liotta, a resident director for the Lyric Opera of Chicago; he had also taught at the University of Washington and elsewhere, and had previously been a guest director at Indiana. The coaching staff was strengthened by the addition of Costanza Cuccaro's husband, the composer and pianist Edwin Penhorwood, who was appointed, on a part-time basis, at the rank of Professor. In 1997, George Calder, who had long been the highly capable Executive Assistant for the Opera Theater, retired; the position was filled by Mark Ross Clark, who had been coordinator of the opera theater at the University of Washington.

The conductor Bryan Balkwill retired in 1992; his slot was not filled until 1994, when Imre Palló, who had conducted both in Germany and the United States (where he was associated especially with the New York City Opera), joined the faculty at the rank of Professor. Starting in 1990, however, the School had enjoyed the services of the noted orchestral and (especially) choral conductor Thomas Dunn, who, since he had already reached retirement age, was appointed to a series of visiting positions. In 1992, the choral faculty was further strengthened by the appointment of Carmen Téllez, who, though born in Venezuela, had done all of her degrees at the School; appointed at the rank of Associate Professor, she was also named Director of the Latin American Music Center. Michael Schwartzkopf was added to the choral faculty (and to Music Education) in 1995; he replaced the retiring Robert Stoll as Director of the Singing Hoosiers.

Abraham Skernick retired in 1991, and another violist, Csaba Erdelyi, left the School the same year. Atar Arad, a former member of the Cleveland Quartet who had taught at Eastman and elsewhere, filled one of the vacated positions, and another first-rank player, Joseph de Pasquale, who had been principal violist with the Boston Symphony and, since 1974, with the Philadelphia Orchestra, accepted a part-time appointment. He was, however, unwilling to relinquish his position in Philadelphia, and in 1994 was replaced on a full-time basis by a third splendid musician, Alan deVeritch, principal violist of the Los Angeles Philharmonic.

In January 1995, Josef Gingold died, at the age of eighty-five. He had continued to teach his more-than-double load of students until illness overtook him a few months before his death. Gingold could never, of course, be replaced; but the hole in the violin roster was filled in 1995 by Mauricio Fuks, a pupil of Galamian and Heifetz, who had, after his concert career was ended by a back problem, gone on to become a celebrated pedagogue. (Webb had previously hoped that Sylvia Rosenberg, a distinguished violin teacher whom he had lured away from the Manhattan School of Music in 1994, would fill Gingold's position. But she found herself unable to endure life outside New York City, to which she perforce returned, after a single year in Bloomington.)

In 1991, Eli Eban, who had been a member of the Israel Philharmonic, joined Campbell and Klug in the Clarinet Department; together they formed the Indiana Clarinet Trio. In the same year, the flutist Kathryn Lukas was recruited at the rank of Professor. The spectacular appointment in flute, though, came in 1994, when the young Dutchman Jacques Zoon, principal with the Royal Concertgebouw Orchestra and widely regarded as the best flutist of his generation, was brought in to replace the retiring Peter Lloyd. In his first year at Indiana, however, Zoon was offered the position of principal flute with the Boston Symphony; he declined, but then accepted the same offer when it was repeated the next year, and so left the School after only two years. He took with him his partner, Iseut Chuat, a brilliant young cellist who had previously studied with Starker and had been appointed to a part-time faculty position simultaneously with Zoon. The year 1993 had seen the appointment of a baroque flutist, Barbara Kallaur, and 1994 that of the bassoonist Kim Walker, who replaced the retiring Sidney Rosenberg as the Bassoon Department. In 1997, Nicholas Daniel, who had been solo oboist of the London Mozart Players and the City of London Sinfonia, and had taught at the Guildhall School, succeeded Marc Lifschey as the Oboe Department; he stayed, though, only until 1999.

As it happened, another distinguished flutist—James Scott—was appointed in the same year (1994) as Zoon, though he was brought in for a different purpose. In the aftermath of the ARC report, Webb had agreed to add an Associate Dean for Instruction and to institute a national search for such a person. The first year of the search bore no fruit, but the next year the committee settled on Scott, who had been head of the music school at Rutgers for a dozen years. This was the first time in forty-seven years that the School had appointed a dean from outside, and the first time since 1973 that it had had a dean without an Indiana Ph.D. The appointment looked to be a superb one; and since Scott, as both an experienced and evidently successful administrator and an eminent performing musician, matched so well the School's needs and its image, it was easy to view him as Webb's likely successor.

In 1994, Harvey Phillips retired. Like Gingold's, his was a hard act to follow. But the School secured an excellent replacement, in the person of Daniel Perantoni, who had performed worldwide as a jazz and classical tubist and had previously taught at the University of Arizona. In 1993 and 1994, the School filled two vacancies on the trumpet faculty by appointing John Rommel and Stephen Burns. (In 1999, Burns was replaced by Marie Speziale, who had previously taught at Cincinnati.)

In piano, the great loss of the early 1990s was that of James Tocco, who resigned from the School in 1992 to take up the position of Eminent Scholar/Artist-in-Residence at the Cincinnati College-Conservatory. Enrica Cavallo-Gulli retired in 1991, though she continued teaching as an emeritus for two years thereafter. The only senior appointment to have followed these departures was made in 1995, when Edmund Battersby accepted a position. But in 1991 the Department had been bolstered by a serendipitous appointment that turned out to be superlative. When Atar Arad joined the faculty, his wife, the Belgian pianist Evelyne Brancart, was recruited as Associate Professor. Surely the main aim of this joint appointment was to secure the husband; but the wife turned out to be an equally valuable addition. A dazzling and revelatory pianist, and a tireless solo and chamber player who appears on the School's stages more often than any other member of its faculty save possibly Leonard Hokanson, Brancart also bids fair to become one of the great piano pedagogues of her generation.

Several appointments, in both applied and academic music, reflected the collective desire in the School to respond to what the 1992 deanship review committee had called the "changing musical milieu." Of these, the most colorful was doubtless the 1993 appointment, on a part-time basis, of the drummer Kenny Aronoff, a 1976 graduate of the School and a Bloomington resident, who had become perhaps the most-sought-after rock percussionist in the world. Following this appointment, the generally staid "Faculty Fanfare" section of the *Music Alumni Notes* was enlivened by announcements such as that Associate Professor Aronoff was featured on the new album "Dance Naked," and had recent releases with artists such as Meat Loaf. His job, Aronoff said, was to prepare students "for the real world, which I'm in right now. I'm in the scene." Obviously not doing it for the money, he continued to teach at the School through the 1996–97 academic year, and subsequently returned to conduct master classes.

The appointment of the rock historian and composer Glenn Gass also proved successful. While still a student, he was appointed (in 1983) Visiting Lecturer, and affiliated with the Jazz Department. Subsequently elevated to the regular faculty, he achieved a tremendous reputation as a teacher, and by the last years of Webb's deanship had become a founding member of the new Department of Music in General Studies, which was created in an attempt to bolster the School's enrollment in the cost-effective area of music instruction for non-majors. The Jazz Department proper suffered a major loss in 1997, when Dominic Spera retired; he was replaced by a saxophonist, Pat Harbison, who was appointed at the rank of Associate Professor. Moreover, the jazz saxophonist Thomas Walsh, who had earned bachelor's, master's, and doctoral degrees at the School, returned to it in 1997 as Assistant Professor in the Saxophone Department (that is, supplementing Rousseau), and the same year Jeffrey Magee, an authority on jazz and black music, was appointed Assistant Professor in musicology.

Major changes continued in the Ballet Department. Bonnefoux and McBride decided they wanted to direct a professional company, and left in 1996 to take over the North Carolina Dance Theater. The Cesbrons remained, with Virginia succeeding Bonnefoux as department chair, and were joined on the permanent faculty by Violette Verdy. A splendid appointee, Verdy had for twenty years been a principal dancer with the New York City Ballet, had performed and taught for major companies throughout the world, and had also been Artistic Director of the Paris Opera Ballet.

In composition, three departures in the 1990s prompted new appointments. Harvey Sollberger left to take a position at the University of California, San Diego, and Frederick Fox retired, the first in 1992 and the second five years later. True to form, John Eaton made a more spectacular exit. In the summer of 1990, at the age of fifty-five, he was awarded a MacArthur Fellowship—the so-called "genius grant" that provides its recipients with a large stipend for five years, so that they may devote themselves exclusively to furthering the socially or culturally significant work that has prompted the award. Having had six of his operas produced by the School, Eaton had been anxious that a seventh one—*The Reverend Jim Jones,* completed in 1987—should be premiered there; after receiving the MacArthur award, he became even more insistent on this point, going so far as to ask the President of the University to give the School's opera production committee his "input" on the matter. The President of course declined to intervene; and the committee declined (for a variety of reasons) to mount the opera in the 1991–92 season. Notified of this decision, Eaton told Webb that he would have to reevaluate his position in the School; by April 1991 he was able to report that he had an extremely attractive offer from the University of Chicago, and that he would accept it unless he could be guaranteed not only that his Jonestown opera would be produced but that all his succeeding ones would also be, within two years of their completion. Webb was unable to meet this condition (or others, relating to Eaton's desire that Indiana match the best features of the Chicago offer), so the composer decamped for the Windy City.

There were, then, a number of positions in composition to be filled in the 1990s. One of these, as I noted earlier, went to David Dzubay (in 1992). Dzubay had been a brilliant student at Indiana, completing bachelor's and master's degrees in trumpet and computer science with high distinction, and a doctorate in composition under O'Brien and Fox; the latter called him "without a doubt" the most talented composition student he had encountered in the School since his 1974 arrival. A second, senior appointment was also made in 1992, bringing to the School Don

Freund, who had earned his doctorate at Eastman and had for twenty years been in charge of the composition program at Memphis State University. (In 1997 the Polish composer Marta Ptaszyńska was appointed to a full professorship, replacing Fox, but she stayed for only a year.)

If the faculty remained first-rate throughout the Webb era, so did the student body—or at least there was enough of the cream (for the sake of which, according to Bain, one had to have all that milk) not merely to sustain but to enhance the School's reputation as a producer of first-rate performing artists. A rapid survey will make this point. The lists that follow consist of alumni of the School (many of whom, of course, also studied at other schools) who have achieved celebrity in the period since about 1970. It omits those already mentioned as having returned as faculty members.

Among singers, one may single out Richard Stilwell, Franz Grundheber, Carole Farley, Nancy Shade, and David Arnold (these five had been at Indiana in the late Bain years), as well as Bruce Hubbard, Sunny Joy Langton, Wendy White, Nadine Secunde, Mark Baker, Susan Patterson, Sylvia McNair, Janet Williams, Heidi Grant Murphy, Elizabeth Futral, Nancy Maultsby, Philip Zawisza, Christopher Schaldenbrand, Emily Magee, and Timothy Noble (who returned as a faculty member in 1999). Moreover, the School's record in the Metropolitan Opera Auditions—that most conspicuous of proving grounds for young American singers—has been far superior to that of any other school. The high-water mark was reached in the period 1984–91, when for eight years in a row at least one of the eleven national winners was a current or former student at the School; in 1986, as I noted in the previous chapter, four of the eleven winners had studied at Indiana—a result unique in the history of the auditions.

String Department alumni from the same era include Eugene Fodor, Gary Hoffman, Edgar Meyer, Nai-Yuan Hu, Joshua Bell, the superlative baroque violinist Ingrid Matthews, and Corey Cerovsek, as well as over twenty concertmasters, among them Jacques Israelievitch of the St. Louis Symphony (and later of the Toronto Symphony), William Preucil of the Cleveland Orchestra, Erez Ofer of the Philadelphia Orchestra, and Daniel Gaede of the Vienna Philharmonic. Among the most recent generation of students, one must mention the bassist Eve-Simone Pastor, who matriculated at the University at the age of thirteen and at fourteen soloed (as Bell also had at that age) with the Philadelphia Orchestra, and Pekka Kuusisto, who in 1995, while still a student at the School, won the Sibelius Violin Competition.

Among pianists, Alberto Reyes had, in the years 1971–73, been a finalist in the Tchaikovsky, Leventritt, and Cliburn competitions; in 1973, Hans Boepple won the Bach Competition in Washington. (Both went on to teach for several years at the School.) The brilliant Canadian pianist Louis

Lortie studied with Pressler in the late 1970s, as did Etsuko Terada, who won the Rubinstein Competition in 1977, and (in the 1980s) another Canadian, Angela Cheng, who won a Brahmsian handful of competition prizes. Frederic Chiu, who studied as an undergraduate with Karen Shaw, became famous for *not* winning the Cliburn Competition, and has gone on to a major career. Jeremy Denk, who spent several years at the School as Sebok's student, returned to it as a faculty member in 1997; a prize winner in various competitions, in 1998 he received an Avery Fisher Career Grant, and the following year the coveted Wolff Prize in chamber music.

Among alumni of the School's smaller departments, one may single out Elizabeth Hainen, principal harp of the Philadelphia Orchestra, Susan Slaughter, first trumpet of the St. Louis Symphony, Sherry Silar, assistant principal oboe of the New York Philharmonic, and Ricardo Morales, principal clarinet of the Metropolitan Opera Orchestra. Patrick Summers, who earned a Bachelor of Music degree at the School in 1986, is Music Director of the Houston Grand Opera. Two young composers of particular note, both Canadians, are Randolph Peters, who was a graduate student in the School in the late 1980s and had his opera *Nosferatu* performed by the Canadian Opera Company in December 1993 (a second opera, *The Golden Ass,* premiered there six years later), and Heather Schmidt, who in 1995, while still a student, fulfilled a commission to write the imposed piece for the Banff String Quartet Competition. One should also acknowledge the fact—perhaps surprising, in view of the notoriously dominant position of performance studies in the School—that its academic-music departments have produced their own substantial share of distinguished graduates. These include a number of award-winning scholars (such as Richard Leppert of the University of Minnesota, and Robert Hatten, who has just returned to the School as a member of the Theory Department) and a number of music administrators—heads of departments or schools of music, state supervisors of music, and so on—greatly exceeding even the number of Indiana-trained concertmasters.

From the time of the Grant Park concerts, the School had frequently been able to display its students beyond Bloomington in ensembles of various kinds; earlier we traced the great tours of the 1970s and 1980s. This tradition continued into the 1990s, still further enhancing the School's reputation. In May 1990, as part of a *glasnost*-inspired music-education exchange agreement between the United States and the Soviet Union (Webb had been a member of the delegation that traveled to Moscow to negotiate the exchange), the Opera Theater gave two performances of Eaton's *The Cry of Clytaemnestra* at the Moscow State Conservatory's Bolshoi Hall, accompanied by a Conservatory orchestra. (The trip mirrored an April visit by members of the Conservatory to Bloomington, where they had presented Rachmaninoff's *Francesca da Rimini.*) With Webb as accompanist, the Indiana students in Moscow also gave concerts in Rachmaninoff Hall at the Conservatory and to a standing-room-only audience at the Pushkin Museum, in conjunction with the opening of a special exhibition from the Metropolitan Museum of Art.

Back in the United States, the remarkable decade of domestic touring that began in the spring of 1981 with the first of the New York ventures was rounded off by additional appearances in that city and in Washington. In October 1990, David Baker took the Jazz Ensemble to the Smithsonian Institution, where they performed an Ellington program. The following March, as part of a Kennedy Center series featuring artists from the heartland, the Chamber Orchestra played at the Terrace Theater. Paul Biss conducted, and Miriam Fried soloed in a Mozart concerto. Two months later, the decade of tours ended as it had begun, with a multiple-event trip to New York. To mark the bicentennial of Mozart's death, Lincoln Center had undertaken to sponsor performances, over an eighteen-month period, of all his works; the School was invited to mount four programs in the series. Two of these were relatively small-scale enterprises —chamber music concerts—but the other two were major events. As in its 1981 New York trip, the School presented a fully staged opera, this time Mozart's early *La Finta Giardiniera,* which was performed in the Juilliard Theater. The event that most clearly bespoke the School's stature in the musical world, however, was the fourth one, a liturgical concert that included (in addition to Symphony No. 34, an early church sonata, and the Ave Verum Corpus) one of Mozart's greatest works, the Mass in C Minor, performed in Alice Tully Hall by the Philharmonic Orchestra, soloists, and a choir comprising the University Singers and the Chamber Choir.

The following year the School returned to Washington for an event that, though renewing its invaluable association with Leonard Bernstein, and in a most conspicuous fashion, unfortunately did not prove to be an entire success. The Maestro had died in 1990; two years later, at the request of his family, the School revived his failed musical of 1976, *1600 Pennsylvania Avenue.* The work, with lyrics by Alan Jay Lerner, had offered an upstairs/downstairs view of life in the White House over the course of American history, as seen by its official residents and its black servants. In its original form, the musical focused on the nation's continuing racial struggles. This uncomfortable material had failed, in the determinedly upbeat Bicentennial year, to please critics in the out-of-town tryouts, and by the time the work opened on Broadway it had been purged of all racial elements and become a merry musical review about life in the White House. Not merry enough, though: it closed after seven performances.

In the different climate of the 1990s, the Bernstein family thought the work merited a second chance, and the School was asked to mount a reconstruction of the original version. Guest director Erik Haagensen, a Lerner expert and a playwright/lyricist himself (but without any directorial experience), undertook the restoration, and the musical was presented by the School's Opera Workshop in April. The invited audience was ominously unenthusiastic—about half its members departed at intermission—but an enthusiastic response by the family and by Roger L. Stevens, who was both one of the original producers of the show and the founding chairman of the Kennedy Center's Board of Trustees, led to a decision to give the work four more performances in the School's Summer Festival (where it played to audiences said to be of unprecedented sparseness), and, finally, despite the sobering omens, a decision to take the semi-staged production to Washington for three performances (August 11–13) at the Center. In prospect, this event generated a good deal of press interest, and all three performances were sold out. The music critics showed up too, and the production was widely reviewed in the local and national press. Excerpts were also heard on NPR's "Performance Today." In sum, the venture put the School once again where it most liked to be: in the American cultural spotlight.

This time, however, it might have been better to have remained in the shade. Although it was possible to extract a number of flattering passages from the reviews, for the most part they simply underscored what had been clearly written (but evidently not read) on the wall in Bloomington. A few reviewers were enthusiastic about the work, but most of them disliked it. Far worse, from the point of view of the School, the response to the *production* was mixed. There was widespread praise for the musical directors (the veteran Robert Stoll and doctoral student Michael Butterman) and for the lead singers—especially the prodigious Angela Brown, who subsequently became one of the School's many Met Audition winners. But Haagensen's staging was not much liked, and for the most part the production was regarded as not meeting professional standards. It was "a basically student production," Bernard Holland wrote in the *New York Times,* and of course it *was:* but for a School accustomed to seeing its touring productions praised for their professionalism, this and the similar phrases in some other reviews made painful reading.

If this venture into musical theater did not entirely pan out, in popular choral music (which had always been at the center of what Bain called the School's "show business") the 1990s brought triumphs surpassing even the previous heights. By 1990, when the Singing Hoosiers marked its fortieth anniversary, the group had performed in twenty-six states and eighteen foreign countries on four continents, and had shared stages with such headliners as Bob Hope, Duke Ellington, and Hoagy Carmichael. Robert Stoll had also led it into a close association with Erich Kunzel's Cincinnati Pops Orchestra, with which in 1989 it had recorded *A Disney Spectacular.* The album rose to the top of *Billboard*'s "Classical Cross-Over Division" and remained there for several months; it also earned a Grammy nomination. This latter honor was repeated in 1992 by another collaborative venture with the Pops, a recording of *The Music Man.* Two more albums (a second one of Disney songs, which also topped the crossover chart, and one of other movie music) were recorded in 1994 and 1995; and that spring Stoll, who was to retire in a few months, capped his career by taking the group, again with the Pops, to a Carnegie Hall concert. In December, under its new director, Michael Schwartzkopf, the group appeared with the Pops in a one-hour PBS broadcast.

All in all, then, it was unsurprising when in March 1994 the School—more precisely, one of its key programs—was again ranked first in the nation. This accolade came in the annual survey of graduate programs in *U.S. News & World Report,* which for the first time that year included programs in music. In particular, the magazine ranked schools offering the Master of Music—the central advanced degree in applied music. In the collective view of the deans and senior faculty surveyed, the program at Indiana was unsurpassed. Thus the School had finished at the top of all four of the national rankings of music schools published since 1974.

Unsettlingly, though, this time Indiana did not have sole occupancy of the highest rung, but shared it with Juilliard and Eastman. Could it be that the School was (if only in the M.M.) in the process of being passed? If so, the causes would not be far to seek, for it was evident—from common sense, reinforced by the various committee reports surveyed above—that the School's reputation depended primarily on four factors: the perceived quality of its faculty, its graduates, and its physical facilities, and its ability to stay abreast of changes in the musical milieu.

The fourth of these was primarily a function (as the committees had insistently observed) of the School's leadership and its administrative structure. The enhancement and even the maintenance of the School's position in the other three depended primarily on its ability to secure adequate financing. Bain, through force of will and because of favorable historical circumstances, had been able to build a great school on the modest resources afforded him by the University administration (supplemented by occasional large private donations), and the tremendous reputation of the School had enabled it to remain competitive for faculty and students into the 1990s, despite the fact that its financial compensation for the first group and its aid packages for the second had been relatively meager, and despite the disarray of its admissions operation.

This last problem had, since the arrival of Gwyn Richards, been greatly alleviated, but the problems with faculty compensation and student aid were far more intractable. Even after Webb's efforts, sustained over the entire period of his deanship, to raise salaries, in the final years of his tenure the preeminent American music school still ranked only fifth in faculty compensation among its chief competitors—and had, almost unbelievably, sunk to eleventh place in the comparison group of thirteen Indiana departments and schools (only Theater and Fine Arts fared worse).

Moreover, an onerous teaching load was guaranteed, even despite the heavy reliance on graduate-student instructors, by the extremely high student:faculty ratio, which in 1992 was 21:1. These circumstances had sometimes prevented the School from recruiting highly desirable prospective faculty members, and if salaries and workload could not be improved relative to the competition—especially if the School's compensatory advantage in reputation were lessening—it would inevitably be the case, over time, that the relative quality of its faculty would decline. Very similar considerations applied to first-rate prospective students, who found themselves courted by other fine schools offering more money, and for whom Indiana's high student:faculty ratio of course meant large classes, and had much to do with the perpetuation of the view of the School as a "factory." In the long run, these weaknesses, if not corrected, must inevitably erode the School's position, however great its past and current glories.

All this had been foreseen, and as a result much more attention had been paid, over the past decade or so, to the matter of improving the School's financial position through tapping non-government sources. Here as in so many areas the burden fell mainly on the Dean, and it increasingly necessitated a change in the allocation of his time and energies.

Webb's predecessor had not devoted much of his time to raising outside money. The usual targets of his fundraising efforts were the officers of the University; as for private-sector donations, once the School had become so famous, he seems to have been inclined to think that whatever was needed would drop like manna onto Apollo's chosen people. According to Dorothy Collins, Herman Wells, who perfectly understood the necessity for constant fundraising from both public and private sources and was very good at the task, took Bain with him on a fundraising expedition only once: a trip to Cincinnati, where he hoped to secure a donation to the School from the Corbetts, the great patrons of the College-Conservatory of Music. But Bain was of no help at all in making the case, because, as Collins tells the story (which she doubtless had directly from Wells), he "just thought his school was so good you don't *have* to make a case: you just get the money." Wells vowed never to take him along again.

At least by 1964, though, Bain had come to recognize the value of sustained private-sector fundraising, and he thus welcomed the formation that year of the Society of the Friends of Music. Spearheaded by Ross Robertson, a business professor who was also an enthusiastic supporter of the School, the Society offered membership in various categories (associated with different sizes of donation), which entitled the members to various perks such as preferential seating for the opera, nearby parking, and passes to dress rehearsals. The Society directed these donations to the support of student scholarships; it continues to flourish, and currently raises about $175,000 each year for scholarships and travel grants.

Webb's administration was from the beginning characterized by increased attention to fundraising. In his first year as Dean, a School of Music Endowment Fund was set up; in the spring of 1974, the School's alumni association launched the first of what were to be annual fundraising drives, directed primarily at raising money for scholarships; two years later, the School established a fund for the benefit of the music library, designed to facilitate the development of special collections and the acquisition of out-of-print materials. (By university policy, the regular acquisitions budget was restricted to current materials.) The inspiration for the fund was a bequest of $131,000 in the will of the long-time music librarian, Ethel Lyman, who had died in 1974.

Doubtless the most charming, not to say quixotic, fundraising venture of the 1970s was the "Take a Chance on Indiana University School of Music" raffle. For $25 each, one could purchase tickets that, with luck, would result in prizes such as an oil painting by Bain (who was an assiduous amateur painter), a duet recital by Webb and Hornibrook, a violin lesson from Gingold, tennis with Pete DeLone, or having one's house painted by Allan Ross. How much money the raffle succeeded in raising is not recorded, but the venture was not repeated.

The same academic year (1978–79), however, witnessed the beginning of a new seriousness about fundraising for the School, when the Indiana University Foundation for the first time appointed an officer (Leonard Phillips) with specific responsibility for Music. As the years passed and the state provided a continually decreasing share of the University's revenues, this connection correspondingly increased in importance. By 1993, the state was supplying only about a quarter of the revenues, so that it had become more accurate, as the Chancellor for the Bloomington campus noted, to refer to the institution not as a state-supported university but as a state-assisted one. This situation was scarcely unique to Indiana: in some state universities, the Chancellor observed, entire departments or schools were privately supported.

In this context, there were increasing expectations on deans to spend a large proportion of their time in fundraising. These expectations were especially marked after the advent, in 1987, of President Ehrlich and his Responsibility Center Management—and Ehrlich's successor, Myles Brand (who took office in 1994), has said that a dean should devote roughly 50 percent of his or her time to fundraising.

To Webb at least, this was an unwelcome trend; he had, after all, turned deliberately away from the world of business and finance in order to spend his life in music. To be sure, he had a tremendous flair for one key part of the fundraising operation, that which creates or reinforces a personal relationship between prospective donors and the school and encourages them to regard it as a worthy object of largess. With Kenda, he was, as I noted earlier, a splendid and indefatigable host. A constant stream of dinner-party guests, often dozens of them at a time, and most of them businesspeople and others with money (their own or their corporations') to spare, were entertained royally at the Webbs'. At least as important to the cause was Webb's adroitness at deploying what had always been the great public-relations engine of the School, performance. As a superb performer himself, who could, moreover, commandeer the talents of other members of the School, he was in this way as in so many others a wonderful ambassador for it. He frequently performed at functions organized to court potential donors, often with some brilliant student of the School, such as the violin prodigies Corey Cerovsek and Tzu Yuan Su, and the soprano Angela Brown. What better way to drive home the School's worthiness as a place to bestow gifts?

The other parts of the fundraising operation were not, however, nearly as agreeable to him. In contemporary university fundraising, elaborate planning precedes the actual solicitation of gifts. It has been determined that prospective donors are much more responsive to appeals for contributions toward the achievement of precisely specified and rationalized ends than to appeals for general-purpose donations; accordingly, much of the labor of fundraising goes into the construction, by "development" officers working with academic administrators, of detailed accounts of just what monies are needed for just what purposes, and why those purposes are worthy. To work of this kind Webb was uncomfortably obliged to devote substantial amounts of time that he could scarcely spare. Nor was he especially comfortable at the *other* end of the fundraising process: though extremely good at putting prospective donors into a state of mind in which they would be susceptible to appeals, he did not relish actually making the appeals. This was particularly the case with respect to the people Kenda and he entertained at their home. They regarded these people, sincerely, as friends; and they did not like putting the touch on friends. All in all, the School's fundraising constituted yet another sphere of activity where the burden on the Dean had, over the years, become insupportable: here, too, Webb needed to delegate more.

Finally the problem was solved (as that in the admissions operation had been) by adding a first-rate professional in the field to the School's non-academic staff. The School had in fact had a development officer on its staff for some years, but the salary attached to the position made it impossible to attract the kind of high-powered, experienced person that was needed. In 1995, though, the IUF agreed to split with the School a salary at the requisite level, and the School was able to recruit as its new Director of Development Barbara Monahan, who had previously performed the same job for the Yale School of Medicine. In the sequel, both Webbs found their lives considerably eased: Kenda told me she only wished Monahan had come ten years sooner.

At the time of Monahan's arrival, the School was in fact just completing a large-scale fundraising operation. From the early 1980s to the middle 1990s, the primary goal of its efforts in this area had been to acquire the wherewithal to build a major new facility that would house both the music library and a new recital hall. The library was spread over seven different locations; and the main one, in the basement of Sycamore Hall, suffered recurrent water damage. Scores and recordings had not, in living memory, been housed in the same building. With Recital Hall as the School's only mid-sized performance venue, many events had to be dispersed to other campus buildings and even to off-campus facilities such as nearby churches.

In 1982, Webb reported to his colleagues on the School of Music Council that the officers of the University thought it very unlikely that the state would fund a new building. Happily, these officers understood that such a facility was a high priority, and in the capital campaign the University launched in 1985, a new music building was designated as a principal target, with $10.5 million earmarked for it. The next year, Webb briefed the Council on the three sites that had been considered during discussions with the University administration: the parking lot behind Sycamore Hall; an annex to the Music Annex (an ugly idea that had also been considered for East Hall's replacement); or (the possibility that Webb regarded as the most desirable) the site of the Wendell Wright Building adjacent to the School. The Wright Building—named after the former Dean of Education who had been a member of Wells's Self-Survey Committee—had been built in 1937–38 to house the laboratory school referred to earlier (the University School), but since the 1960s, when the school moved to new quarters, had been given over to the School of Education and the Department of Speech and Hearing Sciences; however, Education was preparing to move to its own new quarters. Razing the Wright Building would free a truly prime site, which was not only next-door to the School of Music but, occupying the corner of Jordan Avenue and Third Street, formed the southeastern gateway to the old campus.

By 1987, the tentative plans for the new building had it including the library, a small recital hall seating 125, and two 300-seat halls, one of them equipped with a Rosales tracker organ. The projected cost had risen to $15 million. That year also, the first two major donations were pledged: $300,000 from the Irwin-Sweeney-Miller Foundation (that is, Elsie Sweeney's family), and $1,000,000 from the Krannerts, who, like Miss Sweeney, had also made a huge donation for the construction of the MAC. Two years later, another $1,000,000 pledge was secured, from Ione B. Auer of Fort Wayne.

Mrs. Auer's husband had been Senior Vice President of the Lincoln National Life Insurance Company and had also presided over his own investment company; after he died, in 1975, his widow assumed control of the latter, which she operated with great success until dissolving the firm in 1985. For a time, she planned to make a large donation to the Fort Wayne Museum of Art, of which she was a Board member. But this project came to naught, for in the end the Board declined her request that the museum be renamed, in conjunction with the gift, in honor of her late husband, who had had a deep interest in art and been a long-time patron of the museum.

In the aftermath of the collapse of Mrs. Auer's negotiations with the museum (which became a cause célèbre), Peter deVries, an alumnus of the School who was concertmaster of the Fort Wayne Symphony, suggested to Webb that she might be amenable to an alternative proposal for the bestowal of her money. She had a lifelong interest in music; why not attempt to interest her in the new building for the School? With Webb's approval, deVries raised the matter with Mrs. Auer, who was intrigued, and it was arranged for the Webbs to meet her in Fort Wayne—where, over lunch, Charles suggested that in place of an Edward Auer Art Museum there could be an Edward Auer Hall in the new building. After several more meetings, a deal was struck, which varied from the original proposal only in that Mrs. Auer decided the auditorium might better be called the Ione B. Auer Hall: her husband had loved art, but *she* was the one who loved music.

As this anecdote shows, Webb, though not fond of soliciting donations, could do it perfectly well when the need arose; and indeed he was similarly involved in securing the other major donations that made the new building possible. Foremost among these was the $2,100,000 gift of Deborah, Cindy, and David Simon in memory of their mother, Bess Meshulam Simon, an Indianapolis music lover; this became the "naming gift" for the new facility. Yet another gift of $1,000,000 (in addition, that is, to those of Mrs. Auer and the Krannerts) was directed toward the new library: it came from the local philanthropists William and Gayle Cook. Richard Ford contributed $350,000 for the construction of one of the small recital halls; a nephew of Cole Porter, James Cole, together with his wife, contributed $100,000 for a lobby to front Auer Hall. Harold and Robert Janitz also contributed $100,000, for the acquisition of two new concert grand pianos for the hall. Two other major gifts were directed toward landscaping the new facility. In memory of her late husband David, Barbara Jacobs gave $300,000 for the construction of a terrace and plaza on the west side of the building; over the years, the Jacobs, who had supported many of the School's tours, had become by far the largest donors in its history. A gift of $223,000 from Marianne McKinney Tobias, in memory of her deceased first husband Frank McKinney, made possible the dramatic fountain that would front the building's main, east-side entrance. Webb was also involved—though here the Librarian, David Fenske, was the principal mover—in securing the $618,000 IBM contribution to the library's Variations Project (which became a major "testbed" for IBM's Digital Library initiative).

By this time, the plan to build a *new* building had been abandoned in favor of renovating and adding on to the Wright Building. That building was one of the limestone structures that distinguish the campus; Herman Wells, especially, pointed out that the University had never in its history razed one of these. The compromise settled on was to demolish and replace the Wright Building's north wing, and to renovate the rest; one great advantage of this plan was that the substantial size of the building would allow it to accommodate not only the library and concert halls but the academic-music offices located in Sycamore Hall.

By early 1991 the projected cost of converting the building to Music School purposes had risen to $18.5 million, of which only $14.1 million had been raised. (This amount had been garnered entirely from private sources: there was not and is not a dollar of public money in the facility.) To secure the missing millions, the IUF agreed in 1991 to mount a special campaign. Even so, it was decided to reduce the size of the renovated structure, and the School therefore faced the hard decision of whether to eliminate one of the two large concert halls or to reduce the size of the library. It says something about the genuineness of Webb's commitment to the School's academic mission that he supported the former alternative, which was adopted. In the final configuration, the School would have 100,000 square feet of assignable space in the renovated structure. (The building's remaining 22,000 square feet, on the back side, were retained by the Department of Speech and Hearing Sciences.)

The School of Education vacated the Wright Building in the fall of 1992, and construction began on the Center the following spring. In the spring of 1995, the new library and the two concert halls opened; by that fall, the building was near enough to completion that the dedication could proceed. To be sure, there were still various missing pieces, most conspicuously the Auer Hall organ, for which no donor had yet been found, and whose absence was marked by a large blank space in the front of the hall. Nor had all of the final millions for renovating the building been raised. (In 1997, the University undertook to meet the final construction costs from central funds; it was not until 1999 that a naming gift of $400,000 from Mrs. Madie Seward allowed the School to purchase the organ.)

While construction proceeded on the Simon Center, plans for the musical events of the dedication weekend gradually coalesced. The arrangement whereby Kurt Masur conducted the Indiana Philharmonic in the Friday-evening concert came about through the long professional association and friendship between Masur and Menahem Pressler. For years the two had sporadically discussed the possibility of the conductor's visiting Bloomington. Finally, backstage at Carnegie Hall one evening about a year and a half before the dedication was to take place, Pressler made a concrete offer that the conductor accepted: "I told him we are going to have this magnificent library and building[,] and this is an opportunity for the students to experience what it is to play under a great master." The suggestion that a PBS special be filmed at the School came from the network, and was originally unconnected with the dedication. "But then," Webb says, "we discovered it would be possible to tie it all with Kurt Masur, and it just seemed like an opportunity too good to pass up." PBS took responsibility for securing the star performers. Sylvia McNair was especially pleased to come. A PBS special was a sufficient attraction in itself, but to get to tape it at her alma mater made the occasion particularly satisfying. The choice of a piece for the dedicatory concert in Auer Hall was made by the choral director Jan Harrington. "I walked into the hall and it said to me, 'Monteverdi Vespers,'" Harrington reported: the side balconies and the loft above the stage put him in mind of the cathedral choir lofts that Monteverdi and other musicians of his time had used to great effect. As for Joshua Bell, Gary Hoffman, and Edgar Meyer, the main problem, Henry Upper claimed, was tracking them down in the midst of their busy concertizing schedules. Once contacted, they agreed to play without fee—just as well, Webb told the audience at their joint appearance, since "we couldn't afford them." Corey Cerovsek was easier to contact: his family had moved to Bloomington when he entered the School, and he continues to make his home there.

When the Center was dedicated on those five November days in 1995, Webb still had a year and a half to serve as Dean. But the dedication of the facility, in whose creation he had been the main driving force, was the crowning event of his administration, even as for Bain the dedication of the MAC—fourteen months before his own deanship ended—had been, and as the dedication of the Music Building had been for Merrill, thirteen months before the end of *his* deanship. Like those other milestone events in the history of the School, the dedication of the Center brought together all the institution's constituencies for an interlude of celebration and reflection. The current and immediately past Presidents of the University were on hand. The greatest of all the Presidents, Herman B Wells, was also there, attending events in the wheelchair that was, in his last years, his concert seat. In addition to the current Dean as host and master of ceremonies, the eighty-seven-year-old Wilfred Bain was there too, so that the celebration included, in the persons of the present and former Deans and the former President, the three prime fosterers of the School's greatness. Moreover, many of the donors whose gifts had made the Center possible were in attendance, as honored guests for the occasion. All of them must have taken satisfaction from the knowledge that their gifts would make them (or make them to an even greater degree than they had already been) forever a part of the School's magnificent enterprise; and those who gave the largest amounts had the additional satisfaction of seeing the physical evidence of the fact that by their gifts they had grafted their names, or those of the departed loved ones in whose honor they gave, onto the long-lived spreading tree of art. The faculty—in whose collective abilities the School's greatness primarily resides and whose collective eminence is primarily responsible for its reputation—were there, some of them as performers and many others as audience members; many of them were also among the donors. As for the students, some four hundred of them performed in the various musical events. The press, which had from the early Bain years done so much to create the reputation of the School, was there too. Finally, the usual Bloomington audience was there, employees of the University and other members of the community for whom the rich musical life supplied by the School was one of the main attractions of residing in the town.

Celebrating a great moment in the history of the School, the dedication also (again like the other milestone events) inevitably prompted reflections on the institution in relation to its past. The building itself, when added to the four others built under Merrill, Bain, and Webb—the Music Building and its Annex; the MAC; the Music Practice Building—gave the School, as Webb said proudly on various occasions, facilities superior to those of any other music school in the world. This was only as it should be, though, for a school that had become in Bain's time the largest in the world and the best in North America, and that under Webb had not only maintained its size and distinction but had encompassed even more fields of activity in its capacious musical embrace and seen its reputation grow to such an extent that it was not uncommonly regarded as the best *any*where. How far all this was from M. B. Griffith's singing classes, with which formal instruction in music had effectively begun in the University, almost exactly a hundred years before; from Mitchell Hall with its cacophonous decrepitude; or from East Hall with its sweltering nights—where, nonetheless, the foremost American collegiate opera program had grown to maturity.

Such reflections on the School's past and present, as well as on its future and on the nature of the art it serves, were forcefully evoked by the Saturday night performance in Auer Hall. This was the first official event in the new building (the Philharmonic Concert having taken place in the MAC), and the great work chosen for the occasion—Monteverdi's Vespers—took the weekend's survey of Western art music back to its Renaissance origins. Moreover, as Jan Harrington noted, the performance involved a broad range of the School's musical forces; and one of the forces, the University Children's Choir, could be regarded as symbolic of its future, "a new generation of musicians in a new music hall." The work was also appropriate for an event marking the culmination of the stewardship of Charles Webb, since its performance powerfully conveyed the remarkable accomplishments that had stemmed from his determination, announced at the beginning of his deanship, to foster the development in the School of the then largely neglected area of early music.

Much of the history of the School—in which, to recall President Bryan's phrase, the "Empire of Beethoven," originally as alien to the people of Bloomington as that of Genghis Khan, had established a major outpost in the town amid the Indiana cornfields—was, then, implicit in that first performance in Auer Hall. More than that, the reason why all the long and arduous labor of creation had been worthwhile was evident as the first words of the Vespers—"Deus in adjutorium meum intende" ("O God, make speed to save me")—descended from the loft on the angel wings of Alan Bennett's voice, bestowing on all the School's people, the living and the dead, as pure a benediction as this troubled world affords.

Postlude

Charles Webb retired, from the deanship and the University, on June 30, 1997, at the age of sixty-four. He could have remained Dean for one more year, but he was pleased with the idea that the terminal date he chose would mean that the era of Bain and Webb together had spanned precisely fifty years; and family considerations, including especially the desire to spend more time with Kenda, also influenced his decision.

Late June is a slack time at the School, and accordingly the formal commemoration of Webb's long service was moved back two months, to the final Saturday in April. It is suggestive of the feelings toward Kenda in the School that the event was billed as "A Day of Music and Celebration Honoring Kenda and Charles Webb." There were a lunch and dinner with the usual speechifying and, between them, a concert in the MAC by some of the great figures of the School: Starker and Sebok; Susann McDonald; the Gullis; Wise, Campbell, and Hokanson performing Schubert's "Shepherd on the Rock"; and finally three movements of the "Trout" quintet, with Pressler, Fried, Arad, Tsutsumi, and Hurst. At the end, standing at the same spot—front stage right—where his predecessor had stood twenty-five years ago that month at the dedication of the MAC, Webb expressed his gratitude in one of his splendid extempore speeches. He concluded by introducing to the audience all his family, who surrounded him on the stage as he called them out from the wings: Kenda, their children, the four daughters-in-law, and the grandchildren, who at that time numbered five. In the evening, the MAC was again lit, with the Opera Theater's production of John Corigliano and William Hoffman's *The Ghosts of Versailles.* This was only the third staging of the long and demanding work, after its triumphant 1991 premiere at the Met, and the Chicago Lyric Opera production four years later. Corigliano had come to Bloomington to assist in the production; the result must surely have pleased him, for it was one of those spellbinding occasions at the MAC when it is nearly impossible to believe that what one is witnessing is a student production.

As it happened, the spring of 1997 was epochal not just in marking the end of the Webb era but in other ways as well. Two weeks prior to the celebration of Kenda and Charles, there had been a memorial concert for Bain, who had died on March 7, at the age of eighty-nine. (Six days later, Webb wrote to Chancellor Wells to propose that the MAC be renamed in Bain's honor—which it will be, but only, as University policy dictates, ten years after his death.) And also in March, *U.S. News & World Report* published a new ranking of Master of Music programs. Three years previously,

Indiana, Eastman, and Juilliard had shared the top ranking; this time Indiana and Juilliard were still tied, but Eastman was placed ahead of them, by one-tenth of a point on a five-point scale. This was a ranking only of one degree program, and it seemed an odd result in view of the fact that Indiana had, with the opening of the Simon Center in 1995, taken an enormous step ahead in terms of facilities, but whatever one could say by way of mitigating the shock, there was no way around the fact that, for the first time ever in a national survey, Indiana had not been ranked number one; and, as the music editor of the *New York Times*—James R. Oestreich—easily detected a year later, when he spent a few days at the School, that tenth of a point had "registered resoundingly on the school's sensitive Richter scale."

Greater shocks were to come. When the ranking was published—a little over three months before Webb would step down—the consternation attending it was doubtless increased by the fact that his successor had not yet been named. In November 1992, the last of the deanship review committees had urged that a Search and Screen Committee for the deanship be formed in the near future, on the ground that it would probably take several years to secure a successor, given the importance of the position and the small pool of acceptable candidates. The University administrators had, however, ignored this recommendation, and in fact the search committee was not struck until—incredible as it seems—the early fall of 1996. Hurst was named chair; Kurt Masur agreed to be listed as honorary co-chair. The committee held its first meeting on September 23, which was thus the date on which the School formally entered the lengthy and painful period of transition that still, as I write (in the early spring of 2000), continues.

Just as the deanship review committee had predicted, the search committee found (as Herman Wells had in 1938 and 1947) that the pool of plausible candidates was shallow. With the help of a "headhunter," the committee eventually located a dozen individuals whom it regarded as sufficiently plausible to interview; after these interviews, a few candidates withdrew, and the committee was left with a half dozen viable ones; from these, it chose a short list of four.

This list consisted entirely of external candidates. Indeed, the only internal candidate in the group of twelve had been James Scott. When he came to the School as Associate Dean for Instruction in 1994, Scott was, as I noted earlier, easy to regard as a possible successor to Webb: a distinguished performer and a seasoned administrator, he appeared to be a perfect fit for the leadership role in this performance-dominated school. By 1996, however, this outcome had begun to seem unlikely, especially as a result of policy disagreements between Scott and some of his colleagues. As it happened, the distinguished music school of the University of Illinois was searching for a new leader at the same time as Indiana; Scott was offered the position there, and accepted it.

In the earliest stage of its work, the Indiana committee had solicited views as to what attributes were especially desirable in a new Dean. In a November 1996 meeting of the School of Music Council, Hurst had listed the desiderata that had been most frequently stressed by members of the faculty: the School needed "a dean with a vision"; who was "a musician, active either as a performer or as a scholar"; had proven ability as a fundraiser; and could attract first-rate faculty. The committee also heard a good deal about the need for the new Dean to raise the visibility of the School still further, and to be able both to preserve its traditional programs and, simultaneously, to lead it into new areas, especially those involving electronic technology. Among these considerations, unquestionably the overriding one was—and, given the School's ever-increasing dependence on private-sector funding, more or less had to be—that the Dean have an excellent record as a fundraiser. It was in large part because of his accomplishments in this area that, after the campus visits of the shortlisted candidates, the committee finally opted for David G. Woods, who, following six years as Director of the School of Music at the University of Arizona, had for the past six been Dean of the College of Fine Arts at the University of Oklahoma.

Woods, who had been turned up by the headhunter, was content at Oklahoma, and had expressed reluctance to be interviewed by Indiana; moreover, once it was known that Indiana had shortlisted him, Oklahoma did everything in its power to retain him. Thus it was only after protracted and awkward to-ing and fro-ing that he at last accepted the position at Indiana.

The appointment was announced on April 28, 1997 (two days, that is, after the valedictory celebration of the Webbs). Although it was not unexpected by faculty members of the School, who had been avidly discussing the relative merits of the finalists after their campus visits, it occasioned very considerable surprise to outsiders: for Woods was an academic musician. Moreover, his field was music education; that is, the field that for many years had occupied the lowest position in the School's hierarchy, and that would have seemed absolutely the least likely one to produce its next Dean—and within this field, his specialty was early-childhood music education. In professional orientation, then, he was about as far as possible from the high-level performance training and the major classical repertory that had provided the central focus of the School for the past fifty years.

Since the appointment came late in the academic year, Woods was not able to assume his new position at the time of Webb's retirement. Henry Upper was made Interim Dean, and Woods officially took the helm on September 15, 1997.

Once arrived, he began to take vigorous action on a number of fronts where the faculty had claimed, over the years (and had affirmed in their directives to the Search and Screen Committee), that this was what they wanted. Concerned, for example, to develop and articulate a clear vision for the future of the School, Woods began at the grassroots level, in two respects, not only having numerous meetings with faculty members individually and in small groups but also formally requiring each of the School's twenty-four departments to develop a "mission statement." For his own part, he produced, after a year on the job, a "vision statement" for the School as a whole. To be sure, the statement did not go much beyond the particular set of generalities that one would expect from a two-page document on this subject written in the late 1990s: the "agenda for the 21st Century" included "thorough curricular renewal"; further integration of technology into the work of the School; more internationalization and at the same time more effective outreach to Indiana and the nation; more "diversity" in faculty, students, and music; a new emphasis on good teaching and on "the integration of performance, creativity, analysis and musical understanding in all aspects of the curriculum"; and the consolidation of "a solid financial base" for the School.

Woods also acted vigorously on another front that had long concerned his colleagues, namely, the clarification, rationalization, and enlargement of the School's administrative structure. He added a number of middle and upper management positions. At the top end of the structure, Webb's final reslicing of the deanships and directorships (in the aftermath of the ARC report of 1992) had left the School with Associate Deans for Instruction and Administration and a Director of Admissions, in addition to the Directors of Undergraduate and Graduate Studies and the Director of Development. Woods retained the first of the associate deanships, replacing the departed Scott on an interim basis with Hurst, and then, on the advice of a search committee that had considered both internal and external candidates, with Eugene O'Brien. Henry Upper was moved from the Administration portfolio to a newly created associate deanship for External Relations. On the recommendation of the search committee for the deanship of Administration, the School of Music Council reclassified this faculty position as a staff one; it was set at the level of Assistant Dean, and René Machado, who had held a similar position at New York University, was brought in to fill it. Meanwhile, Woods had proposed to the Council that the Admissions position be, in recognition of its importance to the School, reclassified as an associate deanship. The Council endorsed this proposal, and Gwyn Richards became Associate Dean for Admissions and Financial Aid. Unfortunately, the sudden, untimely death of Eugenia Sinor in the spring of 1999 left Woods with a vacancy in the directorship of undergraduate studies.

Other initiatives answered to the desire that Webb's successor further raise the visibility of the School and increase its involvement with new electronic technologies. In the fall of 1999, the School opened a satellite school in Vienna; and by the spring of 1998 the Dean had negotiated an ambitious exchange and distance-learning project with the Royal Academy of Music in London.

These were significant initiatives, but Woods was, when I spoke with him in the summer of 1999, perfectly clear on the point that the most important task confronting him was that of securing sufficient financial support to enable the School to continue functioning at the level it had achieved under Bain and Webb. (Success in that endeavor would in turn be important in achieving his other key goal, that of renewing the School's graying faculty.)

The overwhelming need to shore up the School's finances had of course been clear for a number of years before Woods's advent; it had been an even sharper focus of attention since 1994, when the University had entered the "quiet phase" of a fundraising campaign (publicly launched in 1997) designed to increase the endowment of the institution as a whole by $150 million. Income from the funds secured in the campaign was to be directed primarily toward the creation of scholarships and endowed professorships. These were, as we have seen, precisely the areas in which the School of Music (like, no doubt, other academic units) particularly needed additional funding; the School's share of the $150 million was set at $12 million, of which $6.5 million would go to student aid and $5.5 million to faculty support.

The campaign had, then, been launched before Woods came on the scene, and the School had in fact done very well in it. In September 1995 the new Director of Development, Barbara Monahan, had arrived, and between her efforts and those of Webb, the School's endowment grew remarkably in the last year of his tenure. As of June 30, 1996, the endowment stood at a little over $16 million; eleven months later, it had reached nearly $23 million, and the School had already realized, since the establishment of its campaign goal in 1994, 112 percent of the target. One especially significant gift was that of the Dorothy Richard Starling Foundation, which established, in Mrs. Starling's memory, a Chair in Violin Studies; this was the first endowed chair in the history of the School. (It was bestowed on Franco Gulli.) Before Webb's retirement, commitments had also been secured for three other endowed chairs, all of them sponsored by the Jacobs family, who have been, as I noted earlier, by far the largest donors in the history of the School: established by Barbara Jacobs, one of these chairs bears the name of her late husband, David H. Jacobs; the other two are the Dean Charles H. Webb Chair and the Henry A. Upper Chair. (The inaugural holders of the chairs are, respectively, Mathiesen, Pressler, and Tozzi.)

By the fall of 1999, Woods had secured an additional endowed position, sponsored by Jack and Linda Gill of Houston, in the field of conducting: its income is directed not to the support of a member of the permanent faculty but to visits of notable conductors, brought to the campus for varying lengths of time. He had also had success in other fundraising ventures, including that of securing individual or corporate sponsorship of opera performances. Much of his fundraising had been accomplished without benefit of a Director of Development. Woods and Monahan did not see eye-to-eye, and she left the School in the summer of 1998, after which the Development position remained vacant until the late spring of 1999, when George Bledsoe, formerly of the Indiana University Foundation, was appointed to it.

By this time, though, attention was becoming focused not on long-term financial matters but on an immediate and pressing one: the School's budget was in a substantial deficit. At the present writing, it is impossible to say just how much of this problem should be laid at the feet of the Dean, and how much should be attributed to factors beyond his control: for the first time in this history I am writing about events that are at once so recent and so sensitive that authoritative documentary sources are not available. It seems clear, though, that some of the budgetary woes derived from factors such as salary increases mandated from above and an increase in the tax levied on the School by the central administration for support of the University infrastructure; but it is also clear that part of the problem stemmed from Woods's discretionary expenditures—for one thing, in connection with his actions in rationalizing and enlarging the School's administrative structure. The reconfigured non-academic staff was substantially larger than it had been in Webbs's time, and the budget was simply not adequate to support all the positions.

The administrative restructuring was also the source of another problem that, like the deficit, began to cause tension between Woods and some of his colleagues. Under the new arrangement, the Dean's Office was structured so as to buffer the Dean, two layers deep, from contact with the faculty. When Webb replaced Bain, the subsequent opening up of the Dean's Office had, as we have seen, been extremely well received, though as time passed, some of Webb's colleagues began to think that he could have dealt better with strategic concerns if he were not so open to constant involvement in the School's quotidian business. But now faculty members began to be reminded that there are also negative consequences to having the Dean at a distance from much of this business. The access of individual members to the Dean was substantially reduced: a request to see Woods might result in an appointment for three weeks later. This situation was not good for morale in a faculty where many (though not all, according to the deanship review reports) had been accustomed to having more or less immediate access to the Dean. Moreover, the buffering perhaps prevented Woods from having as full an information flow as he needed: at least the view became common among the faculty that he often made decisions without sufficient consultation. To a faculty that had for several decades been asserting with increasing effectiveness a collective right to be involved in administrative decision-making, this was an unwelcome development; and it was rendered all the more so by the feeling, on the part of some members, that the decisions Woods was making were not always good ones. The School had, over the years, become an extremely complex network of reciprocally affecting parts, especially with regard to its massive performance program, where decisions about such matters as admissions, staffing, and the repertory of ensembles were all interrelated; and a number of faculty members came to feel that Woods—who of course had not previously managed a performance program on this scale (as indeed very few people anywhere had)—sometimes made decisions without due awareness of all their ramifications.

To be sure, Woods had strong supporters, who thought that his innovations were precisely the kind of thing the School needed (and had, for that matter, been loudly *saying* it needed, in the quadrennial reviews of his predecessor's performance); and these supporters included a number of distinguished members of the faculty. But the new Dean's relations with other members, including some in key positions, grew increasingly strained. Among all the points of tension, the greatest was the deficit. In early November, the *Daily Student* reported that it was approaching $2,000,000; nor did Woods's proposals for reversing the trend satisfy his critics.

At a corresponding point early in Bain's tenure, a similarly large amount of faculty discontent with the new Dean had not really mattered. Bain steamed on. But this time the situation was profoundly different, because in the intervening fifty years faculty views had, in general, come to matter very much (Bain himself, it is sometimes said around the School, couldn't be Bain now); and then there was the fact that Woods, unlike Bain, did not have the unqualified support of the central University administration. On December 3, 1999, Woods resigned the deanship, effective immediately.

In accordance with the School's bylaws, at this juncture the Associate Dean for Instruction—Eugene O'Brien—became Acting Interim Dean. Since there would obviously be no permanent replacement until at least the next academic year, and more likely the one after that, clearly an interim arrangement that would be viable for a considerable length of time needed to be enacted. On December 10, the School of Music Council recommended to the Chancellor for the Bloomington campus that he appoint as long-term Interim Dean the other Associate Dean, Gwyn Richards; the recommendation was accepted, and, after some negotiations, Richards assumed the post on December 20.

As one can readily imagine, the weeks leading up to and immediately following Woods's resignation were traumatic and demoralizing for the School. In the subsequent months, though, calm and confidence have been largely restored, owing primarily to Richards's solid performance in the interim position. Having been an associate dean at both the University of Southern California and Indiana, he had had substantial relevant experience and, in particular, had at Indiana turned around a very bad situation in the Admissions Office—where, among other things, he had successfully managed the huge budget for financial aid.

As I noted in the preceding chapter, early in his time as Director of Admissions Richards had added his voice to those that had been calling for the development of a strategic plan to guide the School into the next decades. In the aftermath of Woods's resignation, the Interim Dean has had the opportunity to direct an intensive review of various aspects of the School's operations. As I write, the School is engaged in a systematic examination (some facets of which began under Woods) of fundamental questions pertaining to its mission, size, structure, and curriculum.

We leave the School, then, in a state of flux. But this must always be the case in a history of a living institution: there can be no true ending to such a work, but only a stopping point. Neither the results of the current review nor the identity of the next Dean is knowable at this time—and when these matters are determined, over the course of the next year or so, there will still be no way of telling whether the choices made will have been good ones. The answer to this question will become clear only in a decade or a generation.

What *is* clear is that the basic requirements for the School's continuing eminence will be the constant enlargement of its endowment and the maintenance of the quality of its faculty; success on these fronts is, in turn, vital to success on the third major front, the maintenance of the quality of the students. The signal success of the recent capital campaign indicates that the first of the key goals is realizable; the quality of the most recent appointees indicates that the second also is. To be sure, the great challenge in this second area will be that of successfully renewing a special contingent of the faculty that is in a real way its most important one: the performance superstars who, since the 1950s, have been the primary source of the School's reputation. The School has lost a number of eminent performers in the last decade, including its two most celebrated teachers, Harshaw and Gingold. (The most recent loss of a great luminary is that of Gyorgy Sebok, who, having taught and performed to the age of seventy-seven, died in November 1999, after a brief illness.) And though there have been a few remarkable successes in replacing stars with people of comparable luster—for example, Binkley with Hillier—it is hard to imagine that this will generally be the case, if only because the level of remuneration that eminent performers have become accustomed to is now, by academic standards, simply staggering. Webb likes to drive this point home by noting that when Bain lured Gingold from his post as concertmaster of the Cleveland Orchestra, he was able to offer the violinist a salary comparable to his Cleveland one, plus the various fringe benefits of an academic appointment. Now Gingold's student William Preucil is concertmaster at Cleveland, on a salary of over $200,000.

Moreover, schools located in major cities—especially New York—have an advantage over the rest in recruiting top-rank performers. It is relatively easy for Juilliard to maintain a stellar performance faculty, because being a faculty member there need involve, for any of the myriad first-rate musicians resident in the city, nothing more than accepting as pupils a few of the school's most gifted students. No one expects such faculty members to attend meetings or serve on committees: they are appointed, in effect, on a piecework basis. Needless to say, accepting this kind of appointment involves far less of a commitment, disrupts a performance career far less, than moving to Bloomington or Rochester.

One partial solution to the problem entailed in this difference would be a substantial relaxation of the traditional limits on the "flextime" policy. Bain's and Webb's successes in the recruitment of concertizing artists depended on allowing them to be absent from campus for fifteen teaching days per term. When Bain inaugurated this policy in the 1950s, it was, at least for *university* music schools, an unusual one. But now it is commonplace, and in fact some schools are much more liberal than Indiana in allowing artist faculty to be away from campus. It would, however, be deeply problematic for Indiana to follow their lead, for a basic policy of the School—to which both Bain and Webb attributed much of its excellence—has been that all its faculty members really do *live* in Bloomington and perform the full range of normal academic duties.

There is also the truly fundamental question—which in one form or another now faces all educational and performance institutions devoted to Western classical music—of the proper response to a musical world characterized by steadily declining audiences for classical music, collapsing orchestras, and imploding recital series. In such a world, does it make sense to maintain a classically oriented music school on the scale of Indiana's? Will there continue to be a niche, in North America, for even one such school?

The problems confronting the School as it moves into the new millennium are daunting. But it has the great advantage of being able to confront these problems with a faculty that remains of unsurpassed quality and commitment—and one that has, by this time, substantial (and rapidly increasing) experience in matters of governance. It also has a body of students and alumni whose achievements constantly remind the School and its friends of what its central purposes have been, and of how well it continues to accomplish them. As I lay down my pen, the last report from Bloomington is of a dazzling Opera Theater production, of Britten's *The Rape of Lucretia.* Like all other institutions, the School must, if it is to maintain its stature, continue to evolve in response to its changing environment. But those of us who love it as it is will hope there is not reason for it to change too much, and will find comfort, not merely cause for concern, in the fact that its enormous mass and momentum make it difficult to deflect from the noble course set so many years ago.

Appendix 1: Chronology

The chronology includes a few landmark events in the history of the University, major events in the history of the School, and some landmark faculty appointments.

1824 Indiana University opens

1852 Vocal music included in curriculum for the University's short-lived (1852–58) teacher-training program

1893 Glee Club organized; M. B. Griffith begins teaching "private classes in vocal music in the University buildings"

1902 William Lowe Bryan succeeds Joseph Swain as President of the University

1904 University trustees endorse Bryan's plan to establish a School of Music

1906 Edward Ebert-Buchheim engaged to offer piano lessons and give a series of recitals in Mitchell Hall; University Band and men's and women's Glee Clubs also installed there

1910 Charles Diven Campbell appointed founding Head of Department of Music

1918 Mitchell Hall remodeled

1919 Campbell dies (March 29); William D. Howe named interim Head; B. Winfred Merrill appointed Professor and Head (August 1)

1921 Department of Music becomes School of Music, with Merrill as Dean; annex to Mitchell Hall constructed; Edward Bailey Birge appointed Professor of Public School Music

1922 First degree programs in Music (as distinguished from Arts) established

1923 Gertrude V. Schaupp becomes first graduate in Music; Merrill establishes the Music Series, which, over the years, brings Rachmaninoff, Kreisler, Ponselle, and many other notables to perform at the University

1926 Merrill appoints his daughter Winifred as Violinist, precipitating endless trouble

1928 Ernest Hoffzimmer appointed Professor of Piano (replacing Axel Skjerne)

1929 Lennart von Zweygberg appointed the School's first Professor of Cello

1929 European summer school established (repeated 1930 only); the first "outreach" programs for high school students established

1937 Music Building opened (renamed Merrill Hall in 1989); Herman B Wells appointed Acting President of the University (made President in 1938, served until 1962)

1938 Robert L. Sanders appointed Dean of Music (July 30)

1940 School admitted to full membership in the National Association of Schools of Music

1941 University Auditorium opened; Dorothee Manski appointed

1942 School stages its first full opera, *Cavalleria Rusticana;* Metropolitan Opera presents *Aida* in the Auditorium (April 13; after the war, the Met returned, visiting Bloomington annually from 1946 through 1961)

1946 Bernhard Heiden and Paul Nettl appointed

1947 Wilfred C. Bain appointed Dean (effective July 1); Walter Robert and Myron Taylor appointed; small annex to Music Building opened; Madrigal Dinners inaugurated; number of music majors: 296

1948 Ernst Hoffman and George Krueger appointed (effective second semester of 1947–48 academic year); Spring Festival inaugurates Auditorium organ and includes first fully staged opera of the Bain era: *Tales of Hoffmann,* with Hoffman conducting and Hans Busch, on a visiting appointment, as stage director; Weill's *Down in the Valley* given its stage premiere (July 15); School supplies chorus for Chicago performances of Verdi's Requiem, with Antal Dorati conducting (July 24–25); Berkshire Quartet appointed (Urico Rossi, Albert Lazan, David Dawson, Fritz Magg); East Hall opened (fall; stage area completed early 1950)

1949 First performance of Wagner's *Parsifal* (repeated annually through 1969); Ralph Daniel appointed; Ross Allen arrives as a graduate student (appointed to faculty in 1953); David Baker arrives as a freshman (returned as a faculty member in 1966)

1950 Cecil Smith's *New Republic* review of *Parsifal* brings the production to national attention: "beyond all comparison . . . the most remarkable operatic production I have seen in an American School"; Willi Apel appointed; Singing Hoosiers formed

1951 Marguerite de Anguera, Richard Johnson, and Wolfgang Vacano appointed: de Anguera (resigned 1954) was the School's first appointee in ballet; Johnson, a percussionist, was the School's and the University's first African-American appointee

1952 Sidney Foster appointed; Belles of Indiana formed; number of music majors (1951–52): 483

1953 Frank St. Leger appointed

1955 Menahem Pressler appointed

1957 Walter Kaufmann, Tibor Kozma, and Charles Kullman appointed

1958 Janos Starker appointed

1959 Mario Cristini appointed to a visiting position (permanent position 1961)

1960 Philip Farkas, George Gaber, Josef Gingold, and Martha Lipton appointed; Music Annex—the "Round Building"—opened (dedicated 1962)

1961 William Bell and Juan Orrego-Salas appointed

1962 Margaret Harshaw, Gyorgy Sebok, and Abbey Simon appointed (Simon resigned 1977)

1963 *Aida* performed at the University's football stadium; Eugene Rousseau appointed

1964 *Turandot* performed at the New York World's Fair; Julius Herford appointed

1965 Hans Tischler appointed

1968 Conflagration of East Hall (January 24; in the aftermath, School granted space in Sycamore Hall and other buildings); Jorge Bolet appointed (resigned 1977)

1971 Eileen Farrell, Franco Gulli, Harvey Phillips, and Ruggiero Ricci appointed (Ricci resigned 1974, Farrell 1980); Bain-era enrollment peaks at 1,701 (154 faculty members)

1972 Musical Arts Center opened

1973 Charles Webb becomes Dean (July 1); Max Röthlisberger appointed

1974 Walter Cassel appointed; Andrew Porter first visits the School (to review Busoni's *Doctor Faust*): in 1980 Porter declared the Opera Theater "just about the most serious and consistently satisfying of all American opera companies"

1975 *Change* (winter 1974–75) survey ranks the School first in the nation; Opera Theater stages its first non-English production (*Rigoletto*) and presents *The World on the Moon* at the Kennedy Center's Haydnfest

1977 School tours Bernstein's *Trouble in Tahiti* to Israel; Camilla Williams appointed

1978 School of Music Council created; PBS televises Opera Theater's production of Rimsky-Korsakov's *The Night Before Christmas* (American premiere)

1979 *Chronicle of Higher Education* survey ranks the School's faculty the nation's best; Thomas Binkley appointed; Music Practice Building opened

1980 Nicola Rossi-Lemeni and Virginia Zeani appointed

1981 School's New York City performance series inaugurated with five events, including presentation of Martinů's *The Greek Passion* in the Metropolitan Opera House; Susann McDonald appointed

1982 Leonard Bernstein, spending six weeks at the School, falls in love with it; Early Music Institute performs the Greater Passion Play from the Carmina Burana at the Cloisters

1983 "Music from Indiana" achieves national syndication on American Public Radio; National Association of Music Executives of State Universities survey ranks the School's performance program the nation's best

1985 Jean-Pierre Bonnefoux appointed

1988 Two School orchestras in residence at summer music festivals in France, while another orchestra, with vocal soloists and choirs, presents Bernstein's *Mass* at Tanglewood, as part of the Boston Symphony's celebration of the Maestro's seventieth birthday; Thomas Mathiesen appointed

1989 Philharmonic Orchestra participates in opening festivities of the Bastille Opera House; Patricia McBride appointed

1990 Opera Theater presents John Eaton's *The Cry of Clytaemnestra* at the Moscow State Conservatory

1991 School presents Mass in C Minor and other works in Lincoln Center Mozart bicentennial project; Giorgio Tozzi appointed

1992 School revives Bernstein's *1600 Pennsylvania Avenue* at the Kennedy Center

1993 Martina Arroyo appointed

1994 *U.S. News & World Report* survey ranks the School's Master of Music program first in nation (with Eastman's and Juilliard's)

1995 Bess Meshulam Simon Music Library and Recital center opened

1996 Paul Hillier appointed

1997 Charles Webb retires (June 30); Henry Upper serves as Interim Dean until September 15, when David Woods becomes Dean

1999 Woods resigns as Dean (December 3); Gwyn Richards appointed Interim Dean

Appendix 2: Faculty of the Department and School of Music, 1910–1999

The following list is based on a similar one compiled in 1995 by Catherine Smith and David Cartledge for display in the School's Simon Center; I have supplemented and corrected their list from a variety of sources. I have aspired to include, first, all those individuals who have held non-visiting positions—full- or part-time, tenured, tenure-track, or limited term—at the rank of Tutor or above, and, second, visiting faculty who taught at the School for at least one full academic year (that is, fall and winter semesters). I have not included members of the non-teaching staff.

Undoubtedly I have missed some of the visiting faculty for the period since 1981: at that juncture, the School's Bulletin, whose faculty rosters constitute the main source for my list as for that of Smith and Cartledge, began to be published only biennially. (For the period 1981–94, moreover, it appears to have been the practice to omit from the Bulletin's rosters all visitors other than a handful of long-term ones.) A few regular appointees may also have been missed, namely, any who were appointed in even-numbered years since 1982 and stayed only one year (and thus do not appear in a Bulletin), and whose names happen not to occur in any of my other sources.

"(v)" appended to a name indicates that the individual never held anything other than a visiting appointment at the School. It should be noted, though, that some visiting appointments—for example, that of Daniel Guilet, the original violinist of the Beaux Arts Trio—were renewed for a number of years.

A

Abbenes, Arie
Abeles, Harold
Adam, William
Adams, Jane Johnson Burroughs
Adelstein, Bernard
Aiken, David
Allen, Ross
Amato, Bruno
Anderson, Edwin
Anderson, Linda
Antoine, Josephine
Apel, Willi
Appelman, D. Ralph
Arad, Atar
Aronoff, Kenny
Arroyo, Martina
Arvin, Gary
Auer, Edward
Aufdemberge, Clarence

B

Bailey, Darrell
Bain, Wilfred C.
Baker, Claude
Baker, David
Baker, Edwin
Baldner, Thomas
Baldwin, Frederick S., Jr.
Baldwin, Marcia
Balkwill, Bryan
Barlow, Klara
Bates, Earl
Battersby, Edmund
Battista, Joseph
Bauer, Raymond
Bayless, Eugene
Beach, Phillip
Bell, William
Belnap, Michael
Bennett, Alan
Beriozoff, Nicolas (v)
Berman, Boris (v)
Béroff, Michel
Beversdorf, S. Thomas
Binkley, Thomas
Birge, Edward Bailey
Birmingham, Hugh, Jr.
Biss, Paul
Bitetti, Ernesto
Black, Archie
Blanton, Walter
Block, Michel
Bloom, Myron
Boepple, Hans
Bolet, Jorge
Bonnefoux, Jean-Pierre
Boszorményi-Nagy, Béla
Bowers, Susan
Bowles, Kenneth
Bowles, Michael (v)
Brancart, Evelyne
Bransby, Bruce
Brenner, Brenda
Bricht, Walter
Bristow, Alice
Brown, A. Peter
Brown, Keith
Brown, Malcolm
Brown, Samuel E., Jr.
Brumfiel, W. Howard
Buelow, George
Burkholder, J. Peter
Burns, Joseph (v)

Burns, Samuel T.
Burns, Stephen
Burrows, Elmar
Busch, Carolyn
Busch, Hans
Buswell, James O., IV

C

Calder, George
Campbell, Charles Diven
Campbell, James
Carlyss, Gerald
Cassel, Walter
Caswell, Austin
Cavallo-Gulli, Enrica
Cesbron, Jacques
Cesbron, Virginia
Christ, William
Chuat, Iseut
Civil, Alan
Clark, Mark Ross
Clayton, Kathryn
Clayton, Richard
Cockrell, Virginia Moore
Coker, Jerry
Colón, Emilio
Contino, Fiora
Cord, Edmund
Cordero, Roque
Corra, Arthur
Covington, Kate
Cowart, Robert (v)
Cramer, Bomar
Cramer, Ray
Crane, Dean (v)
Cristini, C. Mario
Cuccaro, Costanza
Cuyler, Louise (v)

D

Daggit, George
Dahl, Ole Steffen
d'Angelo, Gianna
Daniel, Nicholas
Daniel, Ralph
Davidson, Louis
Davies, Dudley
Davis, Agnes
Davy, Gloria
Dawson, David
Dawson, Janna
Dean, Allan
de Anguera, Marguerite
Deis, Jean
deLerma, Dominique-René
DeLone, Richard Pierre
Denk, Jeremy
de Pasquale, Joseph
deVeritch, Alan
Dimitrov, Antonin
Dirié, Gerardo
Dolin, Anton
Doren, Richard
Doty, Gerald
Dubinsky, Luba Edlina
Dubinsky, Rostislav
Dudley, Ray
Duffin, Gerard
Duke, Milton
Duncan, Richard (v)
Dunn, Thomas
Dzubay, David

E

Eagle, Peter
Eaton, John
Eban, Eli
Ebbs, Frederick
Ebert-Buchheim, Edward
Edgerton, Robert
Effron, David
Eisner, Bruno
Ekstrom, E. Ross
Elliott, Paul
Elliott, William
Elvira, Pablo, Jr.
Elworthy, Robert
England, Wilber
Erb, Donald
Erdelyi, Csaba
Erikson, Margaret Sisson
Esposito, Giovanni

Evans, Lucile
Evans, Robert

F

Farbman, Edith
Farbman, Harry
Farkas, Philip
Farrell, Eileen
Felberg, Leonard
Fenske, David
Fiorillo, Marcia
Fleming-May, Lissa
Flower, Jack (v)
Forbes, Vernon
Fosha, Leon
Foster, Bronja
Foster, Sidney
Fox, Frederick
Freund, Donald
Fried, Miriam
Fuerstner, Carl
Fuks, Mauricio
Fulcher, Jane
Fuleihan, Anis
Fuller, Ramon

G

Gaber, George
Gallagher, Edward
Gass, Glenn
Gavers, Mattlyn
Geiger, John
Gelvin, Miriam
Gersten, Frederick
Gersten, Joan
Gilchrist, Doris
Gilfoy, Jack (v)
Gillespie, Wendy
Gingold, Josef
Glidden, Robert
Goetze, Mary
Gordon, Michael
Gordon, Nathan
Gorham, Charles
Gottwald, John
Graef, Richard
Graf, Hans (v)
Green, Barry (v)
Green, Vivien Vincent
Gregory, Ronald
Grinstead, Montana
Grist, Reri
Grodner, Murray
Grossi, Pietro (v)
Grusak, Mary
Guilet, Daniel (v)
Gulick, Henry
Gulli, Franco

H

Hall, Marion
Hammer, Stephen (v)
Hancock, Jory
Haney, Lewis Van
Harbison, Patrick
Harler, Alan
Harrington, Jan
Harris, Roy
Harshaw, Margaret
Hart, Mary Ann
Hartman, Scott
Hass, Jeffrey
Hasty, D. Stanley
Hatfield, Michael
Hatten, Robert
Havranek, Patricia
Havranek, Roger
Hawkins, John
Heiden, Bernhard
Heifetz, Benar
Herber, Mildred
Herford, Julius
Hermann, Joseph
Herz, Gerhard
Higgins, C. David
Hillier, Paul
Hillis, Margaret
Hindsley, Mark
Hoeltzel, Michael (v)
Hoffer, Charles
Hoffman, Ernst

Hoffman, Gary
Hoffzimmer, Ernest
Hokanson, Leonard
Holley, Cecil W., Jr.
Hollinder, Andrew (v)
Holloway, Clyde
Horlacher, Gretchen
Horner, Jerry (v)
Hornibrook, W. Wallace
Houdeshel, Harry F., Jr.
Houser, W. Roy
Howe, E. Dudley
Howell, John
Hugoboom, R. Wayne
Hunkins, Sterling
Hurst, Lawrence
Husch, Gerhard (v)
Huxol, Harry
Hyde, Ora

I

Ik-Hwan Bae
Ilmer, Irving (v)
Isaacson, Eric
Izquierdo, Juan Pablo

J

Jackson, Wayne
Jacobson, George
Janzer, Eva Czako
Janzer, Georges
Jensen, John (v)
Jensen, Wilma
Jeter, John
Johnson, Hugh B., Jr.
Johnson, Richard
Jones, Ted
Jorgensen, Estelle
Josse, Marcel (v)
Juvelier, A. Theodore

K

Kallaur, Barbara
Karnes, Leon
Kashkashian, Kim
Kaskas, Anna
Kastens, L. Kevin
Kaufmann, Freda
Kaufmann, Walter
Kearney, Leslie
Keen, Charles
Keiser, Marilyn
Keller, Homer
Kelley, Dorothy
Kent, Charles
Kielian-Gilbert, Marianne
Kiesgen, Paul
King, James
Kingsbury, C. Lawrence
Kirkpatrick, William C., Jr.
Kirkwood, Grace
Kisler, Marian Hanson Stone
Klein, Leonard, Jr.
Kliewer, Vernon
Klotman, Robert
Klug, Howard
Kneeburg, Don
Kniaz, Abe
Knoll, Richard
Kogan, Pavel (v)
Koning, Leendert (v)
Koogler, William
Kowalski, Henryk
Kozma, Tibor
Krajewska, Marian
Kriza, John
Krueger, George
Kubiak, Teresa
Kullman, Charles
Kummer, Keith
Kunoff, Karla
Kuttner, Michael

L

LaPlante, Rita
Lazan, Albert
Lazarus, Roy
Legêne, Eva
Lenthe, Carl
Lifschey, Marc
Liotta, Vincent
Lipton, Martha

List, George
Lloyd, Peter
Locke, Evelyn Saxton
Long, Newell
Lowe, Melissa
Lucas, James
Lucas, Michael
Luciano, Lynn
Ludwig, Gunther
Lukas, Kathryn

M

McBride, Patricia
MacClintock, Carol Cook
McCraw, Michael (v)
McDonald, James
McDonald, John
McDonald, Susann
McGinnis, Robert
McGough, Edward
McGreer, Dennis
MacInnes, James
Mack, Harold
MacWatters, Virginia
Madison, Thurber
Magee, Jeffrey
Magg, Fritz
Magg, Natasha
Manski, Dorothee
Mannion, Elizabeth
Marsh, Ozan
Marsh, Peter
Martino, Daniel
Masselos, William
Mathiesen, Thomas
Matthen, Paul
Mazzocca, Julio
Melamed, Daniel
Melville, Kenneth
Merker, Ethel
Merrill, B. Winfred
Merrill, Winifred
Miedema, Harry (v)
Milanov, Zinka
Miller, Eleanor Gough
Montané, Carlos
Montecino, Alfonso
Moore, Aubrey
Moore, Dale
Mordenti, Daniel
Mosemiller, Ruby Lane
Moses, Don
Mueller, Herbert
Munier, Leon, Jr.

N

Nagosky, John
Naoumoff, Émile
Neriki, Shigeo
Nettl, Gertrud
Nettl, Paul
Neumann, Frederick (v)
Neumeyer, David
Newman, Anthony
Noble, Timothy
Noblitt, Thomas
Nolting, Betty Ferris
Nomikos, Andreas
Nye, Douglas

O

O'Brien, Eugene
O'Hearn, Robert
Ogdon, John
Orrego-Salas, Juan
Ossi, Massimo
Oukhtomsky, Wladimir

P

Pagels, Jurgen
Pal, Tridib (v)
Palla, Joseph (v)
Palló, Imre
Palmer, Thomas
Parks, Mildred
Paskevska, Anna
Peck, Leslie
Pellerite, James
Pemberton, Roger Max
Penhorwood, Edwin
Perantoni, Daniel
Perlemuter, Vlado

Perry, Marvin (v)
Phan, Phuc Q.
Phelps, Mark
Philips, Marvin
Phillips, Harvey
Phillips, Leonard
Phillips, Norman
Pickett, David
Porco, Robert
Portnoy, Bernard
Potter, Gary
Pratt, Stephen
Pressler, Menahem
Primrose, William
Prout, Kathreen Reime
Pryor, Naomi Ruth
Ptaszyńska, Marta

R

Ragatz, Oswald
Rampaso, Luciano
Rayfield, Robert
Rechtman, Mordechai
Reed, Gilbert
Rehg, Milton
Rehm, John
Reisberg, Horace
Reyes, Alberto
Reynolds, Verne
Rezits, Joseph
Ribla, Gertrude (v)
Ricci, Ruggiero
Richards, Doris
Richards, Gwyn
Ritchie, Stanley
Rivera, Benito
Roach, George
Robert, Walter
Robertello, Thomas
Roberts, William (v)
Rodman, Fontaine
Roesner, Edward (v)
Rogers, Georgia
Rolf, Marie
Rommel, John
Rosenberg, Sidney
Rosenberg, Sylvia
Ross, Allan
Ross, George
Ross, William
Rossi, Urico
Rossi-Lemeni, Nicola
Röthlisberger, Max
Rothmuller, Marko
Rousseau, Eugene
Rowell, Lewis
Royce, Anya
Rudnytsky, Roman
Russell, Colin
Russell, Walter
Russell, William

S

Sabline, Oleg
Sadlo, Milos (v)
St. Leger, Frank
Samuelsen, Roy
Sanders, Robert L.
Sandström, Sven-David
Sankey, Stuart
Savridi, Polyna
Scammon, Vera
Schantz, Ellen
Schellschmidt, Adolph
Schillin, Scott
Schleuter, Stanley
Schmidt, Charles
Schneck, Joan
Scholz, Gottfried (v)
Schumacher, William
Schuman, Henry (v)
Schuster, Earl
Schwartzkopf, Michael
Scott, James
Sears, William
Sebok, Gyorgy
Seidel, Herbert (v)
Selfridge, Cecil
Seraphinoff, Richard
Shadley, Maurice
Shallenberg, F. Robert
Shapiro, Laurence
Sharrow, Leonard
Shaver, Stephen
Shaw, Karen
Shealy, Joyce Lowrie (v)

Shkolnikova, Nelli
Shriner, C. William
Simon, Abbey
Sinor, Eugenia
Sirucek, Jerry
Skernick, Abraham
Skjerne, Axel
Skjerne, Frances
Skoggard, Carl (v)
Skolovsky, Zadel
Skoog, James
Smith, Carol
Smith, Henry Charles
Smith, Larry
Snapp, Kenneth (v)
Snyder, Richard
Snygg, Fran
Sollberger, Harvey
Sollors, Daniel
Solomon, Izler (v)
Spada, Pietro
Sparks, Thomas
Sparrow, Patricia
Spencer, Stacia
Spera, Dominic
Spezialé, Marie
Stahl, Edwin
Starker, Janos
Starkey, Evelyn Saxton
Stedman, W. Preston
Steele, Nancy
Stevens, Robert
Stewart, Lila
Stewart, M. Dee
Stewart, Val
Stoll, Robert
Stotter, Douglas
Stowell, Richard
Strong, Douglas
Stubbs, Darrel
Svetlova, Marina
Swager, Brian
Szmyt, Elzbieta

T

Takahashi, Yuji
Tangeman, Nell
Tangeman, Robert
Taylor, Karen
Taylor, Myron
Taylor, Thomas
Téllez, Carmen
Teraspulsky, Leopold
Terry, Kenton (v)
Thomson, William
Tischler, Hans
Tocco, James
Tong Il Han
Tozzi, Giorgio
Tsutsumi, Tsuyoshi
Tucci, Gabriella
Turkovic, Milan
Turrentine, Logan

U

Umeyama, Shuichi
Upper, Henry

V

Vacano, Wolfgang
Van Buskirk, Carl
Vanderbeke, Patricia
Vaszonyi, Balint
Vené, Ruggero (v)
Verdy, Violette
Vincent, Margaret
Vitale, Vincenzo
Vlassenko, Lev

W

Walker, Kim
Walsh, Daniel
Walsh, Thomas
Warner, Archibald
Waterhouse, William (v)
Watson, Jack
Watts, Jonathan
Webb, Charles H., Jr.
Wee, A. DeWayne
Weinberg, Anton
Weiser, Adolph
Weisz, Robert
Wennerstrom, Mary

Wesner-Hoehn, Beverly
West, Walter
Whetstine, James
White, Allen
White, Chappell
White, John R.
White, Margaret Buehler
Whittenberg, John
Will, Roy
Williams, Camilla
Wilson, George
Wincenc, Carol
Wing, Charles
Winold, C. Allen
Winold, Helga
Wise, Patricia
Wittlich, Gary
Wolfes, Helmuth
Wood, Linda
Wood, Richard
Wood, Thomas
Woodbury, Max
Woodley, David
Woods, David G.
Wright, Elisabeth
Wronski, Tadeusz
Wustman, John (v)

X

Xenakis, Iannis

Y

Yank, Susan
Yaron, Yuval
Young, Christopher

Z

Zai, Sulaiman
Zathureczky, Ede
Zeani, Virginia
Ziegler, Dorothy
Zoon, Jacques
Zorn, Marie
Zumbro, Nicholas
Zweig, Mimi
Zweygberg, Lennart von

Appendix 3: Sources

This appendix is divided into two parts. Section I comprises annotated lists of the major published and unpublished sources for the history of the School. Section II—the Commentary—gives the sources of all quotations in my text (other than those whose source is given in the text itself) and of all claims of fact that might, as it seems to me, prompt either curiosity or dubiety (and for which the basis is not made clear in the text itself).

I. Sources for the History of the School

Published Sources

Bain, Wilfred C. *Indiana University School of Music: The Bain Regime, 1947–1973.* Privately published, 1980. Bain's first annalistic tome (1,206 double-spaced typescript pages) on the School is clumsily written and poorly edited. It is also far from disinterested, representing as it does his attempt to attain control over the history of the School after he had relinquished control of the institution itself. But it is invaluable both as an account of his views and as a revelation of his mentality. It also contains a wealth of information about people and events in the School—though, as with Clark's *History* (below), everything it says needs to be checked against another source. There are copies in the Music Library and the University Archives.

———. *Indiana University Opera Theater 1948–1973*. Privately published, 1990(?). Bain's second tome (1,434 pages), surveying the 145 productions of the Opera Theater in the twenty-six years of his deanship, plus the first seven productions of Charles Webb's deanship. A brief essay about each production includes facts, opinions, and a final evaluation in the form of a letter grade! An especially valuable feature of the work is its photocopies of the programs of the productions and its extensive reproductions, by typescript or photocopy, of reviews. Copies in the Music Library.

Clark, Thomas D. *Indiana University: Midwestern Pioneer.* 4 vols. Bloomington and London: Indiana UP, 1970–77. Clark surveys again the territory earlier covered by Woodburn and Myers (below) and extends the story to 1968. His volumes are comprehensive and readable, but unfortunately they are riddled with errors. Wherever possible, I have checked his claims by reference to other sources; in the Commentary, he is cited only where I have been unable to find another source for a quotation or factual claim included in his work.

Clemens, James W. B. *An Historical Study of the Philosophies of Indiana University School of Music Administrators from 1910 to 1973*. Master of Music Education thesis, Indiana University, 1994. Clemens's thesis is invaluable not only for its interpretations, which are solidly based in his detailed knowledge of archival materials, but also for his extensive bibliography of published and unpublished sources and the transcripts of two interviews—with Herman B Wells and Newell Long—that are appended to the body of the thesis. Clemens conducted these thorough interviews at a time (April 1992) when both men were much better able to speak about the School than they were when I interviewed them in, respectively, 1996 and 1995. The interviews contain valuable information that would have otherwise been irretrievably lost, and students of the history of the School are deeply in Clemens's debt for them.

Collection of news clippings 1945–46. In 1945, someone undertook a scrapbook of newspaper clippings pertaining to the School during the first semester of the 1945–46 academic year. Fifty years later this collection was unearthed by Charles Webb, who passed it to me. (I have deposited it in the University Archives.)

Collins, Dorothy C., and Cecil K. Byrd. *Indiana University: A Pictorial History*. Bloomington and Indianapolis: Indiana UP, 1992. In addition to its many photographs, this splendid book includes a concise narrative of the history of the University.

Indiana Daily Student. The student newspaper, known variously in its early history as *The Indiana Student, The Student,* and *The Daily Student,* acquired its current name in 1914. (In 1920–21, an additional issue—*The Indiana Weekly Student*—was also published.) The most complete collection is on microfilm in the University Library.

Indiana University School of Music: Directory of Endowed Funds and Annual Scholarships. Bloomington: Office of the Dean, School of Music, updated annually. This is a valuable reference work, which includes photographs and brief biographies of the many faculty members, students, and patrons of the School whose names have been enshrined in endowments.

Indiana University Alumni Quarterly. Published 1914–38; succeeded by the *Indiana Alumni Magazine.* There is a collection in the University Archives.

Indiana University Catalogues. There is a collection in the University Archives. From 1923, the Bulletin of the School of Music was printed separately.

Lahrman, Delores M., and Delbert C. Miller. *The History of Mitchell Hall, 1885–1986.* Bloomington: Indiana University Archives, 1987(?). This is an indispensable account—replete with photographs, floor plans, and reproductions of various published articles—of the extremely modest building that housed Music from 1906 to 1937.

Music Alumni Notes. Established in 1973 and published on a semiannual basis (though not entirely reliably) ever since, these bulletins are valuable for their accounts of events in the School; notable achievements of faculty, students, and alumni; listings (with brief vitae) of new faculty; and occasional obituaries and accounts of retirements. There is a collection in the School's Office of Communications, which is, however, missing a few issues.

Myers, Burton Dorr, M.D. *History of Indiana University.* Vol. II: 1902–37: *The Bryan Administration.* Bloomington: Indiana University, 1952. This is an excellent, reliable history of the era of President William Lowe Bryan. Chapter 19 (pp. 226–43) treats music at the University; it begins with Dean Merrill's survey of the nineteenth-century phase of the subject. The volume is a companion to James Albert Woodburn's *History of Indiana University,* Vol. I: 1820–1902 (Bloomington: Indiana University, 1940).

Stempel, Guido Hermann. "In Memoriam: Charles Diven Campbell." *Indiana University Alumni Quarterly,* 6 (1919), 227–32. The obituary contains much detail about the life, work, and character of the first Head of Music.

———. "Music at Indiana University." *Indiana University Alumni Quarterly,* 24 (1937), 109–19. A valuable survey of all phases of musical activity in Bloomington in the years 1897–1937.

Wells, Herman B. *Being Lucky: Reminiscences and Reflections.* Bloomington: Indiana UP, 1980. Wells's engaging autobiography includes, in addition to much information about his administrative philosophy and style, information about his lifelong involvement with music.

Unpublished Sources

University Archives: The Archives include a rich and extensive variety of materials (all open to the public) pertaining to the history of the School. These may be classified as follows:

Proceedings of the Indiana University Board of Trustees: The proceedings include numerous passages pertaining to such matters as budget requests, appointments, and salaries.

Annual Reports of the Deans: For the Campbell and Merrill eras, these are found in the bound volumes of the President's Reports. For the subsequent era, the reports are filed separately.

Correspondence: The Archives house extensive correspondence involving faculty members of the School (especially the Deans). Correspondence to or from the President of the University and members of his staff is in the President's Files.

Faculty vitae: There is an extensive collection of one-page vitae for retired or deceased faculty members of the University.

Faculty files: There are individual files for a number of faculty members; these include especially press clippings.

Photographs: There are extensive files of photographs pertaining to the School: its physical facilities, its faculty members, and its musical performances.

Miscellaneous materials: In addition to correspondence with members of the School, the President's Files include a variety of other materials pertaining to it. The Archives also include a number of files labeled "Music, School of" (most of them with some subtitle), which contain a wide range of materials, especially printed materials such as press reports on School events.

School of Music Archive: The School's own archive houses the files of all former faculty members. (These are the personnel files that, for faculty members still active in the School, reside in the Dean's Office.) There is a plethora of interesting materials in these files, ranging from correspondence to press clippings to salary data, but the archive is not open to the public.

School of Music Office of Publicity files: This office houses extensive files on individual faculty members and notable students, on the School's buildings, on its musical presentations (especially opera productions), and on press coverage of the School. The files are not open to the public, but requests for access are entertained.

Lilly Library: There are four valuable interviews pertaining to the School in the collection of the Oral History Research Project housed in the Lilly Library (the University's rare books library): of Bain (two interviews: John Wolford; Jean Freedman), Ross Allen (Thomas Clark), and Winifred Merrill (Thomas Clark).

Minutes: Minutes of School faculty meetings dating back to 1921—and, in the Bain and Webb eras, including minutes of meetings of the Advisory Council, the Academic Council, and the School of Music Council—are stored in the Music Library.

"A History of Indiana University School of Music, July, 1973–June, 1976": This is a brief (17 typescript pages) annalistic history of the first three years of the Webb regime. Compiled by the then Director of Publicity, Carol Greene, it includes, as appendixes, enrollment statistics, lists of faculty and administrative officers, vitae of new appointees, and faculty obituaries for the period; and it is accompanied by an index of musical programs presented in the same years. The history was to have been continued on an annual basis, but in fact this is the only installment. It was passed to me by Webb; I have deposited it in the University Archives.

Bound programs: The Music Library includes bound volumes of programs of School musical events dating back to the Merrill era.

Naming Day Ceremony, B. Winfred Merrill Hall: The speeches (including significant ones by Herman Wells and Newell Long) and musical selections of this occasion (10/2/89) are available on audio cassette through the University's Instructional Support Services.

Indiana University Photographic Services: The collections in this office include a series of albums of photographs pertaining to the School.

Materials collected for the present work: I have relied heavily on a series of interviews I conducted with active and retired faculty members (and with Herman Wells and Dorothy Collins) in the period 1995 through 1997. I will eventually deposit the tapes of these interviews, together with at least partial transcriptions of them, in the University Archives, together with certain materials collected for my book that are not otherwise available to the public.

II. Commentary

Abbreviations

AC Minutes of the School of Music's Advisory Council (1947–63) or Academic Council (1961–78)

AQ *Indiana University Alumni Quarterly*

BL Wells, *Being Lucky*

C Clark, *Indiana University: Midwestern Pioneer*

Cl Clemens, *An Historical Study of the Philosophies of Indiana University School of Music Administrators*

Cli Collection of news clippings 1945–46

Dir *Indiana University School of Music: Directory of Endowed Funds and Annual Scholarships*

F Minutes of faculty meetings

H-T The Bloomington newspaper first called the *Herald-Telephone* and subsequently the *Herald-Times*

IDS *Indiana Daily Student*

M Myers, *History of Indiana University: The Bryan Administration*

MAN *Music Alumni Notes*

Mit Lahrman and Miller, *The History of Mitchell Hall*

OT Bain, *Indiana University Opera Theater*

R Bain, *Indiana University School of Music: The Bain Regime*

SMA School of Music Archive

SMC Minutes of the School of Music Council
UA University Archives
Wo John Wolford interview with Bain

N.B.: With the exception of a few especially notable items (such as the *New Yorker* profiles of Josef Gingold and Harvey Phillips), and a few facts that may strain credibility, the following commentary does not include the sources of the biographical information I give about faculty members of the School. I have gathered this information primarily from the archival collections listed above, from *Music Alumni Notes,* and from the standard biographical dictionaries of musicians.

Prelude

page 1: The general consent of the profession as to the School's preeminence has its primary attestation in the five survey-based national rankings, either of music schools overall or of particular programs within them, published in the period 1974–97. For these, see the index, s.v. "national rankings." From the late 1960s until recently the School had an undisputed claim to the title of the world's largest music school. Recent enrollment has been in the range 1,600–1,800. But the Berklee College of Music in Boston (focused on jazz, rock, film music, music technology, and the music business) now boasts some 3,000 students, and there are at least two Japanese music schools larger than Indiana's. (The Musashino Academy of Music in Tokyo currently has about 4,000 students.)

1–2: Statistics on the Musical Arts Center and the Simon Center derive from press releases and publicity brochures issued in conjunction with their dedications. Copies are in UA. Details about library holdings are from the library's 1995–96 annual report.

4: Gaines's *The Campus as a Work of Art*: New York: Praeger, 1991.

Beginnings

6: "The Empire of Beethoven": *AQ* 3 (1916), 360. "Expectation . . . on tiptoe": *The New Purchase or, Seven and a Half Years in the Far West,* ed. James Albert Woodburn (Princeton: Princeton UP, 1916), p. 260.

Merrill's survey: M 226–32.

7: "The one sour, discordant note": M 233.

The Glee Club's 1893 Indianapolis excursion is reported in *Indiana Student,* bound volume for 1913, p. 23 (UA). Other information in this and the following paragraph is from C 1.299, 276, 2.58.

8: "Obsessed with the subject": C 2.60–61. "It has been recognized": quoted in C 2.62, which gives the date only as "1907."

9: "By many teachers": *Changes Needed in American Secondary Education,* Publications of the General Education Board, Occasional Papers, No. 2 (New York: General Education Board, 1916), p. 12.

For brief overviews of musical education in Europe and America, see the *New Grove Dictionary of Music and Musicians* ("Education in music") and *The Harvard Dictionary of Music* ("Music Education in the United States").

10: "It is extremely difficult": 11/14/04.

10–11: On Bloomington's lack of civilized amenities: C 2.13, 15, 36; on unvaccinated students, 2.30; on the Governor's threat, 2.31; on the "prehistoric" trains, 2.39–40.

11: Stempel surveys visiting artists in "Music at Indiana University," *AQ* 24 (1937), 109–11.

On Ebert-Buchheim's biography and his work at Indiana: M 233–35, and Stempel, pp. 111–12.

12–13: "We have had": 6/17/10. For Campbell's biography, see especially Stempel's obituary of him, *AQ* 6 (1919), 227–32. "A music fund": *IDS* 4/30/07. Campbell's 1909 letter to Bryan outlining proposed courses in music history and musical form is dated 9/12/09; it is in a UA file labeled "Music, School of: History."

14–15: Campbell's reports to Bryan are in UA; along with other information, these include the enrollment statistics I quote. Information about courses and Assistants in the Campbell years derives from the University Catalogues.

15–16: On Mitchell Hall, see especially *Mit.* "A poor little frame": *Indiana Student,* Vol. 12, No. 5 (2/1886), 114–15.

17: On the Friday Musicale, see *Dir* ("Friday Musicale Scholarship").

"Focal center of activity": "Music at IU," p. 231.

17–18: Programs for the 1916 orchestral concert and for the "Pageant of Bloomington and Indiana University" (and the *Musical America* review of the latter) turned up, among a collection of printed items connected in one way or another with Campbell, in the Dean's Office; I have deposited these materials in UA.

20: "The present financial condition": 7/2/15.

22: On Campbell's death and obsequies, see Stempel's obituary (which includes the memorial resolution), and the collection of Campbell-era items referred to above, which includes several newspaper clippings on these matters.

The Merrill Years

23–24: On Merrill's biography and character: M 238; Clark's interview with Merrill's daughter, Winifred, in the Oral History Research Project (Lilly Library); Clemens's interview with Newell Long (Cl 119–32); Long's remarks on Merrill at the Naming Day Ceremony (above, list of unpublished sources). On average salaries of full professors and department heads: C 2.245.

24: On Bloomington around the time of Merrill's arrival, see especially Forest M. "Pop" Hall, ed., *Historic Treasures: True Tales of Deeds with Interesting Data in the Life of Bloomington, Indiana . . .* (Indianapolis: Ye Olde Genealogie Shoppe, 1979; originally published 1922). Mrs. Hazel's odyssey: *Bloomington Evening World* 3/31/19.

24–25: Music faculty in Merrill's first years: the University Catalogues and Merrill's first report to Bryan (10/19).

25: On Merrill and Mitchell Hall, see Winifred Merrill Warren, "Home at Last," *Indiana Alumni Magazine* 49 (1987), 15–17. *IDS* on Assembly Hall: 12/10/21.

25–26: Merrill on the music business: *IDS* 12/21/26.

26–27: Bryan to Merrill reporting approval of two additional professorships: 3/23/20. Bryan's correspondence with Birge leading up to the latter's appointment is in the President's Files.

27: "In view of the fact": 2/26/21.

Mildred Blake wrote out her reminiscences for me in June 1997.

28–29: Details about course offerings and the curricula of the various degree and certificate programs come from the annual School of Music Bulletins; so also data about student numbers, and about the faculty complement. M 239 records the fact that the first graduating class consisted of two students. There is an obituary of Gertrude V. Schaupp in *MAN* 14.1.5. Merrill noted that there were several hundred students taking music as an elective in a report to Bryan 11/22/23.

29: My description of the University in the 1920s draws on *BL* 31.

30–31: "We saw jazz": *Sometimes I Wonder* (New York: Farrar, Straus and Giroux), p. 75; "Our girls": p. 80.

31: My information about Long as band member and bandleader comes from my interview with the Longs.

"Contemplating bringing an orchestra": M 230. Mitchell Hall radio broadcasts of the Chicago Opera: C 2.287.

31–32: Procedures for selecting visiting artists: F 11/14/23, 2/26/24, 2/23/26. The lists of artists come from the School of Music Bulletins.

32: The programs for the centennial Ceremonial and Pageant, together with an account of the former in the *Weekly Student* for 1/26/20, are included in the collection of Campbell-era items referred to above.

32–33: My account of the School's early orchestra is based on Long's Naming Day remarks; the account of Merrill's versatility as a teacher comes from Long's interview with Clemens, Cl 119. "A delightful person": Long's Naming Day remarks; "a personality": Wells's speech on the same occasion.

33: According to the minutes of faculty meetings, the first cafeteria convivium was held on 2/26/24.

33–34: Merrill's 1925 letter criticizing Skjerne and Birge is found only in a draft copy among Merrill's papers (UA). But an apparent allusion to the letter in one Merrill wrote to Bryan on 7/1/32 suggests that it was sent. All the letters and memoranda discussed in the following pages are in the President's Files.

35: Mary Birge as a power in the Friday Musicale: Bryan to her, 8/11/23. "From the winter": "Music at IU," p. 115. On the tradition of the *Messiah* at IU, under Birge and after his retirement: *IDS* 12/13/45 (Cli). Bryan to Birge expressing his appreciation: 12/12/32.

35–36: My information on Birge as a chamber player comes from Mildred Blake. Eleanor Long on the social rivalry between the Merrills and the Birges: my interview with the Longs.

36: "Bothered his mind": Cl 122. Statistics on (January) 1938 enrollment are from the 1938–39 Bulletin; those on graduates are from F 5/17/38.

37: On highlights of Winifred's performance career: *IDS* 12/8/45 (Cli). See also her obituary, *MAN* 17.2.14. It was Eleanor Long who told me that the Birges' under-appreciation of Winifred was one of the Merrills' grievances with them. "Had less acclaim": Cl 120.

37–38: Sources for Hoffzimmer's career include *Dir* and *IDS* 1/17/46 (Cli). The correspondence discussed here, from May 1932, is in the President's Files.

38–40: "I have been for a long time": 6/27/32. Merrill's reply: 7/1.

40–42: The letters and memoranda stemming from the Grinstead brouhaha are in the President's Files; they span the period 5/25/36 through 7/20/36.

43: "Ornery streak": Cl 119; "some feuds": Cl 119–20; "pretty much handled everything": Cl 120.

44: "Very popular": Cl 128.

45: Motion creating "Music Week": F 1/19/26; motion encouraging recital attendance: 10/27/36; "expected in their own interest": 10/27/36; motion requiring attendance at Music Series events: 6/3/28.

45–46: "The first Invasion": 8/11/29; there is more on the program in M 241 and Cl 125–26.

46: My information about the various outreach programs for high school students derives from M 241 and the announcements in the School of Music Bulletins. Financial failure of the alumni newsletter: F 3/29/38.

Impossibility of finding an organ for Mrs. Chew: F 12/5/27. "The glaring bar": 1939–40 annual report.

47: "Animals got underneath": Cl 126.

48: "It was unanimously decided": F 12/21/25; rescinded 2/23/26.

Myers on hopes for a new building: M 240–41. Merrill's letter endorsing the proposal to move the School to the proposed university auditorium: 1/26/33 (to John C. Bollenbacher); declining quarters in Residence Hall: 1/8/32 (to Bryan). Both letters are in the President's Files.

49: The petition protesting the siting of the new building was received in the President's Office on 10/23/35.

One source for the (apocryphal?) story of Daggett's pique is Wells's Naming Day speech.

50: Merrill's 1937 budget submission is summarized in F 4/20/37; the disappointing result is reported in F 6/1/37.

51–52: Merrill's expanded statement on the School's purpose appeared in the 1938–39 Bulletin.

52–53: Wells's view that Bryan stayed on so long because he couldn't afford to retire: my interview with him.

53: Long on Merrill's disinclination to retire: Cl 127. The 1937–38 enrollment statistics are from the 1938–39 Bulletin.

53–54: Merrill's speech at the dedication of the Music Building is printed in *AQ* 24 (1937), 305–306.

The Sanders Years

96–97: Details of Wells's early life: opening chapters of *BL,* and the UA vita.

97–98: Bryan's retirement and Wells's appointment to replace him: *BL* 89–90. "A fluid and dynamic period": *BL* 95.

98: Influence on Indiana of the Northwestern self-study: C 2.364–67.

98–99: "The quality of the faculty": *BL* 101–102. "First in their home situations": *BL* 101; "besides numerous conferences": *BL* 102.

99: "For a semester or year": *BL* 103.

Consulting Hanson and Lutton: Cl 148. Sanders's dossier, with a brief vita and excerpts from letters of recommendation, is in the President's Files (received 12/21/37).

99–100: Wells's method for choosing between Sanders and Harris: Long (Cl 132). "A very attractive wife": Wells's interview with me. Sanders as the unanimous choice: Long (Cl 132); Wells (to Sanders, 7/28/38).

100: "A rather unconventional appointment": Cl 148.

Sanders's enthusiasm for Burns: Wells to Burns, 8/5/38.

100–101: Sanders's request to replace Geiger with two people: 8/15/38. "Trait in his personality": Sanders to Wells, 9/7/38.

102: Merrill on NASM: F 10/26 and 11/16/37; the question of membership raised again under Sanders: F 9/26/38.

102–103: Long on Sanders as a liberal: Cl 138; "give everybody a chance": Cl 133.

103: Grinstead's suggestion: F 5/8/39. "We had a big table": Cl 146.

104: List of degree candidates: F 5/22/39. "In hearty accord": Wells to Sanders 10/29/38.

105: "These had never been granted": F 10/10/38. Dropping the Ph.D.: F 10/10 and 10/31/38. Distinguishing the M.M. from the M.A.: F 12/19/38, 1/14/46.

Discussion of applied-music requirements: F 11/28/38 and 2/6/39. New five-year degree program: F 12/5/38 and 3/7/39.

106: Loss of credit as penalty for skipping recitals: F 11/24/41; 1942–43 Bulletin.

Statistics on fees and operating expenses: F 3/17/41.

107: Discussion of fees: F 3/28 and 5/22/39.

School's fees unusually high: F 4/10/39. "Forced by financial stringency": 1/9/39. Long on stratified fees: Cl 143.

107–108: Sanders on NASM result: telegram to Wells, 12/28/38; report to faculty, F 1/9/39. Indiana alumni at Eastman: F 5/7/45. "They can't read anything": F 9/29/42. Cello scholarship: F 5/26/41.

108: Eastman's acceptance rate: based on remarks of the NASM examiner, F 4/29/40.

Hoffzimmer-Burns exchange: F 12/19/40.

108–109: Failure to enroll music contest winners: F 9/22, 10/7/41, 5/12/42.

109: Merrill raises specter of a School of Fine Arts: F 5/24/38. Proposed by Self-Survey Committee: report 265 (UA); adds Home Economics: F 12/4/39.

110: Opposition to creation of Junior and Senior Divisions: F 11/6/39. Trustees decree the reorganization: C 2.372.

Degree-program credit for applied music: F 3/11/44; Sanders's 1942–44 report.

110–11: Tuthill's report: President's Files. Tuthill to Sanders: 12/12/40; Sanders to Wells: 12/17/40; "a miracle": 1/3/41.

111: Tuthill's suggestion for Public School Music, and discussion of possibility of more group lessons: F 4/29/40.

111–12: Most of my information on the building of the Auditorium comes from C 3.463–72 ("Hall of Music": 3.465). The quoted version of Wells's auditorium story is from Cl 158.

113: Events in the Auditorium Series: listed each year in the School of Music Bulletin.

114: The reminiscences of Biddle's widow are in UA.

115: It was Ross Allen who told me that the Met's touring productions were the best the company had to offer.

115–16: Met logistics: C 3.474. Cultural dissonance at Gib & Denzil's: Allen interview. Origin of the Antics: C 3.474; *IDS* 5/23/56. "Until 5:05": Allen interview.

116–17: Absences permitted for performers on faculty: F 12/19/40. The account of Hyde's trouble with students is from Long: Cl 133. Hyde to Sanders: 2/29/41.

117–18: Melchior to Sanders: 3/31/41 (in President's Files). Manski anecdotes: from Allen interview; substantiated in conversations with Eleanor Long, Dorothy Collins, Sara Pressler, and others. Bain on Manski: my interview with him.

119: Newell Long on part-timers: Cl 145. My summary of Sanders's appointments derives from the Bulletins. The School's organs: interview with Oswald Ragatz.

1943 enrollment: F 9/23/43. "Horde of students": F 3/15/44.

120–21: Discussion on Jewish émigrés: F 1/8/40. Sanders wrote twice to Wells about Hindemith: 3/7 and 4/30/40. Nettl's appointment file is in the President's Files. Bain's reversal of Sanders's decision not to reappoint Nettl: R 76–77.

121: Shortage of space: F 10/14/46. Enrollment statistics: Sanders's 1946–47 report.

123: "Field man" appointed: *IDS* 12/11/45 (in Cli). More scholarships: F 11/5/45. Clinics: F 12/4/44. Motion recommending a University FM station: F 10/22/45.

123–24: Discussions about opera program: Post-War report, p. 8 (attached to F 10/9/45), F 10/2/44, 11/5/45. "Reasonably satisfactory": Sanders's 1944–45 report.

124: Discussion of trends in music education: F 11/5/45.

125–26: "Things just got too big for him": Cl 139. It was Long who told me that teaching was one of Sanders's primary interests: Cl 138. Clemens's observation: Cl 79. "Didn't know how to simplify his job": Cl 145.

126: Robert T. Ittner reported Sanders's remarks on the burden of administration in a memo of 4/26/45 (President's Files). Letter of resignation: 3/25/46.

126–27: Sanders's pursuit of coeds was, Oswald Ragatz and his wife told me, open. Long on Sanders's discomfort at Indiana: Cl 138–39. "We were *ready*": Cl 133.

The Bain Years I

128–29: "I started": Cl 148–49. Bain's Clark-Brewer dossier and the other materials pertaining to his application to Indiana are in the President's Files. "Well, one day": Cl 149.

129–30: I have collected information about Bain's early life, and about his career before Indiana, from his interviews by John Wolford and Jean Freedman, from various newspaper articles in the Bain file in UA, and from the vita included in his Indiana application. "There's always music in church": Wo 88. "That's the man I'll marry": *H-T* 10/5/83. "I remember the day": Wo 6–7. "The ministry faded": Wo 8.

131: "To see how I worked out": ibid. "At the start": John Rosenfield, *Dallas Morning News* 6/19/47.

132: "Did everything": *IDS* 7/25/64.

"Loved every bit": Wo 15. "Nine years of unmixed success": *R* 11.

"Got more attention": Wo 98.

132–33: Excerpts from the letters of recommendation Bain secured in 1939–40 are included in his 1947 Clark-Brewer dossier.

133: "Limitations": Wo 98. "Remarking to himself": *R* 5.

133–35: "Had indicated his vital interest": *R* 7. "Much impressed": *R* 8. Wells to trustees: 5/27/47. Lutton to Wells: 6/27/47.

135–36: Bain's remarks to Wolford on his theory of education are found mostly in Wo 224–44. "One-eyed specialists" and "conservatory amalgamated into a university": Wo 44.

137: "A thousand times": my interview with Wennerstrom.

The crucial importance of ensembles: F 8/12/47.

138: The third "great post": Wo 113–14.

139: "You have to have a show window": Wo 297; "if they're good at that": Wo 275; "if you're going to be in business": Wo 68.

140: Some "unusual" appointments: Bain to F. T. Reed, 6/27/47. "They had the reputation": interview with me.

"Of the support he had given": *R* 11.

140–41: "To find an individual teacher": *R* 23.

141: "A fine faculty": F 9/30/47. Bain's May assessment of students and faculty: *R* 17, 9. "In the production of voice": Wo 162.

142–43: The massive meeting: 9/30/47. Expanding the summer program: AC 11/19/47; *R* 51–52.

143: "Fabricated a sign": *R* 12.

143–44: "Nothing was happening": *R* 53. Dr. Quarles's address: F 12/2/52. "Participate in music-making": *R* 41.

144: "Not met with any enthusiasm": *R* 40.

145: "Right to review": F 5/15/57. "Maybe two or three times": Wo 147. Faculty members should spend their time in music-making: AC 7/25/68; or research: Wo 157; or in recruiting and teaching students: Wo 161.

146: "Mary Bain says": my interview with Allen. "Counselled": F 10/12/49; "weren't autonomous": Wo 145–46; "the chief of staff": Wo 294. "Except when I disagreed with them": interview with me.

147: Not a single violin major: Wo 27. "A few salesmen": Wo 28. Mary at the A&P: *R* 50.

148: Professional soloists for Requiem: *R* 45. "A lot of influence": *R* 47. "Worn out five copies": Allen's interview with me. My authorities on Bain's Indiana reputation as a choral conductor are Bruno Nettl and Charles Webb.

"Baby-sitting": *R* 73. "Major asset": *R* 74.

149: Sources for Hoffman's biography include the account in his Arthur Judson publicity packet (Bain attached a copy to his strategic memo to Briscoe) and the program notes photocopied in *OT* 21. An "acceptable" violist: *R* 44. "A practical man of the theater": Allen's interview with me. The valedictory tribute of the Women's Committee is included in the Judson packet. Asked Bain to appoint him: Wo 23.

150: "Soon became the rule": *R* 44.

150–51: On the Roosevelt Organ, see *R* 1202–1206 and *IDS* 5/11/48. "The historical aspects": *R* 1204.

151–52: For Busch's biography, my sources include the program notes in *OT* 21, and Charles Webb. Bruno Nettl told me the story of the graduate student's being replaced by Vanelle. Reviews of *Hoffmann: OT* 9–12.

152: Background of the Weill premiere: *R* 60. "His slender wardrobe": *OT* 20. Reviews: *OT* 24–29.

152–53: Background of the Grant Park Requiem: *R* 58. "Tremendous advertising value": F. T. Reed (Wells's assistant) to Briscoe 2/24/48. "The most influential": *R* 58. There is a photocopy of Cassidy's review (7/26/48) in a UA file called "Music, School of: 1948–49."

154: The story of Hastings's colloquy with Wells was told me by Bain. "By calling on him": Wo 30. Collins gave me her views in an interview.

154–55: The quotations from Wells come from *BL* 13, 19, and 34. Webb on Wells's feeling for music: interview with me.

155–56: "Peaks of excellence": *BL* 98, 155, 165. "The administration didn't know": Wo 65.

156: Bain's fondness for Antoine is apparent in *R* 62–63. On Antoine and Carnation: *IDS* 11/12/48. Antoine and the chauffeur: Wo 204.

156–57: Hunkins's departure: *R* 74. "Willing to give": *R* 67.

157–58: Tensions over faculty-wife appointments: *R* 507–509, 714. Student assistants: *R* 70, 74–75. Graduate Assistants teaching 95 percent of elective students: 1949–50 report.

158: Enrollment statistics: Bain's 1948–49 report. Shared studios in Sanders's time: 1945–46 report. Bain to Wells on practice rooms: 8/7/47. "Little more than a shack": *R* 70.

158–59: Sources for the story of East Hall include *R* 53–57; there is a detailed description of the "new" building in *IDS* 3/26/49.

159: "The jam of human traffic": 1949–50 report.

160: The story of Hoffman and *Parsifal* is in *R* 88–90 and Wo 281–84. "The preliminaries": *R* 89. "Chattering like a magpie": Wo 282.

160–61: Allen on Indiana wind players: interview with Clark, pp. 21–22. "Almost staggering": *OT* 47. "Let's see what he can do": Wo 282.

161: Hoffman responsible for dividing the role of Kundry: *OT* 50. Aiken's war service: *OT* 51. The anecdote of Hoffman cutting the third entry in a fugue was told me by Allen; he also told me about Hoffman's rescoring of difficult passages.

161–62: On Elsie Sweeney: *Dir.* A booklet on her among the School of Music files in UA credits her with the idea of making *Parsifal* an annual event.

162–63: Cecil Smith's review of *Parsifal* is reproduced in *OT* 84–85; the *Time* and *Newsweek* accounts are in *OT* 120–21. The *Opera News* review appeared 4/7/52; *Life*'s photojournalism piece appeared in the issue of 5/15/53.

163–64: "Shot up": Wo 109. The draft brochure on the opera program is included among School files in UA.

164: "I am sure": 10/9/48 (President's Files). "Assured . . . of continued financial support": *R* 101.

165: "Very courteously indicated": *R* 100. "One of the most fortunate decisions": *R* 100–101.

166: UA includes a brief account of Allen's life and career written by Charles Webb at the time of Allen's retirement (1988). "A legendary performance": interview with Clark, p. 17.

"We are going to do this": Wo 65, 67.

167: "In keeping with the general desire": *R* 109. Televising Foss's opera: *R* 114. For Thomson and other reviewers, see *R* 112–13, *OT* 105–106. Corbin's review of *Amahl* is quoted in *R* 113.

167–68: Bain's limited familiarity with dance: *R* 91. Mary Maurer's help: *R* 139.

168: “That the music school was going to be”: interview with me. “I had a time”: Wo 103. Stith Thompson’s help: *R* 77.

169–70: For student and faculty discontent in Bain’s early years, my principal sources are my interviews with Bain and Webb. “He had a woman”: my interview with Collins. “Considerable resistance”: *R* 54. “A rough time”: Freedman interview, p. 17. “20 students left”: AC 3/5/49.

170: Bain attributing resistance of inherited faculty to new emphasis on performance: *R* 136. “In record time”: *R* 26. “Might occupy a secondary place”: *R* 127.

“Seemingly not very nice”: my interview with Webb. “Bridge the gap”: *R* 136.

170–71: “All the faculty”: interview with me. “If at any time”: F 9/30/47. “It must be understood”: *R* 136–37. My information about Wells’s support of Bain against the “loyal opposition” comes from an unimpeachable source. “The arrangement did not succeed”: 1950–51 report.

171: “To acquire the influence”: *R* 121.

172–73: “I did not consider him”: Wo 252. Fuleihan’s bantering correspondence with Bain is in SMA. The correspondence relating to Fuleihan’s dismissal is in the President’s Files.

173: Fuleihan’s severance pay taken from library budget: Wo 208.

174: It was David Baker who told me that Johnson was hired at Hoffman’s insistence. “Reached a plateau of activity”: *R* 151.

175–76: Baker’s remarks about the School ca. 1950 are from my interview with him.

The Bain Years II

177–78: “You have only what you create”: F 11/3/48. “Good will”: memo to faculty, 11/8/54. “Music from Indiana” series: F 10/14/47, *IDS* 9/29/48; 1952 radio series: *IDS* 3/13/52; weekly television programs: F 10/7/52.

178: “Constant advertising”: AC 12/3/47; “to the music schools”: F 10/6/48; “to attract undergraduate material”: AC 11/12/49.

178–79: “Award to us a fine reputation”: F 8/12/47. “Ought to be on tour”: F 11/3/48. University Singers: *R* 103–104.

179: “Will play to more people in one season”: Wo 76. “Many people think”: AC 11/1/48. “Show business”: *R* 128. Statistics on off-campus appearances: Bain’s 1953–56 reports.

180: “By any standard”: *Post-Dispatch* 4/16/56.

180–81: Origin of the World’s Fair *Turandot: R* 665. “They’d say”: my interview with Allen.

181: Bain as a slave: *IDS* 8/8/63. Record crowd for *Turandot:* C 3.501.

182: “The preliminary work”: *R* 1187. “The extent of rights and responsibilities”: AC 7/25/68.

182–83: “Now, who . . . would you suggest?”: Wo 181; “people are not going to”: Wo 143; “with a whole lot of persons”: Wo 146.

183: “Just take people”: my interview with Wennerstrom. “Their undergraduate . . . training”: *R* 297. Bain’s argument for inbreeding: *R* 530.

184: “A little black book”: my interview with Pressler. Consulting critics: *R* 266–67. “A hunter for voice teachers”: *R* 284.

“What do you need?”: my interview with Webb.

"Realized that Mr. Kullman's career": *R* 284.

185: Britten: Bain to Wells 8/7/47. "Even Rubinstein": Pressler interview.

185–86: Origins of the flextime policy: *R* 141–44 ("perhaps the first": *R* 143). "Come, you'll love it": Pressler interview.

186: "Here are the people": Wo 52.

186–87: Docking Busch's salary: Bain to Briscoe 9/21/54. Outside performances interfering with ensemble program: AC 11/2/67. "Jumped over the traces": Wo 56.

187: For Bing's view of St. Leger, see *5000 Nights at the Opera* (New York: Doubleday, 1972), p. 145. St. Leger in Hollywood: Wo 287, *R* 202. "He knew every important musician": *R* 202. "Not necessary": *R* 973.

188: "I didn't have the greatest faculty": Wo 110.

"A hundred times": Collins interview—as also for the next two quotations.

188–89: Firestorm over salary position of the School: AC 3/8/73; 1972–73 report to the President.

189: "Give him one assignment": Collins interview.

189–90: "A very nice person": Wo 213. "A big zero": Wo 38–39.

191: "Look-see": *R* 161.

192: Harshaw as a "reigning diva" of the Met's Wagner wing: *R* 532. Bing on Milanov: *5000 Nights,* p. 235. Long courtship of Farrell: *R* 1040–41. Farrell's departure: *H-T* 10/7/79; *IDS* 10/8 and 10/9/79.

193–95: "Old enough": *R* 601. The Spada story: *R* 897–902. "Worried considerably": *R* 316.

196: The Starker subterfuge: *R* 397–98. Bain's doubting letter (with Starker's mildly incredulous reply) is in SMA.

196–97: There is a profile of Gingold by David Blum in *The New Yorker* for 2/4/91, pp. 34–57. "Master musician": Bain's interview with me. "Take any job": *MAN* 18.1.4. Szell's attempt to persuade Bain to take the assistant concertmaster instead: *R* 437; Wo 305–306. "A truly . . . wonderful human being": *R* 438.

198–99: Teraspulsky's unhappiness: *R* 442. Bain's courtship of Ricci: *R* 1048. "Contributed more": Wo 164.

199–200: "A very nice person": Wo 200. "Fresh in my mind": *MAN* 18.1.7.

201: "Any time I meet a composer": Balliett's *New Yorker* profile of Phillips (12/15/75), p. 50. (The profile occupies pp. 46–62.) Two cases of gin: Joseph Roddy, "A School of Note Scores Big Back Home in Indiana," *Smithsonian* 1/86, p. 143.

202: St. Leger and Melba: *R* 237. No plans for Vacano to conduct: *R* 148. Wells and Bain attend the Hoffmans' funeral: *IDS* 1/7/56. The University Archives include obituary accounts of Hoffman from the *IDS* (1/5/56) and the *Indianapolis Times* (1/4/56), as well as the University's Memorial Resolution (1/17/56), which was written by Bain, Busch, and St. Leger.

203–204: "Nothing trivial": Allen interview. Kozma deprecating *Mefistofele:* *R* 824. Kozma's ambition to conduct *Parsifal* without cuts: Wo 274; Allen interview (also for Hoffman's *Rigoletto*). "Infected by the love of music": *R* 478.

204–205: Bain's disappointment with Dimitrov: *R* 1038. Reed's lack of success in recruiting students: *R* 754, 920. Svetlova recommends Dolin: *R* 968.

206: "Nearly every combination": *R* 280. Sousa himself could not satisfy this constituency: *R* 447.

207: The account of Baker's relationship with Bain comes from my interview with Baker.

207–209: My account of the development of ethnomusicology at Indiana depends heavily on information supplied by Bruno Nettl; it also draws on Louise S. Spear's interview with George List, included in *Discourse in Ethnomusicology: Essays in Honor of George List,* ed. Caroline Card et al. (Bloomington: Ethnomusicology Publication Group, Indiana University, 1978). The account of Malcolm Brown's appointment derives from *R* 530–31 and my interview with Brown.

210: "Were on tenure": Wo 164.

211–12: "Central place": *R* 523. Bain's disappointment with Harris's lack of drawing power: *R* 314. Waning interest in Xenakis's lectures: *R* 838; "heroic effort": *R* 937.

214–15: University shrinks 4–5 percent, School grows 13–14 percent: F 10/11/50. "There were many times": Wo 111. Continued high instructional cost: Wo 80–82; AC 10/2/48. Wells asks Mary about Wilfred's enrollment goal: Wo 79. "Contain a sufficient number": *R* 934. "The answer to President Wells's question": *R* 933.

215–16: "If there were that many students": F 9/19/51. Bain lamented and documented the sharing of studios in a memo to Briscoe of 10/12/51.

216–17: "Get us quality practice rooms": Wo 116–17. "The administration really did very, very little": Wo 31. "Always had us sucking off the hind tit": my interview with Webb. "Allocated much less money": *BL* 258.

217: The original configuration of the Music Annex is given in the 1960–61 Bulletin. "Some question": F 9/28/56.

218: The planned square annex to the Round Building is discussed in *R* 526, and in H. F. Gaugh, "Music at Indiana U," *Musical America* 4/64, p. 12.

218–19: "It is a fire trap": AC 3/5/49. How Wagnerian it looked: Allen interviewed by Clark, p. 39. Forty-six pianos: *H-T* 5/25/68. "Could clearly see": *H-T* 12/19/90 (a story on a fire in the Student Building, with a side box on other notable fires at the University). "Bain gets his new building": Wells's interview with me. "Many friends and acquaintances": *R* 1188.

219–20: "Sympathetically consider": AC 5/14/70. "Protested practically every procedure": *R* 916. Ninety-hour limit to ensemble duties: Wo 74; changes in programming practices: *R* 915–16.

220: "Not a complete waste": *R* 974. "Era of Documentation": *R* 973; "a successful war": *R* 974.

221: "Do the cuts": my interview with Allen. Attendance at *Parsifal: OT* 1150–51; economics of it: *OT* 1218. "Twenty years ago": AC 11/6/69. Bain's tribute to Hoffman at the 1973 production of *Parsifal* is recorded in *R* 1174. Bain takes responsibility for canceling *Parsifal: OT* 1150. "A very sad, inappropriate thing": *OT* 1151.

221–22: Bain second-guessing his enrollment policy: AC 1/15/70. "Too many students": AC 9/24/70. Shortage of practice rooms: AC 9/16/71. "The lowest financial ebb": AC 3/18/71. "A previous high administrator": AC 9/16/71. 1972–73 enrollment: annual report. "Ideal": AC 11/2/72.

223–25: Statistics about the new opera house derive from the press package issued for the Dedication Week and from a booklet ("The Musical Arts Center") prepared at the time by Indiana University Publications. There is a section on the creation of the MAC in *R* 1188–97. "Appears to have been designed": Michael Steinberg in the *Boston Globe* 4/19/72. There is a collection of press clippings in *OT* 1326–44.

225: A new opera prohibitively expensive: according to William Mootz, in the *Louisville Courier-Journal* 4/9/72. A bargain price for *Heracles:* Wo 267.

226: "Always be repainted tastefully": Roger Dettmer, *Chicago Today* 4/9/72. "A small town": *Morning News* 4/23/72.

"Marvelous": *New York Times* 4/17/72. "A consistently professional standard": *Chicago Tribune* 4/23/72.

228: Change, winter 1974–75, pp. 42–47.

The Webb Years I

230–31: My primary source for Webb's biography is my interview (series of interviews, actually) with him. Other sources include a profile in the *Indianapolis Star* 3/31/96, and articles in *H-T* 7/23/89 and 11/13/94. "You can play the piano *anytime*": interview with me. "So we got together to practice": *Indianapolis Star* 3/31/96 (a profile of Kenda alongside that of Charles).

232–34: My information on the process by which Webb became heir apparent, and then the successor, comes primarily from my interviews with Bain, Webb, Mary Wennerstrom, Malcolm Brown, and Dorothy Collins. More than sixty possible candidates: *Star* 12/17/72; "undisguised glee": ibid. "Commenting very freely": interview with me.

235: The recording series: *MAN* 1.1.5.

236: Upper appointed at Webb's urging: *R* 979.

Bain's approval of the Festival Orchestra: interview with me.

"Just stayed on": interview with me. Bain's desperation to retain control of the Opera Theater: Webb, interview with me.

237–38: Bain's correspondence with Lynne Merrit, Jr., regarding travel money for the Met Auditions is in UA, as are Busch and Kozma's letters to Ryan. Ryan's briefing of Webb on the matter, and Webb's plea to Busch and Kozma: my interview with Webb.

238–39: Background of Webb's two operatic "heresies": Webb's interview with me.

239–40: "Enigma": Wo 155. "Nobody asks me anything": Webb's interview with me.

240: "Extremely well liked": *IDS* 1/29/75.

241: Webb's daily schedule: *IDS* 9/14/84; *Opera News* 11/84, p. 18; interview. Webb's insistence that his colleagues exhibit high standards: "Message from the Dean," *MAN* 3.1.2; report of the deanship review committee, 1988, p. 4. "A *good* man": interview with me.

242: "Charles was a colleague": Robert interviewed in "Charles Webb: Making Music," a video released 4/24/97, commemorating Webb's service as Dean (Indiana University Radio and Television Services). "An incredibly gifted accompanist": quoted in the report of an administrative review committee. Keiser and McNair on Webb: "Making Music."

243: "Charles was more responsive": interview with me. "I'm trying to allow people": *IDS* 4/24/78.

244: "To explain the responsibilities": AC 9/19/74.

245: Heiden's lament: AC 12/9/76. Fenske proposes standing committee on educational policy: AC 1/13/77.

246–47: Anecdotes of Linden: Webb interview. Discussions of a practice building in Bain's last year: 1972–73 report, p. 32. Practice building becomes top priority: *MAN* 2.1.2. "Do You Really Need This?": interview. On termites in Linden Hall: Webb's 1979–80 report; *MAN* 5.1.1 (which is also the source of "not only handled assignments"). "A live demonstration": 1979–80 report.

247–48: IDS article sampling views on the Dean: 4/24/78.

248–50: Webb explains the new system of administrative reviews in SMC 9/27/79. My information on the composition, proceedings, and findings of the committee derives from its report, given me by Webb. The failure of the SMC to discuss strategic issues is lamented not only in the report of the deanship review committee but in SMC 2/14/80.

250–51: Star interview: 12/17/72. *Musical Journal* supplement: 9/74. New Music Ensemble in Washington: *MAN* 21.1.3. Sources on Binkley include the obituary in *MAN* 21.2.2, 4. "Livid rage": interview—which is also the source of "moving it up a notch."

251–52: On the 1976 excursion to Germany: AC 7/8/76 and *MAN* 4.1.1; on the excursion to Israel: AC 9/10 and 9/23/76; *MAN* 4.1.4, 4.2.1.

252: "Quite simply a brilliant achievement": *Washington Star* 9/30/75. Orrego-Salas in Washington: *MAN* 4.1.3, 4.

252–53: First discussion of New York performance series: SMC 11/16/78.

253: "Receive, hold, manage": Articles of Incorporation, IUF. For William Armstrong's faith in Webb and the New York venture, my source is Leonard Phillips. Phillips to Ryan: 2/17/81.

254: "Several times": *New Yorker* 5/18/81. "As much interest": *New York Times* 4/28/81. "The Indiana University Opera Theater": *New York Post* 4/27/81. A photocopy of Mary Campbell's review is included in a press package prepared by the School in conjunction with its contributions to the 1991 Mozart Bicentennial at Lincoln Center. Unfortunately, the photocopy lacks a date. "Vested concerns": *Opera News* 11/84, p. 16.

255: "Start in August": SMC 1/22/81.

Webb reported the cost overrun, and the IUF's response, to the SMC on 6/25/81.

255–56: "What we heard": *New Yorker* 5/10/82. The documents stemming from the controversy over the passion play are in the President's Files.

257: "Fresh, vital, and rich": quoted in *MAN* 15.1.1 (which does not give the date). "Inherent splendors": quoted (again without the date) in *MAN* 15.1.2.

258: On the Japanese tour: *MAN* 11.2.1, 3; on the French festivals: *MAN* 16.1.7. "Maybe the most powerful musical impression": *Star* 12/18/78. Opening of the Bastille Opera House: *MAN* 17.1.1–2.

259: On the history of "Music from Indiana": *MAN* 14.1.5.

Schonberg's review and article: *Times* 11/25 and 12/8/74.

260–62: The issues of *The New Yorker* referred to in this passage are as follows: 12/23/74 (*Faust*), 12/19/77 (*Night Before Christmas*), 5/22/78 (*Danton*), 3/31/80 (*Porgy, Arlecchino,* and *Clytaemnestra*), 12/1/80 (*Prince Igor*), 8/31/81 (*Jakob Lenz*), 12/14/81 (*Mr. Brouček),* 5/10/82 (*Carmina*), 2/27/84 (*Tom Jones*), 4/15/85 (New Music Ensemble), 5/18/87 (*Tsar Saltan*), 6/6/88 (*Orfeo*).

Peter Brook's view: *The Empty Space* (New York: Atheneum, 1968), p. 32. Brook continues: "I see nothing but good in a critic plunging into our lives, meeting actors, talking, discussing, watching, intervening. I would welcome his putting his hands on the medium and attempting to work it himself. Certainly, there is a tiny social problem—how does a critic talk to someone whom he has just damned in print? Momentary awkwardnesses may arise—but it is ludicrous to think that it is largely this that deprives some critics of a vital contact with the work of which they are a part. The embarrassment on his side and ours can easily be lived down and certainly a closer relation with the work will in no way put the critic into the position of connivance with the people he has got to know. The criticism that theatre people make of one another is usually of devastating severity—but absolutely precise."

262–65: Webb reports possibility of a Bernstein guest appearance: AC 9/10/76. "Lenny was pretty depressed" (and the quotations from Kraut in the following paragraphs): "Making Music" video. Costs of the Bernstein visit: SMC 1/28/82. Almost all the rest of my information about the visit and its consequences comes from *MAN* 9.2.1, 5–7, and from conversations with Webb. "I hope you know": quoted by Webb in SMC 2/11/82. On the seventieth-birthday celebration: *MAN* 16.1.1–4. "This is one of the finest performances I've ever seen": video.

The Webb Years II

266: MAN 3.1.3–4 marked Long's and Robert's retirements with articles about their careers and their plans for the future.

268–70: There is an account of Hokanson's youth and career in *MAN* 17.2.6, and a profile of Susann McDonald in *MAN* 16.2.1.

271: "Arguing among themselves": 8/18/80, President's Files. There is a profile of Bonnefoux in *MAN* 13.1.2.

272: Musicologists' discontent with the process of the MacClintock appointment: *R* 1127.

273: "Best young symphonic composers": *U.S. News & World Report* 11/27/89.

274ff.: My information about the procedures and reports of the deanship review committees of 1984, 1988, and 1992, and the Administrative Review Committee of 1992, derives from copies of the reports given me by Webb (who also gave me a copy of the report of the 1990 Ten-Year Planning Committee).

276: "Having direct responsibility": Upper to Vernon Kliewer 3/20/85 (included with SMC minutes); Webb's comments on the memo: SMC 3/21/85.

276–77: The relative salary position of the School within the University is traced in a chart appended to Webb's 1996–97 budget submission (which he provided to me). On reductions of salary inequities within the School: 1988 deanship review report, Exhibit D. Data on salaries of Associate Instructors: 1990 Ten-Year Plan, subcommittee report 2, pp. 16–17.

282: Copies of at least some of the parental letters complaining about the audition weekends were sent to the President and are to be found in the President's Files. A particularly effective one was sent by Allen and Jeanette Ferdman on 2/14/85.

287–88: Pickett on the need for a strategic overview in the Ten-Year Plan: SMC 3/1/90. "Philosophical projection": 8/9/90. "Open discussion": Attachment to SMC 10/13/94.

288: "Ready musician": interview with me.

290: "A successful administration": interview with me.

294: "For the real world": *MAN* 19.2.2.

295: Eaton invited President Erhlich to intervene with the opera production committee in a letter of 10/8/90. This and the other documents pertaining to Eaton's disappointment and departure are in SMA.

"Without a doubt": *MAN* 17.2.8.

297–98: There is a detailed account of the School's exchange with the Moscow Conservatory in *MAN* 17.2.1–3.

298–99: 1600 Pennsylvania Avenue revived at request of Bernstein family: IU News Release 5/19/92. The history of the original production and the revision is sketched in the Director's Note in the program for the Kennedy Center production. The program and numerous press clippings are included in a collection of materials on the revival prepared at the time by the School's Director of Publicity. Haagensen's vita: program notes. Unenthusiastic response of audience at Bloomington tryout: *H-T* 7/15/92. "A basically student production": *Times* 8/13/92.

299–300: On the various triumphs of the Singing Hoosiers: *MAN* 17.2.9, 19.1.3, 22.1.4.

300: Ranking of M.M. programs: *U.S. News & World Report* 3/21/94.

300–301: Barbara Monahan, the School's Director of Development, reported that it ranked fifth in faculty compensation, in *MAN* 22.2.8. (This issue, for winter 1997, is incorrectly designated 22.1.) Student:faculty ratio: 1992 deanship review report.

301: "Just thought his school": interview with me.

On the Society of the Friends of Music, see *Dir* and an article (on the Society's twenty-fifth anniversary) in *H-T* 7/23/89.

302: Inauguration of alumni fundraising drives: *MAN* 1.2.1. Lyman bequest: *MAN* 3.2.1–2. "Take a Chance" raffle: *MAN* 5.2.7, 6.1.1, 5.

A "state-assisted" institution: SMC 10/21/93.

302–303: Webb's feelings about various aspects of the fundraising process were conveyed to me in our conversations, and supplemented by conversations with Kenda.

304: Library spread over seven locations: SMC 1/17/91.

Unlikelihood of state funding for a new building: SMC 1/28/82. New music building as a priority in capital campaign: *MAN* 12.2.3; SMC 4/11 and 10/24/85. Briefing on sites: SMC 3/6/86. Tentative plans (1987): *MAN* 13.2.2.

304–305: On Ione B. Auer: *MAN* 16.2.3. My other information about her, and about Webb's negotiations with her, comes from him.

306: New projected cost: SMC 1/17/91.

307: "I told him": *H-T* 11/12/95. This and the other newspaper articles referred to in this paragraph are in a collection of clippings on the dedication put together by the Office of Publicity. "But then": *Evansville Courier* 10/29/95. McNair's response: *H-T* 11/19/95. "I walked into the hall": *IDS* 11/17/95. Upper's claim: ibid. "We couldn't afford them": *H-T* 11/22/95.

308: "A new generation": *IDS* 11/17/95.

Postlude

310–11: U.S. News & World Report 3/10/97. "Registered resoundingly": *Times* 4/16/98.

311: My information (none of which is confidential) about the proceedings of the search committee comes from Mary Wennerstrom (who was a member of it) and David Woods. I formed the impression that Scott would not succeed Webb in interviews conducted in the summer of 1996.

312: Hurst on desiderata: SMC 11/21/96.

To-ing and fro-ing: some of it is reported in *IDS* 4/30/97.

313–14: For the summary of Woods's accomplishments during the two years of his deanship, I rely on my interview with him, and on a document produced by his office under the title "Summary and Analysis of 1997–1999 Tenure of Dean David G. Woods." This document includes, as appendixes, Woods's "A Vision for the Indiana University School of Music" (8/98) and the "Joint Vision Statement" of the Distance Learning Project undertaken by the School and the Royal Academy of Music (1/25/99).

314: Endowment as of 6/96: SMC 11/7/96; as of 5/97: SMC 7/26/97.

On the Starling Chair, see *Dir.* At Indiana, endowed chairs are distinguished from named professorships, which require a smaller endowment. Two of the latter, sponsored by Judit Bretan Le Bovit and bestowed on Josef Gingold and Malcolm Brown, existed for a period in the late 1980s, before a disagreement with Le Bovit (who expected the School to devote more of its energies to the music of her father, Nicolae Bretan) resulted in the withdrawal of her support.

315: Concerns about the School's growing deficit and its consequences, and about other aspects of Woods's stewardship, first came to my attention in interviews conducted in the summer of 1999. Subsequently, I discussed these matters with several key members of the faculty, spanning a broad spectrum of views. *IDS* 11/8/99 quotes Woods extensively on budgetary factors beyond his control.

316: *IDS* 11/8/99 reported a deficit of $1.77 million.

317: The salary of the Cleveland concertmaster is a matter of public record.

318: Woods discussed the possibility of relaxing the residence requirement in *New York Times* 4/16/98. Webb and Pressler are quoted in impassioned opposition.

Index

The Preface and appendixes are not indexed. Italicized page numbers refer to illustrations.

GEORGE M. LOGAN, James Cappon Professor of English and former Head of the Department of English at Queen's University, Canada, is a scholar of Renaissance literature and an editor of the distinguished *Norton Anthology of English Literature.*